The
NOKIA
Revolution

The
NOKIA
Revolution

*The Story of an
Extraordinary Company
That Transformed an Industry*

Dan Steinbock

AMACOM
American Management Association

New York • Atlanta • Boston • Chicago • Kansas City • San Francisco •
Washington, D.C. • Brussels • Mexico City • Tokyo • Toronto

This publication is designed to provide accurate and authoritative
information in regard to the subject matter covered. It is sold with
the understanding that the publisher is not engaged in rendering
legal, accounting, or other professional service. If legal advice or
other expert assistance is required, the services of a competent professional person should be sought.

Library of Congress Cataloging-in-Publication Data

Steinbock, Dan.
    The Nokia revolution : the story of an extraordinary company that transformed
an industry / Dan Steinbock.
        p.   cm.
    Includes bibliographical references and index.
    ISBN 0-8144-0636-X
    1. Nokia (Firm)—History.   2. Cellular telephone equipment industry—
Finland—History.   I. Title.

    HD9697.T454 N657   2001
    338.7'62138456'094897—dc21   2001022580

Printing number

10   9   8   7   6   5   4   3   2   1

Finland has quite a few resources. Briefly put, there are two of them: the people and the trees. Exports are obligatory in the future as well. Things must be sold abroad so that living conditions will remain good domestically. This, in turn, requires that we have extensive experience in international business. . . . That is the greatest risk facing the Finns—the small amount of international business experience.

—Kari H. Kairamo, managing director, Nokia (1981)

How was it that an obscure Finnish company, Nokia, emerged as the number-two supplier of cellular telephones in the world, leaving European giants like Philips, Siemens, and Alcatel with mere crumbs?

—G. Hamel and C. K. Prahalad, Competing for the Future (1994)

Until the 1980s, Nokia was a Finnish company, in the 1980s Nokia was a Nordic company and in the beginning of 1990s a European company. Now, we are a global company.

—Jorma Ollila, president and CEO, Nokia (1997)

Nokia's strategic intent is to take a leading, brand-recognized role in creating the Mobile Information Society by combining mobility and the Internet, and stimulating the creation of new services.

—Jorma Ollila, president and CEO, Nokia (1999)

Contents

Selected Acronyms and Definitions

1G	First generation (1G) systems are analog and were designed for voice transfer. AMPS, NMT, TACS, etc., are included among first generation systems. Very few analog systems remain in existence.
2G	Second generation (2G) systems are digital and are capable of providing voice/data/fax transfer as well as a range of other value-added services. These systems include GSM, US-TDMA (IS-136), cdmaOne (IS-95) and PDC.
2,5G	Evolving 2G systems with ever-increasing data rates via new technologies such as HSCSD (High Speed Circuit Switched Data) and GPRS (General Packet Radio Service).
3G	3G systems enable multimedia and are currently being standardized under 3GPP.
3GPP	Third-Generation Partnership Protocol
AMPS	Advanced Mobile Phone System
ATM	Asynchronous Transfer Mode
BCG	Boston Consulting Group
CDMA	Code Division Multiple Access
CdmaOne/IS-95	A digital cellular standard, which applies CDMA to realize large volume traffic and enable numerous users to access a limited bandwidth. Also known as cdmaOne, this system is used in Hong Kong, North and South America, Korea and Japan.
CDMA2000	A radio transmission technology for the evolution of narrowband cdmaOne/IS-95 to 3G adding up multiple carriers.

CEPT   European Conference of Postal and
              Telecommunications Administrations

CMT   Car Mobile Telephone

CSCE   Commission on Security and Cooperation in
              Europe

CTIA   Cellular Telecommunications Industry
              Association (today the Cellular
              Telecommunications & Internet Association)

D-AMPS   Digital Advanced Mobile Phone System

DECT   Digital Enhanced Cordless Telecommunications

EC   European Commission

ECSC   European Coal and Steel Community

EDGE   Enhanced Data rates for GSM Evolution. An
              intermediate technology, still under development,
              which brings second-generation GSM closer to 3G
              capacity for handling data speeds up to 473 kbit/s,
              enabling value-added Mobile Multimedia
              services.

EEA   European Economic Agreement

EEC   European Economic Community

EFTA   European Free Trade Association

EPOC   An operating system for mobile terminals,
              developed by Symbian (a joint venture with
              Ericsson, Matsushita, Nokia, Motorola and Psion).

ERMES   European Radio Messaging System—a pan-
              European–wide area paging network working in
              Europe, the Middle East and Asia.

ETACS   Extended Total Access Communications
              System—the analog mobile phone network
              developed in the UK and available in Europe
              and Asia.

ETSI   European Telecommunications Standards
              Institute

EU   European Union

EUREKA   A Europe-wide network for industrial R&D

FCW   The Finnish Cable Works

FCC	Federal Communications Commission. Regulatory body governing communications technologies in the U.S.
FDMA	Frequency Division Multiple Access. A cellular technology that has been used in the first-generation analog systems (i.e., NMT, AMPS, and TACS).
FRW	The Finnish Rubber Works
GPRS	General Packet Radio Service
GSM	Global System for Mobile Communications
HSCSD	High Speed Circuit Switched Data
HSEBA	Helsinki School of Economics and Business Administration
HUT	Helsinki University of Technology
ICM	Intellectual capital management
ICT	Information, communication, and technology (somewhat parallel to the U.S. designation of the "IT-producing industries").
IMEDE/IMD	International Management Development Institute/International Institute for Management Development
i-mode	A wireless service launched in Japan in spring 1999 by NTT DoCoMo. The service is accessed by a wireless packet network (PDC-P) and the contents are described in a subset of the HTML language.
IMTS	Improved Mobile Telephone Service
IMT-2000	International Mobile Telecommunications
Internet	The collection of interconnected networks that use the Internet Protocols (IP).
IP	A communication protocol commonly utilized by communication hardware comprising the Internet.
ISDN	Integrated Services Digital Network
ISP	Internet Service Provider
IT	Information Technology

ITU   International Telecommunication Union

KOP   Kansallis-Osake-Pankki (today, via Merita, part of
                Nordea)

LBO   Leveraged buyout

M&A   Mergers and acquisitions

M-Commerce   A term referring to mobile commerce, a hybrid of
                e-commerce. Mobile commerce is effectively the
                ability to conduct monetary transactions via a
                mobile device, such as a WAP enabled cell phone.

MCTC   Microelectronics and Computer Technology
                Corporation

MNC   Multinational company

Mobile   A shorthand for mobile cellular systems.

Modem   Abbreviation of modular/demodulator, the
                modem converts digital computer signals into
                analog form for transmission over analog
                telephone systems.

Mobile Portal   A mobile portal implies a starting point which is
                accessible from a mobilephone.

NCU   Nordek Customs Union

NMP   Nokia Mobile Phones

NMT   Nordic Mobile Telephony

NMIT   Nokia's global initiative, Nokia Mobile Internet
                Technical Architecture, aims to provide seamless
                interoperability between all interaction modes,
                any network environment and with any type of
                access.

NRC   Nokia Research Center

NRP   Nokia Radio Phones

NTC   Nokia Telecommunications

NTT   Nippon Telegraph and Telephone

NVO   Nokia Ventures Organization

OECD   Organization for Economic Co-operation and
                Development

OEM   Original equipment manufacturer

PCN — Personal Communications Network. A standard for digital mobile phone transmissions operating at a frequency of 1800 MHz (also referred to as GSM 1800). Adopted mainly in urban areas of Europe.

PCS — Personal Communication Services. In the U.S., refers to digital mobile networks using the 1900 Mhz frequency. In other countries, refers to digital mobile networks using the 1800 Mhz frequency.

PDA — Personal Digital Assistant. A generic term for handheld devices that combine computing and communications functions.

PDC — Personal Digital Communications. A digital cellular standard presently being used in Japan.

PHS — Personal Handyphone System. A digitalized evolution of the earlier analog cordless phone concept which enables outdoor use as well.

PIN — Personal Identification Number. A code used for all GSM-based phones to establish authorization for access to certain functions or information.

PMR — Private Mobile Radio. Generally for use within a defined user group such as the emergency services or by the employees of a mining project.

PSTN — Public Switched Telephone Network

PTT — Historically, the Ministry of Post, Telecommunications and Telegraph. Now a term to describe the incumbent, dominant operator in a country, many of which are being or have been privatized.

PCM — Pulse Code Modulation

SIM — Subscriber Identity Module card. A small printed circuit board inserted into a GSM-based mobilephone when signing on as a subscriber. It includes subscriber details, security information and a memory for a personal directory of numbers.

SMS — Short Message Service. A service available on digital networks. A single "short message" can contain text up to a maximum of 160 characters.

SYL   National Union of Finnish Students

SYP   Savings Bank of Finland (Suomen Yhdyspankki)

TABD   Trans-Atlantic Business Dialogue

TACS   Total Access Communications System. An analog
                    cellular communications system derived from
                    AMPS.

TDMA   Time Division Multiple Access. A digital cellular
                    technology that divides frequency into time slots.
                    Prevalent in 2G cellular with three main versions:
                    North American TDMA (IS-136); European
                    TDMA (GSM); and Japanese TDMA (PHS/PDC).
                    GSM and US-TDMA standards apply this
                    technique.

TD/CDMA   Time Division/Code Division Multiple Access

TEKES   Finland's National Technology Agency

Triple Mode   A combined analog and digital mobile phone.
                    Allows operation of the phone in the existing
                    analog system frequency (8000MHz) and in both
                    digital frequencies (800MHz and 1900 MHz).

UMTS   Universal Mobile Telecommunications System.
                    Based on WCDMA-DS. UMTS is the European
                    term for 3G mobile cellular systems.

US-TDMA/IS-136   US Time Division Multiple Access / IS-136. A 2G
                    system used in the US. Also referred to as D-
                    AMPS (Digital AMPS). First digital system
                    adopted in the U.S. and covers the entire country.

UTRA   UMTS Terrestrial Radio Access. The European 3G
                    mobile standard ETSI has agreed on which draws
                    upon both W-CDMA and TDMA-CDMA
                    proposals. Often applied with identical meaning
                    of WCDMA-DS.

WAP   Wireless Application Protocol

W-CDMA   Wideband Code Division Multiple Access

WTO   World Trade Organization

Acknowledgments

In the early 1990s—after severe restructuring but before the triumph of Nokia as *the* leader of the cellular business—the company's senior vice president of marketing approached me to write Nokia's story. After careful reflection, I came to the conclusion that the project would have required a return to Finland for a period of time longer than was possible for me. I had to decline at that time, but I have continued to follow and study the activities of this intriguing company through the years, recently more than ever before.

In the early and mid-1990s, my research focused on digital convergence, a subject that had become increasingly vital for Nokia. Around 1997, I was engaged in an extensive study on the competitive advantage of Finland. In the course of this project, I was able to hear the views and opinions of several senior managers of Nokia, including Lauri Kivinen, senior vice president, Corporate Communications; Mikko Kosonen, vice president, Corporate Development; and Juhani Kuusi, senior vice president, the Nokia Research Center. About that time, one of my interview subjects, Bengt Holmström, professor in the Department of Economics at MIT, joined the board of Nokia, and Erkki Ormala, former chief planning officer of the Science and Technology Policy Council of Finland, was appointed the company's first technology policy director. I also interviewed some 120 leading Finnish CEOs, strategists, and public-policy implementers. Many of these individuals participated in Nokia's value chain as partners, complementors, buyers, channels, or suppliers; represented firms that serve in its related and supporting industries; or had crafted public strategies for the industries in which Nokia now competes. Finally, I interviewed several internationally known academic researchers, industry consultants, and investment analysts who had studied Nokia or the Finnish telecommunications/mobile cluster. Among others, these interviewees included Michael E. Porter, professor of strategy and competition at Harvard Business School.

In the past years, I have found myself increasingly involved with research and consulting that involves Nokia's core businesses. Additionally, some of my Finnish students at the Helsinki School of Economics and Business Administration (HSEBA) as well as the Helsinki University of Technology (HUT)—several of whom (often the brightest) became Nokia recruits—have either focused on various aspects of the company's activities or used Nokia as a case in their term papers, theses, and dissertations.

Between 1998 and 1999, I served as a strategy consultant for Telecom Italia. More recently, I have consulted for Sonera (formerly Telecom Finland), the leading Finnish telephone concern, and Finland's Ministry of Transport and Communications (MTC). In the public sector, the MTC has been a catalyst in the success of Finnish mobile telecommunications. Historically, the MTC and Sonera have had a fundamental, formative impact on Nokia.

Since 1997, I have consulted for the OECD on the rise of global electronic commerce and the internationalization of the Finnish telecommunications/mobile cluster. Since 2000, I have also consulted for the European Commission on the competitive advantage of European technology challengers. In both cases, I have turned my traditional perspective of looking at these issues upside down. Instead of examining the underlying drivers of success for U.S.-based companies, I have explored the opportunities for European and Asian companies to upset the rules of the game through strategy, innovation, and geographic advantage. In such studies, Nokia may well be a model case.

In August 1999, I joined Columbia University's Institute for Tele-Information (CITI), where my research projects involve global telecommunications/mobile strategies and the mobile Internet. Through this research and the intellectual inspiration of Eli Noam, director, CITI; and Christopher H. Sterling, professor and associate dean for graduate affairs, Columbia School of Arts and Sciences, George Washington University, I have increasingly found myself studying and writing about Nokia's efforts to pioneer the mobile Internet. In Finland and Sweden, dozens of researchers, consultants, and chief executives in the private and public sectors have generously offered their assistance and views in the course of preparing this book. I am grateful for the intellectual assistance and observations of Professor Erkki K. Laitinen and Senior Researcher Rolf Leppänen, University of Vaasa, for their observations on Nokia's management accounting systems; Kaj-Erik Relander, CEO of Sonera Corporation, which is pioneering mobile commerce and services; Research Director Pekka Ylä-Anttila and researcher Laura Paija, the Research Institute of Finnish Economy (ETLA); partners of Holtron ICT Consulting, Mikko Puhakka and Tom Henriksson; partners of Slottsbacken Venture Capital, Leif Rylander and Ulf Svensson; my many colleagues at the HSEBA and HUT; and the many librarians of the HSEBA and HUT who provided valuable source documents and historical studies. I am also grateful to Docent

Juhani Ihanus, Department of Psychology, University of Helsinki, for our e-mail correspondence on the psychology of leadership, and to the dozens of Finnish academic researchers, senior managers, industry consultants, and public-policy analysts who generously gave their assistance but wish to remain anonymous.

I am most thankful to Nokia Corp. and many Nokians whose assistance made possible the use of rich illustrations (historical and contemporary photos, charts, figures, exhibits) in order to explore and describe Nokia's fortunes and aspirations in the course of the past 140 years.

I am deeply indebted to Cara Anselmo, who did great work in reviewing hundreds of manuscript pages. The completion of *The Nokia Revolution* has also kept busy several hardworking people at Amacom Books—particularly Neil Levine, senior acquisitions editor, Andy Ambraziejus, managing editor, and Irene Majuk, director of trade publicity and sales promotion. They, along with the author, have suffered the rollercoaster dynamics of the mobile business in the 3G era.

Thanks to the Latin rhythms of *salsa y sabor* and my many dance partners for giving me the *ache* that kept my spirits up during this project. Finally, and most importantly, thanks to my parents and my brother, *mi familia,* whom I see too seldom and miss daily.

Dan Steinbock
New York City, August 7, 2000

Introduction

Since the end of the 1990s, the Nokia Corporation has been pioneering the mobile Internet. Between the end of 1998 and April 2000, the company's market capitalization more than tripled, from almost $73 billion to $250 billion. By the end of the 1990s, Nokia and the mobile Internet appeared to be the "next big thing."

This book tells the dramatic story of strategy making at the Nokia Corporation, the world's leading mobile phone maker, located in Finland. In this small Nordic country, the cellular and Internet penetration levels are among the highest in the world. Although Nokia is the global leader among mobile equipment vendors and a pioneer of the mobile Internet, surprisingly little is known about this extraordinary company, and even less is known about the public policies that stimulated and nurtured the rise of Nokia into one of the cellular giants of the 1990s.[1]

This book delivers the first comprehensive *strategic* study of Nokia. Because of the company's explosive expansion, systematic accounts are few even in Finland and Scandinavia. No other work in the existing literature can match its scope. Although there are more feature stories on Nokia today than ever before, most simply recycle old stories or revise old newsletters. Some accounts have been published in Finland and Sweden, but these have been geared toward the domestic market, focusing on the Finnish or Nordic role in the cellular story.[2] Yet, Nokia's success is global. By 2000, half of Nokia's 55,000 employees were Finnish, but only 2.4 percent of its revenues came from Finland.

The present story draws from history but is not itself a history. Instead, the focus of the book is on Nokia's current efforts in the cellular and mobile Internet arenas. The objective is to examine how strategy works through history, and vice versa. This study goes behind Nokia's official façade to explore the company's intended strategy and to explain how Nokia operates, how its chief executives think, how and when it listens to its customers. The book goes on to evaluate these attributes with the performance of the company.

Nokia's story is far more than a colorful account of a single company and the historical transformations of its strategy and structure. It also offers insight into what it is like to compete and succeed in a fast-cycle, volatile, intense, and highly uncertain competitive environment while building new capabilities for the digital economy. To established industry leaders in the United States, Europe, and Japan, it offers lessons on how incumbents can take advantage of strategic inflection points and disruptive business models in order to *sustain and renew* their competitive advantages. To industry upstarts around the world, it provides lessons on how new challengers can take advantage of the very same inflection points and disruptive business models in order to *overthrow* the old competitive advantages and create new ones.

The case of Nokia has significant implications for current strategic management theory. For decades, strategy was based on the idea of "fit" between a company's strategy and its external environment. Since the late 1980s, however, resource theorists have stressed the leveraging function of a *mismatch* between strategy and environment. The recent history of Nokia provides a concrete example of a purposeful effort to reconcile and transcend these two theories.

The Legend and the History

Somewhat unexpectedly, Nokia has emerged as a global powerhouse in mobile communications. "The Future Is Finnish," a *Newsweek* headline announced in June 1999. "Finland has a national knack for mobile communications and information technology—and a vision for combining the two."[3] To their great surprise, the Finns suddenly found themselves ahead of both the United States and Japan in the mobile marketplace. The "next big thing" was not taking place in Silicon Valley, but in a distant Nordic country of 5.2 million inhabitants that for years had drawn a blank in opinion surveys. Nokia's leadership in the mobile Internet made Finland's Wireless Valley legendary worldwide. "Just Say Nokia!" urged *Wired* in the early fall of 1999:

> Now Nokia is taking a leadership role in the development of third-generation wireless services, or 3G. In telecom speak, analog cellular was the first wave, and digital networks the second. The third generation of data and voice communications—the convergence of mobile phones and the Internet, high-speed wireless data access, intelligent networks, and pervasive computing—will shape how we work, shop, pay bills, flirt, keep appointments, conduct wars, keep up with our children, and write poetry in the next century.[4]

Nokia seemed to emerge from nowhere as an industry leader. *Newsweek* captured this subtext of the Finnish mobile revolution in this headline: "After 800 Years, An Overnight Success."[5] Of course, that view has little to do with the reality, but it certainly illustrates the way Nokia was initially viewed in the United States.

For decades, many people thought Nokia was a Japanese company based on the sound of its name. The Finns did not mind the misunderstanding; it certainly was better than being an unknown. After all, Nokia did bear some resemblance to the Japanese challengers, and the company's senior managers have studied the lessons of Japanese market-entry models since the 1960s and 1970s. The fact remains, however, that while Nokia's worldwide clout is only very recent, the company itself is almost 140 years old.

Throughout the nineteenth century, Nokia was merely the name of a small mill and river less than ten miles from Tampere, a major industrial city in Finland. In the early twentieth century, the company's name became synonymous with rubber, cable, and electrical power. In the later part of the century, Finnish industry grew with Nokia's rubber boots, toilet paper, and Hakkapeliitta winter tires. Mobile phones came into the picture only in the late 1980s and early 1990s, a very volatile time for Finland, coinciding with the eclipse of the Cold War and the collapse of Soviet trade, a severe recession, and a return to the family of nations. The Finns consider Nokia a company that has stood the test of time and, unlike most Finnish companies, has been able to change and embrace the future.

To the rest of the world, however, Nokia and Finland are enigmas. For decades, Finland has been a puzzle, even to most Europeans. It is in Europe but for centuries it was not part of Europe. Geographically, it is situated on the northern periphery of Europe and has been cursed with a cold climate. In the past, it was often left out of maps of Europe. It is considered one of the Nordic countries, yet it is not part of Scandinavia. Unlike the Swedish, Norwegian, and Danish languages, which share many affinities, the structure of Finnish and its several dialects is different. The geopolitical history of Finland has left the Finns far more open to international influences than the Russians, yet far less so than the Swedes. Unlike the Russians, the Finns have not embraced authoritarian ideologies; rather, they have put their faith in egalitarian ideals. Like the Germans, the Finns tend to respect formal titles and authority, yet the national heroes have often been populist or individualistic mavericks. These characteristics are reflected in Nokia's organization as well. *Fortune* magazine, quite rightly, has called Nokia "the least hierarchical big company in the world."[6] After centuries of historical subordination to Swedish and Russian regimes, the Finns have a high regard for egalitarianism *and* freedom—and so does Nokia.

A Mobile Test Laboratory

In 1998, the number of subscribers to mobile phone services in Finland dramatically surpassed that of fixed-line subscribers. In fact, Risto Linturi, a former principal research fellow for the Helsinki Telephone Corporation, no longer regards his mobile terminal as just a cell phone. In the future, traditional telecommunications will be just one of the handset's many functions. And, by the way, why should the handset be a *hand*set? "A cellular phone will become a general purpose terminal," Linturi says. "It will emerge as a nodal point of all communications. This is the message that Nokia has now begun to increasingly emphasize, but which they have well understood for far longer."[7]

By 2000, the very function of the handset was rapidly changing. Certainly, it served as a traditional phone, but the data explosion that has transformed traditional telecommunications was bound to revolutionize mobile communications as well, even before the so-called third-generation rivalry. Take, for instance, short message service (SMS), a text-messaging feature of GSM (Global System for Mobile Communication) digital cellular phones used throughout Europe. Despite its limited capabilities, SMS was a vibrant business and social phenomenon in Europe, especially in Finland, where teens quickly made it their own. Sonera, formerly Telecom Finland, and its competitor, Radiolinja, offered group messaging capabilities where messages are broadcast to several users simultaneously, creating a sort of mobile chat room. Through Sonera's Zed, the operator's "mobile portal," users could access personal Web pages and configure the services they could get through the phone. These included specific information, lists of numbers for group messaging, personalized ringing patterns, and stylized postcards that could be sent to one's own phone or to a friend's.[8]

By 1999, Sonera, in cooperation with Nokia, was developing the first wireless application protocol (WAP)-based wireless picture messaging service. The two companies were also developing digital image transmission and reception with a WAP phone. In addition, Sonera was launching a host of other services that could be ordered or purchased using a mobile phone. For example, a soft drink, a piece of music, or a car wash could be purchased from a vending machine using a mobile phone and paid for on the mobile phone bill. Meanwhile, Merita-Nordbanken, a Finnish-Swedish bank, became one of the first banks to work with Sonera to explore new financial business opportunities spawned by the mobile Internet.

Using the handset as a general-purpose terminal, the dramatic rise of the SMS, mobile chatrooms and mobile portals, mobile vending and mobile commerce, mobile banking, WAP and WAP-based applications, and so many other dramatic innovations now had worldwide pioneering significance. Most, if not all of these, can be traced to Nokia. What the Finns first embraced at the end of the 1990s would later trickle down to other markets as well. Along with other Nordic countries, the Finns knew far more about the new mobile business than traditional industry giants in the United States or Japan.

Despite its dominance in the computer, telecommunications, and—most recently—Internet industries, the United States has not been the leader in the mobile business. Although wireless technologies have often been first developed and commercialized in the United States, the market momentum has been elsewhere since the 1980s. By 2000, there were four major areas in the mobile industry: Western Europe, Japan, the United States, and China (see Exhibit 1).

Since the 1980s and with the large-scale adoption of the GSM standard, most mobile activities have concentrated on Western Europe. Although Japanese consumer electronics giants and telecommunications monopolies missed the leadership in the second-generation (2G) rivalry (to the great surprise of the Finnish Nokians), a new round of investments has ensued with the arrival of third-generation (3G)

Exhibit 1. The mobile Internet: time line, lead markets, and test laboratories.

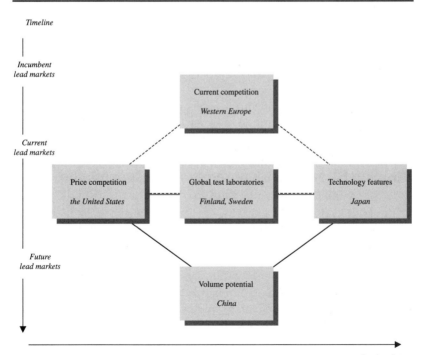

competition. During the 1990s, Japan, then a lead market, became an innovation center where the top vendors would first test new technological features. In the United States, digitalization began only near the end of the 1990s, but the U.S. has remained a lead market due to its large scale and intense price competition. In the long term, China will be critical to all major vendors as well. With its 1.2 billion inhabitants, China is widely considered to be a market with extraordinary untapped purchase power.

Because of its small size, Finland's "Wireless Valley" will never become a major lead market, but as a highly developed telecommunications/mobile cluster, it has become something of a test laboratory for the first movers of the mobile Internet. Through their early-mover experiences in the Finnish market, the industry leaders hope to gain industry foresight and to extrapolate future trends in price, volume, and performance. In this sense, the mobile future may already be Finnish.

Industry giants need their test laboratories. Over time, the stakes in the mobile rivalry have become increasingly risky. At the inception of the 2G rivalry, the leading mobile vendors and operators were competing for relatively small, early-adopter niche markets. By 2000, the incumbent mobile vendors and operators were no longer the only competitors; they had been joined by global computer, telecommunications, consumer electronics, and Internet leaders. Concurrently, industry rivalry drastically intensified due to worldwide deregulation in telecommunications services, privatization of former state telecommunications monopolies, and rapid technology change. Today, competitive developments involve large-scale, late-adopter mass markets. As the financial stakes and profit zones have grown immense, the key players have not been immune to threats of trade war.[9]

Building Strategic Advantages from Capabilities

In the United States, Nokia was first really noticed only in the late 1990s. Indeed, the volume of press exposure the company has received in the past decade far outweighs any earlier business coverage. A simple search of the Dow Jones Publications Library demonstrates that in the second half of the 1980s, *The Wall Street Journal* published only thirty-six full stories on Nokia. In the first half of the 1990s, there were sixty-eight features. During the second half of that decade, the number of Nokia articles soared to 606. Almost one-third of the stories appeared in 1999, the year Nokia publicized its mobile Internet strategy.

Except for the coverage of Nokia's logistics blunder in the mid-1990s (or the loss of $64.3 billion in market capitalization after Nokia's warnings about third-quarter results in July 2000), most articles featuring the company have been sympathetic. In light of the company's extraordinary achievements, the tone is legitimate. In 1999, Nokia's market share continued to grow to 27 percent while it claimed almost 70 percent of the profits in mobile phone manufacturing. By 2000, it had built the world's fifth most valuable brand. Among others, *Fortune* saw fundamental reasons for being optimistic about the company: "While that market cap is but half of U.S. tech superstars Cisco and Microsoft and Intel, one can make at least a plausible argument that, as the mobile phone displaces the PC as the essential appliance of the Information Age, Nokia could shoulder those titans aside."[10]

Despite threats and challengers, it is easy to be a Nokia optimist in the "new economy." In 1998, more mobile phones were sold worldwide than automobiles and personal computers combined. Out of the 165 million phones sold, an estimated 41 million were made by Nokia, and the global market was nowhere near saturation. The Finnish company had become the darling of Wall Street.

Prior to the backlash of July 2000, Nokia's market capitalization amounted to $250 billion. Why were the valuations so high? The conventional explanation might be that such valuations derived in part from Nokia's exceptional historical performance but primarily from its future prospects. Like Wal-Mart in discount retailing or Intel in microprocessors, by 2000 Nokia was far more than just one mobile vendor among others. Rather, some might argue, it had become something of a "capabilities predator,"[11] coming out of nowhere to challenge top competitors in a nascent market. Yet many observers knew relatively little about the company or its capabilities. Thus, an alternative and unorthodox explanation might be that high valuations originated, at least in part, from the expectation that its past triumph would ensure its future success, not from knowledge about Nokia's capabilities. In the company itself, such deductions have not been taken that seriously, but while the Nokians have little faith in fairy tales, they did not discourage the hype either. A triumphant image might deter attacks that otherwise could divert resources.

In effect, Nokia's present success conceals a tragic past. While current business observers understand the role of the company as a profit driver, little is known about the Nokia's history. Perceptions based on the company's current success ignore the critical role of strategic inflection points in Nokia's transformations throughout its history. It is difficult to understand how highly focused competitors leverage their existing capabilities in the future unless one knows *where* those capabilities originate, i.e., the strategic drivers of a company's exceptional performance and shareholder value. Misconceptions of Nokia abound. To most observers, the company remains an enigma because it has been analyzed without regard to history or without appropriate knowledge of the drivers of its performance.

This book endeavors to demonstrate how strategic advantages can be built on the company's existing capabilities. The focus is not on descriptive history but on those strategic transformations that ultimately make or break a company.

Three Stages of Competitive Development: Toward the Mobile Information Society

Nokia was founded during the early industrialization of Finland. It grew along with the national ambitions of a small country that had been ruled for centuries by neighboring Sweden and Russia. Almost 140 years old, Nokia has been created, recreated, and restructured again and again. It has endured Russian oppression, a Bolshevik revolution, a struggle for independence, a civil war, a worldwide depression, two world wars, reparations, cyclical recessions, and the premature deaths of key executives.[12]

What makes Nokia unique is its persistence, the tight linkages between upstream and downstream innovation, and, more recently, dogged efforts to globalize and conquer world markets, often through ingenious leverage. Unlike most Finnish companies, Nokia struggled to determine its corporate strategy during the Cold War, a time when attempts at internationalization were perceived to conflict with Finland's "special relationship" with the Soviet Union. Nokia's strategic history prior to the 1990s must be understood against the backdrop of the Finnish economy and society, just as its more recent strategic story must be viewed within the context of the global economy.[13]

Sustained growth in productivity requires an economy that supports ceaseless upgrading and innovation.[14] Upgrading involves seeking increasingly sophisticated sources of competitive advantage and strategic positions in higher-productivity industry segments. Over the years, Nokia has played a pioneering role in Finnish innovation. In the process, it has worked within a *political* economy that facilitated its strategic efforts until the late 1970s and 1980s, when the objectives of the company and the state diverged.

From the 1860s until the 1950s, the Finnish economy was largely factor-driven; that is, industries derived their revenues from the basic factors of production. Starting in the mid-1950s, Finland opted for investment-driven growth, for political rather than economic reasons. With the eclipse of the Cold War and the country's participation in the European Union (EU), Finland has now rapidly moved toward an innovation-driven economy. At each stage, Nokia has been among the pioneers and first movers in Finland. Never a follower, Nokia has always been willing to take risks (see Exhibit 2).[15]

In Nokia's early years, the focus of operations pertained to the mill; industrial concerns, including those of electrical power, grew thereafter. These efforts took place in a factor-driven competitive stage as well as during the nation's struggle for independence and against Russification (from the 1860s to 1917). In the aftermath of Finland's civil war, Nokia became a part of a three-company coalition, not as a parent but as a subsidiary. Through its new corporate entity, it was involved in forestry, electrical power, cable, and rubber. In uncertain times, diversification is not a bad bet, and it certainly served Nokia well through these decades of turmoil and war, until the reparation years, which saw the stabilization of a special relationship with the Soviet Union and the rise of the investment economy (from 1917 through the mid-1950s).

After the incorporation of Oy Nokia Ab in the mid-1960s, the company began a radical growth strategy while investing in electronics. Though insignificant at the time, this unit would eventually give rise to the company's telecommunications and mobile phone activities. By the 1980s, it also allowed Nokia to approach Western trading partners who led the technology sector. Although the investment economy began shifting under the impact of global finance and new technologies, the political economy of the Cold War did not allow for radical change. To stay abreast of competitive developments, Nokia engaged in frantic M&A activities. Its diversification was extreme; the company found itself in numerous industries, including television, telecommunications, mobile radiophones, information systems, cable, engineering, industrial machinery, paper, rubber, chemicals, and plastic.

Following the eclipse of the Cold War and the collapse of the Soviet economy, Finland was swept by a severe recession. Unemployment figures rose above 20 percent. As the investment economy and its dominant forest cluster began to fade into history, the Finns moved toward the innovation economy, and the telecommunications/mobile cluster emerged rapidly. Since the early 1990s, Nokia has driven the emergence, growth, and expansion of this new, dominant cluster—first by restructuring its activities and divesting itself of the noncore segments, then by focusing its activities worldwide.

Throughout its history, Nokia has employed several corporate strategies. It has been a forest-industry enterprise with a highly focused strategy, a diversified three-company industrial concern, a European-style technology conglomerate that replaced diversification with a growth strategy based on M&A activities, and a globally focused

Exhibit 2. Stages of national competitive development in Finland (from the 1850s to 2000).

	18th Century	1917	1950s	1970s	1980s	1990s
Time line						
National competitive development	*Factor-driven*	⇧	*Investment-driven*		⇧	*Innovation-driven*
Finland's economy	Forestry economy		Cold War economy			Post–Cold War economy
Public telecommunications strategies	Russian suppression	Finnish strategies	Postwar consolidation	Nordic cooperation rise of mobile	Telecommunications Liberalization	Mobile Internet
Telecommunications legislation	Statute of 1886	Amendment of 1919			Telecommunications Acts of 1986 and 1997	
Nokia's corporate strategy	Original Nokia		Three-company conglomerate		European technology conglomerate	Globally focused cellular mobile vendor — Focused mobile Internet vendor

cellular phone maker. Since the late 1990s, it has been transforming itself into a mobile Internet vendor (see Exhibits 3, 4, 5).

With EU membership, Finland left behind the era of the Cold War. Now the changes that Nokia's chief executives had dreamed of for years came true almost overnight. At the EU, the success of the Finnish company that always paid great attention to government and international relations validated the proposition that European firms can achieve sustained advantage in the highly competitive technology sector. Like Ericsson in Sweden or SAP in Germany, Nokia is one of the few thriving European companies in a sector that historically has been dominated by American and Asian companies. In the course of the 1990s, the immense growth of the company made it less dependent on Finland and Europe. Though Helsinki remains Nokia's corporate headquarters, the company competes outside Europe in the Americas and Asia-Pacific. By 1999, Nokia's Finnish sales accounted for only 2.4 percent of its total revenues, yet some 55 percent of the entire production volume still took place in Finland (the corresponding figure for Ericsson was only 3 percent).

By 1999, Nokia seemed "ideally placed to bring the benefits of the convergence of Internet and mobility to the markets."[16] A year later, things looked even brighter. Nokia's operating profit was up 57 percent, to $2.598 billion, while its revenues had increased by 48 percent, to $19.9 billion. "We know that there are no limits to what can be achieved with will, vision, and determination," said Jorma Ollila, chairman and CEO, and Pekka Ala-Pietilä, president of Nokia. "And we have all three in abundance."[17] Amazingly, these developments reflect barely a decade of strategic activity, a decade that began in near bankruptcy. In the early 1990s, the company had seemed adrift until it restructured, refocused, and redefined its strategic intent, stretching resources and capabilities toward the future. However, while most companies fail to sustain *and* renew competitive advantage, that is at the core of Nokia's strategic intent with regard to the mobile Internet.

■ ■ ■ ■ ■

The Nokia Revolution tells the story of the company's strategic transformation in three parts. Part I explores the historical evolution of the company, in particular, its origins in forestry, rubber, and cable; its rise to an industrial conglomerate; and the consolidation of its three core companies. Even more important is the account of Nokia's growth strategy and its struggle as a European technology concern through the Cold War investment stage, the creation of its electronics subsidiary, the subsequent M&A binge, the crash of the investment economy, and the eclipse of the old diversification strategy.

Exhibit 3. Nokia's historical milestones.

The Forest-Industry Enterprise

* 1865 Establishment of Nokia in the forest industry
* 1898 Founding of the Finnish Rubber Works
* 1912 Establishment of the Finnish Cable Works

The Three-Company Coalition

* Early 1920s The Finnish Rubber Works obtains majority control in Nokia and the Finnish Cable Works
* Late 1920s First merger talks end

The European Conglomerate

* 1967 Three companies merge to form Nokia Corporation
* 1977 The Kairamo era begins
* 1979 Mobira Oy (Nokia Mobile Phones), jointly owned by Nokia and Salora, founded
* 1981 Telenokia Oy (Nokia Telecommunications), jointly owned by Nokia and Televa, founded
* 1982 Nokia introduces the first fully digitalized local exchange in Europe
* 1984 Acquisition of Salora and Luxor; Nokia introduces the world's first portable Nordic mobile telephony (NMT) car telephone
* 1986 Nokia introduces an NMT cellular mobile phone and a low-radiation monitor
* 1987 Acquisition of Standard Elektrik Lorenz's consumer electronics operations; Nokia starts designing and manufacturing nationwide pagers; Nokia introduces the world's first NMT pocket phone
* 1988 Koski suffers cerebral hemorrhage; Kairamo commits suicide
* 1989 Acquisition of NKF
* 1990 Nokia introduces the world's first radio data system (RDS) pager
* 1991 The world's first genuine Global System for Mobile Communications (GSM) call made in Finland with equipment supplied by Nokia

The Focused Cellular Phone Maker

* 1992 Ollila is appointed CEO, and increases restructuring and refocusing of operations
* 1992 Nokia introduces its first GSM hand-portable phone
* 1993 Nokia is the first manufacturer to launch hand-portable phones for all existing digital systems
* 1994 Nokia is the first European manufacturer to start selling mobile phones in Japan
* 1995 Nokia General Communications Products formed by consolidating Nokia Cor and Industrial Electronics and Nokia Cables and Machinery
* 1995 Nokia introduces the world's smallest base station for GSM/(DCS) cellular mobile networks, called Nokia PrimeSite
* 1996 Nokia introduces the world's first all-in-one communicator, the Nokia 9000 Communicator

The Focused Cellular/Internet Phone Maker

* 1997–1999 Strategic refocus to mobile Internet; efforts toward "mobile information society"

SOURCE: Based on Nokia's annual reports.

Exhibit 4. Nokia's corporate organization: 1865–1990.

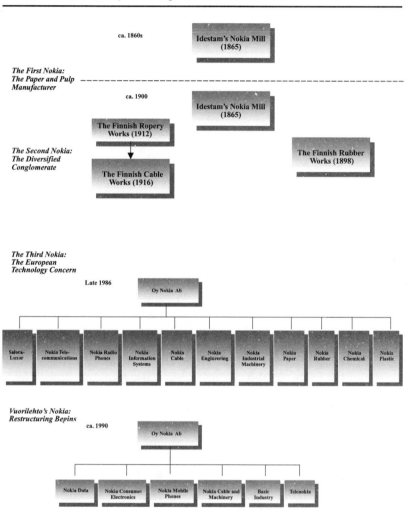

Part II is about the creation and evolution of Nokia's global focus strategy, which transformed the company's existing capabilities into strategic advantages. This discussion concentrates on Nokia's electronics consolidation and Nordic cellular policies; the rapid growth of Nokia-Mobira in the 1G industry environment; and the rise of the digital cellular rivalry among 2G competitors. This section also examines Jorma Ollila's rise within the organization, Nokia's initial framework for global expansion, and the adoption of a strategy that turned a near-bankrupt conglomerate into a flexible and agile process organization. Finally, the section explores Nokia's quest to establish a third way be-

Exhibit 5. Nokia's corporate organization: 1990–2000.

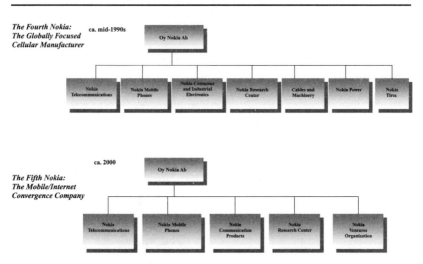

tween traditional competitive strategy and the more recent resource theory. In addition to Nokia's stated strategy, this portion of the book concentrates on the organizational transformation that precipitated its strategic triumphs in the 1990s.

Part III examines Nokia's preparation for the mobile information society; it is about building new capabilities to achieve strategic advantages, and focuses on Nokia's R&D and upstream and downstream innovation. The chapter on R&D tells the story of focusing and globalization in technology development, including Nokia's role in the controversial genesis of the 3G standard (which almost triggered a trade war). This section also delineates the way Nokia builds new capabilities and its motives for strategic coalitions and supplier partnerships (upstream innovation). Additionally, the section explores the key determinants of Nokia's extraordinary success in segmentation, design, and branding (downstream innovation). After the deconstruction of Nokia's strategic configuration into its distinct processes or sets of processes, this section puts them together and looks at them as a whole. The final chapter seeks to unravel "Nokia's secret code," i.e., the drivers of its strategy, while exploring the first-mover advantage inherent in Nokia's preemptive strategy and the inherent vulnerabilities of it (i.e., the preemptor's dilemma).[18]

■ ■ ■ ■ ■

This book was written for an international audience of general business readers interested in the story of Nokia and its strategy and structure; industry practitioners and policy analysts involved in the cellular, telecommunications, information technology (IT), Internet, electronic commerce, and mobile-commerce industries; general practitioners who need to develop a strategy for a particular business; government policy implementers who hope to formulate and execute sound public policy toward competition in emergent industry environments; and trade specialists and policy analysts who seek to facilitate global "rules of the game" in international trade. The book's context is the global competition for industry leadership in the mobile Internet. It should also be of interest to MBA students who must combine economic theory with the practical concerns of individual companies; scholars who need to understand competition and/or business history; general readers and students who are interested in the emerging digital economy, mobile infrastructure, strategy formulation, implementation and valuation in the Internet era; and international audiences who are interested in the primary determinants of strategic leadership in the nascent mobile Internet.

Offering far more than a descriptive account of the company's history, strategy, and industry-specific success, this book provides an evolutionary story of Nokia's strategic success based on its historical, current, and intended future capabilities. It is about new and ambitious challengers that seem to come out of nowhere and yet have been able to gain global industry leadership. It is also about complacent global incumbents, which the new digital economy has rendered surprisingly vulnerable.

Part I
The Diversification Strategy

The Origins of Nokia

FORESTRY drove the Finnish economy from the late nineteenth to the late twentieth century, and even today, Finland remains the world's most forested country. In factor-driven nations, the most successful industries draw advantage mainly from the basic factors of production.[1] In this stage, most Finnish companies in forestry-related industries, requiring little product or process technology, competed primarily on the basis of price. Typically, technology was obtained from other nations rather than created indigenously. Few Finnish companies had direct contact with end users; foreign companies provided most of the country's access to world markets due to modest domestic demand. The Finnish economy remained sensitive to world economic cycles and exchange rates, which drove demand and relative prices.

During this stage, the political economy of the era provided the context for the strategies, rivalries, and industry structures that existed within Finland's business community. Nokia was born amid Finland's struggle against Russification and for independence. The company's founding fathers, in particular Leo Mechelin, the first parliamentarian of the young independent state, led the struggle for national sovereignty. Finland's declaration of independence in 1917 sparked decade-long wars that began with a devastating civil war and resulted in the loss of Nokia's corporate autonomy. The company became part of a three-company coalition in the 1920s. As a subsidiary of a young industrial conglomerate, it had to cope with a barrage of social, political, and economic events, including the Roaring Twenties, the Great Depression, the invasion of the Soviet Union and ensuing wars, and war reparations to Moscow.

After these tumultuous decades, Nokia emerged triumphant in the late 1950s. With a new foreign policy driven by aspirations of neutrality, Finland finally achieved political stability. However, its abundant natural resources no longer supported a high per capita income. The factor-driven economy offered a poor foundation for sustained growth, and as Finland opted for a new stage of economic development, so did Nokia.

From Forestry to Rubber and Cable

Until the 1990s, Nokia's economy and industry reflected those of the Finnish fortunes, albeit with two critical differences. Among Finnish companies, Nokia has always been a pioneer, embracing innovation and risk-taking. It has been driven by bold and grand aspirations.

The creation of Nokia as a small forestry company in 1865 coincided with a tremendous boom in the lumber industry, putting Finland on the road to industrialization. Between 1865 and 1914, the lumber industry spawned a number of associated industries that produced wood pulp, paper, matches, cellulose, and plywood. These industries led to the creation of enterprises that produced textiles, cement, and metal products. Finnish companies at this time were aggressively pursuing export initiatives to supplement the small domestic market, and by 1910 Finland's leading trade partner was Germany, followed by Russia and Britain.[2] Fredrik Idestam, one of Nokia's founders, came of age in this era of entrepreneurial thinking, economic optimism, and new technological opportunities.

Idestam and German Innovation

Born in 1838 to an educated family, Knut Fredrik Idestam attended Helsinki University, graduating in 1863. During his studies at the university, the young engineer had a fortuitous meeting with Leo Mechelin, a chance event that would have a great impact on the history of Nokia (see Exhibit 1-1). Four decades after this encounter, Mechelin, as the country's leading parliamentarian, would play a crucial role in Finland's struggle for political independence, which accelerated in the Great Strike of 1905. Mechelin's constitutional senate, appointed during the strike, was the country's first real parliamentary government. The makeup of the contemporary Nokia would be inconceivable had it not been for Mechelin's active role in government relations, board activities, and capital allocation. From the 1860s to the 1910s, Idestam and Mechelin, Nokia's two founding fathers, supported and complemented each other and were among the "Young Turks" of a new generation of businessmen in Finland.

The political conditions of Finland present an important backdrop to the evolution of Nokia. Following the Crimean War (1853–1856), Finland was joined to Russia by Tsar Alexander I and made an autonomous state. Although its traditions, laws, and constitution remained intact, the tsar replaced the Swedish king as sovereign of Finland.[3]

By the 1860s, technological and political progress seemed to go hand in hand. The first Finnish railway traveling between Helsinki and Hämeenlinna was launched in 1862. A language decree issued in 1863

Exhibit 1-1. Fredrik Idestam and Leo Mechelin: the founding fathers of Nokia Corporation.

Fredrik Idestam   Leo Mechelin

SOURCE: Lars G. von Bonsdorff, *Nokia Aktiebolag, 1865–1965*. (Helsingfors, 1965.)

by Alexander II marked the first step toward making Finnish an official administrative language. As Idestam dreamed of his future in 1863, the Diet of the Four Estates convened for the first time in more than half a century and met regularly to begin legislative work in Finland.[4] The country obtained its own currency, economic development accelerated, and business became less controlled. When the Conscription Act of 1878 gave Finland its own army, the country resembled an independent nation even though it was not one yet.

Unlike Mechelin, Idestam had no political aspirations and, like his father, was more interested in engineering and the metal industry. In late spring 1863, Idestam finished his studies and traveled to Germany. Because of the difficult political circumstances and rumors of impending war, Idestam nearly passed on the opportunity to make the trip that ultimately led to the founding of Nokia.[5] In April 1863, while touring the sights and factories of Germany, Idestam traveled to Mägdesprung, where he had heard that Wilhelm Ludwig Lüders had created a new process to manufacture pulp based on the work of Friedrich G. Keller and Heinrich Völter.

On May 3, 1863, Idestam visited Lüders's factory and persuaded his colleagues to demonstrate the operations of the mill. As they were displaying the new manufacturing equipment, Lüders heard of the presentation and rushed to the scene. He had spent years designing the new process, had invested significant capital in the new machinery, and had no desire to be a gracious host. Lüders ejected Idestam for trying to gather information on a proprietary technology—what he deemed to be industrial espionage. Despite the precipitous end to Idestam's visit, he had seen and heard enough to believe that he could create in Finland what he had seen in Germany.

Bold Dreams, Ceaseless Innovation

Finland's unique maritime landscape in the nineteenth century was both beautiful and potentially useful to industry. Coupled with modern manufacturing technologies, the lakes, rapids, rivers, and seemingly endless forests provided ideal resources for manufacturing pulp to make paper and related products. On May 12, 1865, Idestam realized his vision when he received authorization to build a mill, laying the foundation for the future Nokia Corporation. Over time, the Nokia factory attracted a large workforce, and a town of the same name grew around it (see Exhibit 1-2).

For more than a century, Nokia has been driven by a shared organizational vision of ceaseless innovation and bold dreams, as well as the determination and commitment to vigorously pursue it in domes-

Exhibit 1-2. The mill in Nokia, less than ten miles from Tampere.

SOURCE: National Museum of Finland.

tic and overseas markets. In that regard, Nokia has been an exception among Finnish companies.[6] Through the decades, Nokia's corporate vision, which transcends its founders, has exhibited three characteristics: a context for strategic and tactical decisions; extraordinary effort creating cohesion, teamwork, and community; and self-reliance. The initial conditions were far from easy.

Start-Up Struggles

In the late 1860s, the demand for paper products in Finland far exceeded the domestic supply, even augmented by imports from Russia and Sweden. The domestic paper factories were suspicious of Nokia's products because the company was small and Finnish and lacked the clout of a foreign company. To find success in domestic markets, Idestam would first have to excel internationally, and so he sought customers in continental Europe, particularly Denmark and Germany. This strategy had merit; in 1867 Idestam received a bronze medal in the Paris World's Fair for his groundwood pulp, and sales then took off in England, Russia, and Finland.

To keep the company going, Idestam struggled for financing, and like many other Finnish enterpreneurs of his era, he was dependent on bank loans. "Damn it, the times are so bad!" he wrote to Mechelin in 1865, prior to the purchase of the mill site. "Everybody wants loans, nobody can afford to give them!"[7] Idestam ultimately convinced a group of private investors in Helsinki to finance his operation for a joint note of debt. He also benefited from Mechelin's marriage to the daughter of commercial lawyer J. H. Lindroos, one of the wealthiest men in Helsinki. Mechelin's position as a member of the board of the Union Bank of Finland further added to the financial support of the fledgling company.

The company now under way, Idestam issued forty-one shares in 1867. Mechelin acquired ten, gaining an interest in the company of more than 25 percent. But currency reform, the recession of 1866, and the "Great Hunger" years of the time discouraged expansion. Idestam had met Gebruder Wargunin, a St. Petersburg factory owner, at the Paris World's Fair, who provided the financing that allowed Idestam to build a larger mill near the Nokia River in 1868. But Mechelin remained one of Nokia's most important financiers, sustaining the company over the course of the next two years.[8]

Still, Idestam found little financial relief in Finland and went to St. Petersburg for assistance. Ultimately, it was the commercial trading house of Lindroos that ensured the financial future of Nokia. Mechelin and Torsten Costiander opened doors for Idestam at the trading house. Of the 175 shares, Idestam obtained 100 and Mechelin 30. Together, they controlled almost 75 percent of Nokia. On July 1, 1869, Idestam, Carl Gustaf Mannerheim, Carl Enrooth, and Alfred Kihlman created a limited partnership, rather than a corporation, that enabled Idestam to explore expansion opportunities for Nokia. In February 1871, after months of work with the corporate bylaws, Nokia Corporation (Nokia Aktiebolag) was founded at the home of Leo Mechelin.

Now able to expand his operation, Idestam sought to access the thriving markets of St. Petersburg, Warsaw, Riga, and London. Initially, he concentrated on Russia, Great Britain, and France and built a network of sales agents in each. Having sold the Tampere mill in 1877, he moved all activities to the Nokia region and began to expand; by 1886, he had three paper facilities there. Through his innovative methods, Idestam inadvertently gave rise to something of a pioneering school. Aware that his methods of production entailed strategic advantages, Idestam was very protective of them. Unlike Lüders, *he* would not allow outsiders to learn his secrets of process manufacturing. In 1872 he wrote, "I would like them to be told that, without my permission and under no terms, must visitors be allowed in the Nokia mill."[9]

Mastering the Full Value Chain

By the 1890s, Nokia had grown and diversified. While it was no different in its basic activities from other "paternalistic" Finnish companies of the era,[10] Nokia was unique in its efforts to grow, upgrade, and innovate. A tiny mill had given way to a much larger one, a pulp factory, a large paper factory, and other industrial facilities and was diversifying into electrical power.

In the course of expansion, Idestam exhibited an interest and talent for marketing and advertising, and given the company's reliance on overseas revenues, he engaged heavily in differentiation activities that would set Nokia apart from other Finnish mills. Historically, Nokia's emphasis on differentiation may have originated from a series of ad brochures that appeared in the 1880s (see Exhibit 1-3). Over time, that emphasis would lead to the use of the umbrella brand (Nokia) for the paper, rubber, and cable products sold between the 1890s and 1930s and to the cellular branding investments of the mid-1990s.

While Nokia is well known for its emphasis on innovation, its long-standing focus on differentiation has been less known. What has made Nokia distinctive among its contemporaries is the fact that it has consistently focused on mastering the *full* value chain, from operations and new product development to marketing, sales, and service.

Branding, for instance, has never been considered an exclusively departmental function at Nokia, and the company's current brand umbrella strategy has not been merely an effort to imitate the approaches

Exhibit 1-3. A Nokia ad brochure (ca. 1885) includes a drawing of the original mill and the tiny town.

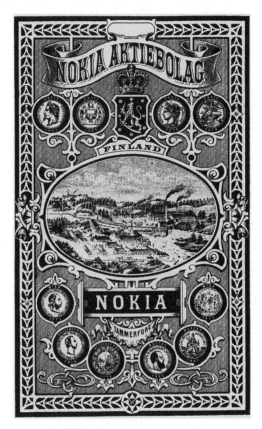

Source: National Museum of Finland.

of its competitors. Innovation in branding, or any other point of differentiation, flows through the entire value chain and requires the active participation of corporate leadership. This philosophy has been a critical element in Nokia's strategic maneuvering that dates back to the company's first efforts to brand itself in overseas markets.

The Second Incarnation of Nokia: The Rise of an Industrial Conglomerate

While Nokia's early years took place in a competitive environment characterized by technological progress and political optimism, conditions were quite different at the turn of the century, when expansion coincided with increasing political turmoil. During the reign of Alexander III (1881–1894) and Nicholas II (1894–1917), nationalist circles in Russia gained increased influence. As part of the Russian Empire, the Grand Duchy of Finland had enjoyed extensive privileges, which had long been a sore point for Russian extremists.[11] The late nineteenth century marked the rise of Russian nationalism and Slavophilic thought, which reflected efforts to integrate the Russian Empire and translated into hard times for Finnish autonomy.

Although leading Finnish politicians supported passive resistance, Governor General Bobrikov, himself a strong advocate of Russification, was assassinated in 1904 by the son of a Finnish senator, and the first period of oppression (1899–1905) ensued, resulting in the demise of the Finnish army.[12] A brief peaceful period preceded the second era of oppression (1908–1917), during which Finland began to develop a democracy. Idestam died in 1916 just as Finland was about to enter an era of independence. He had envisioned Nokia as the most innovative company in Finland. This strategic objective remains strong even today, although little tangible evidence of Idestam's Nokia remains.

The Demise of Idestam's Era: Diversification into Electrical Power

The ability to speak English is a precondition of recruitment at Nokia today; during Idestam's time, much of the correspondence was conducted in German. Speaking the international language of business was important for Nokia given Idestam's overseas market strategy. Nokia's products were first exported to Russia, then to Great Britain and France, and to China, which became an important trading partner in the 1930s. As Nokia became more global, revenues tripled from FIM 1.2 million to more than FIM 3.6 million, while net income doubled from FIM 173,000 to FIM 364,000 between 1895 and 1913 (see Exhibit 1-4). The company benefited from the solid growth that followed the Great Strike of 1905. Through this era, Nokia focused on paper products, in particular groundwood, pulp, paper, and paperboard. The production of groundwood doubled from 2.9 tons to 5.9 tons, and paper production tripled from 2.5 tons to 7.3 tons.

In the operational leadership Idestam was succeeded in the mid-1880s by his son-in-law, Gustaf Fogelholm, the son of a family of liberal reformers. The aging Idestam, then chairman of Nokia, did not support all of Fogelholm's initiatives, especially his persistent efforts to diversify into electrical power. These disagreements led to Idestam's resignation in 1897, when Mechelin, who supported the bold initiative, became chairman. A water-driven power station was built close to the mill, which brought Nokia a new customer, the Finnish Rubber Works

Exhibit 1-4. Nokia's revenues, 1895–1913.

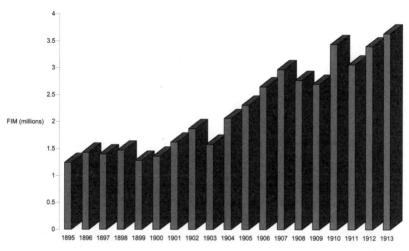

SOURCE: Company reports.

(FRW). Between 1914 and the late 1920s, Nokia's production of electrical power quadrupled; during World War II, demand decreased to the level of the early 1930s, but after the war it soared to more than 300 kWh (see Exhibit 1-5).

As Nokia was moving into new business segments, it was also changing from a family business to a public company. This process has seldom been easy for European family-owned companies. As the saying goes, the first generation creates, the second inherits, and the third destroys.[13] That was not the case at Nokia, where the strategic objective (ceaseless innovation) had transcended the specific industries of the company's operations (i.e., forestry, rubber, and cable).

In the decades following World War I, Finland's economy was closed to foreign competition, encouraging local companies to expand into other domestic businesses. Consequently, Finnish forestry giants went through a period of diversification, but Nokia opted for diversification into electrical power before World War I and was already thriving in international markets. At the same time, Idestam was extricating himself from the company, selling most of his stock to his grandson, who sold some to Fogelholm and most to Carl Gustaf Mannerheim, a legendary Finnish soldier whose name was intertwined with Finland's struggle for independence.

Finland was not directly involved in World War I, although Russian troops were garrisoned in the country. In 1917, Russia plunged into the chaos of revolution, and Finland seized the opportunity to

Exhibit 1-5. Nokia's electric power production, 1914–1945.

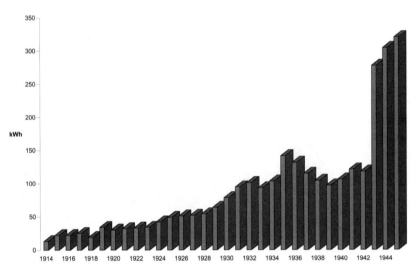

SOURCE: Company reports.

become independent. In January 1918, Finland drifted into a civil war between the "Reds," who wanted to create a socialist Finland, possibly in union with the emerging Soviet Union, and the "White" government troops led by Nokia's former board member, General Mannerheim. The devastating civil war ended in victory for the Whites, i.e., the Finnish government troops, in May 1918.[14] In the course of the civil war, Fogelholm served as the chief of the White troops in the Nokia region. While atrocities were avoided, he resigned in the aftermath of the war and was succeeded by Gunnar Bonsdorff, an engineer and technical director of Nokia.

Unlike most Finnish forestry companies, Nokia was not quite as vulnerable to the consequences of World War I. In the early years of the Soviet revolution, the demand soared for newspaper products, which in the course of the war years had become Nokia's most important segment. With the climax of the Bolshevik Revolution, however, increasing uncertainty and problems associated with the ruble reduced the value of the Soviet demand for paper. Also, with its diversification into electrical power, Nokia was not as dependent on the evolution of international capital markets as were most Finnish forestry companies.

Nokia's diversification should be understood within the context of the company's overall original strategy. Diversification was not solely dictated by the company's efforts to protect existing revenue sources; it stemmed from the company's attempts to find new revenue sources that reflected its commitment to ceaseless innovation.

Cartelization of the Finnish Forestry Business

In the 1920s, Finland's economy still relied on forestry, which accounted for approximately 90 percent of its total exports and one-third of the gross national product. After the Soviet Revolution and Finland's independence, the Finnish paper industry lost its Russian markets. However, it was able to penetrate Western markets rapidly due to the centralized marketing efforts of Finnish paper and pulp producers. To compete with Western big businesses, Finnish companies relied on cooperative networks and cartelization.[15] At the time, Finnish governments protected economic prosperity by instituting conservative fiscal policies and by avoiding large domestic deficits or foreign debt.

Concurrently, Finnish society moved toward greater social integration and progress, mirroring developments in the Nordic region as a whole. However, unlike other Nordic countries, Finnish industry faced obstacles created by the civil war. The Finns had been left behind by Sweden and Norway, who had been able to innovate in marketing and technology because of their wartime neutrality. Furthermore, Nokia's ownership structure was changing again. As the company moved from a family-owned business into a truly public company, the Finnish Rubber Works sought majority control of Nokia.

The Finnish Rubber Works

In the United States, the "rubber fever" of the early 1830s ended as suddenly as it had begun. Many investors lost millions, but a bankrupt hardware merchant from Philadelphia, Charles Goodyear, kept experimenting with rubber. His great discovery, which came to be known as vulcanization, was made in February 1839 when Goodyear created weatherproof rubber, making it possible to use rubber in widely different conditions. In 1898, Frank Seiberling founded the Goodyear Tire and Rubber Company and purchased the company's first plant. A decade later, it was the world's largest rubber company.

In Finland, the arrival of rubber products began late in the nineteenth century. The first products consisted of footwear or rubber-coated fabric goods. At first a luxury of the upper classes, raincoats and galoshes soon invaded both the towns and the countryside, and rubber products expanded from consumer to business markets. Meanwhile, industrialization boosted the use of machinery and equipment, including rubber parts for maintenance, heating plants, waterworks, power plants, hoses, and seals. For decades, galoshes were the main product of the Finnish Rubber Works (see Exhibit 1-6a), which competed with Russo-American rubber factories in the Baltic Sea region.

"Wear Only Finnish Galoshes in Finland!"

Amid Russification and the Finnish struggle for independence, shopkeeper Carl Henrik Lampen and engineer J. E. Segerberg founded Suomen Gummitehdas Osakeyhtiö (the Finnish Rubber Works, FRW) in 1898.[16] The first years of the FRW were tumultuous. The company failed to find markets for its products, the quality of the galoshes did not satisfy the shareholders, and management changed frequently. Despite these problems, business was good. In the days of the independence movement, a Finnish company could rely on nationalist sentiments. As the FRW's ads put it, "Finnish people: Use nothing but Finnish products. . . . Wear only Finnish galoshes in Finland. Available all over Finland!"[17] The company further prospered as it became the first Finnish company to apply Goodyear's discovery of vulcanization.

Exhibit 1-6a. Nokia's early branding. The product flow in the Nokia rapids, 1905.

SOURCE: Tampere Museums, Finland.

With their margins slim, FRW owners Antti Antero and Eduard Polon needed higher volume, but increasing production in the middle of Helsinki was not a viable option. The board of directors suggested moving the factory to the country, and the owners began to explore various options, including partnering with Nokia. As Antero and Polon examined the region around Nokia more carefully, they realized that the energy for their factory could be purchased inexpensively from the Nokia power plant.[18]

Moving to Nokia in 1904 represented a new beginning for the FRW. As the company sought to erase the persistent image of the unsatisfactory early galoshes, buyers began to appreciate the product's enhanced quality and the company's imaginative advertising. Not only did the quality of Nokia's galoshes match those made in Russia, but using Finnish products also made people feel good about their identity. The use of rubber footwear became ordinary rather than prestigious. Unfortunately, like so many other Nokia leaders, Polon could not keep his negative views of Russians to himself. In 1916, he was arrested and deported to central Russia.[19]

In March 1917, Lenin's Bolshevik Revolution ended Polon's political misery, and he returned to Finland to manage the business. In addition to footwear and tires, the company later went on to manufacture rubber bands, industrial parts, raincoats, and other rubber products. Although the FRW had thrived during the war, it now grew even faster and obtained a majority stake in Nokia. In 1922, the FRW bought majority control in the Finnish Cable Works, which was struggling through a serious financial crisis. Through the acquisition, the rubber company sought to ensure access to the cable company's power plant and land as well as exploit the the cable factory's need for massive amounts of rubber.

Branding and Product Proliferation

By the early 1920s, the amount of footwear produced in ten days equaled the amount that had been produced in an entire year at the close of the 1890s. More important, the FRW's branding strategy foreshadowed that of the future Nokia. In response to competition, the rubber unit moved from business to consumer markets, a strategy seen in today's Nokia as it became a global cellular leader by shifting focus from business to consumer markets. Like the FRW, Nokia used advertising to stimulate Finnish sales, even when foreign imports cost less (and were, initially, of higher quality).

Beginning in 1930, the FRW centralized marketing and advertising activities and employed the designs of Göran Wichmann, the first marketing manager of the company. This centralization enabled the company to engage in campaigns that foreshadowed integrated marketing communications six decades later. The company understood the significance of advertising in creating a certain image for rubber footwear and hired some of the best graphic artists in Finland (see Exhibit 1-6b). Over time, the FRW also followed the fashion trends important in women's footwear in the early twentieth century. By 1936, the result of mass customization techniques were reflected in the FRW's sales catalogues, which offered more than 250 different overshoes.

All of these developments—astute management of business and consumer markets, a single umbrella brand, product proliferation, imaginative use of national sentiments to beat foreign imports, centralization of marketing activities, ingenious reliance on image to sell rapidly changing products, accommodation of fashion cycles, and early steps toward mass customization—recurred decades later as well, albeit in Nokia's technology products and customer segments. The branding and segmentation of the FRW had a tremendous impact on Nokia's own marketing strategy in the late 1980s and early 1990s.

The Roaring Twenties were good for the FRW, increasing the manufacturing of footwear and technical rubber. As the company initiated tire manufacturing, it also expanded its product portfolio through pacifiers, balls, erasers, and hard-rubber products. Although Nokia lost its corporate autonomy, its trade name soon became the common foundation for the companies, and in the 1920s, the FRW started to use Nokia as its brand name. Soon, however, a third company, this one in the power industry, would set Nokia on a new course.

The Finnish Cable Works

By the early 1910s, electrical power had been in use for almost a generation. In 1882, the Finlayson cotton factory installed Europe's first electrical lighting, and the first private electrical utility began business in Helsinki two years later, with Berlin following soon after. In 1911, Arvid Konstantin Wikström learned cable manufacturing in Germany, studying the techniques of Werner Siemens. A year later, the young engineer founded the Finnish Ropery Works in the center of Helsinki.[20]

The Creation of the Cable Company

The Finnish Ropery Works represented a new industrial opportunity for Finland. The increasing need for power transmission and telegraph and telephone networks translated into rapid growth. Wikström, a twenty-six-year-old engineer who had studied in England

Exhibit 1-6b. Summer footwear advertisement displaying trendy fashion consciousness, designed by Göran Wichmann, 1933.

and Germany, planned to manufacture insulated electrical cables for lighting purposes.

At first, Wikström had to cope with intense competition as importers engaged in price competition. Ironically, Wikström's problems had less to do with competition than with the negative customs protection that favored foreign importers. Salaries were lower in Finland than abroad, but the customs policy kept raw materials prices high, and the company needed foreign raw materials. While Wikström maintained his optimism, other shareholders were more skeptical.

Meanwhile, Strömberg, Finland's largest electrical business, became a key client of the Finnish Ropery Works and in July 1916 purchased the company. After a year of transition, it re-entered the marketplace as the Finnish Cable Works (FCW). Now fiscally healthy, the FCW soon found clients among the vanguard of Finland's business. Despite the political uncertainty and the civil war, the company entered an era of dramatic expansion.

In the early 1920s, the FCW experienced a serious financial crisis. Failing to fund its expansion, it lost more than 30 percent of its stock equity to Germany. When the company began to manufacture technical and related rubber products, the FRW grew interested in it as a potential rival. Further, a major international rubber concern, Treugolnik, was exploring Finnish markets. The FRW did not want Treugolnik to enter the domestic market and bought a majority stake in the company in 1922. Through this acquisition, the FRW eliminated Treugolnik and effectively consolidated the Finnish market.

The Rise and Fall of Combination Talks: Toward the War Period

In the early years of the twentieth century, Nokia's paper and pulp mill, the FCW, and the FRW were all able to establish footholds and capture the leadership in their respective industries. Similarly, they all managed to exploit the economies of scale in the great Russian markets. In the first years of independence, Finland, like many countries during the era, relied on protectionism to support domestic companies. The FRW and the FCW lost critical Russian markets but discovered customers in Western Europe and the United States. What's more, as high import customs discouraged foreign entrants, the FRW diversified into car tires in the 1930s. Meanwhile, the FCW thrived with the Imatra electrical power project, enabling the company to respond better to German competition.

Finnish ministries, however, could be unpredictable. Unlike many of their foreign counterparts, they did not always favor domestic producers. In new growth-driven industries, they often stressed competition as a way to nurture Finnish industries and permitted foreign rivals to enter Finnish markets, forcing domestic companies to take nothing for granted. Luckily, Nokia's growth was boosted by an export-oriented trade policy as well as the modernization by state-owned companies.

In the forestry era, Nokia's entry into the Russian paper market was facilitated by company networks, industry trade associations, and sales cartels in which Nokia often played a central role. In the first years of national independence, Finnish authorities nurtured cooperation and strategic coalitions among companies to defend the Finnish paper industry against foreign industry giants and their cartels.[21] Competition and cooperation were not perceived as mutually exclusive. Instead, both were subject to considerations pertaining to economic sovereignty. Competition would ensure innovation and upgrading while cooperation would reinforce national independence and cultural identity in global competition.

Nokia's Role as a Subsidiary

In the aftermath of the civil war, Fogelholm resigned as chief executive of Nokia, and Gunnar Bonsdorff took the position. In August 1919, Ingwald Sourander, an engineer who had studied in Germany, Austria, Switzerland, and England, was appointed Nokia's managing director. The 1920s were difficult for the company. High inflation, rising tax rates, and the war years left factories behind the times. While facilities needed upgrading and innovation, new export regions had to be found to replace the Soviet Union, where daily business had become impossible.

A decade later, Gustaf Magnus Nordensvan took Sourander's post as Nokia's chief executive. Nordensvan had the right family connections—his great-grandfather had been one of the founders of Tammerkoski, Finland's oldest paper factory. Unlike his predecessors, he had studied and worked in the United States in the early 1910s. As the center of innovation moved to America, the attention of Nokia's senior managers shifted to the United States as well. Nordensvan's tenure endured for some three decades, during which the significance of power stations accelerated among Nokia's segments and the company became one of the leading players in the business. In the process, Nordensvan had to cope with changing business cycles, drastic environmental changes, recessions, wars, and inflation. Through these years of persistent struggle, Nokia's diversification served to protect the company. When one industry segment was swept by unfavorable business cycles or a difficult competitive environment, another often enjoyed favorable results and beneficial environmental conditions. The careers of Nokia's chief executives reflected and contributed to its evolution. In the first half of the twentieth century, senior managers with a background in wood processing or power stations emerged as the company's leaders.

Throughout his years of leadership, Fogelholm stressed the importance of Nokia's independence to the board and at annual shareholder meetings. With his own stake in the company in mind, as well as that of Leo Mechelin's daughter, Fogelholm had often intervened when the FRW sought to infiltrate Nokia's board. It was not until the Nordensvan era that the relationship of the subsidiary (Nokia) and the parent (the FRW) began to evolve without friction.

Prior to the onset of the Great Depression, Nokia grew rapidly and was generating far greater revenues in the late 1920s than during the Idestam era. In 1895, Nokia's revenues amounted to FIM 1.2 million while net income was some FIM 80,000. In 1928, revenues had soared to FIM 36 million and net income to FIM 3.5 million. Beginning in 1929, Nokia began to feel the impact of the Great Depression, especially in China's shrinking paper markets. These years of recession were followed by solid growth from 1933 to 1937.

From Combination Talks to Three Wars

Beginning in the early 1930s, the issue of integrating the three companies began to surface at board meetings. In addition to its own business segments and through its majority stakes, the FRW controlled both Nokia and the FCW, so why not combine the three? Each company was leading market developments in its respective industry. Ideally, a combination of the three would benefit everyone, but the board was not convinced by such arguments. After lengthy debates, Lars Wasastjerna, the FRW's lawyer, argued that such merger aspirations were not in accordance with the corporate bylaws. Auditors opposed such efforts as well. In April 1937, the board voted against the merger. In effect, they suspected that a combination of the companies would inhibit growth of the FRW at the expense of the two weaker companies. The issue was suppressed, but it resurfaced in the 1960s when Nokia began to move toward the technology sector.

After the rejection of the proposed merger, nationalization swept the industry, but the FRW survived with the least damage. However, the three-company coalition soon had to cope with a national tragedy that transformed the company once again. After a failed coup d'etat by the right-wing Lapua Movement in the 1930s, all political extremes lost support in Finland. In the mid-1930s, the emphasis in Finnish foreign policy shifted from the border states (Poland and the Baltics) to the Nordic countries. Also, the clearing arrangements between Finland and the Soviet Union were first established in the 1930s after the world-wide Great Depression.[22] These peaceful developments, however, came to an end in 1939.

During World War II, Finland fought three interconnected wars: the Winter War (1939–1940), against the Soviet Union after its aggression; the Continuation War (1941–1944), alongside Germany against the Soviets in an effort to reconquer and secure the eastern areas; and the Lapland War (1944–1945), against Germany to drive its forces out of northern Finland.[23] These wars shattered the old political and social orders. Despite the great losses of the war years, the Finns preserved their independence, but neither the nation nor Nokia would ever be the same.[24]

The New *Realpolitik* and Soviet Trade

After the peace treaty of Paris in 1948, Finland assumed a policy of cautious neutrality and *realpolitik*, carefully taking into account its geographical location bordering the Soviet Union. This policy became known as the "Paasikivi-Kekkonen line," named after the two prominent post–World War II presidents, Juho K. Paasikivi and Urho K. Kekkonen.[25]

After the war years, major Finnish companies worked closely with the government to pay the severe reparations by 1952. As Finnish companies expanded production capacity, the government bore the business risks associated with reconstruction efforts by providing low-interest financing, supplying raw materials, and devaluing the Finnish *markka* twice in 1949. The reconstruction became the next joint "national project." In 1950, the foundations for bilateral trade between Finland and the Soviet Union were laid.

Finland was the first market economy to sign a five-year agreement on the exchange of goods with the Soviet Union. This initiative, which lasted from the early 1950s to the collapse of the Soviet economy in 1990, led the Finns to emulate Soviet procedures and institutions and pioneered eight consecutive five-year agreements.[26] Soon 15 to 25 percent of Finland's foreign trade was with the Soviet Union. In the clearing arrangements, market-based considerations played a subordinate role to politics. As an independent state, Finland had had some 40 percent of its foreign trade with Russia. At its peak, Finland's trade with the Soviet Union reached 20 to 25 percent. From the late 1940s to the early 1980s, the price of political independence was an economic autonomy of sorts.

War Reparations and Nokia's Growth

In 1944, Finland's foreign minister, Carl Enckell, signed the agreement on war reparations with A. A. Zhdanov, head of the Allied Control Commission in Finland. These arrangements proved very beneficial to Nokia, which now played a central role as the cable supplier to the Soviets. In the coming years, more than 50 percent of the entire production of the FCW went to the Soviet Union. While the factory could generate more than one hundred miles of cable annually, the Soviets demanded more than twice that amount. Due to exchange controls, the company could not purchase new machinery or expand current facilities in the mid-1940s. The only way to increase productivity was to increase efficiency. This theme, to achieve more with less, resurfaces again and again in the history of Nokia and its subsidiaries.

The Expansion of the Finnish Cable Works

From the 1920s to the 1960s, the FCW was the leading force behind the evolution of the three-company coalition. Between 1948 and 1962, the index value for the FCW's open-wire cable and phone equipment doubled, while that of power cables tripled. Meanwhile, phone cable grew almost eightfold (see Exhibit 1-7a).[27]

Throughout the war and reparation years of 1940–1948, the company steadily increased production capacity, but it did not invest in either marketing or sales. Instead, the war reparations drove rapid increases in distribution. Of the estimated $300 million of Finland's war reparations to the Soviet Union, cable products amounted to about $25 million (8.3 percent). At the same time, trade policies discouraged import markets, allowing the company to gain a dominant domestic position. By the close of the 1940s, the production capacity of the FCW significantly exceeded the domestic demand. Export activities were encouraged to ensure adequate demand in foreign markets.[28]

In the course of the reparation years, the Soviet Union had learned to trust the capabilities of the Finnish company. After the reparations had been paid and the capacity of the factory had doubled, a political relationship was converted into a business relationship. With Soviet exports, the cable business, the cash hole of the 1920s, became the cash cow of Nokia's three-company coalition. Its revenues exceeded those of the two other businesses combined (see Exhibit 1-7b).[29] This success did not come without a price.

During the post–World War II era, technology transfer became far more difficult. Not only was Nokia faced with market and technological uncertainties, it also had to cope with the implications of its special relationship with the Soviet Union. At the Kremlin, the Soviets per-

Exhibit 1-7. The Finnish Cable Works: cable segments and revenues.

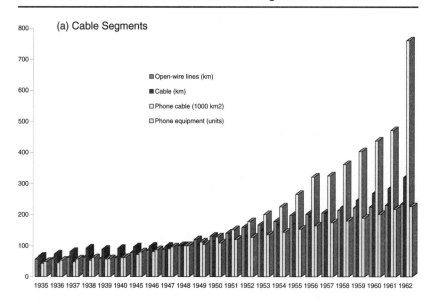

(a) Cable Segments

▣ Open-wire lines (km)
■ Cable (km)
☐ Phone cable (1000 km2)
☐ Phone equipment (units)

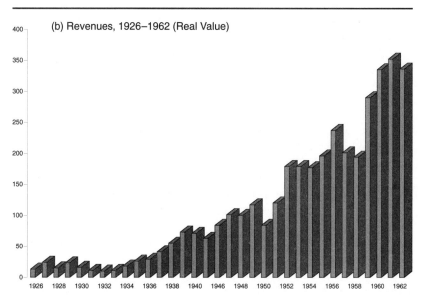

(b) Revenues, 1926–1962 (Real Value)

SOURCE: Company reports.

ceived technology partnerships as political alliances. Unlike most businesses in Western European countries, Finnish companies would not be able to enjoy the benefits of the Marshall program and ensuing technology transfers. While these factors contributed to the extraordinary rise of the German and Japanese economies, Finnish companies had to form their business strategies within the context of political exigencies.

The Three-Company Merger: The Birth of the Industrial Conglomerate

From 1945 to the mid-1960s, the FRW continued to control Nokia and the FCW through its majority stakes. The control, however, no longer reflected the changing revenue mix of the company. As the Nordensvan era ended, Torolf Sörensen, who had been in charge of Nokia's wood-processing units, was appointed managing director of the company in 1959. Prior to his tenure (1950–1958), Nokia had invested FIM 2.7 billion, whereas from 1959 to 1963, investments exceeded FIM 4.8 billion. Once again, Nokia had to turn to the Finnish banks for loans.

Since its creation in the 1860s, the company had relied on foreign exports and overseas customers, not domestic ones. Over the course of decades, it had diversified into new product and business segments as well as a variety of markets in order to survive the harsh business and political cycles of Finland's economy.[30] Between 1880 and 1915, Nokia's revenues increased from FIM 220,000 to FIM 3.4 million. By the mid-1930s, revenues were at FIM 23.3 million. In the aftermath of the war era, Nokia emerged as a far larger company. As Finland moved toward an investment-driven economy, Nokia's revenues exceeded FIM 580 million in 1950, doubling to almost FIM 1.1 billion in the mid-1950s. By 1963, total revenues had tripled to close to FIM 2.9 billion. In 1895, Nokia's mills had produced 2,513 tons of paper, 2,935 tons of groundwood, 531 tons of pulp, and 613 tons of paperboard. By 1963, they produced 39,000 tons of paper, 31,000 tons of paper, and 89,000 tons of pulp (see Exhibit 1-8).

Three decades earlier, the FRW had rejected the idea of merging Nokia and the FCW. Organizationally, the same senior management that comprised the three different boards led the three-company industrial conglomerate. Historically, this arrangement had a political rationale, but in terms of economic efficiency, it made little sense. In the future, each would have to struggle against international entrants in the domestic markets.

A merger, argued the proponents, would strengthen the bargaining power of the new corporate entity, which would provide added benefits in finance, procurement, research and development, and sup-

Exhibit 1-8. Nokia's primary segments, 1895–1963.

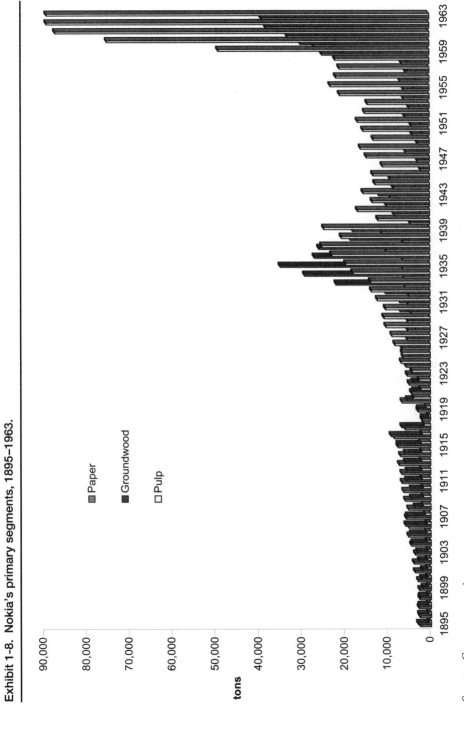

SOURCE: Company reports.

plier relationships. The problem was not how to combine the three companies, but how to gain the acceptance of the companies' two leading banks. Reflecting the old Swedish capital, the Savings Bank of Finland (Suomen Yhdyspankki, SYP) controlled the FRW, and Kansallis-Osake-Pankki (KOP), the precursor of the current Merita-Nordbanken, representing the new Finnish capital, controlled Nokia's pulp factory. To defuse the banks' potential opposition, the merged company's financial control was divided into two. Each bank would have an equal interest in the new entity. In the short term, the arrangement worked, but by the 1980s, it had become a nightmare for Nokia's executives.[31]

The last remaining obstacle involved the chief executive of the FCW, Björn Westerlund, who was against the merger. As he saw it, the new Nokia, *his* cable business, would have to carry a double burden—a maturing company (Nokia's paper products) and a declining company (the FRW). Without better synergies, what was the point of the merger? He saw little value in the rubber business, although his ancestors, the Pentzin brothers, had founded the business. Eventually, Westerlund did agree to the merger, on the condition that *he* would be made the managing director of the new entity.

The merger of the three businesses was formalized in 1967. The new corporate entity was an industrial conglomerate with four major business segments: forestry, rubber, cable, and electronics. The old businesses, in particular cable, ensured Nokia's continued profitability. As some Finnish observers put it, the name of the new company, Oy Nokia Ab, came from wood processing; the management from the cable factory; and the money from the rubber industry. But it was the most insignificant segment of all, electronics, that would ultimately renew Nokia's competitive advantage in the new era.

The Emergence of Nokia's Electronics

"In the past century, Nokia has evolved into a solid company that can look at the future optimistically," concluded a 1965 corporate biography.[32] The company certainly had an optimistic future, but that had little to do with those business segments that had been so carefully developed, protected, and nurtured for an entire century. As Nokia's original setting became a subject of idyllic corporate legends but irrelevant to its daily operations, the company began a transition into electronics, which eventually would take the company into wireless communications. This was a strategic U-turn for a company that, in the 1960s, was still known for its rubber boots, toilet paper, and Hakkapeliitta winter tires.

Over time, the diversification into high technology pushed the company further away from its early markets, triggering the need for new strategy and structure. In the late nineteenth century, process innovation enabled Nokia to enter the forestry business. The company's move into electrical power at the turn of the nineteenth century did not result from a commitment to a particular technology or capability, but to innovation. In the 1960s, electronics represented a similar breakthrough for the company, just as cellular communications would two decades later.

Again and again in the course of its history, Nokia has seized opportunities to enter new and exciting businesses characterized by high risk but great promise for growth. In each case, it has staked its future on massive infrastructural projects, from forestry, rubber, and cable to electronics, cellular, and the mobile Internet. As business and financial stakes have risen, Nokia's scale and scope have increased accordingly.

As chief executive of the FCW, Björn Westerlund had been in charge of the cable business since 1956. As Nokia's managing director, he steered the company through the early phase of the Kekkonen era, building new business relationships with the Soviets. The more Nokia did business with the Soviets and the more the company thrived, the more skeptical he became of the company's ability to sustain growth based solely on these markets. He would have preferred Nokia's Eastern exports to grow at the same pace as its Western exports. The problem, as Westerlund saw it, was that the Soviet Union, as a significant and demanding customer, was developing and building Nokia and its capabilities, yet the Soviet economy was not market-driven. When Nokia's Soviet business reached 20 percent of the FCW's total revenues, Westerlund warned the senior management: "We must be cautious and not allow the proportion of Soviet business [to] grow too much. . . . If one day they'll say *nyet* in Kreml, we'll lose our business overnight."[33]

Westerlund did allow exports to grow, but only on the condition that the other markets grow at an identical pace. Nokia could sell cable to the Soviet Union, but it would have to find new markets elsewhere in Europe, Asia, and Africa, as well as develop new products for domestic markets, in order to avoid dependency on Soviet exports. Some of his managers thought this attitude was too cautious. If the Soviets wanted to pay, why avert the inflow of business? The world had changed. This relic of the war generation was constraining Nokia's growth. True, argued Westerlund, the world had changed, but the Soviet command economy had not. Younger Nokians thought Westerlund was missing a great profit opportunity, but he would not change his mind.

When Westerlund left his job in 1977 and Kari H. Kairamo took his place, approximately 50 percent of Nokia's exports went to the Soviet Union and the other 50 percent to the West. Kairamo had achieved an important market balance within Nokia, and in the early 1990s, when the Soviet trade collapsed, this balance saved the company from catastrophe.

Kairamo's Vision

THE end of World War II was a catalyst for a renewed interest in European unity throughout most of Western Europe, but these dreams did not remain unshaken during the Cold War that followed. As the old Continent was divided into two, Finland found itself not only outside Western capitalism but also not a part of Eastern Europe. For the next four decades, the country would be torn between the two.

Relying on the support of the Social Democratic Party (SDP), Finland's president, Juho K. Paasikivi, preserved the political preconditions of Finnish democracy through diplomacy; and for decades following, every Finnish child learned Paasikivi's maxim: "Acknowledging the facts is the beginning of wisdom." Whatever the aspirations of the Finns, foreign policy and good relations with the Soviet Union were the top priorities in the nation's political agenda. Over time, this axiom became the content of the Paasikivi-Kekkonen foreign policy line and the self-evident truth of Finland's *raison d'etre*.[1] The new era of *realpolitik* began in 1948, when the government signed a Treaty of Friendship, Cooperation, and Mutual Assistance (the YYA Treaty) with the Soviet Union.[2] In order to preserve its political autonomy, so the argument went, Finland had to make political concessions that dictated its economic policies and forced it to stay away from early efforts at European integration, in which the United States played a critical role. The YYA treaty represented a trade-off (see Appendix A). The nation retained its independence but grew insulated internationally.[3]

By the early 1950s, the Finnish Communists no longer held the monopoly on good Soviet relations. If Paasikivi codified the foreign policy preconditions for the investment-driven economy, it was the minister of justice, Urho K. Kekkonen, who designed the economic principles that would guide Finland through that stage. In the early years of the investment-driven growth, from the early 1950s to the late 1960s, Nokia expanded aggressively, which led to the formation of a three-company coalition in 1967. In its third incarnation, Nokia evolved into a technology conglomerate with bold aspirations to become a dominant European player and world-class manufacturer. The phase ended dramatically, however, with a frantic wave of merger and acquisition activities, the sudden death of Nokia's chief executive officer, the eclipse of the Cold War, the collapse of Soviet trade, and Finland's efforts to enter the European Union (EU).

The faster Nokia grew, the more it became constrained by the very premise of the postwar economy, which eventually drove the company to the brink of despair. The story of Nokia's third incarnation chronicles the rise and fall of the Cold War economy.

The Cold War Era: The Rise of the Investment Economy

After the years of reparation, Finnish companies began to invest extensively in their businesses, upgrading to more modern and efficient large-scale facilities.[4] In an investment-driven economy, the government's role is often substantial, and in Finland's case, it was critical. This arrangement had as much to do with the economy as with politics, particularly as it related to foreign policy and national security considerations.[5]

Patience to Prosper

During the Cold War, Soviet trade aligned a substantial proportion of Finland's economy with Moscow's command economy and planning cycles. Such arrangements turned many Finnish companies, even the great ones, into instruments of foreign policy, which then became the sole responsibility of the president and his "inner circle." Through the Cold War, the most influential Finnish executives had to take into account these realities, as business strategies became constrained by geopolitical exigencies.[6] Starting with the reparations, Nokia had played a critical role in Soviet trade, but unlike most Finnish companies, it was not motivated by political ambitions and did not allow Eastern business to monopolize its exports. Instead, Nokia tenaciously stuck to its long-term strategy, which occasionally meant forgoing short-term profits.

New industrial policy ideas were first documented in the *Report of the Committee on Industrialization* (1951) by Finland's Ministry of Trade and Industry, which called for a "coherent and comprehensive program of industrialization."[7] In 1952, Kekkonen, the future president of Finland, published a volume on national industrial policy, *Do We Have Patience to Prosper?*[8] As the Finnish government moved from reparations and emergency measures to comprehensive public policies that promoted industrialization, Kekkonen defined the nature and goals of

Finnish industrial policies through the entire investment-driven stage. In contrast to the prevailing "Nordic model of accumulation," he insisted that the country should *not* borrow capital from the international capital markets.[9]

By design, the cold geopolitical facts—Finland's political semi-isolation from the United States and Western Europe—were rationalized through a new economic policy that based national competitive advantage on the willingness and ability of the nation and its companies to invest aggressively in its own businesses and organizations.[10] This investment-driven model was founded on a national consensus that favored investment and long-term economic growth over current consumption and income distribution.[11] Finland's government took the lead in encouraging investment to create and upgrade factories, although companies would play a growing role in making such decisions in the future. On the surface, Finland's economic turnaround was reminiscent of the kind of Soviet growth achieved through Stalin's and Hrustsev's early industrialization programs or in the more recent "Asian miracle."[12]

The investment stage of economic development forced the most advanced Finnish companies to linger in relatively undifferentiated industries and industry segments, preventing them from full participation in the technology sector. Not all companies were content to wait until the climate changed—Nokia foremost among them.

Kairamo's Rebellion: From Trees to People

Born into a family of wealth, Kari H. Kairamo (1932–1988) steered the transformation of Nokia in the late 1970s and through most of the 1980s (see Exhibit 2-1).[13] He was energetic, charismatic, hardworking, persistent, independent, entrepreneurial, innovative, and rebellious. At times, he displayed the optimistic mania that was the public image of Nokia; at other times, he would fall into pessimism and depression, a side of his personality that became publicly known only after his tragic death in 1988. Ironically, Kairamo's personal fate paralleled Nokia's own experiences from the era of détente until the eclipse of the Cold War. Finland was growing rapidly, and the Finns perceived themselves as the "Nordic Japan." Their dreams were grandiose, their hopes inflated. When the crash finally did come, it was devastating, burying the old order of the Kekkonen era as well as the investment economy.

Among Finnish industrialists, Kairamo was a maverick, yet he was very typical of his family. His great-grandfather was Alfred Kihlman, a priest, educator, and industrialist who had been in charge of a major paper and iron factory in Tampere under Idestam's Nokia. Even more important, Kihlman was among the founders of Finland's first

Exhibit 2-1. Kari H. Kairamo: the creator of the European Nokia.

SOURCE: Nokia 2000. Nokia and Nokia Connecting People are registered trademarks of Nokia Corporation.

commercial banks, the SYP and KOP, the precursors of the current Merita-Nordbanken. Alfred Kihlman's son, Alfred Oswald, was an influential professor, senator, and diplomat who changed the Swedish family name to Kairamo in 1906 at the peak of the national struggle against Russification. Alfred Kairamo married into a Finnish agrarian family and became one of the leading voices of Finnish nationalism and progressive social policies. He was also among the founders of the Finnish Party and the Pellervo Association and indirectly contributed to the rise of Finnish conservatism and the Center Party. His son, Aulis Kairamo, Kari Kairamo's father, was an equally charismatic industrialist who led two of Finland's old-economy giants, Oulu Oy and Kemi-Yhtiö. An engineer by profession and a rebel at heart, he spoke for radical reforms.

After completing engineering studies at the Helsinki University of Technology (HUT), Kari Kairamo worked for Rosenlew and Metex and initially spent summers working abroad. At home, his sister married Pekka Tarjanne, an influential politician and academic, and a key member of Kairamo's inner circle. He found the domestic climate suffocating and moved abroad. In 1962, he represented Rauma-Repola in Poland and two years later was hired by Finnmetex to sell paper and paper machinery in São Paulo, Brazil. In the mid-1960s, Kairamo became a senior vice president of Madden Machine (founded by the giants of the Finnish paper business, Valmet, Ahlström, Tampella, Valmet and Madden Corporation) and represented Finnish companies in the United States. In New York and doing business with Boise Cascade Corporation, Kairamo gained international business experience and enhanced the bargaining power of Finnish companies in the United States. During this time, Kairamo worked mercilessly, an ethic that would remain his model of doing business throughout his career.

Nokia hired Kairamo as a senior vice president in charge of the company's international affairs in 1970. At the time, Nokia was a traditional, hierarchical company, and after his hectic U.S. experience, Kairamo felt bored and became depressed,[14] but he soon advanced rapidly in a company that rewarded determination. His career paralleled dramatic changes in Finnish public policies. When Kairamo began at Nokia, Finland's President Kekkonen initiated efforts at international détente, which provided a spotlight for Finnish companies internationally. As Kairamo's responsibilities grew, deregulation and privatization began to redraw the business landscape across Europe. When his leadership was consolidated at Nokia, Kekkonen had died and Finland had a conservative government coalition for the first time in a generation. At each stage, Kairamo stayed a step or two ahead of public policies and company strategies, positioning Nokia for growth in the new markets and emerging industries.

Nokia was the largest private company in Finland, but Kairamo recognized that Finland no longer sufficed as a market. The company would have to tap into European and global markets. Despite accelerating European integration in the 1980s and the first signs of economic restructuring in the Soviet Union (*perestroika*), Kairamo was impatient. Nokia required new capabilities to exploit change; the key to success, he would repeat in numerous interviews, was lifelong learning and internationalization. Backing up his words with action, Kairamo initiated Nokia's internationalization project and encouraged employees to work overseas. In the 1970s and early 1980s, such ideas were not common in Finland.

As Nokia's chief executive, Kairamo was well aware of his influence. He led by personal example and tenacious persistence that often resulted in maverick behavior, what Kairamo himself called "management by *perkele* [Satan]." It is no surprise that Kairamo legends abound. One example is when in order to end a strike in the paper factory, Kairamo challenged a union leader to a footrace; the two ran around Kairamo's mansion, naked and barefoot in the middle of the winter.[15] Nokia's current CEO, Jorma Ollila, is highly respected, but Kairamo, a charismatic and passionate leader, was loved. The contrast between the two men should not be exaggerated, however. Ollila has shown imagination and the ability to improvise as Nokia's leader just as Kairamo exhibited extraordinary discipline at times, and both have excelled against all odds. Kairamo often criticized other senior executives for being complacent about penetrating international markets. Finland, he pointed out, was insignificant compared to European and international markets. Such boldness was unheard of in the small Nordic country where a sense of national inferiority had been inculcated through centuries of Swedish and Russian domination. Kairamo sought a dynamic fit between Nokia's resources and the environment. Appointed chief executive in 1986, Kairamo established goals that were overextended by design and therefore inherently destabilizing. Such ideas gained broad popularity only in the late 1980s, when Asian business analysts began to publish accounts of the Japanese challengers and the rise of the "Asian tigers." Following the example of Japanese leaders, Kairamo believed overextension to be an imbalanced growth strategy that would stimulate resource accumulation and revitalize organizational vitality. Through leveraged fit, Nokia would not just anticipate and respond to future changes in the environment; it would use those very environmental characteristics that were currently seen as limiting to make its strategy more effective. Kairamo's Nokia endeavored to mobilize its "invisible assets": specific technologies, accumulated consumer information, brand name, reputation, and corporate culture.[16]

When Kairamo was appointed managing director in 1977 and later CEO in 1986, he was not necessarily the logical choice. He competed for the managing director position against Matti Nuutila, but unlike his rival, Kairamo, who had great people skills, was eager to face challenges, passionate about shaping Nokia into an international high-growth technology giant, and willing to fight for the job. After his appointment, things changed at Nokia. Traditional formalities and processes gave way to speed and immediacy. Change and flexibility became important attributes to the company. Kairamo personified the company through the 1980s; after all, it was Kairamo's Nokia that first grasped the pressing need to think in terms of competitive advantage and that fully understood how the company's fate precipitated that of the country.

As far as Kairamo was concerned, it was difficult to draw a line between Nokia and Finland. When he said "we," he often implied both. Like the cautious Finnish politicians, he also learned to use language shrewdly, relying on ambiguous metaphors in order to avoid debates on foreign policy. In the past, Finland had been about trees (comparative advantage, natural resources); in the future, Finland would be about people (competitive advantage, human capital).

> To us, the Finns, internationalization is not an alternative to something else. Finland has quite a few resources. Briefly put, there are two of them: the people and the trees. Exports are obligatory in the future as well. Things must be sold abroad so that living conditions will remain good domestically. This, in turn, requires that we have extensive experience in international business.[17]

To Kairamo, that meant a "kind of Japanese model." The great success of Japanese companies had resulted in increased protectionism worldwide. Finland and Finnish businesses were too small to cause such reactions. Kairamo argued:

> If Finland can change rapidly and if we can keep up with the technology, if we can match the quality and if cost level is not made an obstacle in sales, we will always find room in worldwide markets. But all of this requires internationalization. . . . That is the greatest risk facing the Finns—the small amount of international business experience.

Kairamo spoke for change and speed and eschewed complacency. "We must learn to become fast," he would urge his company. "If, for instance, one isn't fast enough in the most competitive segments of electronics, there just aren't any chances to succeed. We're garnering international experience at an accelerating pace. Our educational level is high. We can become fast."[18] But there was a catch—in order to become fast, Nokia would have to access global markets, and in order to access global markets, it would have to be fast. In both cases, the first requirement was to open doors to Europe. But how could Nokia even dream of achieving such a feat when Finland was both a part of and apart from Europe?

In and Out of Europe

Beginning in the late 1950s, Finland had opened its economy to the two Western European trading blocs, the European Economic Community (EEC) and the European Free Trade Association (EFTA). Expanded trade with the West did not require abandoning profitable exchanges with the East. The guiding principle of Finland's postwar foreign policy was to assure the Soviet Union that it was not a threat, a delicate political balancing act. Finnish commercial ties with the Soviet Union and the other members of the Council for Mutual Economic Assistance (Comecon) continued to deepen after 1960. In the West, skeptics felt that Finland's active neutrality did not go far enough to minimize its relationship with the East. In the East, however, critics argued that it went too far.

As the rearmament of West Germany was achieved through the Western European Union (WEU), the North Atlantic Treaty Organization (NATO) insulated Finland from initial European integration. During 1950 and 1951, the Schuman Plan led to the pooling of coal and steel resources, especially between France and the newly established West German state, thereby serving as the blueprint for the European Coal and Steel Community (ECSC).[19]

Efforts at European integration culminated in 1957 with the Treaty of Rome, which established the EEC. In 1960, the EFTA was founded to offset the EEC. A year later, Finland's EFTA agreement was made possible only because equal terms had been negotiated a year before concerning Finnish-Soviet trade. Finland joined the EFTA as an associate member but enjoyed all the basic commercial privileges by the following year. The EEC internal tariff barriers had been substantially reduced and quota restrictions on industrial products largely eliminated by the 1960s. In 1969, a summit meeting in The Hague reconfirmed political union as the EC's ultimate goal, calling for the implementation of the Economic and Monetary Union (EMU) by 1980.[20]

President Kekkonen had consolidated his power by the 1970s, garnering the support of all major parties from the conservatives to the Communists. In 1973, his presidential term was extended by special legislation that required a two-thirds majority in Parliament. That year also saw Finland's trade agreement with the EEC, but not without Kekkonen's intervention. He guaranteed that the EEC agreement would not harm Finnish-Soviet relations or trade.[21] Instead of countering cyclical fluctuations through a Keynesian fiscal strategy, Finland opted for restrictive economic policies that would restore external balance and restrain inflation.[22]

Finland's economy remained stuck in a devaluation cycle until the 1980s, while elsewhere in Europe barriers fell and trade accelerated. Western observers interpreted Finnish foreign economic policy as focusing on security concerns rather than economic interests, but the reality was more complex. From 1945 to the late 1970s, Finland's foreign economic policy was marked by a precarious balancing act between Eastern and Western trade, from which many Finnish companies benefited as long as the investment economy reigned.

In the early postwar years, Soviet trade served important economic interests in Finland, driving the rapid development of the metalworking industries during the 1950s and helping to absorb farm labor. Similarly, after the 1973 oil crisis, Finnish exports to the Soviet Union provided an essential market during a recessionary period in Western markets. In both cases, Nokia benefited immensely. Reparations made its cable business just as Soviet trade in the 1970s provided a testing ground for its electronics products. Yet, the benefits of Soviet trade and postwar foreign policy had a price,[23] restricting the strategic scope of Finnish companies internationally by blocking their participation in the Marshall Plan and the Organization for European Economic Cooperation (OEEC).[24] When the Cold War economy began to crumble, Finland's most advanced companies felt the pain, and Nokia was among the first of them.

Postwar Technology Catch-Up

After World War II, American leadership prevailed across the international technology sector, and postwar technology catch-up accounted for most of the convergence between the late 1940s and the early 1970s, and the birth of the "convergence club" (the Organization for Economic Cooperation and Development, OECD).[25] In Europe and Japan, the remarkable growth of the postwar years was achieved by technology transfer, high rates of investment, and a range of growth-friendly domestic policies. The master architect of the convergence club was the United States. The Marshall Plan enabled those countries that lost the war to reassert their economic strength during the Cold War.[26] Due to its delicate politico-economic balancing act with the

Soviet Union, Finland missed the first opportunities made possible by the convergence club.

After the Soviet invasion of Afghanistan in 1980 and the advent of the Reagan era, the United States prohibited technology exports to the Soviet Union. At the time, Finland—Nokia, in particular—served as Moscow's primary supplier of "Western technology." Conversely, the future of Finnish electronics depended on U.S.-based technologies. However, NATO was concerned that the Finns were sharing technologies with the Soviet Union. Kairamo had to convince the United States and its allies that critical technology products were not being given to the Kremlin. During the 1960s and 1970s, "Finlandization" had become a cautionary catchword in the West.[27] Although the term was vague, it was used as a foreign policy hammer to stress Finland's inherent geopolitical limitations. Allaying Western concerns was not an easy task.

In Finland, all major foreign and even domestic policy decisions were carried out with an overriding concern for possible Soviet reaction.[28] Not only did the Finnish government avoid taking issue with Moscow's human rights violations, every major Finnish politician had some level of contact with the Soviet embassy, and often had a KGB-based "acquaintance."[29] According to published sources, Kairamo himself was no exception—after all, trade with the Soviet Union was the first step in Nokia's efforts to become an international company.[30]

Richard N. Perle, the U.S. assistant secretary of defense for international security policy, visited Finland in 1984. Nokia had previously built cable factories in Russia; now Kairamo wanted to export Nokia's new DX 200 stations to the Soviets. Serving as Perle's host, Kairamo had the opportunity to discuss U.S. export controls, which were threatening Nokia's technology exports to the Soviet Union. With the assistance of Western technology, argued Perle, the Soviets saved at least $5 million and five years in product development. Still, the American guest appeared to appreciate Kairamo's persuasive diplomacy. After the visit, Perle wrote a gracious letter in which he expressed his confidence that a solution could be found that would minimize the harm to Nokia caused by export controls while securing the defense interests of the West. Later that year, the first DX 200 stations were exported to the Soviet Union.[31]

Despite the positive outcome, as long as Finland was constrained by its special relationship with the Soviet Union, Nokia would not be a credible partner in strategic technology coalitions. In the mid-1980s, for instance, Finland struggled to join the European EUREKA research program. Many Western countries felt threatened by the Finns' participation, fearing that technology secrets might be shared with the Soviet

Union and Eastern Europe. It was only through persistent diplomatic efforts that Finland eventually participated in EUREKA.*

In the early 1980s, foreign ownership remained prohibited in Finland, and international capital was difficult to raise. Kairamo said in 1986:

> Until recently, Finland has been forgotten to the margins of Lapland, at the periphery. Even though we have a positive attitude towards technology, not enough resources have been invested in it. It's only in recent years that we've participated in major international research projects, as members and payers. We have been engaged in cooperation, yet we have often been enjoying the benefits of others.[32]

Because of politics and trade, Kairamo could neither distance himself from the Soviet Union nor approach the United States. So began his quest for a third way: the European integration process that a decade or two before had become politically safe in Finland.

The Third Incarnation of Nokia

Kairamo had the drive and determination to turn Nokia into an electronics giant. In effect, that goal had been discussed since the 1973 oil crisis, when Nokia's board had taken a hard look at the company's prospects. Kairamo later recalled, "We came to the conclusion that we couldn't grow in Finland with cables or tires any more. . . . We decided to keep what we had, but also to put all the new money we could scrape together into high tech."[33] So began the story that ultimately climaxed in Nokia's position as a world power in mobile communications.

From Comparative to Competitive Advantage

Until the mid-1980s, the idea of comparative advantage dominated most of the thinking about international competition, resting on endowments of inputs such as labor, natural resources, and financial capital. In an increasingly global economy, however, these factor in-

*During his visit to Finland in the early 1990s, Boris Yeltsin apologized on behalf of his predecessors for past meddling in Finland's domestic affairs during the Soviet era. In addition to direct Soviet influence in Finland, "Finlandization" stemmed from a political culture created by the Finns themselves under the leadership of President Kekkonen, who himself cherished (and expected) undivided loyalty.

puts were becoming less and less valuable. In national competitive advantage, prosperity stems from creating an appropriate business environment along with supporting institutions that allow a nation to productively use and upgrade its inputs.[34]

Finland was a textbook case, and Nokia provides a company-level example. Scarce natural resources, the energy crisis, and extraordinarily high inflation prompted Finnish interest in the technology sector. To pay for needed imports, Finland depended on export markets in Western and Eastern Europe. To protect those markets, the country had pursued economic integration with both the East and the West and had maintained good commercial relations with the Soviet Union. However, as Finland was reaching its limit of economic growth in the 1970s and 1980s, the very basis of competition was changing. To expand meant incorporating increasingly greater amounts of raw materials, capital, and labor into the production process. Yet the economy needed to grow through better resource management, improved labor productivity, and newer technologies. In international markets, the oil crises of 1973 and 1979 caused particular difficulties for the Finns, who imported more than 80 percent of their primary energy supplies. While Finland suffered less than other Western European countries because of its special trading relationship with the Soviet Union, it was still affected by recession in Western markets and growing technological competition. Furthermore, tighter financial markets made Finland's traditional cycle of inflation and devaluation untenable.[35] Nokia no longer had faith in comparative advantage; rather, it would seek competitive advantage.

The Quest for First-Mover Advantages in Electronics

In the late 1950s and early 1960s, Nokia shifted its focus to consumer and business electronics and modernized its basic industries by expanding into robotics, fiber optics, and high-grade tissues. In the aftermath of the worldwide energy crisis, Nokia, unlike many other Finnish companies, also reassessed its dependency on Soviet trade, which comprised almost 40 percent of its exports. Unlike the Finnish state-owned companies, Nokia kept its independent strategic course, even in the face of official Cold War rhetoric. Luckily, Finland's political role in the détente process favored some Finnish companies, which exemplified the "peaceful coexistence" of Finland and the Soviet Union.

In the 1960s, when its electronics department was researching radio transmission and realizing the future potential of semiconductor technology, the company employed several digital gurus, including Björn Westerlund and Kurt Wikstedt, who maintained good relations with universities, provided a strategic vision of a digital future, and were eager to exploit the commercial uses of new technology. Their activities laid the groundwork for Nokia's role in telecommunications. In 1969, Nokia was the first company to introduce pulse code modulation (PCM) transmission equipment that conformed to standards of the Consultative Committee on International Telegraphy and Telephony (CCITT). By stepping into the digital age early on, Nokia made one of the most important strategic decisions in its corporate history.

Ironically, the contribution of electronics to Nokia's total revenues remained insignificant. In 1967, electronics generated only 3 percent of the Nokia Group's net sales and provided work for only 460 people. In the early 1970s, the majority of telephone exchanges were still electromechanical analog switches, and no general consensus about digitization existed. Nokia's digital gurus sought first-mover advantage in a massive new industry, yet to skeptics their visions seemed more like science fiction.

In 1967, Intel's Gordon Moore formulated "Moore's Law," which stated that the power of the silicon chip would double annually. If the trend continued, he reasoned, computing power would rise exponentially over relatively brief periods of time. As a result, integrated electronics would make electronic techniques widely available. At the time, few understood the phenomenal implications of Moore's Law. "I don't remember any response to the article," Moore recalls. "It was only in the mid-1970s that the industry really understood what was going on."[36] Nokia's electronics unit did understand this phenomenon and began developing the digital switch that eventually became the Nokia DX 200. While skeptics continued to criticize the costly investment in these activities, the successful switch evolved into a multifaceted platform that remains the basis for Nokia's network infrastructure today.

Political Visions, Market Realities: The Valco Debacle

By the late 1960s, the Finns continued to share a long border with the Soviets but believed in the Western ideals of democracy.[37] As Nokia sought to strike the right balance between Western and Eastern trade, a new, radical generation emerged in Finland. The parliamentary elections of 1966 marked a major turning point in Finnish politics and represented a great victory for the socialist parties, which gained their first absolute majority since 1916. Although they still sang the old "Internationale" at party conventions, the new bunch bore little resemblance to the older generation Social Democrats and Communists.

Starting with their landslide victory, Social Democrats were the critical political force in the changing Finland. Despite some instability at the cabinet level, a series of center-left governments came into power from 1966 to the mid-1980s. By the end of this era, some 85 percent of Finland's total workforce had been organized into unions. Meanwhile, the Conservative Coalition Party was kept outside the government for an entire quarter of a century.[38] It was only after the conservatives returned to the government that European integration accelerated and telecommunications deregulation really began in Finland.

As political stability led to the rejection of demands for nationalization, the investment-driven policies stressed economic development that justified the establishment of government enterprises. Nokia, however, was left untouched; it was a business success story and a major Soviet trade partner. While some private companies were organized as government agencies, none underwent nationalization.[39] (True, in the aftermath of the War Years, the state council had appointed a socialization committee that, in 1950, had recommended the socialization of Finnish telecommunications. However, as conditions in Finland gradually improved, socialization efforts failed and the committee dissolved.)[40]

It was during these extraordinary years that younger politicians, motivated by the fear of American multinationals and bolstered by their faith in socialist values, began to consider the idea of a state-owned electronics giant. If the notion had advanced, it might have demolished Nokia's investment in the technology sector. The Finnish fears were hardly unique in Europe. In 1968, Jean-Jacques Servan-Schreiber published a bestseller, Le Défi Américain (The American Challenge), that portrayed a bleak future for high technology. "Fifteen years from now," he wrote, "it is quite possible that the world's third great industrial power, just after the United States and Russia, will not be Europe, but American industry in Europe."[41]

To counter the perceived threat, progressive Finnish politicians envisioned a convergence of rationalist socialist planning and modern high technology. Such ambitions were in no way aligned with the existing capabilities of local companies. Despite the relative success of the country's tiny electronics industry, Finland's balance of trade in electronics products had been strongly negative, and domestic manufacturing remained insignificant until the 1980s.[42] As the Old and the New Continent were viewing each other suspiciously, both ignored the Asian challenge.

By the mid-1970s, progressive politicians considered Valco, a company that manufactured television tubes, to be the country's first competitor in electronics. Yet, given the low profit potential of this sector, existing industry players showed little interest. In 1972, RCA explored the plan but came to the conclusion that it would be a loss leader. After similar studies, Siemens, Toshiba, Philips, and three Finnish television manufacturers—Salora, Lohja (Finlux), and Asa—came to identical conclusions.[43] Their view was not shared by Social Democrats in the Center Party, which believed in the future of a national champion and insisted that the factory be located in a developing region. In the public sector, this reluctance of competitors was perceived as a sign of a market failure (what business today might deem an immature marketplace) that would be resolved when political planners restored order and growth.[44] Industry did not buy the argument. "It is painful for the taxpayer," noted the Finnish *Electronics News*, "to see his work end up in Valco's well, through politics and taxation." The publication suggested that, in the future, the ensuing technology might prove useful only to roast hot dogs.[45]

Just as Silicon Valley was emerging as an entrepreneurial and technological hotbed in the U.S. economy, the Finns were moving in a diametrically opposite direction. Valco was a joint venture between the government (60 percent of the stock), a Finnish private company (20 percent), and Japan's Hitachi (20 percent). However, some key participants nurtured plans that went further. Between 1974 and 1975, Lauri Saari, Valco's managing director, wrote two memos on the "major measures to achieve a state-owned electronics concern." The objective was to establish a major electronics company by 1977. Valco would receive significant public financing and cooperate with Soviet markets. This plan, which became public only near the end of the 1980s, required the socialization of Nokia.[46] The factory was in trouble within a year or two and would never operate at full capacity.

By the fall of 1977, the Finnish state owned 75 percent of Valco, whereas Salora and Hitachi each had a 12.5 percent stake. At this point, any additional costs were attributed mainly to inflation. The Valco debacle had become a tabloid story about political corruption, tax avoidance, Freemasons, and bribery. In August 1978, when Valco's Imatra factory was launched, the prime minister noted that the market future of color television was now brighter than it had been two years prior. The new factory, he declared, heralded the potential of mass production of electronics in Finland. Yet, Hitachi declared it would no longer invest in the project. Only a few weeks later, the government acknowledged the failure of Valco, both as a technological power and as a profitable business. Eero Rantala, then minister of trade and industry, suggested that with the "socialization of Valco" the Finnish state would simply acquire a 51 percent majority stake. In 1979, the factory was closed temporarily, but two years later, 51 percent of Valco's stock was sold to Nokia.

The high-profile failure of the old-style industrial policy resulted in Nokia accumulating its electronics and telecommunications capabilities in Finland *without state intervention*,[47] while the politicians looked to Nokia as their new national champion. Since the early 1970s, Kairamo had been nurturing close relationships with Social Democratic leaders, including Ulf Sundqvist, one of the new radicals, and Finland's minister of Trade and Industry. Sundqvist advocated state-controlled electronics, Kairamo supported Nokia's leading role in electronics, but both agreed on the future significance of the high-technology industry. With the Valco debacle resolved, Kairamo wrote on his beliefs:

> In the developed economies, electronics is not just a strategic, but a central industry determinant of international competitiveness. While investments amount to billions, many favor indirect trade barriers to protect their domestic electronics. This is the case in Western Europe. . . . The challenge of Finnish electronics is in the small and perhaps world's most open domestic marketplace. That is why we can thrive only by retaining substantial competitiveness and by raising exports. That, in turn, requires both fast responsiveness to external changes and a diversified industrial endurance.[48]

Now Nokia set out to expand its electronics business with renewed vigor. While electronics had been only a small part of the cable unit in the 1960s, it accounted for more than 40 percent of sales after the mid-1980s. From the 1960s, Nokia's digital gurus had managed the transition from forestry, rubber, and cable into electronics. But the mere presence of the electronics unit did not cause the change in Nokia's corporate strategy. It was a calculated strategic choice made by Kairamo.

The Birth of the Electronics Concern

At the end of the 1980s, Nokia was considered a technology conglomerate. Today the company is internationally known for its dominance in the mobile communications marketplace. At the beginning of the decade, however, the company was perceived quite differently in Finland. One analyst noted in 1981:

> The great public may see Nokia as a wood processing company (toilet paper) and *hakkapeliitta* rubber boot firm. The image is a false one because Nokia's largest industrial group is metal, which includes cable and cable machinery. Second, due to its diligent foreign acquisitions and the consolidation of British Tissue, it is mainly an international con-

cern; it has subsidiaries through the globe. Similarly, the role of exports and foreign activities is now more than half of its revenues.[49]

Due to its extensive diversification, Nokia was considered a "post-cyclical company."

The analysts were in for a surprise. As Eastern trade steadily diminished in importance, the real M&A spree was only about to begin. By 1983, Nokia's Soviet trade still amounted to some 39 percent of the total, but with accelerating investments in electronics, the importance of Western countries to the company's foreign efforts was rapidly growing. Between 1983 and 1984, Nokia was transformed from a diversified industrial conglomerate into an electronics concern. For the first time in the company's history, the electronics revenues exceeded those of cable, forest, or rubber.[50] "As the size has grown, the issues of electronics have become increasingly important to group leadership," noted Kairamo. "They are now strategic issues."[51]

Nokia's success has its roots in the critical strategic decisions of the late 1970s and early 1980s. Nokia's diversification into electronics is only one part of the story. At the time, many companies invested in new technologies. However, few chose the right strategy in the right industry. And among these, still fewer benefited from appropriate location advantages and favorable public policies.

Growth-Share Matrix

From the late 1950s until the mid-1970s, Nokia's electronics was a cash trap, but years of investment, effort, and intense internal controversy ultimately turned the unit into a success. The determination of Kurt Wikstedt, then chief of the unit, was not shared among the other unit chiefs. His belief in the future significance of electronics was based on American management approaches, the experience curve and portfolio analysis in particular, rather than intuition.

The Boston Consulting Group (BCG) was one of the first consulting companies in the United States to focus on future management. In the mid-1960s, the BCG popularized the experience curve (see Exhibit 2-2a). The concept evolved in technology research as BCG sought to explain price and competitive conduct in high-growth industry segments for clients such as Texas Instruments and Black and Decker. BCG claimed that for each cumulative doubling of experience, total costs would decline some 20 to 30 percent due to economies of scale, organizational learning, and technological innovation.[52]

As long as electronics failed to turn a profit, Nokia's other units perceived the unit as an expensive burden rather than a future bonanza. It was only in 1977, when most of the Nokia Group suffered from a cyclical downturn, that the electronics division began to generate cash, and in 1981, approximately 77 percent of Nokia's electronics revenues came from Finnish markets. However, in just one year that figure was expected to drop significantly—to less than 40 percent— with growth coming from overseas markets. "Electronics has been the right solution for the company," acknowledged Wikstedt. "Its profitability is not as good as we'd like it to be, but this has to do with our vast investments."[53] That was not an understatement. In 1980, the electronics unit invested some FIM 180 million in product development—representing 12 percent of all Finnish R&D. By the mid-1980s, these investments had increased to around FIM 400 million. It was only when Wikstedt was about to retire that the electronics units became profitable, after seventeen years in the red.

Portfolio Analysis

As the experience curve was becoming the new business strategy mantra of management consultants, it also found new applications in corporate strategy. By the early 1970s, BCG defined portfolio analysis on the basis of the experience curve. After experience curves had been drawn for the business units of a diversified company, the relative investment potential of each could be compared by plotting them all on the growth-share matrix (see Exhibit 2-2b). BCG's strategy guidelines urged companies to divest slow-growth/low-share businesses ("dogs") while maintaining a prudent balance between high-growth/high-share segments ("stars") and slow-growth/high-share businesses ("cash cows"). The company also paid close attention to the allocation of some resources to high-growth/low-share businesses ("question marks") that could prove to be future winners.[54]

At Nokia, Wikstedt expanded electronics initiatives based on BCG's growth-share matrix. This matrix permitted senior managers to identify the company's future stars and cash cows. Even more important, it located the longest product life cycles in the telecommunications unit of Nokia Electronics. "That is the cash cow," Wikstedt acknowledged in the mid-1980s. "Radio links, PCM equipment, wired and wireless information transmission generate the money."[55] With some enhancements, he estimated the life cycles of stabilized products to be perhaps ten to fifteen years, although modifications would be needed every two to three years.

The diversified conglomerate sought financial discipline through portfolio management, which was benchmarked from General Electric. Nokia also adopted an active corporate strategy, boldly allocating capital to electronics and telecommunications, both perceived to be "star"

Exhibit 2-2. Boston Consulting Group: experience curve and growth-share matrix.

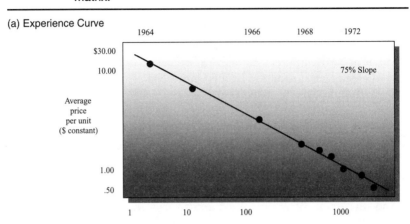

segments with promising prospects for growth. These insights, as well as Wikstedt's ability and willingness to champion them against a chorus of internal skeptics, led to Nokia's success in cellular a decade later. At the time, however, he could only rely on estimates, expectations, future scenarios, and digitalization trend lines based on Moore's Law.

In the 1960s and 1970s, the most innovative Japanese leaders had applied American insights to increasingly global industries. Now, the Nokians were about to do the same for mobile communications. Nokia was small enough to exploit new technologies more quickly and with more flexibility than its mass-producer rivals. As electronics became Nokia's core business segment, the company initiated supplier relationships with L. M. Ericsson in Sweden, IBM in the United States, and Northern Telecom in Canada. Soon thereafter, Nokia engaged in strategic alliances that included a joint venture with Tandy in Texas and South Korea in order to learn more about flexible manufacturing and to ensure market access in the United States.

With bold dreams came necessary risks.

The Acquisition Spree

When the fortunes of Nokia's electronics seemed to reverse in the early 1980s, Wikstedt was already sixty-three years old and ready to retire. In the succession struggle, three names surfaced: Timo H. Koski, Wikstedt's vice deputy; Heikki Keränen, chief of information systems; and Antti Lagerroos (until he was appointed the chief of Salora-Luxor, Nokia's television group). Organizationally, Nokia's electronics consisted of four profit units (see Exhibit 2-3): telecommunications, information systems, industrial automation, and data. Of these units, telecommunications was the largest, led by Sakari Salminen; Koski was in charge of information systems until Kairamo appointed him head of business development for electronics.[56]

To compete with the European national champions, Kairamo began a frantic wave of M&A activities. "We must not stop," he would say to his troops. "We must renew ourselves." The old sources of competitive advantage eroded as new ones emerged. In order to participate in the digital future, Nokia had to sustain its current competitive advantage and continually renew it to ensure future profitability. Kairamo and his senior managers shared the belief that Nokia had to become a technology concern, but that was where the consensus ended.

The Push into Consumer Electronics: Mass Production or Focus Strategy?

As the electronics unit emerged as a cash cow, Nokia's telecommunications expanded rapidly. While Kairamo was upgrading the company's basic segments in chemicals, electricity, machinery, and paper, he was also focusing on consumer electronics. In 1983, Nokia took full control of Salora Oy, a major Finnish company in which it had had a 17 percent stake; it was now Scandinavia's largest maker of color televisions. The acquisition originated from a 1976 deal in which Mobira obtained Salora's radiophones. According to Simo Vuorilehto,

Exhibit 2-3. Nokia's corporate organization (1984).

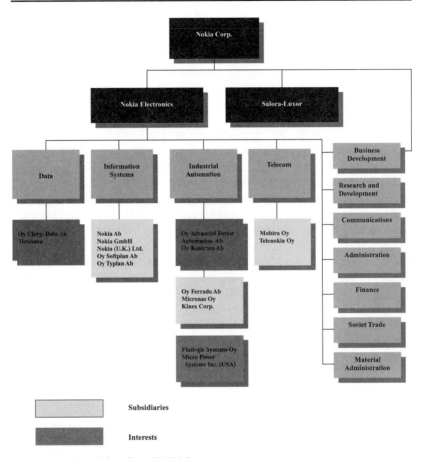

SOURCE: Based on *Talouselämä* 33 (1984).

Kairamo's deputy, industrial, home, and consumer electronics were rapidly converging: "Technology will be largely the same. Mass products, office products, telecommunications and factory automation products will be divided in terms of markets, the buyers. It is important to Nokia to acquire know-how in electronics, in both mass production and marketing practices."[57]

Nokia's other senior managers were not quite as convinced of such future scenarios. While many would have agreed on the convergence projection, they envisioned a variety of implications. Most important, convergence would mean increased specialization. If Nokia were to offer everything to all buyers, it would stumble in the changing markets. The future belonged to new, fast, and focused players, not to old, slow, and vertically integrated conglomerates. Besides, the technologists would add, what did Vuorilehto know? He had been trained in the forestry business.

Despite doubts, Nokia pushed into consumer electronics. Having acquired Salora, it then purchased Luxor AB, Sweden's faltering state-owned electronics and computer concern. The result was one of Europe's largest television manufacturers, an entity that many contemporary observers thought could compete with both Japanese and American electronics giants. Three years later, Nokia acquired Oceanic, a French television manufacturer that Electrolux had bought from ITT in 1980.

Nokia was now Europe's third-largest player in television manufacturing. Because Oceanic exported only 5 to 6 percent of its production, Nokia wanted to use it to access the French and Italian markets, just as it intended to exploit Oceanic's distribution network to export mobile radiophones. Irrespective of bold strategic objectives, the acquisition was a difficult one to manage. Although Nokia's Salora, Luxor, and Oceanic produced about one million television sets annually, individual brands did not contribute to the Nokia brand. Nokia had become a major player in the consumer markets, but few people knew about it because of low brand awareness. Also, in order to exploit scale economies, Nokia would have to move from business-based television manufacturing to country-based production, which required increased organizational complexity.[58]

In 1984, Nokia's electronics generated approximately FIM 1.7 billion, while revenues at Salora-Luxor climbed to FIM 1.8 billion. In the long term, the numbers told only part of the story. In the late 1970s, the Valco affair had been built upon a dream of a state-controlled electronics conglomerate comprising component, telecommunications, process, and biotechnology units. The idea of a unified technology giant may have been natural to politically oriented planners who had little understanding of the markets and who equated vertical scale with market power, but this idea was far from those nurtured at Kairamo's Nokia, where the organization was perceived as a function of existing *and* emerging markets. If markets were specialized and focused, creating a vertically integrated giant was the wrong solution at the wrong time. "Nokia's leadership does not believe in a management organization, which seeks to build a great sub-concern under the group itself," noted Kairamo. "Nokia does not form a great comprehensive electronics concern."[59]

Nokia was after defined and focused business segments that it could turn into profit centers. Indeed, by 1990, Timo H. A. Koski saw Nokia as a corporation consisting of key electronics groups that would operate independently and group leadership that would concentrate exclusively on major strategic issues. Like Wikstedt, Koski wanted strategic decisions to be the responsibility of group leadership, whereas operational responsibility would belong to profit units alone.[60] The problem was that the consumer electronics acquisitions were pushing Nokia in diametrically opposite directions. In fact, despite all its M&A activity, Nokia was a late mover. It had to compete with Silicon Valley in information technology, and the Japanese already dominated the television business.

Certainly, the creation of the Salora-Luxor group at Nokia reflected an effort to exploit technology integration among different fields of electronics, just as it represented the parent's continuing attempts at diversification. According to Kairamo, Nokia's M&A activities were designed for a purpose:

> The idea is that there would be at least a single broad electronics house in Finland. Our electronics is now almost as diverse as the concern itself; it is no longer vulnerable to cyclical threats. All of this began from the vision of a future factory. The next stage was the future office and then the future home. Synergy doesn't come easily. It requires a lot of work and still more work.[61]

A European Technology Concern

Even while launching Europe's first digital telephone system, Nokia continued its aggressive acquisition activities. Some purchases supplemented existing cellular properties, including Mobira, a Finnish mobile phone company and the precursor of Nokia Mobile Phones (see Chapter 4). Others, particularly in television operations, distracted from this focus. The former created gateways to the future, the latter resulted in divestitures. In 1986, Nokia acquired control of Finland's largest electrical wholesaler. It then created the largest IT group in Scandinavia, Nokia Data, by purchasing Ericsson Group's Data Division in 1988.

Nokia reported its best results in 1987 and 1988; it was now a European technology concern. In 1988, M&A activities boosted the company's revenues from FIM 14 billion to FIM 21.5 billion. Acquisitions had significantly altered the company's strategic and geographic focus: Nokia had moved production closer to customers, which translated into an increasing number of overseas manufacturing facilities; less than half of its personnel was Finnish; it financed its subsidiaries vis-à-vis Switzerland; and it had more than one hundred subsidiaries in continental Europe. Between 1982 and 1987, Nokia's market value more than tripled, from FIM 2.272 billion to FIM 8.029 billion—the largest in Finland. Things looked good. Finnish analysts interpreted the competitive situation as follows: "It is difficult to find anybody who could invest FIM 4 billion to take over Nokia. Especially when the headquarters looks secured under the watchful eye of KOP, Pohjola and SYP [the largest Finnish insurance companies and banking concerns]."[62] Ironically, the very same insurance companies and banks eyed Nokia's rapid growth with increasing concern and were already plotting to change Nokia's ownership structure (see Chapter 3).

Yet, Nokia's size and market power reinforced its confidence in the M&A strategy, and the more quickly Nokia grew, the more outspoken Kairamo became. Finland was the company's home base, but the Finnish economy did not allow for appropriate internationalization, and Nokia again had to look beyond its home base. It was time to question the old political truths. In the spring of 1987, Kairamo raised a debate by insisting that Finland should join the European Council. "Since we already participate in almost all practical activities," Kairamo argued, "it is difficult to explain why we are not a member of the European Council. It should be noted that, according to recent press reports, even [the] Soviet Union is seeking common contact with the European Council."[63] Hardly an unreasonable argument. In Finland, however, many old-style industrialists, not to mention the cautious political mandarins, considered such ideas an intervention in foreign policy, which was the sole responsibility of the president.

Although Kairamo was not interested in politics, he was not afraid to meddle in it if that served Nokia's interests. Because of the significance of Soviet trade in the company's exports, he had engaged in diplomacy of his own with the Soviets and quite a few Finnish politicians since the early 1970s. Unlike many other Finnish industrialists, he did not belong to the inner circle of President Kekkonen, an old enemy of Kairamo's own father and a man who seldom forgot his political enemies, yet he nurtured a good relationship with Finland's centrist leadership, especially Paavo Väyrynen, whom many expected to be a future president. In effect, Kairamo's willingness to keep the Soviets happy was noted even by Viktor Vladimirov, a KGB general who presented himself as a loyal follower of the new party chief, Yuri Andropov, and declared Kairamo one of the most important Finnish industrialists he ever had the pleasure to communicate with regularly.[64]

Since the 1950s, foreign policy had developed a rhetoric that was considered the price of national survival. Kairamo was among the first industrialists to question such arrangements, although that was not his explicit objective. Instead, he already envisioned an era in which such rhetoric was irrelevant. He argued:

> I only said my opinion that I don't see any obstacles in joining the European Council. I also said that it would be in

the interest of Finland's image. I didn't make any explicit suggestion, that's not the way I would like to influence things; those things belong to the "politbureau" [sic]. I don't have political aspirations. I do not intend to get into any political group. But of course I want to influence things always when politicians, irrespective of their parties, agree to listen to a representative of the industry. That is my obligation and the obligation of every industrial association representative.[65]

Despite Kairamo's exploits, Nokia remained relatively unknown in Europe, even if it was doing its utmost to popularize its brand name. In one advertising blitz, residents of Stockholm and Oslo were given a business trivia quiz: What company brought electricity to 350 Egyptian villages, makes the most toilet paper in Ireland, and provides all the studded winter bicycle tires in the world? The company was not Swedish, German, or Japanese. It was Oy Nokia. By 1987, the flagship of Finnish industry had 27,600 employees. The $2.7 billion conglomerate was Finland's largest publicly traded concern, with some 47.9 million shares outstanding. Under Kairamo's leadership, Nokia had evolved from an insular maker of pulp, paper, chemicals, and rubber into a growing, international technology leader, focusing on television sets and mobile telephones. Electronics accounted for more than 40 percent of its sales.

Four years before the collapse of the Soviet Union and Eastern trade, Kairamo saw the warning signs quite clearly. As Finland's sheltered Soviet-bloc markets were shrinking, Finnish industry was forced into the more rigorous competition for Western markets. Nokia was leading the way and expected to become Finland's first international company, even if meant moving its headquarters outside Finland. Kairamo was the first to raise this sensitive issue, but he made no formal propositions.

Years *before* Nokia's restructuring and refocusing, Kairamo was already thinking aloud about selling off some of the company's old core divisions to generate cash in the coming years. The company needed investment capital to deter domestic protectionism and resolve the shortage of engineers. It also needed financial muscle to compete with major electronics giants. Despite its domestic clout, Nokia remained something of an anathema in Finland and abroad. In the former, skeptics thought it was too big for a small country; in the latter, it was deemed too small for the big leagues. Kairamo ignored both viewpoints and pushed ahead. Nokia, he told the *Wall Street Journal*, "wants to forget being a Finnish company and become more Scandinavian, more European."[66]

In 1986, investors outside Finland obtained over half of the new shares issued by Nokia. The company's prospects in foreign capital markets also got a boost in early 1987 when the *Eduskunta*, the Finnish parliament, doubled the ceiling on foreign ownership in Finnish companies, from 20 percent to 40 percent. This measure, argued Nokia's then finance director (and future CEO and chairman), Jorma Ollila, would allow the company to issue as many as ten million new shares. The company had become big enough to attract the attention of its competitors, but it had not yet become strong enough to be feared. "Like its homeland, Nokia has an image problem," noted *The Wall Street Journal*. "Outside of Finland it barely has one."[67]

Nokia needed a brand name that would be ubiquitous worldwide. However, few products bearing the Nokia brand name had reached dealers' shelves. Its personal computers were used almost exclusively in larger systems or sold to better known rivals. Competitors like Canada's Northern Telecom and Sweden's Telefon AB and L. M. Ericsson sold equipment supplied by Nokia under their own brand names. Because Nokia seemed invisible, its telecommunications activities were often underestimated. However, as it tumbled through trial and error, it was already carving itself a market niche by its willingness to listen to the customer—a great competitive asset that would become legendary a decade later.

By the spring of 1987, the future looked very bright. Vuorilehto even suggested to Kairamo that he should use his influence with Pehr G. Gyllenhammar for Nokia to acquire Ericsson, yet only a year and a half after *The Wall Street Journal* interview, both Kairamo and Koski were dead.

CHAPTER THREE

The Crash of the Investment Economy and the Struggle for Corporate Control

TWO years before the tragedies of 1988 occurred, Nokia was intent on becoming a leading European technology conglomerate. To prepare the company for international markets, Kairamo focused on what he could best control: the corporate organization. He initiated organizational reform designed to increase flexibility and cooperation while delegating responsibility. What's more, the legendary decentralization and teamwork that exists today at Nokia originated from these efforts. Like Jorma Ollila, Kairamo wanted to demolish hierarchies that prevented the company from listening to its customers. Flattening the corporate organization was not a matter of philosophy or management science; it was a practical instrument based on his belief that the future belonged to an organization that could ceaselessly renew itself and manage change.

Such reforms were certainly needed as the organization had swollen beyond recognition. While Kairamo and other senior managers at the corporate headquarters may have had a clear idea of Nokia's strategy, things often looked quite different at the business-unit level. Tensions mounted as Kairamo and his senior managers initiated reforms. Furthermore, external stakeholders—in particular, banks and insurance companies—had their own plans for Nokia's future.

Ownership and Competitive Strategy

By 1986, Nokia possessed a board, corporate headquarters, and eleven industrial groups, including Nokia Paper and the television group Salora-Luxor, each generating FIM 2 billion in revenues, and Nokia Tele-communications and Nokia Radio Phones (NRP), which brought in FIM 0.6 billion and FIM 0.7 billion, respectively. The new organizational structure reflected Nokia's increasing size and complexity (see Exhibit 3-1), but it also reflected problems that had remained invisible to Finland and the international business community until the turmoil of 1988.

Problems of Corporate Governance

Problems first began with the specialization of Nokia's technology groups. The old electronics unit had branched into four directions: Salora-Luxor, Nokia Telecommunications (NTC), NRP, and Nokia Information Systems. Ultimately, these industry segments would converge. Except for the telecommunications units, they remained quite different for a short while. What's more, as Nokia's most profitable units operated in volatile and uncertain technology industries, risks relating to business strategy were evolving into risks relating to corporate strategy. While Timo H. A. Koski and other executives insisted again and again on a clear distinction between Nokia's business-unit strategy and its overall corporate strategy, the line was often blurred. Worse, organizational arrangements, which originated from the investment economy, conflicted with the role of each. In theory, the supervisory board was responsible for monitoring the executive board and the company, and for developing the company's strategic direction; it conflicted with the obligation of the executive board to manage strategy. However, the strategic boundaries between the supervisory and the executive boards were far from clear. Exacerbating the situation was that the executive board was also responsible for developing operational activities, which created additional tensions between the executive board and members of the business units.

Nokia's ownership relationships complicated the company's strategic management. Those members of the supervisory board who developed the overall strategic vision for the company were believed to be the least informed about its operational activities, yet they had the ultimate financial control over Nokia through share ownership. It was this control more than anything else that was the cause of significant concern to growth advocates Kairamo and Koski during the late 1980s.

Nokia's public façade notwithstanding, the company's top management tier was torn by a struggle for corporate control between the executive board's high-technology growth proponents (Kairamo, Koski, and others) and the supervisory board's financial gatekeepers (particularly Mika Tiivola, Jaakko Lassila, and Pentti Kouri). The high-

Exhibit 3-1. Kairamo's Nokia: corporate organization (1986).

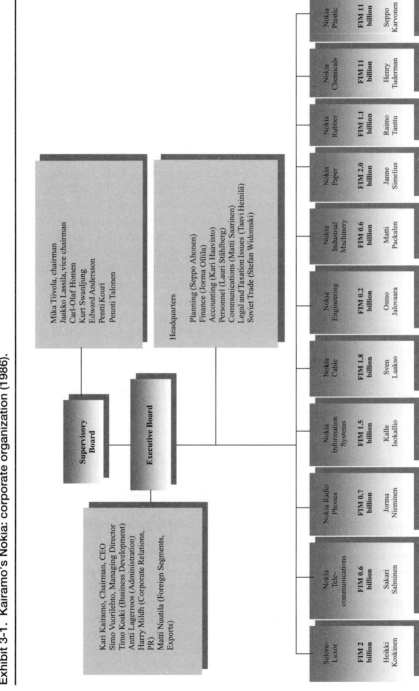

Supervisory Board

Mika Tiivola, chairman
Jaakko Lassila, vice chairman
Carl-Olaf Homen
Kurt Swanljung
Edward Andersson
Pentti Kouri
Pentti Talonen

Executive Board

Kari Kairamo, Chairman, CEO
Simo Vuorilehto, Managing Director
Timo Koski (Business Development)
Antti Lagerroos (Administration)
Harry Mildh (Corporate Relations, PR)
Matti Nuutila (Foreign Segments, Exports)

Headquarters

Planning (Seppo Ahonen)
Finance (Jorma Ollila)
Accounting (Kari Haavisto)
Personnel (Lauri Stählberg)
Communications (Matti Saarinen)
Legal and Taxation Issues (Taavi Heinilä)
Soviet Trade (Stefan Widomski)

Salora-Luxor	Nokia Tele-communications	Nokia Radio Phones	Nokia Information Systems	Nokia Cable	Nokia Engineering	Nokia Industrial Machinery	Nokia Paper	Nokia Rubber	Nokia Chemicals	Nokia Plastic
FIM 2 billion	FIM 0.6 billion	FIM 0.7 billion	FIM 1.5 billion	FIM 1.8 billion	FIM 0.2 billion	FIM 0.6 billion	FIM 2.0 billion	FIM 1.1 billion	FIM 1.1 billion	FIM 1.1 billion
Heikki Koskinen	Sakari Salminen	Jorma Nieminen	Kalle Isokallio	Sven Laakso	Osmo Jalovaara	Matti Packalen	Janne Simelius	Raimo Tanttu	Henry Tuderman	Seppo Karvonen

technology growth advocates had homogeneous strategic objectives, but the financial gatekeepers did not. As long as Kairamo could "divide and conquer," senior management steered the company. As financial stakeholders came together, they gained superior bargaining power. Interestingly, the Finnish business press neglected or misunderstood this battle for corporate governance in 1986, focusing on the similarity between Nokia and its "Americanized organizational style," which they thought had affinities with the large Finnish state-controlled corporations.

> Today Nokia is reminiscent of state corporations, insurance firms and banks because it has a supervisory board. Since Tiivola and Lassila are members of the latter, the lost reputation of supervisory boards should improve. The image of these boards is very low in Finnish business. In state corporations, supervisory boards tend to be largely prize positions for the political pugilists or plotting bases for various interest groups. In great commercial banks and insurance firms, supervisory boards have served as rubber stamps.[1]

After the mid-1980s, Nokia's organization was hardly ideal. In his public statements, Kairamo often presented Nokia's organization as an Americanized corporate structure that just happened to be located in a European country. Yet Finland remained outside the European integration process, and Nokia's structure had become more reminiscent of the Finnish state corporations. This was particularly seen in the relationship between the supervisory and executive boards and the distinction between the chief executive (Kairamo) and the managing director (Vuorilehto).

Kairamo had done his best to insulate the owners of Nokia from the supervisory board, just as he had rejected the idea of senior vice presidents involving themselves with the operational levels of the company. On the one hand, his objective was to eliminate organizational layers between the managing director and the industrial groups. On the other hand, the organizational structure stressed the role of the executive board, which had the strategy authority, over that of the supervisory board, which had financial authority. The shrewd system allowed Nokia's managers to enjoy a level of operational autonomy that had previously been the privilege of the company's largest financial stakeholders only. It also impacted the role of union representatives, who demanded representation in the boards.

Not everyone, however, approved of the new organizational structure. "This year Nokia intends to grow 10% and improve its results," noted one analyst in 1986, with a weary sense of humor. "More taxes and dividends! Hail to the state and *heja* to the Swedish state, which is Nokia's 10th largest shareowner. The greatest one is the pension fund of KOP, which bypassed that of Union Bank of Finland. Power relationships have not crumbled."[2] In the next two and a half years, the antagonism between Nokia's corporate reformers and the financial gatekeepers accelerated. Soon after, the financial stakeholders were swept by Finland's severe banking crisis, in which Tiivola, Lassila, and Kouri played highly controversial roles.

An Ownership Vision

Early in Nokia's history, Leo Mechelin had struggled for an independent Finnish democracy. Almost a century later, in 1987, Kairamo led the talks of the nonsocialist parties.[3] The conservatives returned to the government in 1987, after a quarter of a century on the outside. Harri Holkeri, a longtime conservative politician, was appointed prime minister. Holkeri would go on to play a critical role in the deregulation of Finnish telecommunications, which in turn boosted Nokia's fortunes through the late 1980s.

Through his political activities, Kairamo was eager to influence Finland's Ministry of Trade and Industry. He also wanted to restrict the power of the banks in the economy and privatize the state-owned enterprises and monopolies.[4] Although the competitive environment was finally becoming more favorable to Nokia's internationalization efforts, the corporation itself was drifting toward a power struggle. Through the 1980s, Finland shared many structural affinities with the Scandinavian countries; however, due to its special relationship with the Soviet Union, its economy was more closed and centralized than those of its Nordic neighbors. Because banks provided mostly investment credit, companies became dependent on particular banks, just as the banks became dependent on their major borrowers. The system also gave significant control to state agencies. Further, the Finnish industrial companies and bank groups were deeply intertwined.[5]

From the 1920s to the mid-1980s, protective and regulatory barriers effectively sheltered the Finnish banking sector. Thereafter, the old system crumbled under the globalization of finance and banking. A major step toward deregulation followed in 1986. By the end of the decade, the process resulted in critical changes in Finnish laws and practices for the stock exchange and securities trading, which meant an increase in price competition, transparency, and efficiency.

At Nokia, these developments gave rise to a new ownership approach that stressed the aligned goals of the business units that were concerned with their competitive advantage and financial leadership that was concerned with valuations. The approach anticipated—and to some extent already reflected—the modern concept of shareholder value, which makes a distinction between *formulating* and *valuing* business strategies.[6] Struggling with their conservative financial gatekeepers, the Nokians had come to understand that gaining competitive advantage and creating shareholder value were complementary objectives. The leading proponent of this vision at Nokia was Koski, Kairamo's apparent heir.

While Kairamo remains a legend in Finland, Koski is less remembered. Still, the latter played a significant role in Nokia's technology units and in-house training activities, from efforts at lifelong learning to the launch of Nokia University. He was also among the first management strategists in Finland who truly considered the implications of the post-investment–driven economy, which would emerge after the Cold War.

In the late 1980s, Finland remained an investment economy inhabited by large state-owned conglomerates, a few indigenous major companies, and many family-owned enterprises. Koski tried to prepare Finnish owners and managers for an era when the fate of the small nation would be in the hands of foreign owners. He expected the tenets of U.S. capitalism to affect Finnish companies' search for scale and scope outside their home base. Such ideas were highly contrarian in Finland of the 1980s, and these issues became a source of an extensive Finnish debate a decade later.[7]

Like Kairamo, Koski drew from the theories and studies of U.S. strategic management. His dissertation, *Ownership Strategy and Competitive Advantage*, is filled with notes on competitive strategy.[8] "How can a firm use ownership strategy as a basis for creating competitive advantage?" Koski asked. How could competitive advantage be aligned with strategies that ensured shareholder value? His belief was that it was the responsibility of corporate management to create an ownership structure that supported this alignment:

> New investors—especially foreign investors—can influence the overall investment criteria of the total owner/investor group. As a result, they can have an impact on corporate strategy by affecting corporate management's capability to restructure and its power to make decisions. Corporate management must, therefore, plan ownership strategy in such a way as to ensure the matching of the ownership portfolio with the business portfolio, and the matching of ownership structure with business dynamics.[9]

At the time, the Soviet Union was undergoing dramatic economic restructuring (*perestroika*), and Finland was still heavily engaged in Soviet trade. Foreign ownership of Finnish companies was highly restricted, and only a handful of Finnish companies thought of seeking international investors. Thinking forward, Koski was struggling with issues that were expected to surface in major Finnish corporations: the post–Cold War era, normalized Soviet trade, derestricted foreign ownership, rapid internationalization, and accelerating foreign direct investment. Along with strategies for sustaining competitive advantage and managing the overall organization, he needed to create an appropriate ownership strategy, a crucial issue for an ambitious company that hoped to remain "Finnish" even after internationalizing its operations.[10]

Ownership Strategy and Competitive Advantage reflects Nokia's chaotic M&A phase and anticipates the impending struggle for corporate control. Koski's tone is hurried and frustrated, but determined. More than an academic treatise, it was Koski's effort to conceptualize the most frustrating obstacles that he, as well as Kairamo, saw as threats to Nokia's future, namely the traditional Finnish banks and insurance companies. Nokia's senior management perceived the role of these domestic financial stakeholders to be redundant and declining; a transition into foreign ownership was imminent.[11] In 1987, new legislation allowed for an increase in foreign ownership that was in keeping with the globalization process of Finnish industry. But to Koski, it was too little, too late.

The Demise of the Old Capital Investment System

From the post–World War II reconstruction period to the late 1980s, Finland's political economy had been structured by its geopolitical location and the Cold War. With the collapse of Communism and the breakup of the Soviet Union, the country seized the opportunity to join the European integration process. The rapid pace of history, not business strategies, accounted for the crucial shifts in Finland's external and internal capital markets.

Competitive strategy, competitive advantage, and national competitive advantage are linked together through the determinants of investment, which can be categorized as the macroeconomic environment, capital allocation mechanisms, and external and internal capital markets.[12] By the late 1980s, Finland's capital investment system had become inefficient, inflexible, and unresponsive. It showed low rates of corporate profitability. These problems were the result of four decades of domestic and international intervention, investment-driven growth, and the absence of efficient competition in the economy (see Exhibit 3-2a and b).

Investment behavior in the external capital market is shaped by

Exhibit 3-2. The changing capital markets in Finland.

(a) External Markets

Secure Corporate Position   →   Maximize Measurable Investment Returns

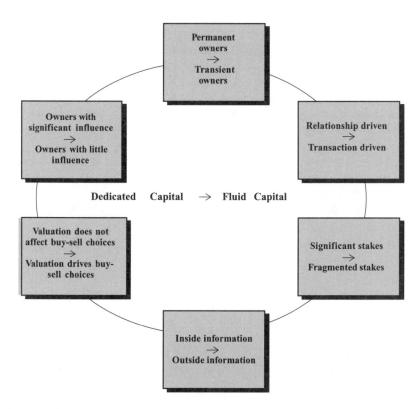

four attributes: the pattern of share ownership and agency relationship; the goals of owners, agents, and lenders; monitoring and valuation methods; and the influence of owners and agents on management. Until the early to mid-1990s, the Finnish system was defined by *dedicated capital*. Funds supplied by external capital providers did not move rapidly from one company to another. The owners were principals who held significant stakes in their companies. Because the owners were virtually permanent, they sought long-term appreciation of their shares to be held in perpetuity. Traditionally, these goals had been defined by the principals and major financial groups. Suppliers and customers owned stakes in each other that were designed to solidify their business relationships rather than to profit from shared own-

Exhibit 3-2 (continued).

(b) Internal Markets

Maximize Measurable Investment Returns   →   Secure Corporate Position

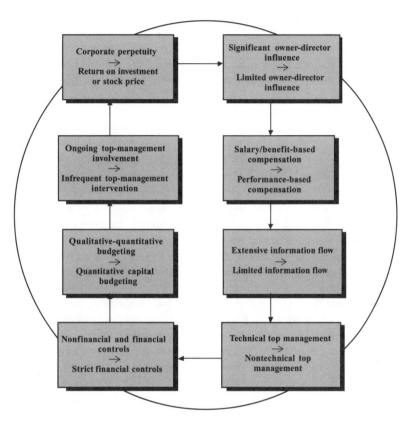

Source: Dan Steinbock, *The Competitive Advantage of Finland* (Helsinki: ETLA/SITRA), 1998. Based on Michael E. Porter, *Capital Choices: Changing the Way America Invests in Industry* (Washington, D.C.: Council of Competitiveness and The Harvard Business School, 1992).

ership. In this system, owners held significant stakes for long periods. Consequently, they had incentive, power, and legal permission to gather information within their companies. Eager to monitor the company's profit potential, the owners became increasingly powerful, commanding the attention of management, accumulating inside information on the company, and influencing managerial conduct.

An internal capital market is a system by which corporations allocate available capital from both internal and external sources to investment projects within and across business units. This market tends to mirror the external capital market. The four attributes that shape investment behavior in the internal capital market tend to parallel those that shape the external market. In the past, the Finnish system had intended to secure the position of the corporation and the company's continuity. Information flow was extensive, and financial criteria played a less significant role in investment decisions. The perpetuation of the enterprise was reinforced by permanent employment and interlocking directorates. Somewhat similar to Germany, supervisory boards in Finland consisted of bank representatives and other significant financial and nonfinancial owners—a practice highly suspect to the institutional investors who invaded Finnish companies after 1993.

Finnish companies also practiced a form of decentralization that allowed information to flow among multiple business units, suppliers, and customers. Typically, managers who had technical backgrounds and spent their careers with one company advanced through tenure and possessed an in-depth knowledge of the company's relevant businesses. Financial control and capital budgeting were part of the management process, but both were technical considerations subject to the company's long-term position in the industry. It was a hands-on system in which top managers were involved in all important decisions.

By the late 1980s, the internal capital market in Finland displayed many characteristics similar to those of Japan and Germany. Unlike them, however, dedicated capital was inefficient in Finland. This inefficiency can be traced back to political rather than market determinants, including the Cold War, the investment economy, Finland's relationship with the Soviet Union, highly centralized planning, and marginality vis-à-vis international business.[13] By the 1990s, however, European integration, the changing nature of competition, and the increasing pressure of globalization had forced the country's capital investment system toward far greater fluidity. Dedicated and fluid capital allocation systems are polar opposites. Even with accelerating European integration, the transition from one to another has taken decades in most of Western Europe, and the process has not occurred without significant friction. Due to the eclipse of the Cold War and Soviet trade, the very same transformation swept through the Finnish economy in just a few years. Nokia's fate precipitated changes in other Finnish companies as well.

The End of the Kairamo Era

When Kairamo arrived at Nokia in the early 1970s, the company was far too dependent on domestic revenues. Exports and foreign activities accounted for only 20% of total sales. Therefore, his first objective was to stabilize the ratio between the two. By 1980, exports and foreign activities increased to more than 50% of total sales. At the same time, the company initiated a thorough transformation (see Exhibit 3-3).

In 1980, when Kairamo clearly understood the need to invest in people rather than trees, Nokia's personnel had grown to 20,500 from 12,400 in 1973, and revenues had quadrupled to FIM 4.5 billion from FIM 1.092 billion. Cable (35 percent) and forestry (32 percent) were the strongest segments, but rubber (19 percent) also remained a major segment, and each was maturing quickly. In contrast, electronics (14 percent) had begun a steady but not yet significant expansion. (Exhibit 3-3a, b, and c illustrate the steps in Nokia's transformation.)

Near the end of the 1980s, Nokia was a very different company. Between 1980 and 1988, Nokia's personnel more than doubled to 44,600. At the same time, revenues quadrupled to FIM 21.8 billion. In the process, electronics (59 percent) became the primary business segment of the company, while cable (18 percent), forestry (14 percent), and rubber (8 percent) served as support segments. In addition to internationalization and focusing on electronics, Kairamo advocated corporate training and education issues. "European industry, as well as the cost structure of products, has become increasingly knowledge-based," he would argue in one speech after another. In effect, he discovered these themes before most chief executives in Europe did.

> When one speaks of structural change, one too often exaggerates the circumstances into a polarization between the "high-tech" industry and traditional hard industries. . . . Yet, all industries live in a rapidly changing world where the competition is becoming more intense. What is essential, then, is the continuing change and renewal, in other words, adaptability vis-à-vis new circumstances and market opportunities. . . . There are no longer mature industries; rather there are only mature ways of doing business.[14]

Kairamo was able to act on this belief after Pehr G. Gyllenhammar, CEO of Volvo, introduced him to the Roundtable of Industrialists, a select few chief executives, including Percy Barnevik of ABB. The Roundtable saw the need to subordinate national interests to the economic imperatives imposed by globalization. In light of Nokia's future developments, the views of Wisse Dekker, chairman of the supervisory board of Philips and a founding member of the Roundtable, would prove prophetic:

> Europeans have always been exporters, of course. But either we have exported to one another's countries, or we have ex-

Exhibit 3-3. Nokia expansion, 1967–1988.

(a) Personnel

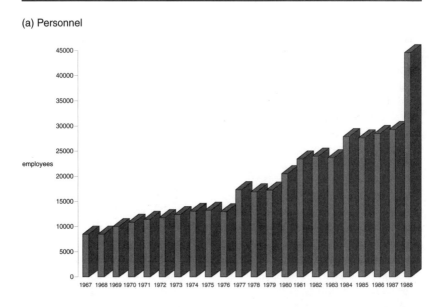

(b) Business Segments

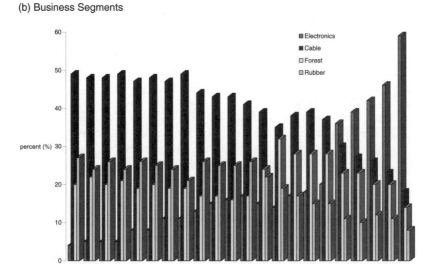

Exhibit 3-3 (continued).

(c) Revenues

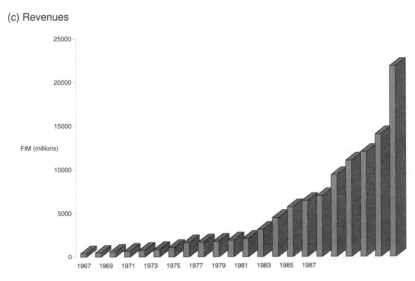

SOURCE: Company reports.

ported across the ocean. Now we have to compete globally, which means actually introducing products at the same time in markets around the globe. That's a new phenomenon. So are the product-development challenges that confront managers in information industries like electronics: the fact that the product life cycle is so short; the fact that the investments you have to make are so large and the time you have to recover your costs and make money is so very short.[15]

In the United States and Japan, educational institutions endeavored to meet the needs of companies through corporate learning and training programs. In Europe, universities and academic institutions ignored such needs, believing that they were the responsibility of independent education and autonomous research. The Roundtable assigned Kairamo to lead a committee to draft an educational policy for Europe.[16] When the University of Bologna, Italy, founded a team called the European University–Industry Forum, Kairamo was selected to be its vice chairman; his role was to "intensify cooperation between business and higher learning,"[17] and to that end he founded Nokia University in Finland. Yet amid all this enthusiasm, the pressure of Nokia's M&A and increased turmoil in Europe began to affect Nokia's executives.

A Death and a Suicide

Timo H.A. Koski, managing director of Nokia's electronics and Kairamo's right hand in the Nokia University project, was expected to receive his Ph.D. degree from the Helsinki University of Technology in May 1988. Anticipation of that event had already led to a personal conflict with Kairamo, who was concerned about Koski's choice of subject matter for his dissertation: ownership, a highly sensitive theme for Nokia. Even more important, perhaps, Kairamo felt uneasy with the idea that Koski, along with several other senior executives, were positioning themselves as leaders within the company even though he was CEO.[18] Tragically, in April 1988, Koski suffered a lethal cerebral hemorrhage on a plane at Heathrow Airport in London. Koski, a visionary and able diplomat adept at resolving conflicts with the board, had been widely expected to succeed Kairamo at Nokia.

With his heir gone, Kairamo took charge of the Nokia University project in addition to managing the company's M&A activities. In his public statements, he had always stressed risk management and rational expansion, yet even as the Cold War was coming to an end and Europe was rapidly changing, he seemed to be taking greater risks, to the point where the company's growth was no longer under control. Nokia's debt stood at $2.6 billion, although its 65-percent debt-to-equity ratio was considered average for European companies. Divestments, a stock offering, and Nokia's $733 million in cash were assumed to cover the costs of the acquisitions of 1987. Publicly, Nokia was portrayed as a growth company and a challenger to U.S. and Japanese players. "But Kairamo's work isn't finished," reported *Business Week*. "He wants to dominate Europe's cellular phone business and, someday, America's, too. In fact, Nokia, whose U. S. headquarters is just under the nose of American Telephone & Telegraph Co. in Basking Ridge, N.J., plans to spend up to $1 billion soon to expand in the U.S., either with an acquisition or a joint venture."[19]

As times became more difficult, the struggle for corporate control at Nokia intensified. When Kairamo was invited to serve on the board of Volvo, he drafted a plan with Gyllenhammar for what was then the most expensive Nordic business deal in history and would have made Volvo Nokia's largest shareholder. By the fall of 1988, Nokia and Volvo agreed on a plan that would diminish the financial control of Finnish banks and financial institutions. When Kairamo met Gyllenhammar for the last time in November 1988, he said briefly, "They don't want it," referring to the Finnish banks' opposition.[20]

Kairamo anticipated the worst regarding Nokia's future when he lost the vote on the plan to the board. In early December, board members held a meeting on the potential restructuring of Nokia's electronics unit. Once again, Kairamo felt betrayed by the banks. After the meeting, he remarked to Vuorilehto (who was to become Nokia's CEO in the near future), "It won't end here. Those two will meet tonight." Then he pointed to the chief executives of Finland's two major banks, Mika Tiivola, director of SYP, and Jaakko Lassila, director of KOP.[21]

Reportedly, Kairamo thought that the banks were exploring spinning the conglomerate off into pieces, although the banks denied such allegations. Tiivola claimed he had suggested that Kairamo take a vacation, arguing that Kairamo himself had pondered a time-out. In addition to Kairamo's concerns regarding the actions of the bank officials, he was also concerned about Vuorilehto's activities. While Vuorilehto was expected to retire in just two years, Kairamo was convinced that he was trying to overthrow Nokia's current management and establish himself as its new leader. In the past, Kairamo would have quickly neutralized any perceived threat, but this time he was oddly passive; this indecision would contribute to Nokia's impending roller-coaster ride. On December 11, 1988, Nokia's board members learned that Kairamo was about to travel to Thailand for a vacation, but that afternoon the chairman hanged himself.

Barbarians at the Gate: From Banks to Kouri's "Northeast Plan"

Apparently, Kairamo also knew of the plotting by Pentti Kouri, a controversial Finnish investor and a one-time advisor of George Soros, who was a controversial international investor himself.[22] In the early 1980s, Kouri had been one of Finland's most promising economists. Like Jorma Ollila, he had studied at Atlantic College in Wales and developed a close relationship with the Center Party and Paavo Väyrynen, an ambitious career politician whom many thought would succeed President Kekkonen. At the age of 21, Kouri became the youngest economist recruit of the International Monetary Fund. When Ollila left student politics for Citibank in the 1970s, Kouri completed his dissertation at the Massachusetts Institute of Technology (MIT), which led to academic work at Stanford and Yale. In 1979, when Ollila was advancing at Citibank, Kouri was appointed professor at New York University[23] and, ever the businessman, followed closely the hostile takeovers of the 1980s. Kouri thought of Nokia as a parallel to R. J. Nabisco and other takeover targets, just as he perceived himself as a corporate raider.[24]

As his international business career took off, Kouri was appointed to the board of directors of the Sanoma Corporation, Finland's powerful newspaper empire. At Nokia, Kairamo was equally impressed with the economist who had become the youngest member of the board.

While Kairamo may have thought that Kouri would help him better influence the board, the bankers soon grew frustrated with the vocal newcomer and his many proposals that they considered self-serving. But the economist appealed to Kairamo because he had little interest in old economy segments and supported the intensified push into electronics.

Kouri became an advisor to George Soros, and in the mid-1980s, Soros took a minority stake in Kouri's investment company, Kouri Capital. Soros also had a Finnish stock portfolio valued at FIM 300–400 million, which included Nokia stock. Unlike Finnish institutions, Soros worked with fluid capital. But when he was eager to sell, it was hard to find buyers in the narrow Finnish markets, and eventually Finnish banks and companies aligned to keep Soros out. In 1987, Soros sold his stake in Kouri Capital, and as a result, Kouri became one of Nokia's major owners, but unlike other board members, Kouri was an active participant.

When Nokia announced it would sell its industrial electronics to Catalyst, few knew that Kouri Capital owned the little-known company. The proposed deal brought out in the open the latent tension at Nokia. Mika Tiivola, chairman of Nokia's board and also chief executive of Union Bank (SYP), the financier of Kouri's acquisitions, refused to finance the purchase. Now Nokia would have to find foreign investment capital in order to marginalize the bargaining power of the Finnish banks.

However, even as Kairamo was struggling to access global markets, Kouri was working on a leveraged buyout (LBO) initiative of his own. The objective of the plan was to slice Nokia into pieces that would then be sold in the markets. Despite a significant stake in the company, he needed more capital to execute the plan; reportedly, Finnish banks, particularly KOP, knew about Kouri's intentions.* Nokia, however, was not Kouri's primary target. Instead, he was buying chunks of the Union Bank, under an assignment from KOP. A takeover plan did not materialize, but the event proved costly to the Union Bank, which was forced to buy back its own stock for FIM 2.8 billion ($644 million) in the biggest cash-and-stock deal ever in Helsinki markets.

The Wall Street Journal concluded:

> The transaction shuffled ownership in Union Bank of Finland, the nation's biggest bank; a large insurer; and two blue-chip industrial companies. Kouri walked away the big

*A few years later, Lassila, the CEO of KOP, had to resign, reportedly because of Kouri's deals.

winner. And he continues to keep the staid Finnish establishment off balance. . . . Last week's battle between Mr. Kouri and Union Bank gave Finnish investors a taste of tenacious takeover tactics long familiar in international markets. Such tactics are likely to become more common in Helsinki as deregulation proceeds and curbs on foreign ownership fall. . . . It was bad enough that Kouri is a well-known ally of [the KOP], which breached a longstanding gentlemen's agreement by taking such a large, potentially unfriendly stake in Union Bank, its direct rival. His holdings were even more distressing, because Union Bank had planned to acquire Sampo and create Scandinavia's first full-fledged financial-services holding company, with banking and insurance units under the same roof.[25]

For his part, Kouri received more than FIM 1 billion in cash as a partial payment. In addition, Union Bank and affiliates ceded to him a 25-percent stake in the forestry concern Rauma Repola Oy and a 3.5-percent stake in Oy Nokia. That boosted Kouri's stake in Nokia to about 5 percent. What's more, the arrangement resulted in KOP's allies holding approximately 28 percent of the voting stock, compared with roughly 22 percent for Union Bank.[26]

The Wall Street Journal noted, "Analysts in Helsinki said they [didn't] expect [the KOP] interests to try to raise that stake much anytime soon. Kouri already has served on Nokia's supervisory board and isn't expected to take a more active role at the company."[27] The assumption was in line with Kouri's past investment activities. Though an advisor to many large Finnish companies, he remained more of an investor than a manager. However, the assumption was a mistake, for Kouri targeted Nokia for the "Northeast Plan," an educational institution conceived of by Paavo Väyrynen that involved Kouri's acquiring Nokia and selling the consumer electronics segment. In the future, Nokia would focus on the mobile communications and cable businesses only.* While many Finns considered this ambitious plan a betrayal, that interpretation is too narrow. In effect, the plan shared certain affinities with Kairamo's own visions for the company and was the precursor to the restructuring strategy initiated by Ollila in 1992.

---

*In the aftermath of Nokia's power struggles, the Finnish press debated extensively on the plotting by the banks and Kouri's Northeast Plan. Yet the first nonfiction book that explored these issues—*Boken om Nokia* (in Finnish, *Nokian valtatie*) by Bruun and Wallen—was published in *Sweden* and only thereafter translated into Finnish.

Nokia's Roller-Coaster Ride

It was only after Kairamo's suicide that the Finns learned about his manic-depressive inclinations. Prior to the suicide, he had failed to bring Volvo into Nokia and had to accept the board's opposition. For years, he and Koski had been frustrated by the banks and insurance companies, which they felt constrained a true growth strategy. Kairamo may have thought that the banks had finally managed to gain control of Nokia. In a suicide letter, Kairamo himself indicated that his death was due to a manic-depressive disease. He also offered recommendations on how to deal with his suicide without harming Nokia's interests. The suicide, he said, had to do with him, not with Nokia. Then he signed his letter, "Sick."[28]

As was so often the case in Finland during the Cold War era, the Finns themselves were not aware of the facts, which were suppressed in the name of national interest. At Nokia, Vuorilehto, Harry Mildh, and Paavo Rantanen suppressed the news of Kairamo's death. According to the press release published by Nokia, Kairamo had suddenly passed away at home. Most Finnish media and newspapers bought the story, except for *Helsingin Sanomat*, the largest morning newspaper in the country. Two days after the press release, the paper published a front-page feature reporting that Kairamo had committed suicide following a strange deal with Nokia's chief executives. Janne Virkkunen, editor-in-chief, and several journalists had struggled with the story. In order to confirm its report on the suicide, the newspaper agreed to refute all speculation on the presumed crisis at Nokia, including rumors that the company's financial woes had led to Kairamo's suicide. "I think it was a good deal, for both," Vuorilehto recalled a decade later in the anniversary book of the economic journalists. "*Helsingin Sanomat* did the right feature. At no point did the matter come out in a way that would have harmed the company. We had enough time to inform on the facts—that is, the finances and prospects of Nokia—and not the rumors, which others were working on and which had no news value."[29]

The investors and analysts, however, were dependant on the freedom of the press. Kairamo had seen himself as a pioneer and had hoped to prepare Nokia for a great transformation. In retrospect, he was also a transitional figure—too close to the past, too far from the future. Tragically, he and his closest executives were aware of their historical role; they could identify the problems but could not overcome the economic, financial, and political obstacles. Between the late 1960s and late 1980s, the segment revenues of Nokia's cable, as a percentage of total revenues, dwindled from 50 percent to 20 percent, while those of forestry declined to less than 20 percent after a temporary surge. Similarly, rubber plunged from nearly 30 percent to about 5 percent. As all three major segments declined, electronics soared from less than 5 percent to more than 60 percent. Such changes do not occur without significant turmoil. Nokia's sales rose rapidly, but profits plunged because of the extraordinary price competition in consumer electronics.

So began Nokia's restructuring and financial roller coaster.

The Vuorilehto Interlude: From Diversification to Restructuring

Restructuring efforts at Nokia were initiated by Simo Vuorilehto and completed by Jorma Ollila, who also envisioned and directed the company's refocusing strategy. Interestingly, Kairamo himself had considered both strategies as early as 1981. Meanwhile, analysts had been wondering whether Nokia had diversified too broadly and engaged in too many M&A activities. In the long run (read: in an innovation economy), Kairamo emphasized, the precondition of success meant focusing. In the short term (i.e., in an investment economy), he viewed diversification as a useful means of hedging one's bets and as a buffer against the whims of the investment economy.[30]

So long as the economic facts of life—technology, trade, and politics—did not reinforce specialization, Nokia continued diversifying. "Undoubtedly, the developments of the 1970s show that diversification has been of use to Nokia," argued Kairamo. "Of course, paper towels and cable machinery share no functional linkages. But to my mind, Nokia's basic characteristic as something of a supermarket is one reason why the company has been more successful than other companies in Finnish industry on average."[31] At the beginning of the 1990s, the telecommunications and mobile phone divisions were the supporting pillars of the company.

Despite the depth of the recession, Nokia recovered quickly as its new CEO, Simo Vuorilehto, started streamlining its businesses. Vuorilehto was a tough-minded engineer who rose through the ranks of Finland's big pulp and paper industry (see Exhibit 3-4). He lacked experience in electronics, and he did not share Kairamo's ambition to make Nokia a more international company. Between 1988 and 1989, the company reversed its position completely, shifting its activities from aggressive buying to selling, and in just a few months, 10 percent of Nokia's revenues were gone (see Exhibit 3-5a and b). Nevertheless, the streamlining proceeded in a strategic manner. Even as Nokia's revenues diminished, Vuorilehto did not sell or divest those businesses he considered strategic, in particular consumer electronics, data commu-

Exhibit 3-4. Simo Vuorilehto: Nokia's interim chief executive.

SOURCE: Nokia 2000. Nokia and Nokia Connecting People are registered trademarks of Nokia Corporation.

Exhibit 3-5. Vuorilehto's restructuring begins (1988–89).

(a) From Buying to Selling

Nokia's Buying Binge

1988	Segments	Revenues FIM (mil.)	Personnel
Standard Elektrik Lorenz AG (Germany)	Consumer electronics, components	4,000	8,900
Ericsson (Sweden)	Information technology	3,500	5,000
Oy Dava Ab (Finland)	Information systems	550	550
Deeko Plc (England)	Paper products	130	400
Renucci S.A. (France)	Paper products	23	50
Oy Edacom Ab (Finland)	kassapaatejarjestelmat	40	100
Eke-Robotersysteme GmgH and EKE Automation Oy (Germany, Finland)	Industrial robotics	16	30
Suomen Sähkotuonti Oy (Finland)	Electrical power and importing	69	48

1989			
Wullum Dekk A/S (Norway)	Car tires	53	60
British Tissues Ltd (England)	Paper products	760	160
Atlas Lace Paper Corp. (England)	Paper products	40	160

Nokia's Selling Binge

1988	Segments	Revenues FIM (mil.)	Personnel
Maksutieto Oy (Finland)	Credit and payment information	8	30
Oy Nokia Ab Vammala (Finland)	Rubber processing	4	12
Jaromet Oy (Finland)	Processing machinery	30	42
Savion Tehdas (Finland)	Processing machinery, rubber	50	124
Rotabyte Oy (Finland)	PC importing	30	22
Nokia Footware (Finland)	Shoes, manufacturing	8	15
Videotex activities (Finland)	Application software	3	4
Nokian Sahkolaitos (Finland)	Electrical power	85	85
Nokian Kalanteri, Suomen Parketti (Finland)	Carpeting	240	375
Nokia Data (Finland)	Information processing, consulting	4	11
Kalku factory, etc. (Finland)	Rubber processing	255	617
Holmsund Golv AB (Sweden)	Carpeting	80	130
Factory (West Germany)	Rubber production	135	400
Carpet manufacturing (Finland)	Carpeting	15	35
Nokiaís soft paper production	Paper products	2,235	4,200

Exhibit 3-5 (continued).

(b) Loss of Revenues

	Revenues before 1988		Revenues in 1988*	
	FIM (mil.)	%	FIM (mil.)	%
Consumer electronics	5,968	27.4	5,968	31.4
Data	4,877	22.4	4,877	25.6
Mobile	1,118	5.1	1,118	5.9
Telecommunications	1,526	7.0	1,526	8.0
Cable and machinery	4,075	18.7	4,075	21.4
Basic industry	4,749	21.7	1,931	10.2
Internal sales	-494	2.3	-479	2.5
Total	21,819		19,016	

*Nokia's 1988 revenues minus the sold business activities (floors, paper, most of technical rubber production).

SOURCE: Abbreviated with some modifications from *Talouselämä* 24 (1989).

nications, mobile phones, and telecommunications. Instead, he sold Nokia's basic industrial units. Meanwhile, the losses incurred by consumer electronics alone reduced Nokia's revenues by hundreds of millions of Finnish marks. As the company was swept by restructuring, Siemens saw it as an attractive takeover target. "The Finns were thrilled when Kairamo and his troops initiated their European invasion," noted one observer. "But friends disappeared as problems increased. In the spring [of 1989], investment analysts noted that some media had become too enthusiastic in their gloomy depictions of Nokia's situation."[32]

Vuorilehto's restructuring did not result in the expected profitability, and Nokia's image continued on its downward slide. A low point was reached in 1990, when the Finns who lived in the original Nokia region suggested in the local newspaper that the company should pay royalties for the abuse of its good name. Between 1984 and 1989, the average annual growth of Nokia's common stock was only 1 percent, whereas that of the preferred stock was 14 percent. Many owners had believed in Kairamo's impassioned rhetoric of European invasion and bought the stock; now they felt betrayed and were eager to get back at least some of their investments.

Despite restructuring, Nokia still had 170 organizational units (see Exhibit 3-6). While NTC was doing well, NMP, led by Ollila, was not as fortunate. Like so many other units, this more recent business

Exhibit 3-6. Vuorilehto's Nokia: corporate organization (ca. 1989).

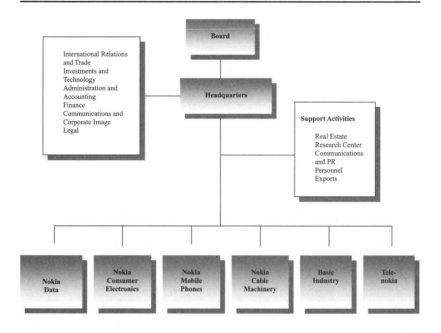

was quickly burning capital. In the good old days, that would not have been a concern, but now it was. As one observer said, "Jorma Ollila was sent to the trenches from the headquarters, but Vuorilehto's scythe already hovered threateningly above the mobile phones group."[33] In order to raise capital, the company sold Nokia Data to the IT services company ICL in 1991. Buying activities continued, but in a more focused manner, with the purchase of Technophone, a U.K. mobile phone manufacturer that had been a strong competitor of Nokia.

The financial community applauded the restructuring. Nokia was no longer buying new and exciting companies; it was busy divesting old and failed units. Vuorilehto was far more cautious and conservative than Kairamo. As long as the two played together, Nokia benefited. One drove visions, the other implemented them. With visions gone, Nokia's corporate strategy focused solely on restructuring. The new senior management did not react with a sense of urgency. Even as Vuorilehto took charge, he portrayed the situation as neither difficult nor worrisome. What was even worse, Vuorilehto deprived the Nokians of the very motive that had driven them for years—the vision of a growth-driven European Nokia—and gave nothing in exchange. Vuorilehto tried to address the employees' concerns, writing in the corporate newsletter:

With Kari Kairamo, we had very similar ideas to develop Nokia. Things were taken care of in good mutual understanding. We have achieved a lot during the recent few years. Last year, growth was extraordinary. Major acquisitions in West Germany and Sweden have contributed to our revenues and strengthened our positions in Europe. Of course, it takes a while to digest two significant acquisitions. The close timing of these deals was partially due to external reasons. Still, we've already got far in the technical quality, practical know-how and market expertise of our products, and these things will ensure our success in the future as well.[34]

Few believed the message.

By the end of December 1989, a *Wall Street Journal* headline announced, "Nokia's Bold Strategy May Be Unraveling." Vuorilehto acknowledged to the *Journal* that Nokia "miscalculated the time needed to integrate the acquisitions," but he also insisted that things were turning around at the company. Long-vacant management posts had been filled. The company had taken the first step toward divesting its paper division and was seeking a buyer for its rubber subsidiary—disposals that would provide badly needed funds for electronics expansion. "We think we have some breathing space for the moment," said one anonymous senior executive. "But in two to three years we'll have to consider divesting or spinning off at least one, and maybe two, of the electronics businesses to raise funds to invest in the others." Influential board members were pressing for faster action. *The Wall Street Journal* suspected that directors had lost confidence in Vuorilehto as the right man to lead Nokia out of its current difficulties. (Apparently, Vuorilehto had lost his confidence in Nokia as well. When he was replaced with Ollila, he sold a chunk of his Nokia shares to buy a yacht. When the share price went through the roof in the late 1990s, he realized he had given up a fortune. "I have the world's most expensive yacht," he acknowledged.) The sense of urgency for more drastic restructuring grew rapidly, and Nokia continued to divest itself of noncore operations.

Such ideas were not far from Kouri's intended raid in the late 1980s. Unlike Kairamo or Ollila, however, Kouri presumed that Finland would *not* join European integration. This belief was well in line with the isolationism of his political mentor, Paavo Väyrynen, but in conflict with the objectives of European big business. It also led to some rather odd and grand political visions. "Nokia must align with Ericsson and Motorola," Kouri said in 1990. "We need bigger units. Finland's and Sweden's business must be integrated. We must re-create a Swedish-Finnish superpower that will cover the Baltic countries, Poland, and Karelia. . . . Sweden and Finland must not join the European Union. As Eastern Europe will change entirely, it is far more beneficial to stay outside the EU."[35]

By 1990, however, Kouri had become irrelevant at Nokia and had sold all of his stock. Mika Tiivola, chairman of Nokia's board, announced to Kouri that he would not be re-elected. Although Kouri had sold all financial interest he had in Nokia, he had not forgotten about the Northeast Plan. Instead, he initiated negotiations concerning Nokia with Hitachi, Marubeni, and three American banks. In Kouri's odd vision, Nokia would be taken over by a consortium led by KOP. He was not without allies within Nokia. Antti Lagerroos, chief of NMP, participated in the talks, a decision that cost him his job (Ollila would take his place). After months of negotiations, when the papers were ready to be signed, KOP's Lassila suddenly withdrew from the initiative. The Northeast Plan abruptly ceased to exist. The American banks and Japanese companies felt fooled by Kouri, who became something of a persona non grata in two continents. Soon thereafter, Kouri Capital went bankrupt while Kouri found himself demonized as the personification of everything that had been excessive in Finland's booming 1980s.

Financial markets were not adequately aware of Nokia's future prospects, and the awakening caused by Kouri's adventure was devastating. By the early 1990s, the company also found itself amid Finland's worst recession since the 1930s—the result of a tumultuous political and economic shift from the Cold War era to European integration.

From the Eclipse of the Cold War to the Collapse of the Soviet Trade

In the late 1980s, the Finns felt proud of their country and its achievements. The gross domestic product had risen faster than the OECD average. The inflation rate was under control, and the country enjoyed low levels of unemployment (4 to 5 percent). The gross public debt was less than 20 percent of the GDP. The Finns prided themselves on their social policy, which they felt served as a model for the rest of the world. True, growth of labor productivity had declined since the mid-1970s, but much less on average than in other industrialized countries. As measured by GDP per capita, Finland was one of the richest countries in the world, and the Finns thought of themselves as the "Japan of the North." Financially, deregulation was rapidly opening the economy. Internationally, the Finns regarded their country as a bridge between the capitalist West and the socialist East. With economic reform under way in Moscow, even the foreign policy analysts felt more relaxed.

Until the early 1980s, the financial markets were tightly regulated. Over the course of the decade, practically no fiscal or monetary policy measures were taken to moderate the expansionary effects of the economic boom. As a result, the effects of liberalization expanded. When a tighter monetary policy was introduced in 1989, it only resulted in greater foreign borrowing. The country was living beyond its means and pricing itself out of global competition.

Between 1987 and 1991, after a quarter of a century of opposition, the conservatives joined the Social Democrats in a government coalition. The key principle of the government program, governable restructuring, reflected the optimistic view that Finland could move from an investment-driven to an innovation-driven economy without major transitional problems. In reality, the nation was heading into a period of turmoil it had not experienced since the Depression years.

By the early 1990s, Finland's GDP was in the red, and as a result of sluggish economic conditions, the inflation rate had plummeted below the EU average. The unemployment rate had usually remained below the EU average since the 1970s, but it hit close to 20 percent by 1994. Such figures would have been inconceivable even two years before.[36] While high unemployment reduced tax revenues, it also generated significant social volatility. The gross public debt of GDP exceeded 60 percent. The welfare state that had come into existence in the 1960s had failed in the face of the 1990s recession. Now the image of Finland as the "Japan of the North" was simply embarrassing. Due to improper management, financial deregulation directly contributed to the hardships of the economy, and it would take years for Finnish banks to regain profitability. With new foreign ownership laws, Finnish companies were drifting into foreign hands. Bankruptcies discouraged private initiatives and big business was paralyzed. The country grew dubious about its impending membership in the EC, nostalgic about its past, and fearful of its future.

As measured by GDP per capita, Finland was still a wealthy country, but no longer one of the richest. Between 1950 and 1973, Finland enjoyed a 4.9-percent growth rate of real GDP, less than the corresponding growth in Japan and Germany but more than in Sweden and the United States (3.6 percent). Between 1973 and 1989, growth stagnated in most major industrial nations, including Finland (3.1 percent). In 1989, the Finns' standard of living was about 80 percent of that of the Americans. Four years later, it had declined to less than 70 percent—a level the Finns had not seen since 1973.[37]

As the Soviet foreign trade regime was depoliticized during the second half of the 1980s, political trade had simply become unaffordable to the Soviet Union. Now, only trade based on economic and commercial criteria was acceptable. Curiously enough, while the untenable nature of Soviet trade had become evident to Russian economists, many Finnish politicians, decision makers, and trade administrators ignored the changes, which contributed to the severity of the recession in the early 1990s.[38] The old Finnish-Soviet political economy had given rise to substantial distortions in the economy, domestically (public interventionism) and in foreign trade (the high proportion of Soviet trade).[39]

When the political conditions that gave rise to the investment economy collapsed at the turn of the 1990s, so went the "old ways" of Finnish life. By the early 1990s, the Finnish economy lingered in a severe recession as unemployment numbers jumped to record heights. The banking crisis reached its peak in 1992, when loan losses hit 4.6 percent of GDP.[40] In 1993, the closed Finnish economy rapidly crumbled, and the EC opened accession talks with Finland. After World War II, foreign ownership of Finnish companies was tightly regulated, but now foreigners were allowed to buy shares of Finnish companies without restrictions. Between 1989 and 1994, the proportion of foreign-owned companies among the top 500 Finnish companies increased from 14 percent to 23 percent. Trade between Finland and Sweden increased substantially through mutual acquisitions.

Throughout the twentieth century, the small Nordic country had been defined by its historical relationship with the Soviet Union. When the latter ceased to exist, the Finns sought to redefine themselves through European integration. In the past, Finnish business had been defined by the Finnish-Soviet *political* economy.

In the future, it would be defined by the EU political *economy.*[41] In 1992, as Vuorilehto's cadre of executives was shown the door, the forty-one-year-old Jorma Ollila was appointed CEO, and Nokia made the important strategic decision to focus on mobile communications, divesting its noncore operations.[42] At first, Ollila continued the restructuring, but it was only one aspect of his strategy. In a year or two, the Global System for Mobile Communications (GSM) was expected to take off, and Nokia would ride its momentum. In Ollila's vision, it was the digital cellular business that would drive revenues and boost profits.

Part II
The Global Focus Strategy

Restructuring Nokia: The Focus Strategy

ALL relevant accounts (i.e., Internet users per capita, digitalization rate of networks, and cellular phone subscribers per capita) showed that Finland had become one of the "world's most wired countries, possessing a highly educated and technologically savvy population. It also boasted the world's highest relative Internet and cellular penetration. Finland achieved an even more intriguing milestone in February 1997: the country had more than thirty mobile telephone subscriber connections per one hundred inhabitants to its credit.[1] Yet, it was only when Nokia's stock price began to soar that international analysts and the business press noticed these achievements. While the company was portrayed as a newcomer that emerged from seemingly nowhere, many of these advancements stemmed from decisions related to Nokia's diversification and Nordic and EU policy making throughout the 1960s, 1970s, and 1980s. Interestingly, such decisions were based on Finland's solid and somewhat unique telecommunications infrastructure, which originated in the late nineteenth century.[2]

Instead of an upstart, Nokia was an old-timer thriving in a new and emergent industry. Historically, the European initiatives were based upon Nordic cooperation, which was the real catalyst of the thriving European cellular business in the early 1990s. In Finland, it was preceded by Nokia's consolidation of Finnish radio, television, and electronics industries in the postwar era.

Nokia, Electronics, and Telecommunications

The electronics industry in Finland can be traced back to the 1920s, which saw the rise of radio manufacturing and the creation of the Finnish Broadcasting Corporation. Nokia's leadership position in the cellu-

lar industry began with cable and the consolidation of Finnish electronics in the postwar era.[3] The success of the State Electric Works
(Valtion sähköpaja), the Finnish Cable Works, and Salora illustrate the
incremental advances in Nokia's electronics business, a process that
began with the launching of the Finnish Ropery Works in 1912 and
reached its apex with the creation of Nokia Mobile Phones in 1991 (see
Exhibit 4-1). It was only after the consolidation and integration of these
individual businesses and the growth of the cellular industry that
Nokia emerged as a serious challenger in the early 1980s.

The Post–World War II Consolidation

Between 1945 and 1980, Nokia consolidated both state-controlled
and privately owned units of those Finnish businesses that had played
a crucial role in electronics, radiophones, and television through the
postwar era. These efforts were motivated by Nokia's success in electronics, the failures of public-sector high-technology ambitions, and
Kairamo's dogged obsession in the late 1970s to turn Nokia into a technology business.

The State Electric Works, Televa Oy, Telefenno Oy, and Telenokia Oy

Beginning in 1945, the State Electric Works (Valtion Sähköpaja),
originally launched as a research laboratory of the Finnish Defense
Forces in 1925, served as an industry catalyst, changing its name to
Televa in 1962 in an attempt to blur its profile as a public-sector organization.[4] With the state retaining a majority interest, Televa was reincor-
porated in 1976 as Televa Oy, with Pekka Tarjanne as its chairman.
(Tarjanne would later serve as chairman of the International Telecommunications Union.) A year later, Televa Oy and Oy Nokia AB
launched Telefenno Oy, a joint venture intended to coordinate marketing and R&D.[5] Televa Oy was taken over by Nokia in 1981, who renamed the company Telenokia Oy. At this point, Kari Kairamo became
chairman of the board, and Televa's radiophone unit became a department of Telenokia Oy. Prior to the acquisition, the revenues reached
more than FIM 17 million (see Exhibit 4-2a).

Nordell & Koskinen, Salora Oy, and Mobira Oy

Launched as a radio manufacturing company in the 1920s, Salora
began producing televisions in addition to radios in the early 1950s,
with radiophone manufacturing following a decade later. In 1972, the
company obtained its own manufacturing unit and three years later

Exhibit 4-1. The precursors of Nokia telecommunications.

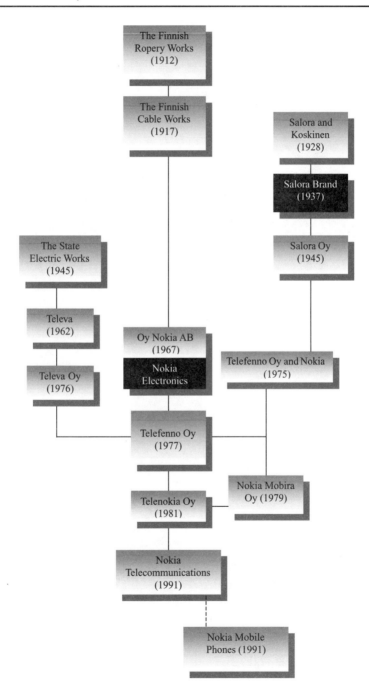

Exhibit 4-2. Nokia's precursors: Televa revenues, 1962–1980, and Salora revenues, 1972–1978.

(a) Televa Revenues

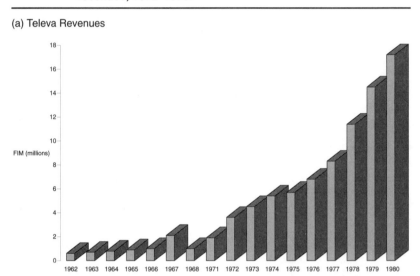

(b) Salora Revenues

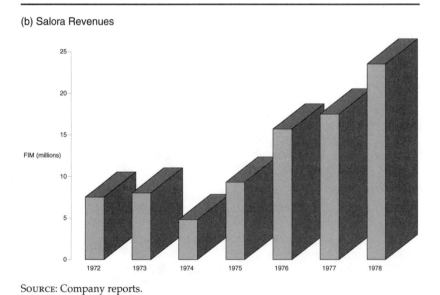

SOURCE: Company reports.

began exporting its radiophones internationally. At this time, Nokia and Salora agreed to coordinate and cross-market their branding and promotion activities. Nokia would market Salora's mobile phones under its brand, while Salora would market Nokia's professional mobile radio base stations and handsets. Between 1972 and 1978, Salora's revenues tripled from FIM 7.5 million to FIM 23.5 million (see Exhibit 4-2b). At the time, Jorma Nieminen moved from Salora's radio products development to the development of radiophones in 1971, eventually taking charge of the independent unit in 1974. These marketing activities resulted in increased cooperation between the two companies, leading to a joint venture, Mobira Oy (as in *mobile radio*), in 1979 (see Exhibit 4-1).

The Finnish Cable Works and the Electronics Unit

In 1960, the FCW diversified into electronics, focusing on calculation activities, the sale and leasing of computing systems, and manufacturing electronics equipment. Concurrently, Nokia began importing the computer systems of Elliot in the United Kingdom and Siemens in Germany. As Nokia began researching radio transmission technology, a French computer company, Machines Bull, selected Nokia to be its Finnish agent in 1962. At this time, activities at Nokia were divided into computing and electronics.

The electronics department was something new in Finland. Led by managing director Björn Westerlund, this department built upon old customer relationships with the Finnish Defense Forces, Posts and Telecommunications of Finland, and the Soviet sales organizations (see Exhibit 4-3). With the merger of Nokia, the FCW, and the Finnish Rubber Works creating the Nokia Corporation in 1967, the electronics unit of the FCW became the newly formed organization's electronics group.

By 1970, Nokia's new corporate organization encompassed numerous subsidiaries and four industry groups: cable, wood processing, rubber, and electronics. In turn, these groups included an array of profit units. At this point, Nokia's key customers consisted of taxi companies, industrial concerns, shipping companies, the PTT, transport organizations, fire departments, and utilities. By the mid-1970s, Nokia used an American license to begin manufacturing manpack phones in Oulu, located deep in the Artic circle, which led to the transfer of the radiophone factory from Helsinki to Oulu as well. Over time, these strategic decisions led to the rise of Nokia's cellular activities in northern Finland.

Between 1966 and 1974, the revenues of Nokia's mobile phone unit soared from FIM .4 million to FIM 10.7 million (see Exhibit 4-4).

Exhibit 4-3. The Finnish Cable Works (ca. 1960).

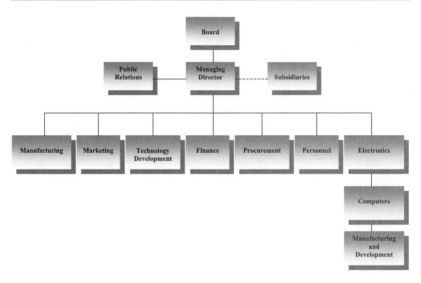

SOURCE: Abbreviated and modified from Eige Cronström et al., *Puoli vuosisataa kaapeli-teollisuutta 1912–1962* (Helsinki: Suomen 1965), p. 397.

Exhibit 4-4. Nokia mobile revenues (1966–1978).

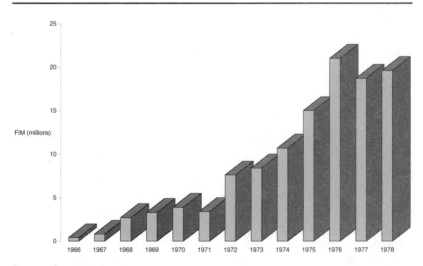

SOURCE: Company reports.

Coordinated marketing activities between Salora and Nokia resulted in revenues of almost FIM 20 million by the end of the 1970s. In 1978, Nokia and Salora began negotiations on increased cooperation concerning radiophones. A year later, these talks resulted in the launch of Mobira Oy, the precursor of today's Nokia Telecommunications (NTC).[6] While the consolidation of the Finnish radio, television, and electronics industries was an important step in creating emerging markets, it was the type of Nordic cooperation seen between Nokia and Salora that gave rise to and nurtured the nascent wireless industry.

Nordic Cooperation

Cooperation exists among Denmark, Finland, Iceland, Norway, and Sweden as well as the autonomous territories of the Faroe Islands, Greenland, and Åland. It is based on the shared values, perceptions, and conditions of geographical location, climate, language, religion, politics, mixed economies, welfare states, and environmental concerns. These efforts were initiated when the Nordic Social Democrats drafted a far-reaching declaration on Nordic cooperation in 1945.

With no military ties, Sweden was reluctant to take part in the growing institutional cooperation and attempted to develop Nordic cooperation instead. In Finland, geopolitics complicated these initiatives. With the gradual relaxation of tensions among the superpowers, Finland joined the Nordic Council in 1955. The Treaty of Helsinki of 1962 gave birth to the Nordic Convention on Cooperation, which defined the achievements and goals of the regional policy. This agreement was followed by the formation of the Nordic Council of Ministers in 1971. Over time, this cooperation gave the citizens of Nordic Europe many reciprocal rights in one another's countries. Economic cooperation, however, did not proceed quite as smoothly.

During the Cold War, the Finns enjoyed the advantages of free and open trade within the European Economic Community (EEC); they first experienced the benefits of a common market through Nordic cooperation. The explosion of the cellular business in the early 1990s was a result of the Nordic initiatives.[7] From the earliest introduction of dispatch radio services, the major Nordic countries adopted an unusually progressive attitude toward all forms of mobile communications.[8] In contrast to other European countries, they heavily promoted mobile use and encouraged the use of the available spectrum of mobile technology. The Nordic topography favored mobile communications due to the wide dispersion of much of the population in remote places. However, conditions pertaining to competition were even more important to the growth of communications in Finland.

It is not comparative advantage, but competitive advantage that explains the rise of the thriving Nordic cellular industry vis-à-vis pro-gressive public policies and the institution of the car mobile telephones (CMT), Nordic Mobile Telephone (NMT), and Global System for Mobile Communications (GSM) networks.

Progressive Public Policies

While in many European countries a monopolistic approach has limited competition, in Finland the high number of independent local operators has ensured demand across several suppliers (see Exhibit 4-5a), whereas a competitive and pro-technology approach to telecom-munications contributed to the early use of mobile technology.

Beginning in the 1880s, local telephone companies were formed and operated by local cooperatives. This history was intertwined with the political economy, just as the history of Finland and Nokia were connected with the Soviet Union throughout the Cold War. By allow-ing private companies and cooperatives to dominate local telecommu-nications since the late nineteenth century, the Finns were not so much boosting the efforts of the private sector as trying to keep Russian au-thorities away from this emerging industry.[9]

In the late 1990s, almost fifty local telecommunications com-panies, called the Finnet Group, operated in Finland. Domestic manu-facturers were not sheltered from foreign competition and, with demanding operations and progressive customers, strengthening mar-ket forces generated a vital telecommunications equipment industry. Nokia thrived in this competitive environment and gained an early foothold in the telecommunications marketplace with the development of the digital switch that eventually became known as the Nokia DX 200. Since the 1980s, the approach has resulted in an extraordinarily high rate of mobile penetration (see Exhibits 4-5b and c).

Nokia-Mobira and the Booming 1980s

Initially, the strategic objective of Nokia-Mobira was to combine re-sources in order to ensure the long-term competitiveness of the Finnish radiophone industry. Managing director Jorma Nieminen and market-ing director Kari-Pekka Wilska took control of the company, whose revenues amounted to approximately FIM 50 million. Although Hel-sinki remained its home base, Salo was chosen as the company's corpo-rate headquarters and the center of radiophone manufacturing, with base stations and other PMR equipment manufacturers located in Oulu. Through the 1980s, Nokia-Mobira designed, manufactured, and marketed mobile end-user equipment, while Nokia Cellular Systems focused on the system infrastructure. By the 1990s, these two subsidiaries evolved into Nokia Mobile Phones and Nokia Networks.

The Evolution of Cellular Networks

Today, the success of cellular communications is often attributed to contemporary technological innovation and strategic marketing ingenuity. In fact, wireless communications has a century-long history, originating with Guglielmo Marconi's first wireless message in 1898 and Lee de Forest's first transmission to an automobile in 1906. A press release for the De Forest wireless envisioned, "Hereafter [we hope] it will be possible for businessmen, even while automobiling, to be kept in constant touch."[10]

Throughout the first half of the twentieth century, cellular saw many incremental improvements, including the adoption of mobile radiophones by the Detroit Police Department in the 1920s, the British invention of radar in the mid-1930s, the military use of radio telephony during World War II, and the introduction of the first commercial mobile radio telephone services by Bell Systems in the United States in the late 1940s. Relying on other enhancements, such as full duplex, direct dialing, and FM channel bandwidths of 25 to 30 kHz, the Improved Mobile Telephone Service (IMTS) triggered a race toward a mobile future.

The late 1960s and early 1970s witnessed the development of the first analog cellular systems.[11] These were not based on a new kind of technology but on the more efficient use of existing IMTS technologies, particularly the microprocessor and the digital control link developed in the 1970s. Work began on second-generation digital cellular systems toward the end of the 1980s. These systems featured a digitized voice signal, an increased service capacity, and dramatically reduced costs compared to those of analog systems.[12] Indeed, cellular standards have evolved through three platforms: *first-generation analog* (1G) networks, *second-generation digital* (2G) networks, and *third-generation* (3G) networks. All leading mobile vendors and operators were preparing for the 3G networks in the late 1990s. The cellular industry is typically divided into two parts: cellular infrastructure (base station and switches) and mobile terminals (handsets). From the very beginning, Nokia has operated in both of these segments, but most of its recent success derives from handsets.

First-Generation Mobile

Relying on analog transmission for voice communication, most 1G mobile systems were introduced in the early 1980s. These networks

Exhibit 4-5. Finland's telecommunications sector: the number of Finnish telephone companies (1900–1999), mobile subscribers (per 100 inhabitants, 1980–1999), and analog mobile networks (1980–1999).

(a) Finnish Telephone Companies

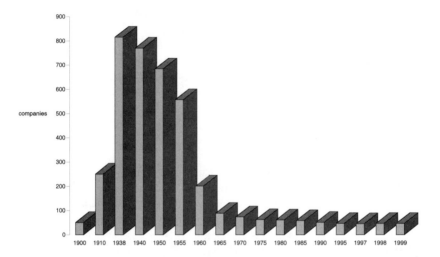

(b) Mobile Subscribers

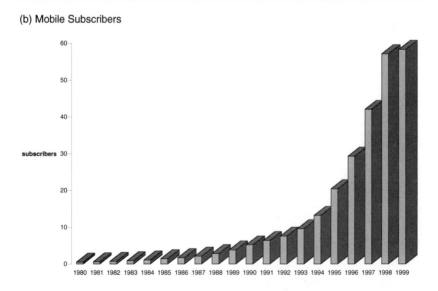

Exhibit 4-5 (continued).

(c) Analog Mobile Networks

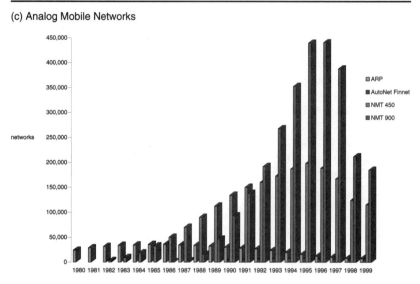

Source: Finnish company reports, Finland's Ministry of Transport and Communications.

were confined primarily to outdoor coverage, had limited capacity, and included heavy car phones. At this point, both large and aspiring mobile equipment vendors focused on business customers only. One of the key industry standards, the Advanced Mobile Phone System (AMPS), was launched in Chicago in 1983. Over time, the AMPS became the most popular analog system and remained the second-largest system worldwide until the late 1990s, with fifty million subscribers mainly residing in North America. The Total Access Communications System (TACS) was introduced in the United Kingdom in the mid-1980s and had fifteen million users worldwide by the late 1990s.

Prior to these standards, a wide variety of 1G proprietary systems existed in France, Germany, Italy, and Japan but were rarely sold outside their home countries. The Nordic countries introduced the earliest 1G system, NMT, to an international audience. Developed by telecommunications operators, authorities, and equipment makers from the Nordic countries and elsewhere, the NMT operated in the 450 MHz bandwidth and, later, in the 900 MHz bandwidth. At the end of the 1990s, NMT was still used by approximately 4.5 million people in forty countries, including the Nordic countries, Asia, Russia, and other Eastern European countries. NMT inaugurated the Nordic countries' leadership in the worldwide mobile cellular market and provided a critical window of opportunity for Nokia.

Car Mobile Telephone (CMT) Network

In 1968, largely in response to the expansion of highway traffic, the Finnish government authorized the construction of a national mobile network based on manual CMT technology. Three years later, Finland's PTT first offered mobile phone services on its CMT network, and by the late 1960s, the capacity of VHF networks could not accommodate demand, highlighting the need for a more effective system.

Nordic Mobile Telephone Group

The Nordic Mobile Telephone Group was established in 1969 with the purpose of developing a new mobile telephone system. Interestingly, it began by drafting system requirements based on market needs rather than technical parameters. The original NMT design objectives were:

- Fully automatic operation and charging
- System and terminal compatibility among Finland, Sweden, Norway, and Denmark
- Full roaming capability among all Nordic countries
- Mobile-to-mobile calls in addition to mobile-to-fixed and fixed-to-mobile
- Sufficient capacity to last for many years
- High reliability, particularly for signaling features such as call charging and number transmission
- Similar use and same facilities as a conventional fixed telephone
- Low-cost infrastructure and mobiles
- Conversations protected against interception
- Open specifications, with no exclusive supplier rights.

From the very beginning, mobile communications was promoted in the Nordic regions as a working tool rather than as a status symbol. This strategic initiative was dictated by the public-service values of the Nordic PTTs, which integrated mobile operations with the rest of their activities. With the low price for fixed subscriptions, revenues would be highly dependent on adequate traffic levels and cost-leadership strategies.

Nordic Mobile Telephone

The first commercial NMT 450 system was launched in Sweden in October 1981. That year, Finland's PTT began constructing a new mobile network based on the NMT standard, operating in the 450 MHz frequency and began offering commercial analog NMT 450 services in 1982, which allowed subscribers to make calls to anywhere in the Nordic region from outside Finland. Concurrently, the development of handheld mobile phones contributed to a growing number of NMT subscribers. Although the other Nordic countries soon followed suit, these various systems were not interlinked. It made commercial sense to develop a common network and to standardize the technology. The result was NMT, the world's first multinational cellular network. Its successful introduction in many other countries both in and out of Europe triggered the rapid expansion of the mobile phone industry. In 1984, in response to increasing congestion, a new mobile network design that utilized the 900 MHz frequency band was developed by Finland's PTT and used commercially two years later.

Paradoxically, it was the egalitarianism inherent in the public policies of Nordic countries that prepared the pioneering companies of the region for mass-market competition in the 1990s. Because consumer needs, such as availability, price, and usability, had been considered during the initial planning of the network, mobile phones moved quickly from business-to-business to consumer markets. As mobile phones found their way from high-end business markets to low-end consumer markets, Finnish teenagers stopped referring to mobile phones as *juppinalle* (translated freely, "yuppie toys") and started calling them *kännykkä* or *känny*, initially a Nokia trademark meaning an extension of the hand. While American operators and equipment makers struggled to understand the demographics of teen use of the handheld, Nokia and Finnish operators had already engaged in extensive market segmentation, gaining first-mover advantages in this emerging marketplace.

Nokia and NMT

Nordic countries first began to develop the NMT network in 1969, and by the spring of 1977, equipment manufacturers joined the process. Two years later, Mobira manufactured the first NMT base stations to Finland's PTT.

The First Steps

As Nordic countries began their NMT cooperation, Nokia increased its radiophone activities accordingly. In the process, Mobira began to invest in NMT mobile phones and base stations while harvesting overlapping products and marketing activities. As England and Sweden launched their first networks in 1981, Mobira entered these markets, even if its most important customers were in Finland. Concurrently, Nokia consolidated the industry. Telenokia had been created in 1981; a year later, Nokia purchased a minority stake in Salora and 50 percent of Mobira's stock equity through Telenokia.

Established in 1979 as a joint venture with Salora to supply phones for Finland's fledgling mobile phone network, Mobira saw its fortunes soar when Scandinavian countries formed the Nordic Mobile Telephone System in 1983. As Mobira became part of Nokia Corporation, Telenokia's radiophone unit was moved into Mobira.[13]

With the Nordic launch of NMT, Nokia had consolidated the business dramatically in just a few years. With revenues expected to soar, Nokia dominated the NMT business in Finland (with the support of Televa) and began to move into Scandinavian markets (through Salora) while augmenting Soviet exports in the Nordic countries and Western Europe. In 1982, Jorma Nieminen presented his celebrated vision of the early radiophone business, reflecting the views of Mobira's senior management and anticipating Nokia's triumphant tone in the late 1990s.

> . . . NMT represents a critically important development phase in worldwide scale. . . . It has already changed the general thinking and views on radiophones. It has become understood that NMT is only an example of the direction which must be taken. The ultimate objective must be a worldwide system that permits the indefinite communication of mobile people with each other, irrespective of the location.[14]

Mobira's marketers and top management pushed other European countries to adopt NMT, and Finland's Ministry of Trade and Industry encouraged the use of the technology. In fact, as early as 1983, Minister Esko Ollila had discussed the matter with France's Minister of Industry and Research. If a common cellular infrastructure were to be built in the mid-1980s, argued Ollila, the launch of a European-wide system would not have to be postponed until the next decade. Yet, Nordic hopes for a European NMT faded by 1983, when regional heavyweights—the United Kingdom, France, Germany, and Italy—introduced different standards.

As European integration accelerated in the late 1980s, the EU began to push competition in the mobile industry as the first step in a phased liberalization and embraced the GSM standard. While GSM did emerge as a semiglobal standard in the 1990s, a decade had been lost. The evolution of diverse standards should have allowed U.S. and Japanese rivals to catch up to their European challengers, but neither did. In the United States, regulators stumbled; in Japan, the bubble economy imploded.

From Business Markets to Consumer and Foreign Markets

Mobira's advertising reflected new market realities. NMT was no longer portrayed as an engineering accomplishment but as a necessary tool to cultivate the business-to-business market (see Exhibit 4-6). Nieminen and other senior managers understood that the niche phase was disappearing as the pressure to appeal to a mass market increased. In the early 1980s, it was important to attract emerging business markets, just as the early 1990s saw the shift from business-to-business to consumer markets.

The 1980s signaled a dramatic increase in growth for Mobira, with revenues growing an average of 50 percent annually. New markets were emerging worldwide and developing rapidly. In comparison, Mobira's R&D expenditures in the late 1970s accounted for 5 to 6 percent of its revenues; by the late 1980s they had increased to 9 and 11 percent. Concurrently, the company was building base stations as well as radiophones. Between 1979 and 1987, revenues soared from FIM 49 million to FIM 1.084 million (see Exhibit 4-7). In the process, the proportion of exports in total revenues increased rapidly as well. By 1983, exports accounted for 35 percent of revenues, and in 1987 they represented almost 75 percent.

Mobira's first cellular phone, the Mobira Senator, was a "me too" product. This product was supposed to be small, light, and easy to carry, but in fact, there was not adequate time for development: "The basic decision was to be first in the market with NMT phones; we made it quick and dirty," recalls Mobira's marketing director, Kari Pekka Wilska. "So no particular attention was paid to such features as the radio unit or ease of installation. The only goal was to have the product finished before the NMT system opened."[15]

In the mid-1980s, the Mobira Talkman, the first transportable phone, contributed to the company's excellent business results. This breakthrough product was launched in the spring of 1984. "The new Talkman does not bind your calls into the car," promised the advertisements. "You can take the phone wherever you go." Talkman precipitated accelerating miniaturization, weighing only 5 kilos (see Exhibit 4-8). Rapid market growth forced Mobira to accelerate the rate of product development, reorganize the company, and increase management seminars and quality training. These investments paid off; Mobira was fourth in the market with 13 percent, behind Motorola, which had an estimated 21 percent of the market in the mid-1980s, but ahead of Ericsson in sixth with 6 percent (see Exhibit 4-9).[16] In the United States,

Exhibit 4-6. A Nokia breakthrough product: the Mobira NMT car phones.

Source: © Nokia 2000. Nokia and Nokia Connecting People are registered trademarks of Nokia Corporation.

Exhibit 4-7. Mobira's revenues (1979–1987).

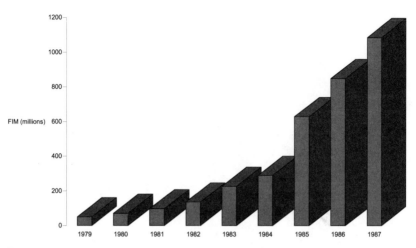

SOURCE: Company reports.

the cellular market lagged behind Europe. In the long term, however, no major mobile vendor could ignore the scale and scope of the highly competitive U.S. markets.

As the U.S. market evolved, Mobira needed a strategic partner with an existing distribution network. In spring 1984, Tandy Corporation proposed a joint venture to make mobile phones in Korea, and Mobira quickly agreed. The two set up a manufacturing plant in South Korea to distribute phones in the United States through Tandy's RadioShack outlets under the RadioShack brand name. In retrospect, this venture proved critical. On the one hand, the timing was favorable. By 1986, approximately 200 American cities utilized the AMPS network, and Nokia was able to tap into the U.S. market through RadioShack. In the long term, the alliance was important in another respect as well. Through Tandy, Nokia was quickly able to learn about overseas manufacturing activities that proved important as the company was preparing to enter the Asian market. Joint ventures may have been the quickest way to build volume, but they were also risky. Mobira's penchant for partnerships diminished its profit margins, and without a strong brand-name image, the company would have been left "vulnerable to being shut out of a market had there been a falling-out with a partner."[17]

Nokia-Mobira Oy

"In 1979 when Mobira was established," recalls Kari-Pekka Wilska, marketing director of Mobira, "we were told: you boys will die

Exhibit 4-8. The Mobira Talkman (1984).

SOURCE: © Nokia 2000. Nokia and Nokia Connecting People are registered trademarks of Nokia Corporation.

Exhibit 4-9. Mobile phone market shares (1985).

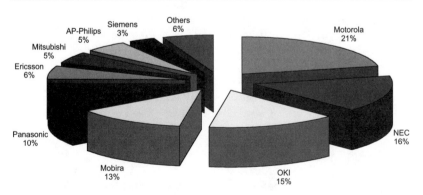

SOURCE: Mobira's 1985 estimate based on annual reports.

when the Japanese enter these markets . . . they will kill you when NMT starts . . . in 1985 you will be chewed up and spat out."[18] Two years later, Nieminen, Mobira's CEO, expected cutthroat competition as well: "Mobira faces open competition and lacks shelter from pressures from any direction. As in open-sea sailing, when you confront a storm, you have to be able to face it. There will be no available shelter."[19]

In 1986, Mobira Oy was renamed Nokia-Mobira Oy and became an autonomous industrial group within Nokia. In turn, the activities of Nokia-Mobira were reorganized in order to focus on NMT and PMR operations as well as activities in the United States, Europe, and Oulu. Concurrently, Nokia launched its first handset, Cityman, for the TACS customers in England, which ultimately became their export breakthrough product (see Exhibit 4-10).

Meanwhile, the company instituted organizational changes aimed at increasing efficiency. If the Japanese were entering the industry, there was no time for complacency. In 1980, Nokia-Mobira was made up of two factories: one for mobile phones and pagers, the other

Exhibit 4-10. The Cityman, Nokia's first handset.

Source: © Nokia 2000. Nokia and Nokia Connecting People are registered trademarks of Nokia Corporation.

for support stations in dedicated networks and standard radiophones (see Exhibit 4-11a and b). The new organizational structure fragmented production into a number of relatively small units, which ensured flexibility and entrepreneurial motivation. However, this fragmentation also resulted in duplicating production costs, which meant a higher cost structure. In the emergent phase of market evolution, growth compensated for these higher costs.

In 1987, Nokia-Mobira grew 28 percent to $269 million, claiming 13.5 percent of the $800-million cellular phone market, making it the world leader. Since competition had cut the price of cellular phones in half, Nokia began looking for ways to strengthen its margins. One plan was to expand its base-station installation business. It also redirected resources from older analog cellular products to next-generation digital cellular phones and base stations. Nokia-Mobira joined forces with France's Alcatel and West Germany's AEG to devise a system for Europe that it hoped would become an international standard for the digital cellular network of the 1990s.[20]

To ensure that Nokia could influence standards, Kairamo sought greater market share. He had bold plans to enter the U.S. market, where Jan Loeber, a former ITT marketing executive and the first non-Finnish member of Nokia's board, wanted to boost the company's sales to $500 million in five years and to 10 percent of the parent's revenues and profits by 1995. Again, the entry strategy required that

Exhibit 4-11. Nokia-Mobira Oy: growth expectations and organizational efficiencies (1987–88).

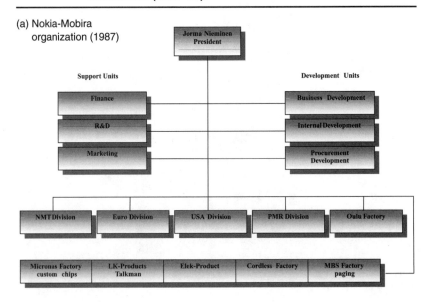

(a) Nokia-Mobira organization (1987)

Exhibit 4-11 (continued).

(b) Nokia-Mobira
organization (1988)

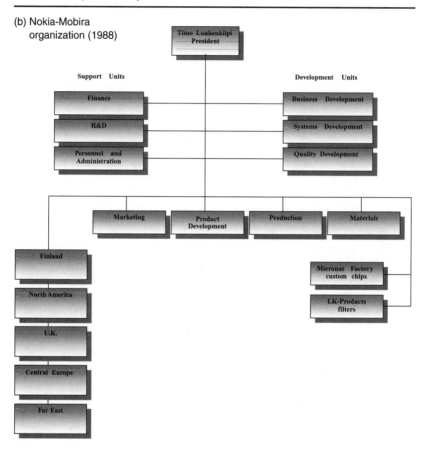

SOURCE: Based on annual reports.

the company partner with or acquire a major American telecommunications supplier. According to Loeber, "We could hit $300 million by the middle of spring if the deal is done. We want this first deal to be big, to make a statement." At the very least, he expected Nokia's U.S. sales to grow 60 percent in 1988, to $100 million.[21]

As price pressures rose in the late 1980s, Nokia-Mobira could not compete with its main rivals. The organizational obstacles of the Finnish company reflected European-wide problems. Between 1978 and 1986, the worldwide telecommunications industry grew rapidly, but the EC's share of world exports declined from 40 percent to 20 percent. The fragmentation of European production stemmed from the continued application of different national equipment standards and approval policies.[22]

Kairamo was eager to stress branding prior to the anticipated GSM explosion, insisting on the world market and on a single brand name—Nokia—for its diverse product line. In order to avoid being outpriced in the growth markets, the company had to drastically improve its operational effectiveness. Further, Nokia-Mobira had stumbled in its early move into the U.S. market. "Price competition is nowhere as tough as in the U.S. markets," lamented Mobira's marketing director Wilska:

> That was the biggest surprise to me. . . . The competition is ruthless. It is cash flow thinking. . . . If the cash flow directs the business, then all kind of issues arise. There is all kind of misconduct in the markets. In the U.S., we talk about totally different sorts of margins. . . . The whole business base there involves huge volumes, and if you don't succeed in entering the volume business, then you'd better forget it.[23]

The Spin-Off of Benefon and the Future of Telenokia

Strategic disagreements, pressures within the company, and U.S. market missteps led to the resignation of Jorma Nieminen, managing director of Nokia-Mobira. The timing of his departure created additional difficulties. After Koski passed away and Kairamo committed suicide, the company desperately needed strong and decisive leaders. Unfortunately, not only did Nieminen leave the company, but he also recruited several of its senior managers to his new company, Benefon.

Nokia's new president, Timo Louhenkilpi, helped the company refine its organizational structure to achieve greater operational effectiveness. The revised organizational chart reflected Nokia-Mobira's rapid geographic expansion along six different units: Finland, Scandinavia, North America, the United Kingdom, Central Europe, and the Far East. In the long term, these geographic segments would form the nucleus of Nokia's globalization initiative. As the subsidiary began to seek synergies through interrelationships with other Nokia groups, Nokia Cellular Systems was established as an independent company. In 1987, Telenokia decided that GSM systems would serve as the strategic instrument in the company's expected growth scenario beginning in July 1991. The next year, Telenokia Oy was renamed Nokia Telecommunications Oy. The company was reorganized in January 1995 into cellular systems, network and access systems, and system platforms and customer services.

Second-Generation Mobile

The earliest 2G digital systems were developed in the 1980s, but they were not introduced into the marketplace until the early 1990s. Digital cellular offered several advantages over analog: increased capacity, the transfer of both voice and data through the radio spectrum (e.g., short message service [SMS], e-mail), and improved security. The 2G networks went hand in hand with smaller and lighter handsets with longer battery life, and outdoor/indoor coverage. Mobile cellular was no longer perceived as distinct but complementary to fixed public switched telephone network (PSTN) systems. The market focus shifted from early-adopter business segments, to late-adopter business segments (including small and medium-size companies), and to early-adopter consumer segments.

In the new standards rivalry, TDMA IS-136, introduced in late 1991, served as the digital enhancement of analog AMPS technology used in the 800 and 1900 MHz frequency bands. Code division multiple access (CDMA) IS-95 consisted of a family of digital communication techniques that increased capacity by using the whole radio band, with each call allocated a unique code. Personal digital cellular (PDC) was the second-largest digital standard in the world for mobile systems, though it has been used exclusively in Japan since it was introduced in 1994. Led by the Nordic markets, the Europeans opted for GSM, a technology pioneered by Nokia and Ericsson. This became the first commercially operated digital cellular system. First, however, the competitive environment in Finland went through a drastic transition, without which Nokia's future success would have been less certain.

The Emergence of the Innovation Stage

The elections of 1991 gave Finland its first purely non-socialist government since 1966. As Social Democrats moved to the opposition, the centrist-conservative Esko Aho government adopted an export-oriented economic strategy designed to revitalize exports and industrial production and sought to curb national and public debt. At the same time, the government encouraged structural reforms such as increased competition and decreased rigidities in labor markets.

Due to a severe recession and the collapse of the Soviet Union in the early 1990s, Finland took several decisive steps toward a new national industrial strategy that endeavored to strengthen its economy and establish itself as a competitor in the rapidly changing global telecommunications and mobile industries. The small Nordic nation was at a turning point. It had to cope with a severe economic crisis, adjust to the competition spawned by European integration, and yet strive to benefit from rapid advances in technology. The task was complicated by high foreign debt, a rapidly climbing public debt, and, most important, one of the highest rates of unemployment in Europe.

In order to expedite the transition, the proponents of the new national strategy advocated market-driven solutions to resolve these problems. The external imbalance could be corrected solely by rapid growth in exports and the creation of a new capacity. While the national restructuring and focus on new and emerging clusters conflicted with the driving principles of the old investment economy (public sector investments), it paralleled Nokia's own restructuring and refocusing on mobile communications (private sector innovations).[24] Yet, even as Finland moved toward a more market-based industrial strategy between 1992 and 1995, it was not as much creating a new national economic policy as it was adapting to major European developments.[25]

European integration provided the kind of business environment that Kairamo and his executives had envisioned would serve as a catalyst for Nokia's new expansion. Although Finland's trade with Western Europe developed slowly in the early postwar years, by the 1980s it had become more important than the country's trade activity with the East. In 1986, Finland became a regular member of the European Free Trade Association, and the Soviet Union finally recognized that the organization posed no threat to its security or trade interests.[26] By the 1990s, these initiatives had laid the foundation for cellular leadership in the Nordic region with the rapid expansion of Nokia in Finland and Ericsson in Sweden.

Historically, EU member states have been heavily engaged in industrial policies. Until recently, many lacked proper competition policy as well as merger legislation. The vision of the internal market was based on free-market principles that conflicted with the European Commission's initiatives. With the recessionary environment of the early 1990s and the rise of regionalism in international trade, the competitiveness of the European companies became the subject of great debate and concern in the Community.[27]

These European developments coincided with Nokia's own refocusing that resulted in increased profits by the mid-1990s. In the EU, the rise of the GSM standard, the Nordic cellular industry, and Nokia and Ericsson in particular were perceived as showcases for the great potential of pan-European competitive advantage. However, the EU's commitment to market-driven industrial strategies was neither dogmatic nor consistent. As long as Commission President Jacques Delors supported the Single Market program (1984–1994), market liberalism prevailed. In the mid-1990s, the new president, Jacques Santer, brought a somewhat different vision to the agenda. The perception that European companies were threatened by the high-technology industries of the United States and Japan did not result in aggressive market innovation and entrepreneurship. Instead, it encouraged European investment programs in IT industries.[28]

It was at this time that Nokia developed its concept of the mobile information infrastructure, which seemed a natural extension of both the EU "information society" efforts and the Clinton-Gore administration's national and global "information infrastructure" initiatives in 1993 and 1994. Skillfully designed, Nokia's strategic approach sought to benefit from both initiatives without confining itself to one or another.[29]

In Finland, Nokia's explosive growth contributed significantly to the transformation of the economy. From the late nineteenth century to the late twentieth century, wood/paper and metals had dominated Finnish industry. By the mid-1990s, the telecommunications/mobile sector was the fastest growing cluster in Finland, and it was expected to expand dramatically in its estimated export share. Rapid expansion was stimulated by the liberalization of world telecommunications markets, yet Finnish public policy and Nordic cooperation had nurtured the wireless segment since the late 1960s.

Despite growing domestic opposition, the Finnish electorate in October 1994 voted to accede to the EU (56.9 percent to 43.1 percent). On January 1, 1995, Austria, Finland, and Sweden joined the EU, enlarging its membership to fifteen states. Finland's membership in the EU signaled the beginning of the innovation stage of competitive development. In this stage, companies not only exploited and improved technology and methods from other nations but also created their own. As a result, companies in an innovation-driven economy compete internationally in more differentiated industry segments. Ideally, thriving industry clusters become self-reinforcing.[30]

For small companies with global ambitions, first-mover advantage and a dynamic *strategy* may be the only ways to enter and dominate international markets. However, as Nokia's experience indicates, the competitive *environment* must change accordingly. An investment economy seldom gives rise to successful innovation-driven companies that exhibit sustained competitive advantage. Similarly, Nokia's success came only after Finland, through painful restructuring, had left behind the investment economy. Indeed, it would be very difficult to envision Nokia's GSM triumph without the parallel transition of the Finnish economy toward more market-driven solutions.

Global System for Mobile Communications

For most of the 1980s, the wide variety of analog cellular systems fragmented the equipment market and prevented most users from roaming between countries. Unlike the Americans, however, the Europeans managed to implement market integration. The need for such a unified European cellular standard was recognized by the French PTT and the German Bundespost as early as 1981.

With the gradual unification of the European markets at the end of the 1980s, the European Conference of Postal and Telecommunications Administrations (CEPT) decided to develop a common standard for digital mobile telephony, the GSM.[31] In 1982, in a move promoted primarily by the Nordic countries and the Netherlands, CEPT formed a new standards group, Groupe Special Mobile, with the mandate to specify radiotelephone systems for Europe. Perhaps the most successful program in the history of European telecommunications, it provided the foundation for the Finnish GSM expansion and Nokia's cellular success from around 1993 to 1997, as well as the accompanying emergence of Finland's telecommunications/mobile cluster (see Exhibit 4-12).

The GSM was as much about the market-driven strategies of Nokia and Ericsson as it was about the political activities associated with the European integration. It was derived from a pan-European political initiative backed by the European Commission together with telecommunications operators and equipment manufacturers to promote regional harmonization among cellular networks. The European Telecommunications Standards Institute (ETSI), created in 1989, became responsible for GSM standardization. GSM used time division multiple access (TDMA) technology and operated in the 900/1800/ 1900 MHz frequency bands. In 1991, Radiolinja, a Finnish mobile operator, launched the first GSM network. Thereafter, all European countries adopted the GSM standard, and it became popular on other continents as well. By April 1999, it was the dominant cellular standard, with more than 45 percent of worldwide mobile subscribers (see Exhibit 4-13a–d).

Nokia and the GSM

For all practical purposes, the story of GSM commercialization chronicles Nokia's success. The project was dubbed the Great Software Monster by engineers debugging the slew of new applications required to support such ambitious features as international roaming, call forwarding, and SMS messaging. From the very beginning, Nokia has been one of the main developers of GSM technology. After his own stint as manager of the GSM team, Ollila appointed a new manager: "The GSM project was in disarray. There was a lot of disillusionment with the spec and the difficulty of the technology," Ollila recalls. "People were saying we wanted a racehorse, but some committee got into the design process and we ended up with a camel. But we continued because we believed in digital."[32]

The first GSM call was made in Finland in 1991 using a Nokia phone on a Nokia-equipped network. That same year, Nokia agreed to

Exhibit 4-12. The Finnish telecommunication/mobile cluster (ca. 2000).

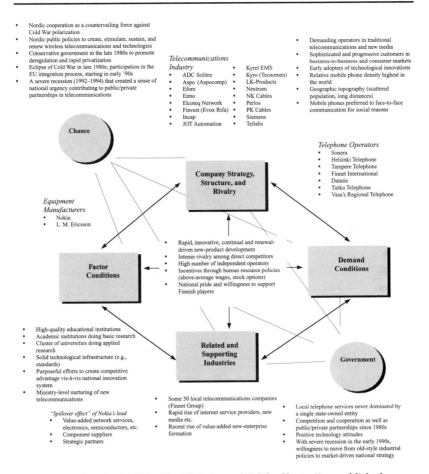

- Nordic cooperation as a countervailing force against Cold War polarization
- Nordic public policies to create, stimulate, sustain, and renew wireless telecommunications and technologies
- Conservative government in the late 1980s to promote deregulation and rapid privatization
- Eclipse of Cold War in late 1980s; participation in the EU integration process, starting in early '90s
- A severe recession (1992–1994) that created a sense of national urgency contributing to public/private partnerships in telecommunications

Chance

Telecommunications Industry
- ADC Solitra
- Aspo (Aspocomp)
- Efore
- Eimo
- Elcoteq Network
- Finvest (Evox Rifa)
- Incap
- JOT Automation
- Kyrel EMS
- Kyro (Tecnomen)
- LK-Products
- Nextrom
- NK Cables
- Perlos
- PK Cables
- Siemens
- Tellabs

- Demanding operators in traditional telecommunications and new media
- Sophisticated and progressive customers in business-to-business and consumer markets
- Early adopters of technological innovations
- Relative mobile phone density highest in the world
- Geographic topography (scattered population, long distances)
- Mobile phones preferred to face-to-face communication for social reasons

Telephone Operators
- Sonera
- Helsinki Telephone
- Tampere Telephone
- Finnet International
- Datatie
- Turku Telephone
- Vasa's Regional Telephone

Company Strategy, Structure, and Rivalry

Equipment Manufacturers
- Nokia
- L. M. Ericsson

- Rapid, innovative, continual and renewal-driven new-product development
- Intense rivalry among direct competitors
- High number of independent operators
- Incentives through human resource policies (above-average wages, stock options)
- National pride and willingness to support Finnish players

Factor Conditions

Demand Conditions

- High-quality educational institutions
- Academic institutions doing basic research
- Cluster of universities doing applied research
- Solid technological infrastructure (e.g., standards)
- Purposeful efforts to create competitive advantage vis-à-vis national innovation system
- Ministry-level nurturing of new telecommunications

"Spillover effect" of Nokia's lead
- Value-added network services, electronics, semiconductors, etc.
- Component suppliers
- Strategic partners

Related and Supporting Industries

Government

- Some 50 local telecommunications companies (Finnet Group)
- Rapid rise of internet service providers, new media etc.
- Recent rise of value-added new-enterprise formation

- Local telephone services never dominated by a single state-owned entity
- Competition and cooperation as well as public/private partnerships since 1880s
- Positive technology attitudes
- With severe recession in the early 1990s, willingness to move from old-style industrial policies to market-driven national strategy

SOURCE: Dan Steinbock, "The Finnish Telecom/Mobile Cluster," unpublished paper, Harvard Business School Case Project, 2000.

NOTE: The companies listed under italic headings are Finnish telecommunication companies that were among the 500 largest Finnish corporations (the "Talouselämä 500") in 2000. Overall, the cluster consists of equipment manufacturers, such as Nokia, and other component producers, electronics concerns, and software companies, as well as telephone operators. See "Suomi Nokian kännyssä," *Talouselämä* (1999).

supply GSM networks to nine other European countries. In 1994, Nokia was the first manufacturer to launch a series of hand-portable phones for all major digital standards (GSM, TDMA, personal communications networks, Japan Digital), the Nokia 2100 family, and was supplying GSM systems to fifty-nine operators in thirty-one countries by August 1997. In addition to mobile voice telephony, GSM technology enabled the versatile development of new services, including the

Exhibit 4-13. GSM and world cellular subscribers (1992–1999).

(a) World Cellular Subscribers

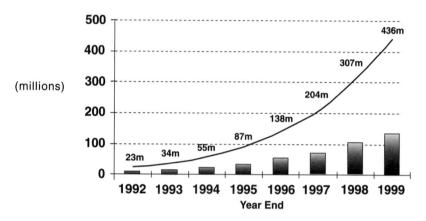

(b) GSM 900/1800/1900 Subscribers

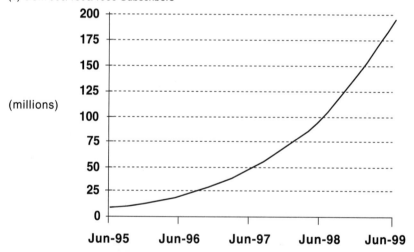

SOURCE FOR EXHIBIT 4-13(A–D): EMC world cellular database.

NOTE: Subscriber statistics demonstrate the numbers of people using GSM at different frequencies and in different global regions. The current count is 200 million, which is phenomenal customer growth running at twice the industry's predicted level.

Exhibit 4.13 (continued).

(c) GSM 900/1800/1900 Market Share by World Regions

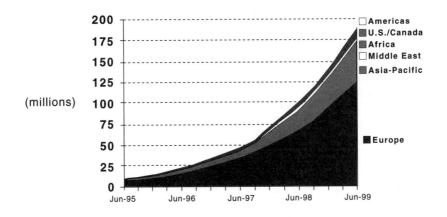

(d) Digital Subscribers

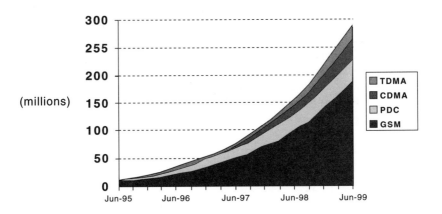

packet-switching technologies used to transmit high-speed data over wireless telecommunications networks. Phenomenal market growth doubled the industry's predicted level. Between 1992 and 1999, the number of world cellular subscribers soared from 23 million to an estimated 436 million. Between 1995 and 1999, the number of GSM 900/1800/1900 subscribers increased from a few million to close to 200 million. Initially, Europe accounted for most of the market share, but by 1999 the proportion held by Asia-Pacific had increased significantly. Similarly, GSM continued to play the most critical role among the four major digital cellular technologies. Among prepaid subscribers, GSM represented 77 percent, far more than PDC (15 percent), CDMA (12 percent), or TDMA (9 percent). In the process, Nokia's success mirrored that of the GSM (see Exhibit 4-14). At this crucial stage, international players had practically no opportunity to enter the Finnish market due to foreign ownership restrictions. Finland's capital allocation system was restructured only after the breakup of the Soviet Union in 1991—through the changes in foreign ownership legislation in 1992 and membership in the EU in 1995.[33]

This institutional context has been crucial for the success of leading Nordic cellular companies, such as Nokia and Ericsson. The Nordic public policy institutions made the first strategies that gave rise to the industry.[34] However, industry attractiveness is a necessary but not a sufficient determinant of company success. Just as there are profitable growth industries in which individual companies fail to gain profitability, there are unattractive industries in which some companies thrive. Every company is shaped by its industry structure, but a truly great company also *shapes* the structure itself in ways that allow it to attain competitive advantage.

Nordic public policies contributed to a favorable industry environment, but it was companies like Nokia and Ericsson that made the environment a source of competitive advantage. At Nokia, this process did not begin with the restructuring of the early 1990s or the public policies in the 1970s and 1980s. The success originated from the consolidation of Finnish cable, electronics, and television production in the postwar era and, ultimately, from the achievements of the Finnish Cable Works in the early twentieth century.

Exhibit 4-14. Nokia's global breakthrough phases.

	First-Generation Rivalry			Second-Generation Rivalry		Coming of the Third-Generation Rivalry
	Competition with global manufacturers in the Nordic countries (1981–1984)	Leap to international markets (1985–1988)	Stagnation and deterioration in markets entered (1989–1990)	Recapturing lost positions and entry into global markets (1991–1992)	Rapid growth and domination of 2G markets worldwide (1993–1998)	Early transition to mobile Internet (1998–2000)
World market position	Fluctuates	Improves	Deteriorates	Improves	Increases	Increases
Position in markets entered	Improves	Improves and deteriorates	Deteriorates	Improves	Increases	Increases
Geographic expansion*	Nordic countries (5)	UK, Continental Europe, North America, Asia (20)	Few significant markets (30)	Middle and South America, Australia, former Soviet Union and East European countries (70)	All lead markets in Europe, Americas, Asia-Pacific (130)	All lead markets in Europe, Americas, Asia-Pacific (more than 130)

SOURCE: For 1981–1992, Matti Pulkkinen, *The Breakthrough of Nokia Mobile Phones*, Acta Universitatis Oeconomicae Helsingiensis, Series A-122 (Helsinki: HSEBA), p. 123. For 1993–2000, the author.
*Total number of countries selling NMP phones at the end of the phase.

CHAPTER FIVE

Strategic Intent

BY the close of the 1990s, Finland was not just aware of but had become self-conscious about its newly discovered clout in mobile communications. Due to the impending convergence of mobile and Internet industries, the country had suddenly become something of a worldwide test laboratory for the leading European, American, and Asian telecommunications and mobile giants.[1] "If you think the U.S. is a leader in moving from wired communications to wireless, take a look at Finland," urged *The Wall Street Journal*. "Nearly half of Finns now use wireless phones, more than double the rate in the U.S. . . . Many American manufacturers and service providers see a day when, as in Finland, the wires in our homes and under our streets serve primarily as data-hauling networks, while much of the talk moves over the airwaves."[2]

By 2000, the new Finnish mobile startups saw themselves as the "next big thing," and the Finnish business press redefined the nation as the "Wireless Valley."[3]

Jorma Ollila's Nokia

If at the peak of the diversification era, Nokia was characterized by the charismatic and colorful leadership of Kairamo, the refocusing era was defined by the results-driven and sophisticated leadership of Nokia's current CEO and chairman, Jorma Ollila. In August 1998, *Business Week* published a flattering cover story on Nokia. The feature opened by drawing a parallel between the Finnish sauna and Nokia's strategy:

> Behind his gentlemanly demeanor, Jorma Ollila, CEO of Nokia Corp., is a man of extremes. As his wife, Liisa Annikki, tells it, her husband fires up the Finnish sauna a good 15 degrees warmer than she likes it, all the way to 212F—hot enough to boil a pot of tea. It was a week after Easter when

the Ollilas drove north from Helsinki for their first trip this year to the family's lakeside cabin. Ice was still floating on Lake Pukala, and the kids challenged their father to dive in. Emerging from the sauna, Ollila paused, then plunged naked into the icy lake.

Ollila, a 47-year-old former banker, lives by the plunge. He believes people get comfy and complacent and that it takes a dive into the unknown, or a push, to tap into their strongest instincts—those that guide survival. Six years ago, as an untested CEO, he bet the 133-year-old Finnish conglomerate on cellular phones, challenging rivals Motorola Inc. and L. M. Ericsson. In the struggle that ensued, Ollila's Finns outdid themselves. Fast and focused, with a canny eye for design, Nokia wrested market share from entrenched competitors and emerged as the most profitable player in the industry.[4]

The metaphor of an existential gambler made a great intro, but it was not exactly to the point. Inadvertently, the *Business Week* story may have established a formula used for those Nokia profiles that followed. The story would be quite dramatic if it were not for the fact that such sauna habits are quite typical in the Finnish lifestyle. With little concrete knowledge of Finnish conditions or the small country's history, and without a more intimate understanding of Ollila's personal history, many writers have filled empty gaps with anecdotal curiosities. Thus was born a new myth of Nokia: the arctic hero that invaded world markets. This stereotype had little to do with facts, but it fit the tourist's expectations. The company's execution of its global growth strategy created the perception that it was poised for endless growth in the stock market.[5]

Ollila does not have an image as a man of extremes; he is respected as a thorough strategist who understands business, finance, and industry (see Exhibit 5-1). He can be impatient and confrontational, but does not engage Nokia in business conflicts that the company cannot win. Yet his career does have a certain dramatic flair, which has been exaggerated by Nordic tabloids and almost entirely neglected by the international press.

The Early Years: Student Politics and Citibank

Jorma Jaakko Ollila was born in August 1950 in a region of Finland known for the persistence of its people and as a strong bastion of the Center Party. His father was an engineer who owned an electronics business until he started working in Finlayson's textile business, and

Exhibit 5-1. Jorma Ollila: the man who made Nokia a global industry leader.

SOURCE: © Nokia 2000. Nokia and Nokia Connecting People are registered trademarks of Nokia Corporation.

his mother was from an agrarian family. The future CEO of Nokia was the first of five children, growing up in a family where both parents were the first students in their families. To the Ollilas, education was perceived as the key to success.

The young Ollila was a bright student. After studying in Vasa, Finland, he earned at the age of 17 a scholarship to Atlantic College, a new Welsh boarding school founded by German educator Kurt Hahn to bring together the world's future leaders. He began his studies at Helsinki University of Technology in 1969, majoring first in engineering physics and then switching to applied mathematics and systems theory. He also began to study economics. In 1970, he met his future wife, Liisa Metsola, a bright, ambitious nursing student who later created a career of her own as ministerial councillor in the international affairs unit of Finland's Ministry of Social Affairs and Health.

The official biography jumps from these early years to Ollila's Citibank career, which began toward the end of the 1970s. One decade is lost. This is not uncommon among the boomer generation of Finnish business and political leaders.

In the early 1970s, pro-Moscow attitudes in Finland were so strong that many Finns who had fought against the Soviet Union felt the country was close to losing its democratic ways. For a while, Ollila, the young Centrist, aligned himself with the student radicals who spoke of a "proletarian revolution," whether they really meant it or not. During this time, Ollila established himself as a leader.

In the 1966 parliamentary elections, major gains by the left had allowed the Communists and the Social Democrats to return to the government. Meanwhile, the conservatives were left outside the government for a quarter of a century. In student politics, Finland did not see a rise of the humanistic and culturally progressive New Left.[6] Instead, the democratic impulse of the leftist coalition soon deteriorated to virulent and narrow-minded middle-class radicalism as the campuses were swept by neo-Stalinists (*taistolaiset*). With the support of the minority of the Communist Party as well as the Soviet Embassy, this group pressured even the moderates to join the "progressive popular front." If one refused to follow the party line, one was against peaceful coexistence with the Soviet Union. No ambitious young student who cherished political aspirations could afford such transgressions.

When Ollila studied at the Faculty of Social Sciences of Helsinki, the peer pressure for neo-Stalinist conformity was at its peak; the student-faculty councils consisted of neo-Stalinists alone. As "Finlandization" became a negative watchword in the West, Finland remained an independent and neutral Western democracy, but most political parties allowed Soviet views to infiltrate the highest levels of the Finnish political economy. Self-censorship reigned in the press. Among enterprising politicians, clandestine contact with KGB operatives made a mockery of the official rhetoric of independence.

In 1971, Ollila joined the Conservative Coalition, a typical choice for students at the HUT. He soon switched to the Center Party, which represented the interests of rural Finland but had a strong presence in national politics. Ollila earned a degree in political science from the University of Helsinki while serving as chairman of the National Union of Finnish Students (SYL). For a career-conscious student, it was a highly desirable position that could be used as a bridge to influential party or government bureaucracies. As a member of the Center Party, Ollila obtained his position in a political deal with the neo-Stalinists. As a centrist chairman of the SYL, Ollila contributed to those very issues that the advocates of "Finlandization" had warned European politicians about. The SYL adopted the pro-Moscow line, and student leaders spoke glowingly in support of the "peaceful coexistence of Finland and the Soviet Union" and the "democratic forces" of Vietnam, Chile, and Cuba. They traveled in the Soviet Union, worked for the progressive forces of Chile and Greece, and participated in the International Union of Students (IUS), a pro-Moscow organization that most Western countries had denounced and abandoned as politically corrupt, with the exception of Finland.

Ollila represented the SYL at peace festivals in Moscow, East Berlin, and Havana. Despite the vocal protests of some non-Communist Socialists who were advocates of Soviet dissidents, the SYL remained quiet about the policies of the Brezhnev era. However, as far as Ollila was concerned, the role of the chairman was a "very pragmatic thing." In retrospect, these events held a certain irony. In 1973, Finland was expected to agree to a free-trade agreement with the EEC, the precursor of the contemporary EU. At the time, Kari Kairamo argued that the EEC moved too slowly, just as there was inadequate cooperation between businesses and academia. Under Ollila's leadership, the SYL felt that the EEC moved too quickly and in the wrong direction. The SYL condemned any potential agreement with the EEC, which it considered "essentially an undemocratic community, whose goals conflict with Finland's social objectives."[7] Almost two decades later, Ollila was appointed to the European Commission as a member of the Competitiveness Advisory Group, just as he joined the European Round Table of Industrialists.

As a bright and active student, Ollila was eager to build a career that would take him to the highest echelons of Finnish society. Unlike some centrists, he did not leave the Center Party. If student radicalism were to be the voice of the era, he would seize the opportunity. Further, the new Finnish politicians needed to gain credibility in foreign policy, and that was achieved only through Moscow.

Of course, the transition from a radical student politician to a Citibank banker and CEO of Nokia is full of irony. However, a far more interesting way to look at this personal transformation is to understand it as a gradual evolution rather than an abrupt reversal. The very same negotiating skills that Ollila demonstrated in the early 1970s were crucial to Nokia's financial deals in the late 1980s and its technology coalitions in the 1990s. In each, he has successfully mediated vastly different, often hostile organizations in adverse circumstances.

Most important, Ollila's personal background differed from that of the neo-Stalinist leaders. Many of them were born into established families of bankers, educators, or politicians. Unlike these privileged "rebels," he had to work his way to positions of leadership. Not surprisingly, Ollila soon grew weary of the narrow-minded political leftism of his era. When he left his post in November 1974, his farewell speech was a thinly veiled warning. The undemocratic political minority posed a threat because it favored measures that might undo the SYL itself: "The worst is that a certain political student organization forms itself a view, which it knows the other will surely oppose and which, then, is launched as the only progressive position, while others are labeled reactionary."[8] In the end, neo-Stalinist radicalism never really appealed to Ollila, who was far too independent and intelligent to buy into the ideological orthodoxy and who, unlike many other student politicians in Finland, had an *international* outlook.

Industry Experience: From Corporate Finance to the Cellular Business

Following his studies, Ollila worked in the headquarters of the Center Party, focusing on international affairs. In 1976, he earned a master's degree in political science from the University of Helsinki, where he wrote a thesis entitled "International Trade under Uncertainty." This academic choice was rather typical of one who harbored dreams of a future in the political bureaucracy. But such a position was no longer Ollila's primary objective. He then studied at the London School of Economics, where he earned a master of science degree, and at HUT, where he earned a master's degree in engineering in 1981. His engineering thesis, "Optimization of Economic Growth," complemented his earlier thesis in exploring the theme of future international business.

At Citibank, Ollila's career progressed, but he continued to keep in close touch with the Center Party, with Paavo Väyrynen in particular, an influential centrist politician. A one-time protégé of President

Kekkonen, Väyrynen was considered a serious candidate for the presidency; critics considered him a political opportunist. By the mid-1980s, Ollila served as a member of the board in Citibank Oy, the bank's Finnish subsidiary. According to Kari Mannola, Ollila's manager at that time. "Jorma is intellectual in the sense that he grabs the theory and puts it into practice rather than philosophizing."[9]

Nokia was one of Citibank's key clients. As a young and ambitious account manager, Ollila marketed his bank to Finnish industry leaders, including Nokia. "It was the era of the liberalization of money markets," he recently recalled. "One learned how the economy works, how one can analyze companies, and how capital movements influence things."[10] Ollila was assigned to analyze the state of Nokia's business conditions at the peak of Nokia's internationalization and M&A activities. He discovered problems in its foreign activities, arguing that the company's organizational structure did not meet the requirements of the current competitive environment and that Nokia needed a thorough organizational transformation. In September 1984, Kairamo invited Ollila to a meeting, and a few months later he hired Ollila as Nokia's vice president of international operations.

In addition to the Helsinki Stock Exchange, Nokia joined international stock exchanges in Stockholm, New York, London, Paris, and Frankfurt. By 1987, its stock equity capital amounted to FIM 1 billion. However, through their 40 percent interest in Nokia, the two major Finnish banks (SYP, KOP) and the leading insurance company (Pohjola) had effective control of the company. Ollila became Nokia's chief financial officer and joined the board in 1986. As CFO, it was his task to ensure capital for the company's new acquisitions, including those of Ericsson Data, Oceanic, and Standard Elektrik Lorentz. In 1988, Nokia issued stocks for Finnish investors. "Become an Owner of Europe," urged the campaign, which generated FIM 800 million. As far as Kairamo and Koski were concerned, these activities were vital to Nokia. In order to open the doors to Europe, Nokia had to eliminate the Finnish banks' control, or at least reduce their bargaining power on the board.

Around 1987, Nokia's mobile business had begun losing money, and the subsidiary had arrived at a critical crossroads. Struggling for strategic positioning in a growth market, it manufactured phones in small-scale series, not in the tens of thousands like its mass-producer rivals, such as Motorola. For years, Kairamo and Koski had considered the future of Nokia contingent on the operations of the mobile subsidiary, but after 1988 both men were gone. It was left to the board and Nokia's new leadership to decide if the subsidiary were to evolve into an important niche producer or seek to conquer world markets. At the subsidiary, disagreements about its future strategy divided employees, triggering the spin-off of Benefon and a migration of talent.

Under Vuorilehto, Ollila got his first taste of competition in the mobile industry by heading the cellular phone division in Salo. "In early 1990, Simo called me and asked me whether I'd like to be in charge of Nokia Mobile Phones. Could I make it," Ollila recalled. "I said that, look, it won't be easy, but that I think I would. OK, that's it, he said. That's about how long that conversation took. . . . "[11]

Along with Kouri, Lagerroos, the previous managing director of the cellular unit, had challenged the group leadership. When Lagerroos was forced to leave the company, Ollila assumed his postion in February 1990. "What I was told by my seniors was, 'Look, you get six months to make a proposal on whether we sell it or what we do with this business. After four months I said, 'No, we're not going to sell this one.' "[12]

In 1982, Nokia Mobile Phones had exported CMT terminals to Nordic countries, but by 1987, it was exporting them to twenty-four countries in Europe, North America, and Asia. The company was in the red in the years prior to Ollila's arrival but became profitable during 1981 and 1982 as well as during 1990 and 1992. By 1992, it was exporting its products to seventy countries and had doubled its share of the global market to 20 percent.

In retrospect, however, the timing enabled Ollila to avoid Nokia's power struggles and focus on the GSM project. He understood its potential for Nokia, and re-entered the leadership arena at a more opportune time. In the late 1980s, he saw Europe heading toward a digital standard for mobile phones, which would provide manufacturers with a vast, unified, and pioneering home market. If Nokia could focus its resources on mobile communications, it could exploit first-mover advantages to compensate for a lack in economies of scale and scope. As markets opened up, Ollila reasoned, even companies in small countries could become world players—if they had the right focus. Ollila's people and management skills also played a crucial role in the success of the subsidiary, particularly during the early 1990s, when the phone business had become paralyzed by low morale and disorganization due to defections at the subsidiary and chaos at the headquarters.

As Finland was swept by a severe recession, Nokia struggled to survive. Between 1991 and 1992, its net income was negative, yet its operations remained relatively good and liquidity somewhat standard. The crisis was primarily strategic, secondarily financial. Nokia's poor profitability illustrated the collapse of the old strategy. If the company did not reposition itself quickly, what began as a strategic crisis would soon become financial as well. The co-CEOs, Vuorilehto and Kalle Isokallio, argued about the details of restructuring but the board was willing to gamble the future of the company. In 1991, Nokia's leading shareholder had tried to sell its stake to Ericsson. Ironically, even the Swedish rival was no longer interested. Further, the banks and financial institutions that had been at odds with Kairamo and Koski had a positive view of Ollila, a former banker. They felt they understood him and he, in turn, communicated well with them. Ahti Hirvonen, the new CEO of SYP, had been the first to suggest Ollila for the position of Nokia's CEO. Casimir Ehnrooth, chairman of the board, and Yrjö Niskanen, vice chairman of the board and new director of Pohjola, were solidly behind Ollila.

Ollila was a popular candidate among many stakeholders because he appeared to know what to do in the mobile phone division, and Nokia seemed intent on its corporate refocusing efforts in the cellular business. After all, Ollila had been able to listen to employees at the Salo factory, communicate his vision, and persuade workers to share it. He had also managed to streamline the R&D department that was stumbling to prepare for the GSM standard. In press interviews, he calls that unit "my university."

In late November 1991, Ollila met with Ehnrooth and Ahti Hirvonen. The owners of Nokia had many questions for Ollila, but most had a common theme: *Can Nokia be saved?* Ollila, in turn, presented his argument: If the company focused on mobile phones and opted for GSM, Nokia could be saved. In mid-January 1992, Ollila got the job. A month later, KOP (SYP's rival) sold its entire Nokia stake (8.5 percent) for FIM 542 million. This enabled Ollila to give his undivided attention to Nokia rather than concern himself with the relationship between the two banks. Nokia's owners gave Ollila the opportunity to move ahead without interference, but if he failed to turn the company around, they would intervene.

Following the boardroom shakeup in 1992, Ollila and Olli-Pekka Kallasvuo, acting as CEO and CFO, respectively, began to strategize a new course for the company. "It was Olli-Pekka and me, sitting in the head office trying to figure out what to do," Ollila recalled. "We had unhappy Finnish shareholders, unhappy international shareholders. The only thing you could do is to start building a base for very meaningful stock performance."[13] Ollila would focus the company by having Nokia concentrate solely on the wireless business, perhaps the single most important strategic decision in the history of Nokia.

In late August 1992, Ollila was working on transparencies for still another weekend seminar on Nokia's strategy. He quickly scribbled a title, "Nokia 2000," and four words. According to corporate legend, these four words became the shorthand that would guide the company as Ollila began to restructure the unwieldy conglomerate: *Focus, Global, Telecom-Oriented, High Value-Added.*[14]

Nokia's Strategic Intent

Restructuring at Nokia did not start with Ollila. It began soon after Vuorilehto became CEO in 1988, but Ollila continued and completed this phase in the mid-1990s when the last noncore properties were divested. Unlike Vuorilehto, whose industry experience stemmed primarily from wood processing, Ollila had managed NMP since the late 1980s and understood the strategic importance of the industry, especially in long-term strategy. He also knew that mere restructuring would not suffice and that the company would have to refocus its activities. He had a very clear idea of the complementary functions of strategy formulation and valuation, but his reasoning went even further: the company required organizational transformation, new kinds of capabilities, the ability to build strategic advantages on these capabilities, and the globalization of these efforts.

Customer Transition and Process Organization

By the close of the 1990s, Nokia's brand name connoted product innovation, flexibility, and rapid responsiveness—the result of years of purposeful strategic management and a few bold and risky decisions. For Nokia, the key to *all* strategic considerations was listening to the customer, yet the customer was often a moving target.

Customer Transition

In the 1980s and 1990s, the rules of the game changed dramatically in mobile communications, as Nokia moved from regulated to deregulated markets. In the past, traditional PTTs had been Nokia's key customers, but starting with deregulation in the United Kingdom in the early 1980s and the breakup of AT&T in the mid-1980s, government authorities were rapidly being replaced by new telecommunications operators. As the identities of these key customers changed, so did the basis of the competition (see Exhibit 5-2).

As compliance-driven PTTs faded into history, deregulated markets and privatized national telecommunications monopolies gave rise to new telecommunications and mobile operators, which favored integrated turnkey solutions on common platforms and were business- and marketing-driven. In the process, order and delivery cycles became less predictable and far more competitive. As these competitive pressures demolished the old order in national and regulated markets, they also brought about new and attractive opportunities.

Soon Nokia found itself competing in an increasingly global market that favored total integrated solutions, boosted rapid price erosion,

Exhibit 5-2. Changing rules of the game.

Old Rules   *New Rules*

Traditional PTTs   New Telecommunications Operators

- Compliance-driven   - Deregulated, privatized

- Orders to a particular product   - Integrated turnkey solutions on
  line   common platforms

- Knowledgeable technical   - Business- and marketing-driven
  workforce
                                                          - Lower predictability in order and
- High predictability in order   delivery cycles
  and delivery cycles

Competitive Pressures

- National   - International, global

- Steady price evolution   - Rapid price erosion

- Focus on product lines   - Total integrated solutions

- Slow delivery   - Fast delivery

- Low level of service   - High level of service

and required fast delivery and top-quality service. While its rivals de-
layed critical decisions, Nokia could not afford to postpone its refocusing efforts. Whereas its competitors only slowly let go of the traditional
PTTs as customers, Nokia jumped at the new opportunity. Between
1986 and 1991, Nokia created a foothold in key European markets by
relentlessly pursuing emerging markets or those in which deregulation
of telecommunications services had led to the entry of new operators.
In the United Kingdom, Nokia was among the first to establish relations with a number of new operators and became their leading supplier of transmission and switching systems. Allying itself with upstart
cellular providers like Orange in Great Britain and E-Plus in Germany,
Nokia stole business from the traditional telecommunications suppliers. Similarly, when the EC took its first steps toward telecommunications deregulation in the early 1990s, Nokia entered key markets. In
1994, when the Federal Communications Commission (FCC) in the
United States prepared to launch auctions for a new generation of

wireless personal communications services (PCS), Nokia had already established its U.S. unit. Unlike the mobile subsidiaries of the large global giants (e.g., Alcatel, Northern Telecom, L. M. Ericsson, Siemens, Motorola), Nokia's mobile unit was considered midsize, but that ensured the kind of flexibility and responsiveness that benefited from emerging and deregulated markets. Furthermore, many new operators found Nokia's corporate culture similar to their own; the Finnish company was more agile and entrepreneurial than the large incumbents. Whatever the company might lack in scale and scope, it gained in speed and timing. By the late 1990s, Nokia was known for its ability to listen and respond to market developments in a rapid, efficient, and flexible manner. That would not have been possible without its reorganization and the new IT strategy that gave Nokia the right strategy and the right structure at the right time.

Logistics Crisis

In 1996, Nokia issued a warning that profits would be significantly lower than the previous year due to the sluggish mobile phone business. The loss in that business area offset improvements in the telecommunications business area, which had reported higher profitability in the previous period. In May 1996, Nokia recorded a 70-percent plunge in first-quarter pretax profit, to FIM 399 million (about $84 million), as sales of mobile phones and related gear slowed. While sales increased 11 percent to FIM 7.93 billion, operating profit plunged 62 percent to FIM 512 million.

Nokia had become the darling of American investors in the early 1990s, but its results were testing the nerves of the investment community. "Nokia has been caught in a cycle of inflated hopes and exaggerated disappointments," noted *The New York Times*.[15] As he had done earlier that year, Ollila blamed the tumbling earnings on problems at the group's flagship mobile phone business, which recorded an operating loss on slower sales growth and pricing pressures. Some anonymous Finnish analysts went even further, calling the results a catastrophe. "We'd expected pretax profit at around FIM 800 million, but Nokia didn't even reach half that level," commented one analyst to *The Wall Street Journal*.[16]

Nokia's problems stemmed from three years of hypergrowth. In 1995, the company added 7,000 new employees to meet the increasing demand for its phones in Europe and Asia, but it had difficulty assimilating the new recruits. Productivity, which had climbed 15 percent in 1994, advanced only 3 percent as Nokia encountered problems with suppliers and late deliveries of components. In addition to losing control of logistics, the market for digital handsets in the United States did not grow as much as anticipated because of a regulatory delay. Meanwhile, analog phone manufacturers cut prices as much as 50 percent. Ollila was racing to implement new controls and increase Nokia's response time for regional markets. He insisted all bottlenecks would be gone within six months: "It's not an insurmountable problem."[17] Although Nokia's shares fell 18 percent on the Helsinki Stock Exchange, Ollila expected the telecommunications operations to achieve strong growth and good profitability, just as the performance of mobile phones was expected to gradually improve.[18]

Despite market anxiety, Nokia remained true to its focus strategy amid its difficulties in process control and logistics. The logistics problems of the mid-1990s stemmed from the company's reorganization a few years before. In order to cope with the transition from business to consumer markets, Nokia's internal organization had to catch up and adapt to its external environment. The company had to upgrade and innovate its existing IT strategies, which then had to be aligned with the new strategic direction.

The Creation of a Process Organization

In 1992, Nokia's vice president of corporate planning, Mikko Kosonen, launched an IT strategy study that helped move the company toward process-based management and supported the need for new logistics information systems. The study identified two core business processes common to all businesses at Nokia Telecommunications: product development and customer commitment (i.e., order fulfillment). This realization led to the institution of a new account management structure that would serve as an interface between the customer and all NTC divisions, not just between the customer and a single product line, as the former system had in the past.

The goal of the process perspective was to increase NTC's customer orientation, with processes analyzed and improved *from the customer's point of view*. It led to new performance measures that augmented traditional financial measures, such as profitability and market share, with ones focusing on customer value.[19] "[Using] traditional financial measures is like driving a car by looking at the rearview mirror," commented one NTC manager. "We need proactive measures that address the critical success factors of the financial results. For us, there are three basic critical success factors: customer satisfaction, operations efficiency, and people involvement."[20] In the early 1990s, Nokia's reorganization and refocus toward telecommunications and mobile communications and, later, its concentration on customer satisfaction fueled the company's growing profits and market leadership. Only a few years later, product innovation, flexibility, and rapid responsiveness became widely recognized as the cornerstones for Nokia's global growth. Organizationally, these initiatives were built on sophisticated management, control, and human resource management processes at Nokia's headquarters as well as at NTC and NMP. In both, the focus was on product development and customer commitment processes. The two initiatives were tightly intertwined and glued together by an IT-driven account management structure.

At Nokia, innovation has not been perceived as an exclusive function of R&D or product development; instead, it has been thought of as something that can and should pertain to the *entire* value chain. "Business activities can consist of many kinds of innovations," Matti Alahuhta, chief of NMP, argued in 1999. "They may be associated with technology and products, but companies can differentiate in any other part of the value chain as well. For instance, superior logistics may form a fundamental base for the competitiveness and growth of a company."[21]

By the end of the 1990s, the company had learned that efficient logistics were vital to its business strategy, organizational capabilities, and corporate value. It was a simple lesson, but a difficult one to execute. In terms of operational effectiveness, Nokia's execution was solid until late 1995, when the stock plummeted by half due to a series of logistics problems at NTC. Through the early half of the decade, the company struggled to survive its extraordinary growth as market changes put pressure on NTC to provide a uniform customer interface, accelerate organizational learning, and leverage its size on a global scale. Armed with the results of the 1992 IT strategy study, NTC instituted a new organization-wide operating mode focusing on product development and customer commitment.

As delays postponed the implementation of the new operating mode, logistics problems ensued. In the first quarter, Ericsson reported a 28-percent increase in pretax profit, citing strong growth in its mobile communications business. Similarly, Motorola, the world's largest mobile phone company at that time, also surprised the market with a better than expected 3-percent increase in first-quarter net income, buoyed in part by cost-cutting measures. Unlike its rivals, the Finnish company had to come to terms with continuing logistics and supply problems in addition to the severe price erosion that all were facing; Nokia stumbled worse than its competitors. Furthermore, demand seemed to be slowing in the United States, although Europe and Asia remained hot markets. After growing about 25 percent for most of 1995, mobile phone sales in the United States slowed in the final three months of the year.

By the mid-1990s, Nokia's operational processes could be divided into two broad types: business and corporate processes.[22] Business processes are associated with the physical or virtual creation of the product, its sale and transfer to the buyer, and postsale servicing. In practice, they can be divided into upstream and downstream processes. This parallels Nokia's distinction between product development and customer commitment processes. Usually, companies excel in one or another, but rarely equally in both. The mobile cellular industry was not an exception. Where, for instance, Motorola and Ericsson have excelled in upstream innovation, Nokia's focus has been on downstream innovation. Corporate processes reinforced these primary activities by providing purchased inputs, technology development, human resources management, and a variety of company-wide functions. At Nokia, these processes can be seen in management, performance measurement and control, human resource management, and R& D activities (see Exhibit 5-3a).

Nokia's process chain consists of a system of interdependent processes that are related by two kinds of links, those *within* the chain and those *between* the company's chain and those of other vertical participants (e.g., partners, suppliers, channels, and buyers). Vertical participants have played a vital role ever since the company opted *not* to invest in semiconductors or component production. Just as Nokia has sought to create long-standing relationships with its end-buyers through the customer commitment process, it has nurtured tight and mutually beneficial relationships with its suppliers and channels. Additionally, the company has managed to take advantage of technology partners through standards coalitions, which have essentially functioned as de facto horizontal suppliers (see Exhibit 5-3b).

As the new IT strategy was finally implemented and the process organization was in place, the risk of recurring logistics problems was reduced (though not entirely eliminated), and the company's stock began an upward climb. The next step was to turn the thriving company into an industry giant, but for this Nokia would need the appropriate resources.

Ambitions Versus Resources

At the time that Ollila moved from Helsinki to Salo and began to explore the issues of NMP, two high-profile management consultants, Gary Hamel and C. K. Prahalad, published a highly influential essay in the *Harvard Business Review* entitled "Strategic Intent."[23] The piece addressed problems that involved many industries and covered those very same issues that had occupied Nokia's senior managers since the late 1980s.[24]

Hamel and Prahalad argued that few companies have had enviable track records anticipating the moves of new global competitors.

Exhibit 5-3. Nokia's process chain.

(a) Corporate and Business Processes

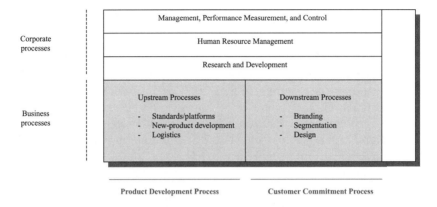

SOURCE: Dan Steinbock, "Dynamic Advantage" (forthcoming). The process chain is a variation of the value chain as developed in Michael E. Porter, *Competitive Advantage* (New York: The Free Press, 1980).

(b) The Process System   Nokia

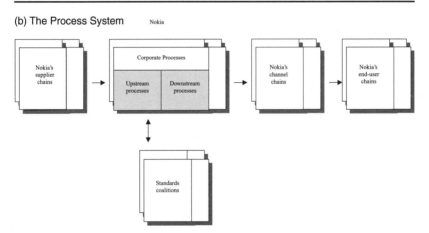

The problem stems in part from the very frameworks that these companies use in competitor analysis. In particular, resourcefulness, "the pace at which new competitive advantages are being built," rarely enters in. Assessing the current tactical advantages of known and familiar rivals would not help the existing industry leaders to appreciate the resolution, stamina, and inventiveness of potential competitors. As the two argued,

Companies that have risen to global leadership over the past 20 years invariably began with ambitions that were out of all proportion to their resources and capabilities. But they created an obsession with winning at all levels of the organization and then sustained that obsession over the 10- to 20-year quest for local leadership.[25]

As far as Ollila and his executives were concerned, Vuorilehto's restructuring was typical old-style strategic planning. It was necessary to overcome the crisis that stemmed from past mistakes and excesses, but it was not enough to cut costs. In order to generate the revenues a successful company required a future-driven strategy. It is easy to understand Nokia's senior management's interest in Hamel and Prahalad's "strategic intent": it justified focused investments and provided a direction; it was clear about overall objectives and flexible about the means of achieving these objectives; and it did not shun orchestration but left room for improvisation. This was precisely the kind of language that Nokia wanted to hear in the early 1990s.[26]

Amid the restructuring, Nokia needed strategic intent that would motivate every employee, not strategic memos drafted at headquarters for the investment community. The language of strategic intent was not just about financial controls, things that Ollila knew thoroughly; numbers would never provide the employee objectives that could ensure their personal commitment.

Kairamo had given Nokia a vision that made the company unique and distinctive. Vuorilehto had taken it away. Ollila would give it back.

True strategic intent implies a sizable stretch for an organization. Nokia's current capabilities and resources would not suffice, thus forcing the company to be more inventive and making the most of limited resources. There was an extreme misfit between resources and ambitions. But it was Nokia's new strategic intent that *created* this mismatch. In the early 1990s, Nokia purposefully used strategic intent to define its fundamental challenge, which stretched the organization into a focused cellular leader.[27]

Competing for the Future

The concept of strategic intent was not mere hyperbole at Nokia. As the company began its transformation, Gary Hamel was a frequent visitor at Nokia headquarters.[28] It was then, too, that Hamel and Prahalad were completing their business classic, *Competing for the Future*.[29] In this bestseller, Nokia was portrayed as a winning company building gateways to the future. On the one hand, the authors identified Nokia as one of those companies that had managed to put national competition in perspective. Companies like Nokia, Unilever, Ericsson, and BMW no longer viewed Europe as home, but as simply one more market. On the other hand, Hamel and Prahalad used Nokia as an example to validate their arguments on resourcefulness:

> How can it be, then, that so many companies fail to anticipate the future? What prevented DEC from seeing the opportunity for personal computers? Why did Canon see and commit to the opportunity for small, personal copiers rather than Xerox? How was it that an obscure Finnish company, Nokia, emerged as the number two supplier of cellular telephones in the world, leaving European giants like Philips, Siemens, and Alcatel with mere crumbs?[30]

The answer, the authors maintained, was in developing industry foresight:

> Industry foresight must be informed by deep insight into trends in lifestyles, technology, demographics, and geopolitics, but foresight rests as much on imagination as on prediction. To create the future a company must first be capable of imagining it. To create the future a company must first develop a powerful visual and verbal representation of what the future could be.[31]

In addition to restructuring efforts designed to cut costs, Nokia had to find a way to create revenues, which translated into industry foresight. The three fundamental themes of *Competing for the Future*—dynamics of globalization, strategy and structure, and volatile environments—rang a bell in the Finnish company, which now incorporated strategic intent into its three phases for future competition. These phases involved competing for intellectual leadership, shaping and shortening the migration paths between the current markets and industry structure and those in the future, and competing for market power and position once the new opportunities took off and the new industry structure began to form. Each phase called for its own additional requirements (see Exhibit 5-4).

Despite its home-base advantage, Nokia ultimately had to deal with larger, better financed competitors and had to manage competitive engagements in light of its need to conserve scarce resources. In this regard, Nokia emulated Japanese companies, building layers of advantage, searching for loose bricks, changing the terms of engagement, and competing through collaboration. In each case, it has enjoyed the benefits of competitive innovation. Yet these experiences have

Exhibit 5-4. Nokia's strategic intent: some efforts and potential problems.

Definitions	Sample of Nokia's efforts	Potential problems
Building layers of advantage. The wider a company's portfolio of advantages, the less risk it faces in competitive battles.	Manufacturing strategy: speed in anticipating and fulfilling market needs, category innovation, product proliferation in valued categories.	Difficulties in demand anticipation, costs of continual R&D, complexity inherent in the management of high product variety, etc.
Searching for loose bricks. Exploiting the benefits of surprise through staking out underdefended territory.	First-mover principles: as rivals were still learning multiphone capabilities, Nokia was already coupling mobility and the Internet.	First-mover disadvantages, costly early-mover strategies, investments in wrong technologies, backing wrong standards, etc.
Changing the terms of engagement. Refusing to accept the frontrunner's definition of industry and segment boundaries.	The reverse of the previous principle: by staking out new market space, the company subverts traditional industry and segment definitions.	The reverse of the previous principle, high risk and capital allocation in staking out new market space, costly cannibalization, wrong timing in obsoleting, etc.
Competing through collaboration. Through licensing, outsourcing agreements, and joint ventures, a company may win without fighting.	Strategic coalition building: particular recent strategic alliances (e.g., Symbian, Bluetooth, WAP, etc.).	Successful coalition building without success in profit extraction, costly coalition management, diverging interests, etc.

SOURCE: Definitions based on Gary Hamel and C. K. Prahalad, *Competing for the Future* (Boston, Mass.: Harvard Business School Press, 1994), Chapter 2.

been relatively recent, intertwined with a single technology generation GSM. The Internet revolution would test these principles—each of which also had disadvantages (see Exhibit 5-4).

Strategic intent may stem from economies of scale and scope, both of which may facilitate entering global markets. Capturing economies of scale traditionally has been a matter of volume, whereas scope demands substantial interbusiness coordination that senior management must nurture. Perhaps it was to create, maintain, and nurture such coordination that Ollila switched the jobs of his innermost circle of senior management in July 1998. Pekka Ala-Pietilä, Ollila's right hand and the handset chief who had overseen development of the 6100, became vice chairman in charge of new ventures. Sari Baldauf, the former top Asia-Pacific executive, would head up development of Nokia's 3G products. Alahuhta, the ex-infrastructure executive, was given global responsibility for handsets. Olli-Pekka Kallasvuo, Nokia's leading executive in the United States, would return to Helsinki to become CFO. "I want to remove people from their comfort areas, to remove stubbornness that gets built into the minds of the people," Ollila said. "Switching also helps people learn from one another. Infrastructure can learn from handsets about the speed and product life cycle of consumer electronics. And the phone people can learn customer relations from infrastructure. It's cross fertilization."[32]

The rotation took place as the company moved from a cellular-driven strategy to a mobile Internet-driven strategy, which revitalized the company's mission. As part of developing a strategic intent, the company sought to create a sense of urgency.[33] Nokia's senior management believed that a management hierarchy fostered an elitist view that could disenfranchise most of the organization, and Ollila and senior executives were suspicious of the myths surrounding some of the most successful top managers.[34] "No politics, a lot of trust, realism with equality between people, titles are not important—teamwork with openness is," explained Alahuhta, the president of NTC, who had worked for the company for two decades. "There is a Finnish word, *nöyryys*, which means humility, humbleness, that you take pride in the past but don't project it into the future."[35]

The idea of strategic intent provided a new way for thinking about the future of an ambitious company in a small country. Nokia would need to rely less on its actual resources and concentrate on building its resourcefulness, just as it would exploit the pace at which new competitive advantages are being built in order to deter its rivals. The idea also stressed global opportunities and threats rather than solely domestic ones. From the mid-1970s through the 1980s, Japanese companies were able to create new global brand franchises.[36] Nokia was eager to follow their example.

Global Focus

BY 1998, Nokia's workforce had increased by almost 30 percent, its sales by 51 percent, and its operating profits by 71 percent. "Nokia's performance has been as startling as its transformation," the *Economist* reported in October 1999. "If it continues to grow at this pace—and the management has set a target for increasing net sales by 25–30% a year—the company's revenues will exceed the budget for the whole of Finland in a few years."[1]

What so stunned the *Economist* was the fact that, for a company with such deep Finnish roots, Nokia had globalized so thoroughly and seemingly with such ease. It sold its products in 140 countries but conducted itself as the very antithesis of the heartless multinational conglomerate, tailoring its products to fit every local quirk.

Yet about half the company's 55,000 employees, the entire group executive board, almost all board directors, and the overwhelming majority of its senior management were located in Finland. Nokia did everything it could to encourage a global mindset within the company, including making English its official language and requiring senior managers to work abroad. Additionally, more than half of the company's R&D was conducted outside its home country. Also, Nokia thought like a consumer-products company, introducing new models annually, changing colors according to fashion, and encouraging phone users to customize their phones with clip-on covers.[2]

The higher Nokia's stock price soared, the more the company gave rise to a storm of speculation by financial analysts and business journalists on the secret of its success. Certainly, the determinants that the *Economist* referred to—global mindset, corporate culture, R&D, segmentation—all played a role in Nokia's accomplishments, but *what* kind of a role? And *how*, more exactly, did they contribute to the company's worldwide success?

Global Growth Strategy for a
High-Technology Challenger

Nokia's group executive board continues to play a critical role in Nokia's strategy-making process. In 2000, Matti Alahuhta, a board member and president of NMP, wrote a dissertation on the global growth strategies of small and medium-size companies of the 1990s. This work illustrates many central tenets of strategic thinking at Nokia's headquarters—right before the great restructuring. In the early 1990s, Ollila and the board did not just refocus the company, in terms of its *businesses;* they also repositioned it, in terms of *global* growth.[3]

In the late 1990s, Matti Alahuhta had become president of NMP while taking charge of the company's operations in Japan. A company veteran whose career really took off in the late 1980s, he had become intrigued by the subjects of growth and globalization at NTC and was encouraged by the executive president, Sakari Salminen, to finish the dissertation. Alahuhta spent a year on the faculty of the IMEDE/IMD as an executive-in-residence while he served as a member of the NTC management team. He completed his dissertation on global growth strategies amid the rising turmoil at Nokia's headquarters in the late 1980s in the aftermath of Koski's and Kairamo's deaths.[4]

Alahuhta's dissertation work is intimately connected with Nokia's strategic transformation in the early 1990s and illustrates some of the basic principles of Nokia's globalization. Even more important, through Alahuhta and some other chief executives the company connected with Europe's leading management researchers, who were intrigued with Kairamo's growth strategy. They would later follow Nokia's restructuring and refocusing efforts with increasing fascination. At the IMEDE, Alahuhta defined the research field with Professor Jean-Pierre Jeannet, a pioneer of global growth strategies and one of Nokia's more high-profile consultants.

Near the end of the 1980s, Alahuhta argued that global strategies had been studied mainly in the context of big multinational companies (MNCs). As current market trends led to greater global uniformity in many industries, these MNCs were able to seize attractive opportunities. But where did this leave challengers like Nokia, who suffered a mismatch between ambitions and resources? What if this mismatch could be used as leverage? Indeed, global strategies for small and medium-size companies had been largely ignored in research literature. Alahuhta would focus on these companies, which represented the future. His objective was "to identify strategy patterns for global growth of high technology challengers."[5]

In global competition, shorter product life cycles forced companies to place more emphasis on R&D, as well as to recognize new opportunities and exploit them more quickly with successful timing. With cellular telephones, for instance, the competitive life cycle of a product had already shrunk to less than three years by the late 1980s. Since markets had become increasingly uniform, the winners would be those companies that operated in several markets simultaneously, timed their new product development (NPD) correctly, and thereby gained both higher volume and quicker learning.

From Low-End Niches to High-End Segments

According to Alahuhta, basic internationalization patterns had changed significantly in the course of the 1980s. While needs in several industries had become more uniform across countries, new customer needs had also emerged. Mobile phones reflected both trends. At first, the mobile radiophone business had been a national industry with tailored, simple voice-based systems. However, changes in the industry drastically accelerated upon acceptance of common European specifications. Today, far more is known about innovation that accelerates new product development.[6] The new frameworks allow a rephrasing of Alahuhta's theses. Due to the emerging "dominant design" (common Nordic and European specifications in the nascent mobile industry), the requirements for a national tailoring decreased.

As strategic thinking was developing in the late 1970s and early 1980s, most industries were mature and experienced a relatively low level of competition. Strategists favored formulations that stressed structure over change, stability over vacillation, and certainty over uncertainty. These formulations matched the environmental characteristics of the era. Today, industry environments are evolving far more rapidly and tend to be far more heterogeneous. Most important, the pace of penetration with regard to more recent technological innovations—cellular phones, PCs, and the Internet, for instance—has been accelerating rapidly.[7]

In the fluid phase of industry development, both incumbents and new entrants seek to produce a dominant product design that is expected to capture the allegiance of the marketplace. The rate of *product innovation* in an industry or product class tends to be highest during these formative years, when less attention is given to processes, and the rate of *process innovation* is slower. In mobile communications, this meant moving toward segmentation in the business-to-business markets either by buyer groups (e.g., power companies, police, fire departments) or by product variety (e.g., systems, mobile phones, data terminals). Anticipating Nokia's emphasis on segmentation in the late 1990s, Alahuhta maintained that the objective of such global segmentation should be to maximize exploitation of global market opportunities with a product that has universal appeal (see Exhibit 6-1a).

To Alahuhta, the issue of the company's size was critical in high-technology industries, especially in computers and telecommunications. His reasoning was that these industries were rapidly going global in all of their activities. Many were dominated by major MNCs. Given short product life cycles and high R&D expenditures, economies of scale were critical. Only major rivals could cover these high investment allocations with their ever-increasing volumes. Unlike MNCs, however, small and medium-size companies had no such advantages. To successfully engage in high-growth strategies, these companies would have to rely on focused strategies, at least initially. In his dissertation, Alahuhta described the kind of focus approach that Nokia adopted in the early 1990s (see Exhibit 6-1b):

> Small companies may have good short-term niche opportunities. With a successful choice of a strategy geared to a specific target segment, a small company can achieve a better fit to that market segment than its bigger, less tightly focused competitors. However, after the initial quick growth period, markets are typically re-segmented to a set of niche segments within an industry. This re-segmentation can change the structure of competition so that the small competitor has a threat to lose its strong position. In this way, most of the high technology industries are changing to a set of niche markets. . . .[8]

This attack mode was rooted in Japanese strategic thinking. Alahuhta was also familiar with Michael Porter's ideas on global segmentation. "Global segmentation, which captures the advantages of a global strategy but marshals resources by focusing on a narrow segment, is frequently a viable option for a smaller multinational or domestic competitors," contended Porter in 1986. "The strategy has been quite common among multinationals from smaller countries such as Finland and Switzerland. It is also frequently the first step in a sequenced strategy to move from a domestic to a global strategy."[9] At the time, Porter may have had in mind the Finnish forestry multinationals, whose experiences were well known at Nokia.

Having studied the lessons of the Japanese, the Finns prepared to compete in global market segments. However, unlike the Japanese, the Finns would not be able to mount large-scale attacks in many industry segments. As Nokia saw a niche opportunity, it tailored its strategy to the narrow segment (see Exhibit 6-1a). Unlike its major rivals, it could exploit its small size; it was faster, more flexible, and more responsive than its larger competitors. While the strategy was tailored to a niche market, its objective was more ambitious. Nokia would use this niche as a lever to gain access to the entire market (see Exhibit 6-1b).

In the course of this competitive effort, Nokia moved from the low-end to high-end markets. Initially, it provided cellular products to such groups as the Finnish Defense Forces and public organizations, but as the phones became smaller and more efficient, Nokia could target business markets in Nordic countries, Europe, and ultimately the world. As Nokia established its dominance in the business-to-business market in the early 1990s, it expanded its global reach to tap consumer markets worldwide in the latter half of the 1990s.

Industry Shift, Early Entry, and Market Leadership

Like its Japanese models, Nokia did not consider the niche opportunity as an end in itself. As Alahuhta put it, "Exploiting a niche opportunity can be a temporary, but seldom a final, solution." The premise was to show precisely "how small and medium-size high technology companies can achieve global growth and become big companies in their segments." Certain competitive environments facilitated such expansion better and more quickly than others. Those opportunities that seemed to offer the most potential contained strategic inflection points. As far as Alahuhta was concerned:

> One such opportunity might be exploitation of industry shifts that change the rules of the game, so that, expressing it in a pointed way, all companies start from a market share of zero. . . . Nokia Mobile Phones exploited the shift to cellular radio, and was quick to move to new, emerging lead markets when market characteristics changed, being now one of the global market leaders.[10]

Unlike Ericsson and Motorola, Nokia's major rivals in the 1990s, the company looked to thrive and expand in circumstances of *disruptive* industry change. Sustaining change benefited the incumbents; disruption worked for the challengers. When other companies hesitated, Nokia would push ahead decisively. Such strategic inflection points presented unique and irreversible opportunities, which only first-movers could fully exploit.

In the course of his research project, Alahuhta found that strategy patterns for global growth were different for fast-growing high-technology challengers in fluid industries than in mature industries.[11] Silicon Valley companies exemplify the former model and Japanese consumer electronics giants the latter (see Exhibit 6-2). Global growth

Exhibit 6-1. Niche opportunities and small companies.

(a) Narrow Focus Strategy: Exploiting Niche Opportunity

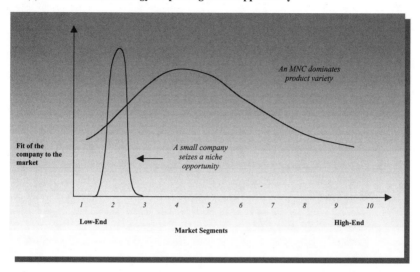

(b) Broad Focus Strategy: Exploiting Segment Opportunity

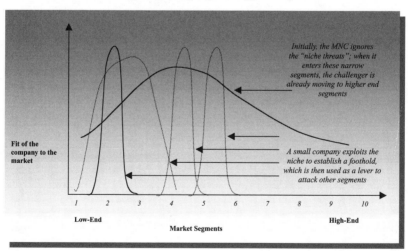

SOURCE: (A) based on Matti Alahuhta, *Global Growth Strategies for High Technology Challengers*, Acta Polytechnica Scandinavica, Electrical Engineering Series No. 66 (Espoo: The Finnish Academy of Technology, 1990), p. 17.

Exhibit 6-2. The stages of the global growth of high-technology challengers in high-growth and maturing industries.

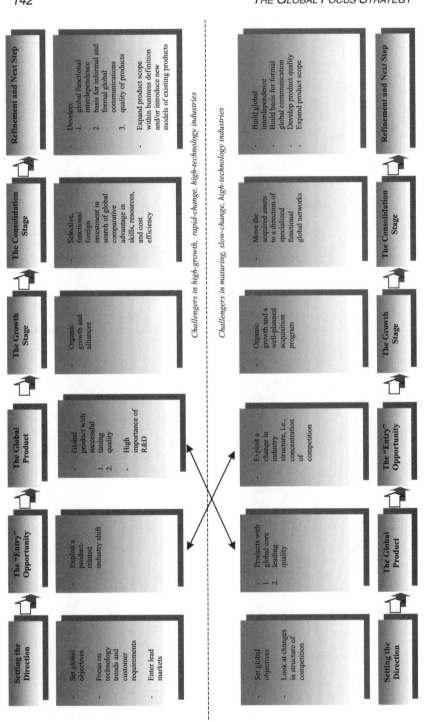

SOURCE: Matti Alahuhta, *Global Growth Strategies for High Technology Challengers*, Acta Polytechnica Scandinavica, Electrical Engineering Series No. 66 (Helsinki: 1990), p. 136.

strategies for high-technology challengers encompassed several critical determinants, each of which precipitated Nokia's success in global wireless markets (see Exhibit 6-3):

1. *Set global objectives and enter lead market early.* Fast-growing challengers establish a global orientation and objectives prior to the start of the high-growth phase. They enter lead markets during the early phases of their evolution.
2. *Exploit industry shifts.* In order to achieve fast-paced growth, global challengers exploit first-mover advantage, optimizing industry shifts.
3. *Develop global products.* In order take rapid advantage of industry shifts, global challengers must develop an innovative, high-quality product and achieve rapid geographic spread for that product.
4. *Build selective, functional foreign investments.* Global challengers must also accumulate selective foreign assets in order to sustain their competitive strategies. Also, due to the short product life cycles, companies must proceed with several closely spaced investments. Finally, these investments seek global comparative advantages, which can be critical to challengers because of their need for global learning.
5. *Nurture global coordination and learning.* Global challengers must nurture global coordination and increase learning, which tend to occur with distribution of skills and development of global functional networks and a global mindset.

Overall, some of these characteristics emulate global strategies of major MNCs. Others are specific to the global growth strategies of small and medium-size challengers only. These strategic guidelines served Nokia well, particularly during its early years of globalization when the company was still building capabilities for the impending struggle over the cellular leadership.

Global Focus and "Horizontal Tigers"

By the mid-1990s, Nokia's strategy was about *global* focus. It was an extraordinarily bold and ambitious strategy crafted by the Finns, who had gained extensive experience in international business. Through Alahuhta's research, Nokia's approach was reciprocally shaped by the global business paradigm of Jean-Pierre Jeannet.[12]

Exhibit 6-3. Exploitation of an industry shift: selective, functional foreign investments.

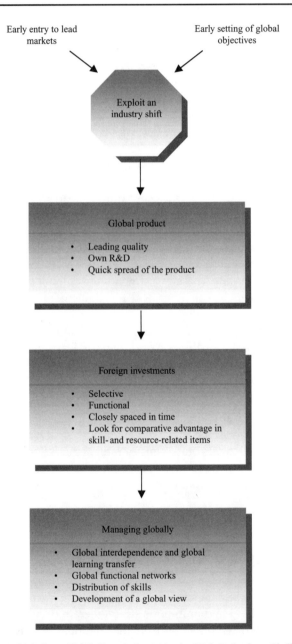

SOURCE: Matti Alahuhta, *Global Growth Strategies for High Technology Challengers,* Acta Polytechnica Scandinavica, Electrical Engineering Series No. 66 (Helsinki: 1990), p. 50.

The Fall of Vertical Dragons and the Rise of Horizontal Tigers

Throughout the 1980s, Jeannet had been developing an approach that fit within the category of global strategies. In changing environmental circumstances, the old-style vertical giants—the "vertical dragons" in Jeannet's terminology—had been descending, while the new-style horizontal players—the "horizontal tigers"—had been ascending. By his own account, he "formed the idea of global focus that resulted in the concept of the 'horizontal tiger' "at Nokia:[13]

The future is with the horizontal tigers, and companies will have to carefully pick the businesses they desire to globalize while finding ways to reduce their exposure to others by divesting or floating them off. As we observe the changes among large, traditional corporations through reorganization, we are witnessing a wholesale shift from the broad-based, unfocused business to the focused niche company with their superior promise to accommodate the global imperative.[14]

In this respect, the lessons of Nokia and Coca-Cola stress the value of focus when facing strong global competition. In the 1990s, both companies were embroiled in strong global rivalries that required them to pursue all large and relevant key markets. (In the case of Nokia, this meant accelerating activities in China.) Building a beachhead in most markets demanded considerable financial and managerial resources. In practice, both Nokia and Coca-Cola leveraged their limited resources by narrowing the business focus while maximizing the coverage of the international markets. To Jeannet, *that* was the most important lesson for achieving a global mindset. In order to make limited resources stretch around the globe, companies would have to concentrate on fewer businesses, but expand those businesses worldwide.[15]

At Nokia, the global focus of mobile cellular evolved quickly after the critical decisions were made by the Ollila regime around 1992. By the mid-1990s, the role of the Finnish home base was declining rapidly while the significance of overseas markets grew. To speed Nokia's international growth, Ollila encouraged his managers around the world to act locally in foreign markets and to develop an acute understanding of local cultures. One outcome of this wide-ranging policy was the creation of a strategy panel comprising Ollila, the company's business-unit bosses, and its heads of R&D and strategy.[16]

Being a global player required that Nokia learn how to market itself appropriately in a multitude of fragmented markets. As a result, the company continued to invest heavily in advertising. In the United States, for instance, it created an ad spoofing itself, aired on MTV in an attempt to attract Generation Xers. It also sponsored ads that aired during the Sugar Bowl to capture older, professional viewers. Unlike Motorola and Ericsson, which were concentrating on developing new technologies, Nokia concentrated on keeping close to its customers.

Mobile Equipment Vendors: Industry Rivalry

By 1998, the telecommunications equipment market was worth an estimated $191 billion, of which mobile accounted for just over one-quarter. Still, the contribution of mobile to total equipment sales was rising rapidly in the high-growth wireless markets. The mobile equipment market consisted of two key product segments: mobile terminals (handsets) and infrastructure (base stations and switches). In 1998, sales were roughly equally divided between the two.

Mobile Terminals

Sales of mobile handsets worldwide reached an estimated 163 million units in 1998, reflecting increased growth by more than one-half in a year's time. Digital handset sales accounted for 85 percent of total mobile phone sales. With a market share of 23 percent, Nokia became the dominant mobile phone vendor for the first time in the history of the industry. "We are the only company in the world selling phones that work in every major cellular standard," Olli-Pekka Kallas-vuo, Nokia's forty-five-year-old CFO and president of the company's U.S. division, told *Fortune*. "We were first to segment our product line, first to build a brand identity, first to understand that design was essential in this business, and first to make sure we could take advantage of the efficiency of global manufacturing in a business where R&D costs are high and can only be recouped with worldwide volumes."[17]

While Motorola continued to lead the analog segment, Nokia grew most quickly (82 percent) in the digital arena, dominating the second-generation rivalry. Together, the three leading mobile vendors—Nokia, Motorola, and Ericsson—controlled 57 percent of the total market. In 1999, Nokia continued to outpace its competition as the world's leading mobile vendor, giving the company a head start in the race to sell new product lines of Internet-ready cellular phones to consumers. That year, the company expanded its global market share to 26.9 percent. With almost three out of every ten handsets sold worldwide being Nokia products, the company stretched its lead over its closest rivals—Motorola, Ericsson, and Samsung.

Total sales of cellular phones were expected to rise 45 percent to 410 million units in 2000 from 283.6 million units in 1999.[18] In 1998, Western Europe enjoyed the highest handset sales with 33 percent of the total. The United States was second with 17 percent and Japan third with 16.5 percent of the total. In 1999, sales doubled in Latin America. In Europe, sales jumped 70 percent while North America and Asia saw increases of about 60 percent and 50 percent, respectively. Again, Nokia dominated the industry. Spurred by its ability to introduce models quickly and distribute them better than their rivals, the company sold 76.3 million phones, nearly doubling its total sales of 38.6 million a year earlier. It also sold a large proportion of higher-profit-margin models.

Nokia's triumph was not flawless. The company experienced delays in introducing its wireless application protocol (WAP) phone. It also encountered some problems in attacking the U.S. market for the CDMA digital standard. In both cases, the company seemed to pick up the pace by the end of the year. While eager to regain a strong position in the digital phone market, Motorola saw its market share slip to 16.9 percent from 19.5 percent. It had difficulties with the supply of certain components and lacked an extensive portfolio of products that could compete with Nokia's state-of-the-art offerings. Ericsson did not possess an extensive product range either. As a result, its market share fell dramatically from 15.1 percent to 10.5 percent. Concurrently, Samsung saw its market share rise to 6.2 percent from 2.7 percent. It sold plenty of CDMA-based phones in its home market of South Korea but also did well marketing GSM models in Europe and the United States.[19]

Beginning in 2000, the leading mobile vendors were expected to attack maturing and new markets with cheaper phones while pitching new Internet-based devices elsewhere. Analysts were waiting for a rapid rollout of new services and technologies that would allow data to be viewed on cellular phones. In 1998 alone, 100 million new mobile users were added worldwide, many of them on prepaid schemes. Projected forward, this trend indicated that the number of mobile cellular subscribers worldwide would overtake fixed-line subscribers before the end of 2010.[20] New marketing strategies can be credited for Finland's reaching this milestone as early as 1998, even with a high level of maturity. In the past, a family would have obtained one fixed telephone connection. By the end of the 1990s, it was conceivable that each member of the family might have his or her own mobile phone, a scenario that became Nokia's explicit objective.

Infrastructure

Wireless infrastructure includes all parts of a wireless network except the mobile handset (e.g., mobile switching offices, base stations, and the links between them). While handsets were marketed to end users, infrastructure was sold to mobile operators. In 1998, half a dozen major companies accounting for more than 80 percent of industry revenues dominated the infrastructure segment. The major products were base stations and switches. Minor players provided various ancillary products and specialized services, including antennae, customization, network design, and consulting.

Most infrastructure vendors, even in 2000, were characterized by the type of technology they specialized in due to regulations, standards rivalries, and national telecommunications monopolies. As a result, Nordic vendors dominated the GSM market, which prevailed in Europe. In the United States, American manufacturers and Ericsson had a larger share in the TDMA market, and vendors from Korea dominated the CDMA market. With deregulation, privatization, and increasing competition, most infrastructure vendors sought to position their products in international markets. Except for the United States and Japan, most markets were simply too small to sustain the growth of the market leaders.

Finnish and Overseas Segments

Between 1990 and 1999, Finland's position as Nokia's dominant geographic market area declined dramatically, diminishing from FIM 6.6 billion to FIM 2.8 billion (see Exhibit 6-4a). In absolute terms, the decline ended around 1996, but in relative terms, the Finnish results fell far behind the others. Over the same period, Nokia's sales in Europe climbed from FIM 13.6 billion to FIM 60.3 billion. In Asia-Pacific and the Americas, however, sales soared. Europe accounted for 60 percent of Nokia's sales in 1990 and Finland for 30 percent, whereas the Americas and Asia-Pacific markets amounted to 3 to 4 percent each (see Exhibit 6-4b). In 1999, Europe still accounted for 52 percent of sales, but those of the Americas and Asia-Pacific amounted to 25 percent and 21 percent, respectively (see Exhibit 6-4c).

In Ollila's era, the role of Finland has become relatively insignificant in terms of overall revenues. Between 1993 and 1999, overseas revenues climbed from 85 percent to 97.6 percent, while those in Finland declined from 15 percent to 2.4 percent (see Exhibit 6-5a). However, it would be naïve to view the role of the Finnish market in Nokia's operations in terms of revenue alone. As a lead market, Finland played a strategic role for the company. It remained the company's corporate headquarters and the center of R&D leadership and personnel. Viewed in terms of Nokia's employment figures, the picture was more complex and subtle (see Exhibit 6-5b). As Kairamo orchestrated the dramatic growth strategy, the number of Nokia's personnel overseas increased beyond that in Finland. In the peak year of 1988, Nokia had more than 21,500 employees in Finland, but over 23,000 employees overseas. In 1992, when Ollila took the leadership of the company, Nokia had some 13,750 employees in Finland and 13,000 overseas. By 1999, the number of the former had climbed to almost 23,200 and the latter to more than 28,000. Finland represented only 2.4 percent of Nokia's net sales, but more than 45 percent of Nokians were employed in Finland.

By 2000, the global mobile phone market continued to grow rapidly, and the ensuing strong increase in the sales of NMP further consolidated Nokia's top position in mobile handsets. In infrastructure, Nokia continued to be the world's largest GSM 1800 supplier and one of the two largest GSM 900 suppliers, with increasing focus in broadband and Internet Protocol (IP) network solutions. By 1999, Europe accounted for 53 percent of Nokia's net sales (58 percent in 1998), the United States and Canada 25 percent (21 percent in 1998), and Asia-Pacific 22 percent (21 percent in 1998). The four largest markets—the United States, China, the United Kingdom, and Germany—represented collectively 47 percent of total sales. Digital convergence drove industry developments. Western Europe pioneered the new wireless technologies, while North America was the major market in terms of volume. In the long term, the market focus would shift drastically toward the East. Nokia saw its greatest future market potential in Asia. Typically, Nokia's first 3G products were first introduced in Japan. Finland had become a test laboratory. The U.S. market represented price competition, while the Japanese market was about technology experimentation in cutting-edge products. In China, low penetration provided extraordinary potential for volume.

China's Volume Potential

Nokia has been adept at leveraging its limited financial and managerial resources to gain a foothold in lead markets. The strategy of narrowing the business focus to leverage resources but aggressively enter international markets made China critical to Nokia's future—and a source of another tragedy within the company.

Explosive Growth and Anomic Crises

Loyal to its strategic view of market making, Nokia viewed geographic segments in terms of *long*-term potential. In China, for instance, Jiangxi Posts and Telecommunications Administration (PTA) and NTC signed an agreement to supply the first phase of a GSM network in October 1995. The network was put into operation in the first

Exhibit 6-4. Nokia's net sales by market area.

(a) Net Sales by Market Area, 1990–1999

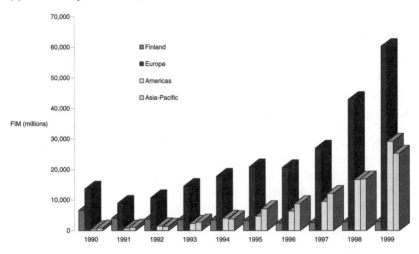

(b) Net Sales by Market Area, 1990

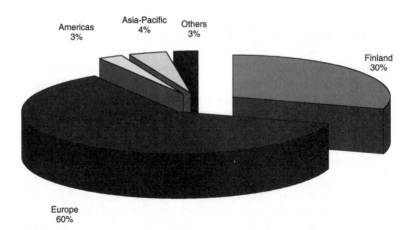

Exhibit 6-4 (continued).

(c) Nokia's Net Sales by Market Area, 1999

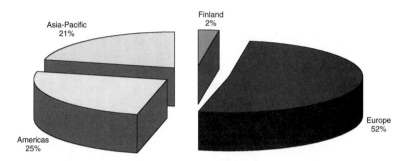

Finland 2%

Asia-Pacific 21%

Europe 52%

Americas 25%

SOURCE: Company reports.

half of 1996. A few months later, Beijing Nokia Mobile Telecommunications Ltd. and Jiangxi PTA signed another contract, valued at approximately $35 million, to expand the latter's GSM network. By the fall of 1996, Nokia's GSM/DCS technology was being supplied to fifty-two operators in thirty-one countries.[21]

These developments hardly occurred overnight. Nokia first arrived in the Chinese market around 1985, but growth began only in the late 1990s. Because Nokia was not well known, it was a very difficult market to tap at first. As a result, Nokia sent Topi Honkavaara to head the local office. When the veteran Nokian arrived in Beijing, the company's sales were less than FIM 1 million; when he left, revenues amounted to FIM 2 billion. Known as a tough manager, difficult but diligent and loyal, Honkavaara built the operation from the ground up and eventually became an expert on doing business in China. Unfortunately, difficulties between Honkavaara and Nokia headquarters worsened in the early 1990s. Reportedly, he and Ollila did not get along, and when the company moved from a diversification to a focus strategy, the cellular unit brought new kinds of Nokians to China. The values of the new Nokians did not mesh with the old subsidiary, and Honkavaara was invited back home, demoted, and allegedly left with empty promises until he committed suicide.[22]

Nokia's transition from a diversified technology concern to a globally focused mobile vendor did not occur without friction, loss, and tragedy. The implications of this transition phase have been ignored in the international press and addressed mainly in the tabloids in Finland. While no company is immune to personal intrigues, it would be naïve to trivialize or attribute these tragedies to personal demons alone. In fact, they appear to be a function of the organiza-

Exhibit 6-5. Nokia's sales and personnel, 1986–1999.

(a) Sales by Markets

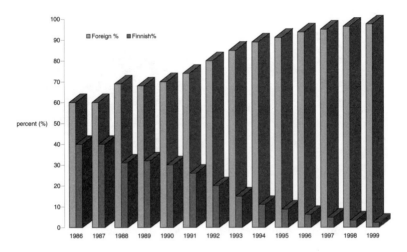

(b) Personnel in Finland and Overseas

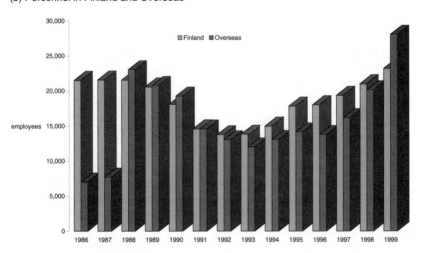

SOURCE: Company reports.

tion's inability to operate positively in highly demanding growth conditions. These tragedies have a common denominator; in each case, explosive growth resulted in willingness but inability to manage it. The deaths of Koski, Kairamo, and Honkavaara, as well as the personal tragedies of less visible employees in high-growth organizations, are not only individual downfalls but also reflections of tensions inherent in strategic intent.

Many transformational organizations experience growing pains, but extreme personal responses of individuals to transition require deeper analysis. When the *mismatch* between current resources and ambitious dreams appears insurmountable, the result can be physical exhaustion, mental agony, even a Durkheimian *anomie*. Organizational demands seem to present conditions in which individual goals have been betrayed by organizational norms or perhaps are no longer regulated by organizational norms at all. As the promise of upward mobility turns into a reality of downward regression, anomic crises ensue, revealing the darker side of a bold and daring strategic intent.

Competition for the Chinese Market

"In 1995, our annual revenues amounted to $200 million," said Matti Vesala, chief of Nokia Networks' production in China. "In the course of the next three years, these revenues tripled."[23] Despite Asia's currency crisis, Nokia increased its investments in China through the end of the 1990s. In October 1998, Ollila and Paavo Lipponen, prime minister of Finland, visited Beijing to open Nokia's new R&D center. By then, the company had already built seven factories in China, and it was building GSM networks in nine of China's twenty-three key regions. The number of Nokians in China had climbed to 3,000, and prospects for the future seemed excellent. In the long term, Ollila noted, China might well become Nokia's leading geographic segment. Although China had a population of 1.2 billion, there were only 22 million cell phones in use.

Over the years, Nokia's partnership with the Finnish government greatly benefited from the arrival of Finnish companies in China. For instance, Finnish security-software companies enjoyed the clout of Finnish neutrality, which has been crucial for the sale of encryption products. The market-driven strategies of Finland's public sector impressed even Chinese authorities. In January 2000, Olli-Pekka Heinonen, the Finnish minister of Transport and Communications, agreed to assist Wu Jichuan, the minister of Telecommunications of China, in the codification of telecommunications regulation.

By 2000, Nokia's revenues in China had climbed to approximately $2.3 billion, and the company had invested at least $1 billion in the promising market. This rapidly growing market provided excellent opportunities for strategic maneuvering. Between 1997 and 1998 alone, the number of cell phones in China doubled. Insofar as Ollila was concerned, Nokia's physical presence in the market location was vital; the company was already manufacturing half of its Chinese products in China.

As Nokia opened access to the Chinese market, the company's suppliers, partners, and other software companies followed in its footsteps. The invasion of Finnish companies accelerated late in 1999, when the United States and China were able to agree on the terms of China's membership in the World Trade Organization (WTO). By 2000, F-Secure was establishing a sales organization in Beijing and a subsidiary in Hong Kong. Stonesoft was seeking resellers in Beijing while establishing an office in Hong Kong. Nedecon and Nixu were preparing entry into the Chinese market, and other Finnish players— Comptel, Elektrobit, Jutron, Aldata, and Opus Capita—were also exploring the market. In advance of these smaller software companies, Nokia's suppliers, such as Elcoteq, Perlos, and Ojala, had already established themselves in the new market. The list of veteran entrants also included Novo (IT), Teleste (cables), and JOT Automation (production automation).[24]

The consensus among Finnish industry observers was that China had leapt into mobile communications through its mobile investments, bypassing the traditional fixed-line infrastructure. Approximately 43 million Chinese were already using cellular phones, and penetration in urban markets had climbed to 28 percent. In Beijing, Nokia was participating in the 3G test network. Of course, Nokia was not alone in the emerging market. It faced tough competition from rivals Ericsson and Motorola, which had had footholds in China for far longer. By the end of 1997, Nokia's market share was estimated at 22 percent, against Ericsson's 35 percent and Motorola's 26 percent. In 2000, Motorola still had 32 percent of the market, but its leadership was based on the 1G analog phones. Nokia's share had climbed to 30 percent and stood on its 2G digital products.

"Until the 1980s, Nokia was a Finnish company, in the 1980s Nokia was a Nordic company and in the beginning of 1990s a European company," said Jorma Ollila in 1997. "Now, we are a global company."[25] Ollila's words have often been used to illustrate Nokia's rapid internationalization. However, there is more to the story. It is strategic intent rather than the idea of locational advantage that truly drives Nokia's strategic considerations. With this strategic intent, *focus* is the key word. "The world belongs to the focused companies," affirmed Ollila in 2000.[26]

Soon, even globalization no longer sufficed as a driver of growth for Nokia. It was about to engage in unique positioning by exploiting the two most powerful drivers of the early twenty-first century: ever greater mobility and the Internet. Around 1997, Nokia began strategic maneuvering in the emerging mobile Internet. That meant still another transformation for the company. (It was also a time of personal loss for Ollila himself; his mother passed away.)

In the development of a global focus strategy and the design of a mobile Internet strategy, Nokia has continued to build on strategic intent. "Today the most important thing in the high-technology markets is change," argued Alahuhta in 1999. "If the company remains flexible, taking advantage of changes makes possible growth, which can be significantly faster than market growth, even for longer periods of time."[27]

Seeking to avoid the historical emphasis of resource-based strategies and static characteristics of classic competitive strategy, strategic intent represented Nokia's efforts at a new management paradigm. These efforts, however, were not shaped by a flavor-of-the-month management consultant nor by Ollila alone. They evolved naturally in Nokia's group executive board, which was responsible for Nokia's strategic market making.

Strategic Market Making

NOKIA was considered a global cellular leader by the end of the 1990s. Listed on the New York, Helsinki, Stockholm, London, Frankfurt, and Paris stock exchanges, the company's operating profit was up 57 percent to EUR 3.9 billion, sales increased by 48 percent to EUR 19.8 billion, and its market capitalization exceeded EUR 209.4 billion. Yet, Nokia's financial history reflected the turmoil of the company's rapid growth. After a high of $6.1 billion in 1990, its revenue hovered between $3.7 billion and $4.1 billion for three years (see Exhibit 7-1a); net income was in the negative between 1991 and 1992 (see Exhibit 7-1b). Once the strategic focus of the company was established, revenue more than doubled, from $6.4 billion in 1994 to $20 billion in 1998, and net income climbed from $632 million to $2.6 billion. Through the end of the 1990s, Nokia's net profit margin amounted to 12 to 13 percent, reflecting a significant increase over the 1 to 2 percent of the decade before (see Exhibit 7-1c). During the restructuring and early refocusing phases between 1989 and 1993, the number of employees dwindled from 41,300 to 25,800 but then doubled to 51,200 in 1999 (see Exhibit 7-1d).

Nokia increased its handset operating margins by 5 percent, reaching 23 percent in 1998, even though handset prices were falling by an average of 20 percent a year.[1] In the process, Nokia's stock price improved greatly, in three distinct phases (see Exhibit 7-2). Restructuring and poor results kept Nokia's stock price low until the mid-1990s. As the company shifted from restructuring to cellular focus, the stock rose from $10 in 1995 to $20 in 1998. At this point, Nokia first registered on the radar of investment analysts, and the company's stock price began to rise. With strategic efforts at the mobile Internet between early 1998 and the spring of 2000, Nokia's stock soared from $20 to nearly $180–$200. This was an extraordinary performance when compared to the other major corporations (Standard & Poor's 500) and the digital economy (NASDAQ).

Business Segments

In 1999, Nokia was comprised of three business groups: Nokia Networks, Nokia Mobile Phones, and Nokia Communications Products. In addition, Nokia included a separate ventures organization and a corporate research unit, the Nokia Research Center (NRC). The company had R&D in fourteen countries; production in eleven; and a global network of distribution, sales, customer services, and other operational units.[2]

Nokia Mobile Phones

In short order, Nokia Mobile Phones had become the world's largest mobile phone manufacturer selling products in over 130 countries. With 163 million phone handsets sold worldwide in 1998, Nokia had an estimated 30% market share versus Motorola's slightly lower percentage.[3] The company developed sophisticated mobile phones and accessories for all major analog and digital (GSM, AMPS, CDMA, TDMA) standards. Nokia mobile phones were developed to make communicating easier, and to provide beauty in design. Similarly, product development was geared to "unsurpassed functional and technological design." Many of the standard features that are now considered generic were originally developed by Nokia, including large graphics displays, signal and battery indicators, colored covers, and ringing tones. By amortizing design costs over multiple countries, the company was able to boost profitability even as its sleek, functional designs contributed to competitive differentiation.

Despite difficult conditions, sales of NMP grew from FIM 2.3 billion in 1990 to FIM 6.3 billion in 1993. As the company settled on its strategic course, sales increased from FIM 10.7 billion in 1994 to FIM 27.6 billion in 1997 and more than FIM 78.4 billion in 1999 (see Exhibit 7-3a). The unit's operating profit illustrated its success even better, increasing from FIM 950 million in 1997 to more than FIM 18.4 billion in 1999 (see Exhibit 7-3b). With a comprehensive product portfolio that covered all consumer segments and standards, Nokia Mobile Phones was in a strong position to shape and define those trends driving the mobile information industry.

Nokia Networks

In 1990, Nokia Telecommunications was still driving the company's revenue growth with FIM 2.5 billion in net sales. During the company's restructuring phase, group sales were slow but steady,

Exhibit 7-1. Nokia's historical results, 1989–1999.

(a) Revenues

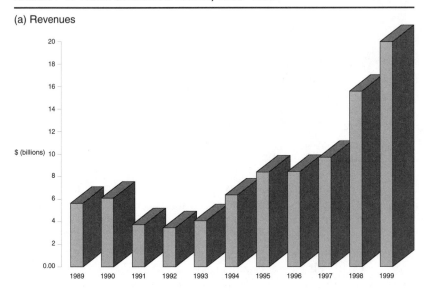

(b) Net Income

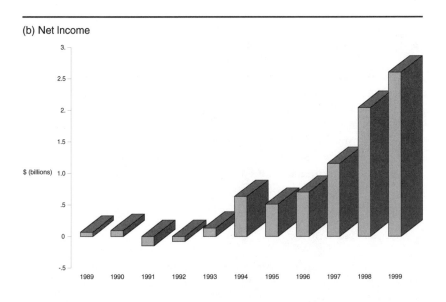

Exhibit 7-1 (continued).

(c) Net Profit Margin

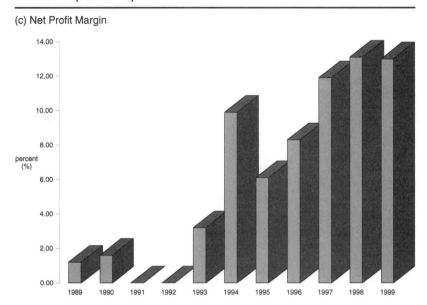

(d) Employees

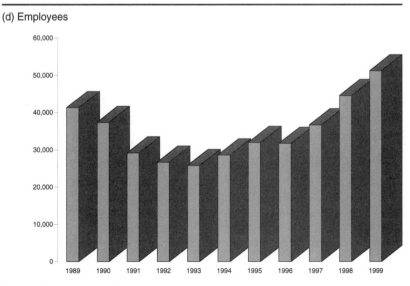

SOURCE: Company reports.

Exhibit 7-2. Nokia's stock price, 1992–2000.

Nokia (1992–2000)

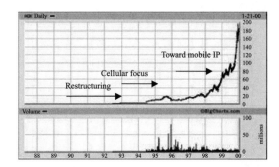

*Nokia vs. Standard &
Poor's 500 (1992–2000)*

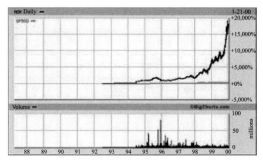

*Nokia vs. NASDAQ
(1992–2000)*

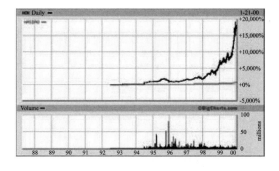

reaching FIM 6.9 billion in 1994. As the company discovered its strategic course, the pace picked up again. Between 1995 and 1999, the
group's sales more than tripled, from FIM 10.3 billion to FIM 33.7 billion (see Exhibit 7-3a). Unlike sales, the group's operating profit consistently exceeded that of Nokia Mobile Phones, until 1997. A year later,
however, the group's profit was still strong at FIM 6.4 billion, but only
a third of that of the mobile unit (see Exhibit 7-3b).

By 2000, Nokia Networks, formerly Nokia Telecommunications,
was a leading supplier of data, video, and voice network solutions,

Exhibit 7-3. Nokia segments (1990–1999).

(a) Sales

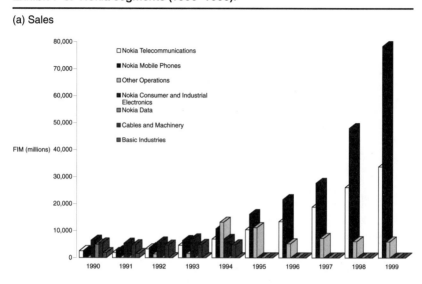

(b) Operating Profit/Loss

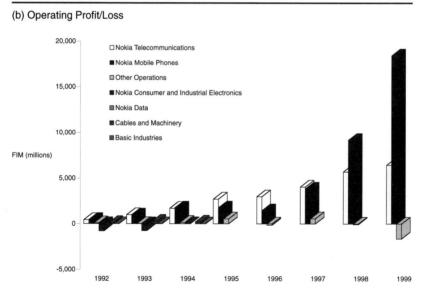

SOURCE: Company reports.

seeking to meet the needs of operator customers and Internet service providers. It was also a leading supplier of mobile, fixed-access solutions, broadband, and IP network solutions, providing service creation, network management, systems integration, and customer services.

Nokia Communications Products

"Internet Protocol, or IP, is just a computer communication protocol," acknowledged Kent Elliot, senior vice president and general manager of Nokia Internet Communications, in 1999. "But it is changing the world we live in."[4] Nokia saw an extraordinary opportunity to pioneer not just a business segment or even an industry segment, but a veritable infrastructure—the *mobile* digital economy.

Global IP mobility was Nokia's strategy for achieving its goal of creating a variety of innovative applications and services. In turn, these products and services would create the applications platform of choice for a wide range of communications, mobile commerce, and entertainment services. Concurrently, the Nokians saw a critical inflection point in the very nature of technology. In the past, new technology markets were initially driven by the technology itself. With global IP mobility, applications would drive growth, eventually becoming independent of the technologies. Through the mobile IP, Nokia saw itself moving from a technology-based to a more user-based approach. The company identified three strategic cornerstones that would guide its entry into digital space: human technology, seamless solutions, and virtual presence.

> This is only the beginning. Global IP Mobility will change our world a lot more yet. We have only just begun to move into digital space. We have only just begun to push the limits. More and more services will go digital. They will become more available to more people. And in a greater variety of situations. The new ways of doing things will become the norm and not the exception. Many activities will be transformed. Buying and selling will be increasingly via e-commerce or m-commerce. At Nokia we believe there are no limits.[5]

In 1999, Nokia's segment of "other operations" showed an operating loss of EUR 273 million. This loss was related in part to the performance of Nokia Communications Products and substantial investments in new business opportunities at Nokia Ventures Organization (NVO). The 3G market represented tremendous opportunities, but Nokia was not alone in recognizing its potential. To compete in this marketplace, Nokia would have to build new capabilities from scratch and prepare for yet another organizational transition. The potential payoffs were extraordinary, but the company would have to risk its present to achieve its future.

Nokia Ventures Organization

The mission of the NVO was to push the limits of Nokia's growth beyond the scope of its current businesses and to introduce and develop new business ideas. The organization provided an arena to discover and develop new business ideas inside and outside Nokia. At the end of 1999, the NVO consisted of five main parts:

- Nokia Internet Communications
- Nokia Home Communications
- Nokia Mobile Display Appliances
- Nokia Ventures Fund
- Nokia Venturing Unit

The first three were structured to take advantage of the opportunities in what Nokia considered the emerging mobile information society. Each reflected the convergence of wide-area mobile communications and local-area computing, creating innovative types of high-speed mobile multimedia and seamless services for use at work and home.[6]

How, then, did Nokia hope to dominate the mobile Internet in the early twenty-first century? Just as the company used strategic intent to overcome the mismatch of its resources and ambitions, it sought to leverage strategic leadership through its group executive board, a bold strategy not for the weak of heart. When Nokia released its annual report in spring 2000, some Finnish industry observers and investment analysts found it a spine-chilling read. The dominant mobile vendor seemed to be rushing into the unknown without a second thought. "You begin to get the creeps when you read Nokia's CEO Jorma Ollila and President Pekka Ala-Pietilä assuring you that we are breaking through the restrictions of time and place and no one can know for sure what mighty forces are sweeping us along."[7]

Nokia's Strategic Leadership

Sustained competitive advantage is notoriously difficult to achieve in mobile communications, an industry in which new technology generations have rapidly mitigated historical advantages. However, Nokia's persistent determination to choose and focus has distinguished the company from its rivals since the early 1990s. Unlike its current competitors (e.g., Lucent, Nortel, Ericsson, Siemens, and Alcatel), Nokia has not pursued the worldwide wireline telecommunications markets in a major way. Instead, it has kept its strategic focus exclusively on cellular business.

In the course of its history, Nokia has never relied on a single strategic framework. In this regard, the Ollila era has not been an exception. But, as we have seen, in certain periods, some fundamental strategic choices have been preferred at the expense of others. In a historical sense, Nokia's strategy has recently come full circle. After all, when the company emerged in the 1860s, it focused on wood processing, although diversification was under way before the end of the nineteenth century. Through the 1990s, Nokia again refocused on a single industry segment. In both cases, Nokia has consistently embraced change and pioneered new industries.

In the 1860s, Idestam crafted the company's strategy, but he was not alone in this effort. For decades, Mechelin served as his loyal supporter and coach, and the two also relied on a small circle of trusted friends. When Ollila began to refocus Nokia, he was not alone in crafting the company's strategic direction. For years he discussed and debated strategic issues with a small circle of veteran Nokians and the group executive board, whose teamwork has served as a model for other teams at different management levels throughout the company.

To personalize a company's corporate strategy means ignoring the complexities inherent in strategy making, industry environment, and institutional constraints. The tendency to reduce the strategy of a major public corporation to the persona of its chief executive is too simplistic. Yet, this trivial method is common in business schools and among many investment analysts and media observers. In the case of Nokia, it would be particularly naïve to personalize Ollila's strategic initiatives, because teamwork and egalitarianism have had such an important role in the company. Indeed, one of Ollila's undeniable strengths has been his ability to delegate authority. Yet, Nokia's strategy making is not a grassroots activity either. Ultimately, the strategy is envisioned, developed, debated, implemented, and measured by the company's group executive board.

The Group Executive Board

In addition to Ollila, the board encompassed eight chief executives in the year 2000 (see Exhibit 7-4a), including the president of the group executive board Pekka Ala-Pietilä (president of Nokia Communications Products), Sari Baldauf (president, Nokia Networks), Matti Alahuhta (president, Nokia Mobile Phones), Olli-Pekka Kallasvuo (executive vice president, CFO, Nokia Group), Yrjö Neuvo (executive vice president, chief technology officer, Nokia Mobile Phones), Veli Sundbäck (executive vice president), Anssi Vanjoki (senior vice president, Nokia Mobile Phones), and Mikko Heikkonen (president, Network Systems, Nokia Networks). In Finland, the careers of these board members have been followed with the same awe and fascination that the speculations of the sovietologists used to have in foreign policy through the Cold War.

Most members of the board were born in the 1950s, and most are alumni of the Helsinki School of Economics and Business Administration (HSEBA), the country's leading business school; the Helsinki University of Technology (HUT), the country's leading technology school; or both. Several hold doctorate degrees and many began their careers as academic researchers. As a group, the members are hard workers and in many ways share Ollila's tough work ethic. They distance themselves from publicity and enjoy peaceful family lives. They are all dedicated Nokians, driven not just by success and money but by more intangible rewards—prestige, lifelong learning, and professional respect—the traditional staples of Finnish values. They exemplify Finland's boomer generation in ambition, moderation, and work habits, and most have worked their entire professional lives for the company. Not a single board member has been associated with professional misconduct or negative publicity. These Nokia insiders work well together, and each brings a unique and distinctive quality to the board (Exhibit 7-4b).

As president of the board and president of Nokia Communications Products, Pekka Ala-Pietilä is Ollila's right-hand man and his successor at NMP. Ala-Pietilä joined the computer division as an applications consultant in 1982. In the 1999 Annual Report, he coauthored the "Letter to Shareholders" with Ollila for the first time, a gesture that did not go unnoticed by Finnish business observers and analysts, i.e., "Nokiologists." Ala-Pietilä is acknowledged to be Ollila's heir apparent.

By 2000, Ala-Pietilä concentrated his operational responsibilities on future challenges, which he portrayed as "digitalization, mobility, and the Internet." When he took Ollila's post in NMP in 1992, he was barely thirty-five years old. The young executive contributed to the rapid resolution of the logistics problems in the mid-1990s. When Nokia launched the new Communications Products group in 1998, he was put in charge. Shunning publicity, Ala-Pietilä avoids other board memberships and is known for his dedication to Nokia.[8]

Sari Baldauf's name is synonymous in Finland with Nokia's international expansion. In 1999, she oversaw Nokia's operations in China. She had been an academic prior to joining Nokia in 1983 as part of a

Exhibit 7-4a. Nokia's group executive board, February 2000.

Chairman Jorma Ollila, 49
Chairman and CEO of Nokia Corporation.
Group Executive Board member since 1986.
Chairman since 1992.
Joined Nokia 1985.

President and CEO, and Chairman of the Group, Executive Board of
Nokia Corporation 1992–1999, President of Nokia Mobile Phones
1990–1992, Senior Vice President, Finance of Nokia 1986–1989.

Member of the Board of Directors of Ford Motor Company, ICL plc, Otava Books and
Magazines Group Ltd and UPM-Kymmene Corporation. Deputy Chairman of the Board of the
Confederation of Finnish Industry and Employers and member of The European Round Table of
Industrialists.

Holdings in Nokia: 3,784 shares and stock options for 1,252,000 shares.

Pekka Ala-Pietilä, 43
President of Nokia Corporation.
President of Nokia Communications Products.
Member since 1992. Joined Nokia 1984.

Executive Vice President and Deputy to the CEO of Nokia Corporation and President of Nokia Communications Products 1998–1999,
President of Nokia Mobile Phones 1992–1998, Vice President, Product Marketing of Nokia Mobile Phones 1991–1992, Vice President,
Strategic Planning of Nokia Mobile Phones 1990–1991.

Member of the Board of Directors of Alma Media Corporation. Member of the Board of
Economic Information Bureau and Finnish-Japanese Chamber of Commerce.

Holdings in Nokia: 2,400 shares and stock options for 556,000 shares.

Dr. Matti Alahuhta, 47
President of Nokia Mobile Phones.
Member since 1993.
Joined Nokia 1975–1982 and 1984.

President of Nokia Telecommunications 1993–1998, Executive Vice
President of Nokia Telecommunications 1992, Senior Vice President,
Public Networks of Nokia Telecommunications 1990–1992.

Chairman of the Board of Federations of Finnish Electrical and Electronics Industry, Vice Chairman of the Board of the Federation of Finnish Metal, Engineering
and Electrotechnical Industries and of the Technology Development Center, Ministry of Trade
and Industry, and member of the Board of The Central Chamber of Commerce of Finland and
the Advisory Board of the International Institute for Management Development (IMD).

Holdings in Nokia: Stock options for 476,000 shares.

Exhibit 7-4a (continued).

Sari Baldauf, 44
President of Nokia Networks.
Member since 1994.
Joined Nokia 1983.

Executive Vice President of Nokia APAC 1997–1998, President, Cellular Systems of Nokia Telecommunications 1988–1996, Vice President, Business Development of Nokia Telecommunications 1987–1988.

Member of the Board of Technical Research Centre of Finland and Finland-China Trade Association, and member of the National Committee for the Information Society Issues.

Holdings in Nokia: Stock options for 476,000 shares.

Mikko Heikkonen, 50
Executive Vice President and General Manager,
Customer Operations of Nokia Networks.
Member since 1998.
Joined Nokia 1975.

President, Network Systems of Nokia Telecommunications 1997–1999, President, Network and Access Systems of Nokia Telecommunications 1995–1996, Senior Vice President, Area Management of Nokia Telecommunications 1993–1995, Senior Vice President, Cellular Systems of Nokia Telecommunications 1988–1992.

Holdings in Nokia: Stock options for 358,000 shares.

Olli-Pekka Kallasvuo, 46
Executive Vice President, CFO of Nokia Corporation.
Member since 1990.
Joined Nokia 1980.

Executive Vice President of Nokia Americas and President of Nokia Inc. 1997–1998, Executive Vice President, CFO of Nokia 1992–1996, Senior Vice President, Finance of Nokia 1990–1991.

Chairman of the Board of Directors of Nextrom Holding S.A. and Nokian Tyres plc, member of the Board of Directors of F-Secure Corporation and Finnish Broadcasting Company. Member of the Board of Telecommunications Industry Association (USA).

Holdings in Nokia: Stock options for 488,000 shares.

Exhibit 7-4a (continued).

Dr. Yrjö Neuvo, 56
Executive Vice President, CTO of Nokia Mobile Phones.
Member since 1993.
Joined Nokia 1993.

Senior Vice President, Technology of Nokia 1993–1994, National Research Professor of the Academy of Finland 1984–1992, Professor of Tampere University of Technology 1976–1992, Visiting Professor of University of California, Santa Barbara 1981–1982.

Vice Chairman of the Board of Directors of Vaisala Corporation, Member of the Board of Finnish Academy of Technical Sciences, Member of the Finnish Academy of Science and Letters and Academiae Europae, Foreign member of Royal Swedish Academy of Engineering Sciences, and Fellow of the Institute of Electrical and Electronics Engineers.

Holdings in Nokia: 4,160 shares and stock options for 489,180 shares.

Veli Sundbäck, 53
Executive Vice President, Corporate Relations
and Trade Policy of Nokia Corporation.
Member since 1996.
Joined Nokia 1996.

Secretary of State at the Ministry for Foreign Affairs
1993–1995, Under-Secretary of State for External
Economic Relations at the Ministry for Foreign
Affairs 1990–1993.

Chairman of the Board of Directors of Huhtamäki Van Leer Oyj and member of the Board of Directors of Nextrom Holding S.A. Vice Chairman of the Board of the International Chamber of Commerce, Finnish Section, and Chairman of the Trade Policy Committee of the Confederation of Finnish Industry and Employers.

Holdings in Nokia: 400 shares and stock options for 436,000 shares.

Anssi Vanjoki, 43
Executive Vice President, Europe and Africa,
Nokia Mobile Phones.
Member since 1998.
Joined Nokia 1991.

Vice President, Sales of Nokia Mobile Phones 1991–1994,
Suomen 3M Oy 1980–1990.

Holdings in Nokia: 8,000 shares and stock options for 294,000 shares.

Exhibit 7–4b. The group executive board: positions and roles.

Nokia's Board of Directors			**JORMA OLLILA** Chairman of the Board and CEO, Nokia			**PEKKA ALA-PIETILÄ** President and member of the Executive Board, Nokia and President, Nokia Communications Products

International Market Builder	Global Expert	Finance Specialist	International Trade	R&D Expert	Future Influencer	Educator
SARI BALDAUF President, Nokia Networks	**MATTI ALAHUHTA** President, Nokia Mobile Phones	**OLLI-PEKKA KALLASVUO** Executive Vice President, Chief Financial Officer, Nokia Group	**VELI SUNDBÄCK** Executive Vice President, member of the Executive Board	**YRJÖ NEUVO** Executive Vice President, Chief Technical Officer, Nokia	**ANSSI VANJOKI** Senior Vice President, Nokia Mobile Phones	**MIKKO HEIKKONEN** President, Network Systems, Nokia Networks

SOURCE: Information based on Nokia's annual reports.

three-year research project on international business. That same year she published a study on disinvestment.[9] As president of NMP, Matti Alahuhta is responsible for the company's most important unit as well as Nokia's operations in Japan. He joined Nokia in 1975 as an R&D engineer for Nokia electronics, and his dissertation on global growth strategies has reflected and shaped Nokia's globalization. Olli-Pekka Kallasvuo is Nokia's CFO, overseeing its business operations in the United States and assisting Ollila with the development of Nokia's initial refocusing strategy in 1992. Through the tumultuous first half of the 1990s, Kallasvuo also served as chairman and board member of the Helsinki Stock Exchange.

Also in the early 1990s, Anssi Vanjoki initiated Nokia's branding strategy, which has played a significant role in the company's differentiation efforts. Since 1994, he has been in charge of NMP in Europe and Africa. Originally an academic researcher, Yrjö Neuvo joined Nokia Group in 1993 as senior vice president of technology. Through the late 1990s, he was particularly active in product development as executive vice president of NMP. He is the man most identified with Nokia's R&D, playing a critical role in stabilizing the 3G standards. Finally, Mikko Heikkonen, president of Network Systems at NTC, participated in continuing education programs in Finland and abroad.

In addition to its sophistication in the marketplace, Nokia has proven itself to be shrewd when it comes to government relations. After the mid-1990s, Paavo Rantanen, Finland's former ambassador to the United States and Nokia's principal diplomat, was succeeded by Veli Sundbäck, an executive vice president in charge of Nokia's international trade relations. It was Sundbäck who lobbied successfully for the WTO Basic Telecommunication Agreement in which seventy-two governments agreed to liberalize their telecommunications markets to various degrees. Having begun his career in Finland's Ministry for Foreign Affairs, Sundbäck was influential in Finland/EC relations, Finnish-EC and EFTA missions, and GATT and OECD negotiations within the EU. When Martti Ahtisaari was nominated for president of Finland, Sundbäck succeeded him as secretary of state in the Ministry for Foreign Affairs from 1993 to 1995.

With their diverse backgrounds in finance, industry, R&D, engineering, manufacturing, and international business, the key members of the board—Ollila, Ala-Pietilä, Alahuhta, Baldauf, and Kallasvuo—function not just as individuals but as an integrated whole. As one observer has put it, "The five have worked together for so long that they can converse in a kind of shorthand. 'We communicate daily,' Alahuhta says of Ollila. 'But our communication is very compact.' The five are also seen by many at Nokia as an inseparable unit. Around Nokia, you don't hear so much talk about Jorma this or Jorma that. It's almost always Matti and Sari and Pekka and Olli-Pekka and Jorma, or some combination."[10] Further, this group serves as the "collective mind" behind Nokia's overall strategy. It is supported by a board of directors that now works *with* rather than *against* the company's strategic management.

The Board of Directors

Through the 1970s and 1980s, Kairamo and his executives rebelled against the board, which to their minds sought to restrict Nokia's drive to grow and expand internationally. Through the 1990s, the board was far more understanding and sympathetic toward the strategic objectives of the company. As chairman of the executive board, Ollila is accountable to Nokia's board of directors, and as a former banker, he is very much to the board's liking. After all, it had fully supported his appointment in 1992. Meanwhile, Finland's financial crisis had transformed Finnish banks and financial institutions; by outlook, they had become more international. By 2000, the board consisted of seven members representing financial institutions (Iiro Viinanen, Pirkko Alitalo, Vesa Vainio), international companies (Paul J. Collins, Robert F. W. van Oordt), and academia (Edward Andersson, Bengt Holmström) (see Exhibit 7-5).

Casimir Ehrnrooth, CEO of Metra Corporation and an industrial leader of the forestry era, had been Ollila's strong supporter and sparring partner in the past. By 2000, his closest confidant was vice chairman Paul J. Collins, a Citibank veteran. But Ollila was no longer just a Finnish industry leader; he had become known worldwide. Among European corporate leaders, Ollila's close circle consisted of the chief executives of the mobile giants, including Vodaphone CEO Chris Gent, Telefonica CEO Juan Villalonga, and British Telecom CEO Peter Bonfield. In the winter of 1999, along with former U.S. Secretary of Treasury Robert Rubin, Ollila assumed a seat on the board of the Ford Motor Company. Nokia had developed automotive wireless communications with Ford for years. Unlike many other new European CEOs, Ollila was motivated by a Protestant work ethic: "A CEO is tempted to go to dinners and irrelevant affairs to give speeches and to give interviews," he observed. "It is, however, the beginning of a downhill slide when one starts basking in the glow of publicity."[11]

After the resignation of Ehrnrooth in 1999, the new board of directors elected Ollila chairman of the company. He resigned from his position as president of Nokia but remained the company's CEO. Ala-Pietilä, previously deputy CEO and head of Nokia Communications Products, was appointed new president. Ollila consolidated his position as the ultimate strategic authority of Nokia. In Finland, Ollila's

Exhibit 7-5. Nokia's board of directors (2000).

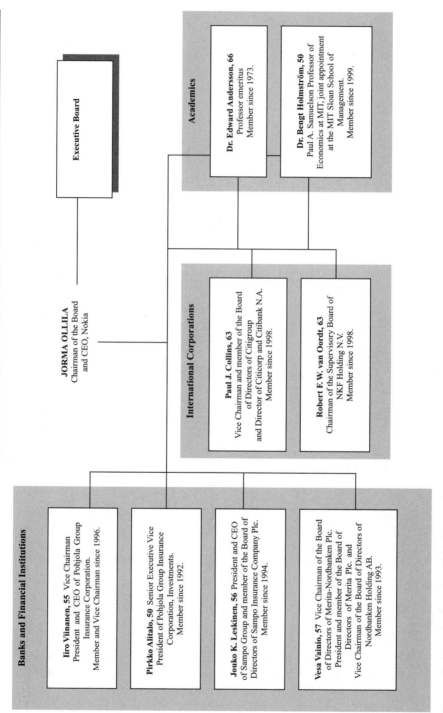

SOURCE: Information based on Nokia's annual reports.

dual roles gave rise to something of a debate. In the United States, the combined roles of chairman and CEO have often been considered effective if the chief executive has integrity and a proven track record. Yet, accumulated power at the top has also resulted in abuse. "Power is a dangerous thing," argued veteran business journalists in Finland. "When it is accumulated, the world around tends to go silent. It is easy to agree with power. Who, from now on, will present the critical questions at Nokia? To whom will Jorma Ollila report? Which one of Nokia's board members will dare to challenge one of the world's most successful chief executives? How to monitor a CEO and chairman, who has only succeeded?"[12] The phrasing of these reflections may illustrate inflated expectations.

Anglo-Saxon corporate governance arrived in Finland only after the collapse of the investment economy.[13] In the consensus-driven country, strong leadership has been perceived as potentially vulnerable to abuse. Nokia's justification for the change derived from the premise that, as an international corporation, Nokia would have to abide by international business rules. That did not pacify critics who claimed that Nokia was drifting toward an "enlightened dictatorship." Typically, most Finnish critics chose to remain anonymous.[14]

Ideally, board members should be outsiders to ensure true neutrality in accordance with appropriate corporate governance. In practice, the issue may be far more complex, especially with the rise of the technology sector since the early 1980s. After all, Nokia operated in the mobile cellular industry that was characterized by rapid change. In such a business, board outsiders were not likely to be informed industry specialists or able to monitor its developments regularly. In Nokia's case, some of the criticism by Finnish observers may have been motivated by allegations of Ollila's "thin skin" vis-à-vis public criticism.[15] In business, he has shown a great ability and willingness to delegate responsibility, and furthermore, actual strategy making was the function of the executive board. "The objective [at Nokia] is to always have decisions made by the people who have the best knowledge," Alahuhta has said.[16] As a result, the company was not only less hierarchical than most large corporations, but decidedly *anti*-hierarchical. The objective of meritocratic management was to encourage creativity, entrepreneurship, and personal responsibility.

In Finland, then, the criticism reflected a fear of the return of the highly centralized power structures and insider deals that characterized the investment economy. It was a uniquely Finnish reaction to Nokia, which was still perceived as a Finnish company (although most of Nokia's stock was held by international institutional investors that included American and European funds). By 2000, these investors owned an estimated 70 to 80 percent of Nokia.[17]

Toward a New Management Paradigm

Over the years, Nokia has not only relied on the thinking of internationally known consultants such as Hamel and Prahalad and academic luminaries such as Michael E. Porter; it has also developed some strategic lessons on its own that have remained in relative secrecy. These lessons have been motivated less by disinterested academic pursuits and theoretical dogmas than the practical issues of corporate and business strategy, yet the proposed resolutions have theoretical and empirical significance far beyond Nokia, addressing the type of problems with which most fast-cycle companies in the highly volatile technology sector struggle. What makes Nokia's strategic reflections particularly fascinating is that they represent the "third way" sought by Ollila and the group executive board. The strategic considerations have been less about competitive strategy *or* resource theory than the effort to transcend both.

The Quest for the Third Way

As Ollila and his group executive board gained more experience in the industry and began to ponder the transition from the traditional cellular business to the mobile Internet, strategy inevitably became a subject of increasing reflection. Strategic intent was clear about the ends and flexible about the means. It meant strategic maneuvering in an emergent industry in which industry definition remained a moving target. Of course, cellular had been a complex growth business, but mobile Internet was even more complicated. In the latter case, strategic intent required an even greater stretch to match the company's capabilities with its objectives and to make the most of limited resources.

In January 1999, Ollila addressed the Finnish Strategic Society on the topic of Nokia's strategic intent.[18] The strategy work at Nokia Group, he said, aimed at a "new management paradigm." This paradigm was designed to cope with developments and challenges in dynamic markets, in particular digitalization and globalization of the communications industry, deconstruction and horizontalization of business systems, market making and standardization, increasing role of brand and corporate image, and the right timing and speed (see Exhibit 7-6).

Nokia's new management paradigm combined two major schools of thought in strategic management: the resource-based view (Hamel and Prahalad) and the market-based view (Porter's competitive strategy). As far as Nokia was concerned, both might be necessary, but even together they remained insufficient. From Ollila's standpoint, resource-based strategies focus on unique competencies. In this para-

Exhibit 7-6. Nokia's view of developments and challenges in dynamic markets.

Digitalization and Globalization of the Communications Industry
- Convergence of telecommunications, data communications, IT, and media
- Emergence of new businesses
- Consolidation

Deconstruction and Horizontalization of Business Systems
- Dynamic "coopetition"

Significance of Market Making and Standardization
- Proactive "driving" of market growth parameters
- Ecosystems thinking

Increasing Role of Brand and Corporate Image
- Lifestyle marketing and segmentation
- Good corporate citizenship

Right Timing and Speed
- New type of management and leadership needed

SOURCE: Based on Rolf Leppänen, *Nokia Group: Case Study in Strategic Steering System,* TEKES Research Project A/555, p. 6.

digm, companies compete by maximally leveraging their competencies on old and new market spaces. Nokia thought this paradigm was "too slow and history-focused." Conversely, Ollila argued that market-based strategies focused on the most attractive existing segments. In this paradigm, companies compete by differentiation, low cost, or specialization. As Nokia saw it, this paradigm takes the market as a given and places too little emphasis on renewal. Instead of either strategy, Nokia preferred to build upon what Ollila called "market-*making* strategies." These, he argued, emerged from the new kinds of management challenges that faced global companies operating in quickly changing markets (see Exhibit 7-7).

Nokia's paradigm was based on several perceived imperatives. First, eager to exploit discontinuities, Ollila believed that network effects contributed significantly to economic success. When one company adopted a new and meaningful way to operate, others in the industry would follow. Through the 2G rivalry, it was this imperative that had motivated Nokia's efforts to influence the competition and its evolution proactively. Second, an industry leader could create new markets and shape old ones through timing, cooperation, and standardization. To implement new ideas and strategies, organizations had

Exhibit 7-7. Nokia's market-making paradigm.

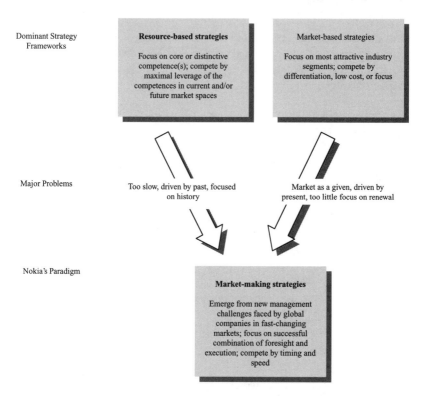

SOURCE: Based on Rolf Leppänen, *Nokia Group: Case Study in Strategic Steering System*, TEKES Research Project A/555, p. 17.

to embrace change. In practice, this imperative was inherent in the ideas of concurrent engineering that Nokia had adopted from the Japanese in the late 1980s. If product development, sales, and production units engaged in significant cooperation, changing markets and product platforms were bound to pose organizational challenges as well. Third, Ollila did not believe that competitive advantage should be built on a single factor. In order to succeed in dynamic markets, a company needed to build on several competitive advantages simultaneously.

Unlike resource theorists, Ollila's Nokia could not afford to look only inward; it had to cope with dynamic markets and therefore ceaselessly monitor environmental shifts and changes. Unlike market theorists, the company could not look only outward either. To adapt to and shape dynamic markets, Nokia had to ceaselessly build new capabilities. Indeed, the story of Nokia serves as a practical illustration of a critical transition from the requirements of *sustained* competitive advantage, to *renewed* competitive advantage.

In Nokia's new management paradigm, the focus was on a successful combination of foresight and execution, and competing depended on timing and speed (see Exhibit 7-8). Competition for future markets and successful innovation required Nokia to come up with the right answers to the "what" and "how" of strategy. The "what" required foresight: reading the market and the right timing; the "how" translated into excellence in execution, speed in anticipating and fulfilling emerging customer needs, quality in products and processes, and openness to new ideas and solutions. Hence the goal of Nokia's senior management was to combine winning foresight and excellent execution in a balanced way. "When something has been achieved, developments are already somewhere else," argued Ollila. "I'm always looking at the next challenge."[19]

Nokia's management paradigm can best be understood as a rephrasing of classic strategy and innovation management within three strategic time perspectives (long, medium, and short [see Exhibit 7-9]). Overall, it stressed the role of strategic fit between interdependent activities (harmony among all elements). In the long term, Nokia's

Exhibit 7-8. Nokia's winning foresight.

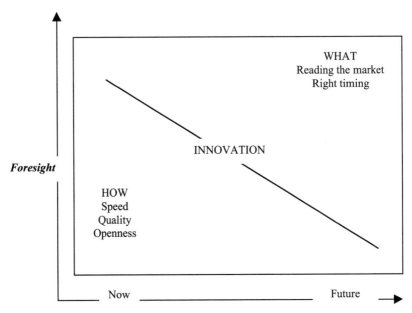

Excellence in Execution

SOURCE: Based on Rolf Leppänen, *Nokia Group: Case Study in Strategic Steering System,* TEKES Research Project A/555, p. 14.

Exhibit 7-9. Framework for strategy development.

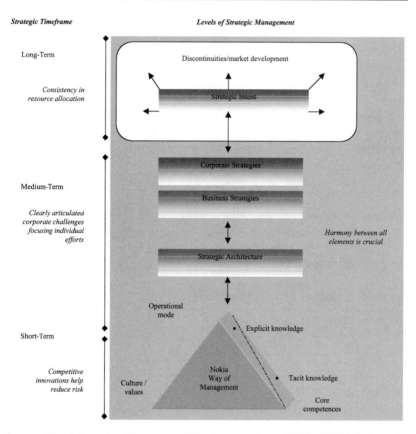

SOURCE: Based in part, with some modifications, on Jorma Ollilla, "Nokia's Strategic Intent," speech delivered at the Finnish Strategic Society in Helsinki, Finland, 20 January 1999.

paradigm stressed consistency in resource allocation and incorporated both continuous and discontinuous market developments.[20] In the medium term, it encompassed corporate strategy (where to compete) and business strategies (how to compete) in addition to strategic architecture (technology life cycles) and sought to articulate the central corporate challenges while focusing on individual efforts. Just as Intel and Microsoft have taken advantage of the implications of Moore's Law in microprocessors, operating systems, and application software, Nokia has exploited the momentum of technology generations in the mobile cellular business since the creation of its electronics division in the 1960s.[21]

In the short term, Nokia's paradigm highlighted the role of competitive innovation, which helps reduce risk, and represented Nokia's way of management, operating mode, culture, values, and core competence (explicit and tacit knowledge). In daily operations, then, the "Nokia Way" has played a crucial role in keeping the company on track. The process started with meetings across the world to brainstorm Nokia's priorities. The results of these meetings were conveyed to top managers, who distilled the discussion into a strategic vision for the company. This vision was then communicated back through the ranks by means of PowerPoint presentations. These presentations provided a strategic guide to the current road map. Among others, Ilkka Raiskinen, a vice president on Nokia's project in digital convergence, argued that employees would not put up with the Nokia Way meetings if they did not convey valuable information. "Our people are also reading Dilbert," he said. "So you get that feedback quite soon: Is your vision statement a quote from Dilbert or does it convey a message?"[22]

Strategic Inflection Points and Dominant Designs

In the medium term, Nokia's paradigm consisted of corporate and business strategies and strategic architecture. Since the 1980s, this architecture has evolved in four phases articulating the central corporate challenges:

- First generation: analog cellular (early 1980s)
- Second generation: digital networks (late 1980s to early 1990s)
- Third generation: data and voice communications, i.e., convergence of IP/cellular (late 1990s to early 2000s)
- Fourth generation: wireless/wireline broadband transparency (2010 and beyond)

At each stage, developments have conformed to the typical characteristics of innovation dynamics and dominant designs.[23] At first, mobile equipment vendors and customers experimented with products and manufacturing. As new entrants have joined rivalry with uniquely designed products, incumbent leaders have sought to perfect their original designs and exhaust competition by rapidly introducing new models as part of an extensive product portfolio. At first, customers have not been wedded to any specific design or company, but with the emergence of a dominant product design, the experimentation has diminished and competition consolidated. As a dominant design has surfaced, the competitive environment once characterized by many companies and many unique designs has been replaced with an environment that contains only a few companies with largely similar product designs.

This framework of innovation and dominant design has been relatively well known since the early 1970s. While the cellular industry has conformed to the general characteristics of the framework, there have been two significant differences that have been peculiar to the mobile business. Until recently, the framework has been applied in industries that have been market-driven or located in the United States or both (i.e., cars, typewriters, PCs, operating systems). In contrast, the mobile cellular industry emerged within the context of traditional telecommunications, which was usually, but not always, regulated and nationally specific. Second, the framework has usually been applied in industries where relatively few radical changes have been incorporated into the system following the emergence of a dominant design. Increasing segmentation has served as a basis for differentiation. To some extent, the mobile industry exhibits similar characteristics. With each new technology generation, performance has improved significantly, prices have eroded, and perceived quality has been enhanced. The transition from one generation to another has been relatively dramatic, comparable to a shift from mainframes to minicomputers or from PCs to Internet-enabled systems. As a result, the most competitive developments can be situated in the nodal points between a declining technology (e.g., analog mobile) and a new, substitute architecture (e.g., digital cellular).

Historically, these strategic inflection points have created the winners and losers of the industry; witness the rise of the Nordic players in the course of the first generation, or Nokia's handset leadership in the second generation as Motorola lost ground by continuing to focus on analog systems. Such strategic inflection points also gave rise to Intel Chairman Andrew S. Grove's motto, "Only the paranoid survive."[24] Intense competition and the Schumpeterian "creative destruction" alert the CEO against attacks by other companies, both rivals and partners, and to inculcate this vigilance in the workforce. Not surprisingly, Ollila has remarked on the significance of Grove's motto in his own management views.

How, then, has Nokia benefited from technology cycles? Since the 1960s, the company has sought to take advantage of not just each technology generation but in particular the strategic inflection points separating one from the other, at first instinctively and later through strategic management (see Exhibit 7-10). In the first generation, Nokia made use of its electronics division, gained first-generation advantages in analog mobile, and benefited from Nordic cooperation. During the second generation, the company entered an era of rapid growth, gained advantages in digital cellular, made a successful bet on GSM as the major standard, and reaped the benefits of EU support. In the early phases of the 3G rivalry, Nokia continued rapid growth and solidified its strategic leadership while seeking first-mover benefits in the nascent

Exhibit 7-10. Nokia and four technology generations.

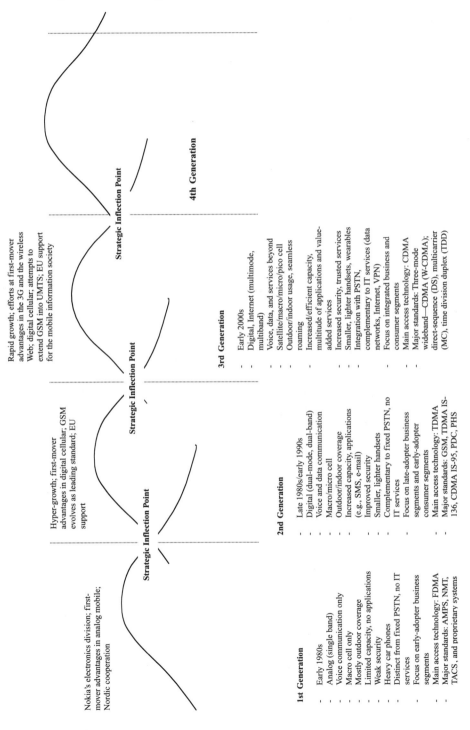

Nokia's electronics division; first-mover advantages in analog mobile; Nordic cooperation

Hyper-growth; first-mover advantages in digital cellular; GSM evolves as leading standard; EU support

Rapid growth; efforts at first-mover advantages in the 3G and the wireless Web; digital cellular; attempts to extend GSM into UMTS; EU support for the mobile information society

Strategic Inflection Point

Strategic Inflection Point

Strategic Inflection Point

4th Generation

1st Generation
- Early 1980s
- Analog (single band)
- Voice communication only
- Macro cell only
- Mostly outdoor coverage
- Limited capacity, no applications
- Weak security
- Heavy car phones
- Distinct from fixed PSTN, no IT services
- Focus on early-adopter business segments
-- Main access technology: FDMA
-- Major standards: AMPS, NMT, TACS, and proprietary systems

2nd Generation
- Late 1980s/early 1990s
- Digital (dual-mode, dual-band)
- Voice and data communication
- Macro/micro cell
- Outdoor/indoor coverage
- Increased capacity, applications (e.g., SMS, e-mail)
- Improved security
- Smaller, lighter handsets
- Complementary to fixed PSTN, no IT services
- Focus on late-adopter business segments and early-adopter consumer segments
-- Main access technology: TDMA
-- Major standards: GSM, TDMA IS-136, CDMA IS-95, PDC, PHS

3rd Generation
- Early 2000s
- Digital, Internet (multimode, multiband)
- Voice, data, and services beyond
- Satellite/macro/micro/pico cell
- Outdoor/indoor usage, seamless roaming
- Increased/efficient capacity, multitude of applications and value-added services
- Increased security, trusted services
- Smaller, lighter handsets, wearables
- Integration with PSTN, complementary to IT services (data networks, Internet, VPN)
- Focus on integrated business and consumer segments
-- Main access technology: CDMA
-- Major standards: Three-mode wideband—CDMA (W-CDMA); direct-sequence (DS), multicarrier (MC), time division duplex (TDD)

3G markets. Concurrently, the company proactively worked the industry forums to influence attempts to extend the GSM standard into the UTMS space while obtaining EU support for its "mobile information society."

When Kairamo began to push Nokia from diversification to technology in the late 1970s, his mantra was to the point: "Finland has few resources. Briefly put, there are two of them: the people and the trees."[25] In the early 1990s, a small company needed big talent. The old Nokia had been about comparative advantage and natural resources. The new Nokia would be about competitive advantage and human capital. Second, the company had to cope with a problem common to many technology companies: how to attract, recruit, nurture, and retain highly skilled technical talent. In addition to issues pertaining to human capital and technology, Nokia had to resolve human resource management (HRM) problems stemming from the company's rapid globalization. Nokia's strategic intent would never have succeeded without its people. At the company, human resource issues have been treated as strategic issues as well.

Human Resource Management

HRM encompasses value activities such as recruiting, hiring, training, development, and compensation. It supports both business and corporate processes (e.g., hiring of programmers) and the entire value chain (e.g., stock options and compensation as reward mechanisms). In most companies, HRM activities occur in different parts of a company, but dispersion of these activities may lead to inconsistent policies. Although its strong corporate culture and values have often promoted coordination, Nokia was not an exception—especially as its customer base migrated away from Finland while most of its production and R&D remained there.

The Nokia Way

New employees at Nokia receive a booklet that spells out the Nokia Way, including this message from Ollila himself:

To You from J. O
Nokia's way of operating—
Connecting People

Nokia unites people
In open, honest cooperation.
It offers equal opportunities
To develop skills and know-how.

Nokia unites people
All over the world
By manufacturing innovative
Products and solutions.
Its goal is customer satisfaction.

THE MORE YOU WILL DO FOR NOKIA,
THE MORE NOKIA CAN DO
FOR YOU

When Ollila initiated Nokia's transformation in 1993, the Nokia Way played a critical role in communicating the company's evolving vision, strategy, and values.

"The value definition discussions began in business units," said Riitta Weiste, chief of Nokia's human resource development in Finland. "At first, the analysis focused on the factors that had been the pillars and strengths of the unit. Of course, unit leadership participated in the discussions, but so did the personnel. Afterwards, Nokia's corporate leadership analyzed each unit's efforts in order to define the Nokia values."[26]

Nokia's value debate also gave rise to the slogan, "Connecting People." (As the company began to globalize and more and more Nokians found themselves overseas, the travel-weary Finns came up with a slogan of their own, "Disconnecting Families."). At Nokia, the company's values are sometimes taken so seriously that Finnish journalists joke that they are holy.

Contemporary Nokia was built on Kairamo's dictum that people should replace trees. The success of the company has relied on attracting, developing, and retaining the most talented people. It has also required an environment that nurtures creativity and the collective realization of individual ideas.[27] Despite its rapid growth, Nokia has continued to stress a corporate culture more typical of an independent, innovative, and creative start-up. The objective has been to maintain this culture no matter how large the company might become. The Nokians think the best way to achieve this goal is through leadership rather than traditional management. This leadership begins with disseminating Nokia's values to everyone in the organization:

1. A drive to achieve customer satisfaction.
2. Respect for the individual.
3. Willingness to achieve and belief in continuous learning.
4. Encouraging sharing (information and responsibility) and open-ness (to each other and to new ideas).

These values are extended worldwide, with some local differences. Additionally, Nokia recognizes three fundamental principles in its operations: always working according to strict, ethical principles; serving the society in which the employees work; and protecting the environment in which one works and lives.

The New Nokians

An argument could be made that Ollila's Nokia has little to do with Kairamo's Nokia. It is not just a different company; it is inhabited by a workforce very different in terms of age and background.

At its peak in 1988, Kairamo's Nokia had almost 44,600 employees, more than 21,500 of them in Finland. After restructuring, the workforce had been cut to 26,800 people, with fewer than 13,800 in Finland. Between 1993 and 1999, the workforce doubled in number and grew in diversity. At the close of 1999, Nokia employed almost 55,300 people in fifty countries, compared to more than 44,500 in forty-five countries a year before. A third of Nokia's employees had worked in the company for less than two years(!). "We will not become a company with more than 100,000 people," said Ollila in one interview after another. In order to retain first-mover advantage, Nokia would have to remain flexible. Big companies, Ollila argued, were too slow. Instead of hiring more people, Nokia would outsource more of its processes.

Nokia's human resource executives define the company as "an international company with a Finnish soul."[28] In 2000, almost 42 percent of Nokia employees were located in Finland, 25 percent in other European countries, 19 percent in the Americas, and 13 percent in Asia-Pacific. Two out of five Nokians worked in Finland. While the role of Finland has remained important in terms of personnel, its growth since 1997 has been more rapid outside Finland, a trend expected to continue. As Nokia continued its global and corporate expansion, the workforce was expected to become increasingly diverse.

Despite its legendary competitiveness in Finland, Nokia's experience in the United States taught the company the meaning of intense competition. "[In the United States], people want comparisons, they want positive results, comparisons between factories, and they want to win," said Rauno Granath, Nokia's site general manager in Dallas–Fort

Worth. "One might say that 'as good as' means not good; instead, one has to be 'better than.' "[29]

In Ollila's Nokia, most of the employees are young, with an average age of thirty-one. To emphasize the international outlook of the company, all are required to speak English. By the late 1990s, the mood at headquarters appeared to be extremely upbeat and highly energetic. Instead of emphasizing job titles, Nokia claimed to downplay internal politics and to promote teamwork. The interview process for job candidates was rigorous, with extensive questioning by both executives and employees to ensure that the recruit was a good fit. Indeed, Ollila exemplified the kind of conversational intensity and directness that was highly reminiscent of the corporate culture at Intel and Microsoft. "Downright scary," comment some Nokians who do not know how to handle the CEO's famous "stare."

Strategic Flexibility and Cross-Functional Teams

Nokia believes that the combined competencies of the whole organization, its operational mode, and efficient processes, served as the foundation for future success and growth. The Nokia Way has often been characterized as a flat, networked organization facilitating speed and flexibility in decision making. Equal opportunity, openness, and respect for individuals and their ideas are regarded as essential elements when dealing with customers, suppliers, or other Nokia employees.

"Investing in people" has been a key method of improving the company's operational performance, management, and appraisal processes. It has involved discussions concerning objectives, performance measures, strengths, professional development, training needs, and feedback on individual performance. In terms of the future, the company's most important challenges include identifying and further developing competencies and promoting strong networking skills to absorb various individual skills into Nokia's collective know-how. To achieve these goals, the company encourages job rotation within the company—from Ollila's executive board to all levels of the workforce.

At Nokia, daily work is often carried out in cross-functional teams. Social interaction skills and the ability to understand different cultures have long been emphasized in various courses offered through Nokia Learning Centers. With employees of thirty nationalities, the NRC reflects the truly global company of the future. To ensure achievement of its goals, Nokia obtains regular feedback from all of its employees through its annual "Listening to You Survey," administered by an independent company.

Nokia's strategists consider environmental change critical to challengers that aspire to overthrow incumbents. While product development, marketing, and branding are important aspects of doing business, they alone are not enough to overthrow the market leaders. Winners have to move quickly. Within a changing environment, time is the scarcest resource, so Nokia established a measure for success: "return on time." It is this measure that guides organizational processes and poses different requirements for productivity, quality, and fast throughput. The Nokians have identified three critical challenges for companies operating in a rapid-growth environment, challenges that hold particular importance for NMP.[30]

1. *Create organizational conditions for rapid growth.* A rapid-growth company must first create an organizational structure that will enable the kind of expansion and increased number of employees that growth requires without slowing or stifling core processes in the organization. The structure of smaller companies supports rapid growth, but big companies may accomplish this if they are formed of small, entrepreneurial cells, as evidenced by General Electric in the early 1980s or ABB in the late 1980s. While both have demonstrated that it is possible to combine scale economies with small-company advantages, neither has been in a business where rapid growth is the condition of survival. In the 1990s, NMP adopted the kind of value management that had been tested in GE and ABB in order to "glue" the small cells to the organizational whole. However, rather than adopt a formalized plan for such management, the Nokians favored a tacit agreement that allowed strategic flexibility and thus rapid growth.

2. *Don't recruit, marinate.* A rapid-growth company needs new employees. Under the pressure of multiple-year rapid growth, it is easy to make significant mistakes in employee recruitment (e.g., recruiting criteria, employee assessments, and the scale of required personnel). Recruiting criteria, in particular, should be kept clear. A rapid-growth company needs employees who can be aligned quickly with the processes and values of the company. Additionally, these employees must be capable of dealing with the kinds of unpredictability and uncertainty that come with rapid growth. At NMP, for instance, the focus was not just on recruiting but on "marinating" that begins with orientation and ends with highly refined team training. The boundaries between the concepts of "work" and "learning" are eliminated. Marinating also includes the annual "road show" conducted by the corporate leadership. Nokia's executives first took their strategy and objectives on the road in 1995, presenting them to every fourth employee in the course of a day. These meetings facilitated interaction between the company's leadership and its personnel.

3. *Reinforce humility*. The Nokians are painfully aware of the industry history as a cycle of success and failure. As companies boost capabilities that ensure success in the current marketplace, they often render themselves vulnerable to rigidities that can lead to future decline. Because the success of a rapid-growth company is critically dependent on strategic inflection points, times of radical transition provide the window new competitors need to overthrow industry incumbents, hence the importance of broad scanning of environmental changes, ceaseless analysis and critique of core processes, and understanding change mechanisms through inflection points (e.g., scenarios and hypothetical alternative development paths). Renewed success is not possible without rapid and responsive identification and interpretation of external changes. Nokians are trained to respect humility rather than arrogance.

Networking, customer satisfaction, teamwork, and continual learning—these characteristics surface again and again in depictions of the Nokia teams (of five to seven employees) and allow the large, international company to operate like a small one, rapidly and with great flexibility.[31] A recent focal point of Nokia's learning program was failure. Unsurprisingly, perhaps, the usefulness of analyzing *failures* as a part of organizational learning parallels Nokia's strategic shift toward the mobile Internet. On the one hand, this attitude made possible an entrepreneurial environment where occasional failures come with the territory. On the other hand, failures provided important learning experiences as the company moved from digital cellular toward the mobile information society.

Intellectual Property Resources

In the future, Nokia expects to become a "knowledge company," perceiving human capital to be critical in value creation and value extraction. The company seeks to understand how to use the knowledge (intellectual capital) of its employees (as well as suppliers, channels, partners, and even rivals) as a major source of competitive advantage.[32] The mobile vendor learned the lesson of what it now calls the "intellectual property resources strategy" the hard way.

By the end of the 1990s, IBM had one of the most extensive patent portfolios worldwide earning more than $1 billion in license revenues annually. Yet, the ability and willingness to commercialize intellectual capital emerged only in the 1980s, when managers, academics, and consultants began to view a company's intangible assets as its intellectual capital and as a significant source of competitive advantage. On the surface, these ideas were not exactly foreign to Nokia. Hiroyuki

Itami attributed the successful performance of Japanese challengers to these companies' intangible assets in the early 1980s. The idea of hidden competitive determinants in human capital—though vague and only tentatively developed—inspired the slogans of Kairamo and the urgings of Koski. The first "knowledge company" formulations evolved in Sweden.[33] By the 1990s, these approaches found expression in the *Knowledge-Creating Company* by Ikujiro Nonaka and Hirotaka Takeuchi, two management researchers who saw Japanese companies' superior innovation on the basis of their knowledge-creation capabilities. The linkages between the Finns and the Japanese were institutionalized soon thereafter.[34]

It was not theory but business practices that motivated Nokia's quest for intellectual capital and knowledge creation. At the end of the 1980s, Motorola accused Nokia and its U.S. partner, Tandy, of breaching Motorola's patents for hand portables, taking the complaint to the U.S. International Trade Commission in spring 1989. The judicial process was a learning experience for the Finnish company. Near the end of 1989, the patent lawsuit was dropped as the two companies settled the dispute and Nokia obtained licenses for some of Motorola's patents. At the time, the Nokians interpreted the complaint as a "legal means to compete for world leadership," not a real technical disagreement. Over time, however, Nokia adopted Motorola's patent posture, thereby protecting its own intellectual capital. In the late 1980s, even though Nokia had evolved into a diversified technology conglomerate, it filed only ten patent applications per year. Inventions were considered occasional chance events. "The view of corporate leadership was that it just didn't make any sense to hire people to invent things," recalls Esko Friman, then chief of the industrial group. "So the patent engineer sat alone in his room. Essentially, there were no conflicts, but nor were there license revenues."[35]

Because product cycles evolve very quickly, the Finns thought that by the time they were granted a patent the products would be declining. This perspective changed drastically with the Motorola court case that concerned the most important of the GSM patent license agreements. Now that Nokia understood the strategic function of patent information, the company went on to create its own patent portfolio. "We understood that the entire company abounded [in] inventions," recalls Friman, "it's just that nobody had made a note of it before. So we created training and reward systems and sought to improve the appreciation for patenting."[36] These efforts paralleled Nokia's earliest investments in global branding in the early 1990s. Again, the Finnish mobile vendor thought in terms of its *entire* value chain, not just of distinct and separate company functions. Since accelerating price erosion would be a reality in the marketplace, Nokia could use patent strategy to protect its upstream innovation, whereas branding strategy served to insulate its downstream innovation. In both cases, the ultimate objective involved, as industrial economists would put it, "monopoly rents."

Typically, while Motorola's suit may have provided a legal model for patent infringements, the Finnish company chose to emulate Japanese companies in developing its patent strategy. In Japan, industrial productivity had been growing more rapidly than in the United States. In fact, Nokia has drawn comparisons between its patenting program and that of Toshiba. Nokia filed approximately 800 patent applications in 1998 and 1,000 a year later. With more than one hundred employees working in its patent office and patents being filed domestically and abroad, patents had become another important part of doing business at Nokia. The number of patent applications at Ericsson exceeded 1,000 in 1997; Motorola filed 2,000 applications annually by 1999, and even Alcatel filed about 700.

Attracting and Retaining the Best and the Brightest

Through the latter half of the 1990s, both independent and in-house research indicated that, overall, Nokia had very good relations with its people. Nokia's human resource policies had played a vital role in attracting the best and the brightest; its employees were said to be "the most technologically savvy individuals in all of Scandinavia." Nokia's 34,000 employees were paid above-average wages, and all received a bonus of 5 percent of their salary if profit growth beat 35 percent per year. More than 2,000 executives also received lucrative stock options. The company continued its general shift toward performance-based compensation as the stock options scheme was extended from 2,000 to 5,000 individuals.[37] In addition, Nokia instituted various other performance-based incentive plans.[38]

Through stock options, Nokia had also generated quite a few millionaires, which led to a national debate on options and income polarization.[39] While the motivations of this debate may be understandable, it led to no viable alternative solutions. Stock options was an important tool for attracting and retaining top talent and has become an industry-wide practice among technology companies. "Resources must be moved to growing industries," argued Bengt Holmström, an MIT economist and Nokia board member. "Stock options make it possible to recruit executives in market-driven change."[40] Yet he and many other Nokians expected options to lose their attractiveness when the ongoing technological and economic change stabilized.

While rewards and incentives were critical to attract and retain appropriate talent, even options were no assurance of employee satisfaction in a country where quality-of-life issues matter greatly. Reijo Paajanen, for example, managed Nokia's Wireless Business Products unit and was considered the founding father of the famed Nokia Communicator. In 1999, the unit was moved to Nokia Internet Communications in the United States. That move translated into new opportunities as well as relocating to Silicon Valley, but what might have been a paradise to many was a nightmare to Paajanen, who left Nokia and launched his own start-up in Finland. "I don't want to be a busy cell phone father who's always traveling," said Paajanen. "I want a good life with my family."[41] Like many Silicon Valley companies competing for the best talent in the United States, Nokia had to dedicate great attention to developing incentives and rewards that worked for its employees located worldwide. "Values keep an international company together, like a glue," argued Ollila. "In building commitment, they are a far better instrument than money or options."[42]

Nokia also had a university program that maintained relationships with more than one hundred universities and institutions of higher learning worldwide. The program included activities that ranged from sponsoring research to encouraging employees to take part-time teaching positions. To make learning as efficient as possible and to unify its training processes across the company, Nokia established its first of four Nokia Learning Centers in 1998.[43]

Due to the company's rapid growth, Nokia recruited approximately 12,000 new employees in 1999 alone, and the pace was expected to continue. Hallstein Mørk, who was in charge of global HRM (and had himself been recruited only in 1998), remarked, "As history has shown, success includes its weak spots." "One can avoid the threat of complacency by setting new, tough objectives."[44] Mørk was the first non-Finnish senior vice president among Nokia's senior executives, though not a member of the group executive board. Over time, he expected globalization to change the face of the company's group leadership as well. In practice, a truly global HRM strategy had been implemented in very few companies. At Nokia, Mørk saw different challenges. "A continuing, drastic pace of growth requires that we must be able to appeal to people, as an employer. Therefore, we're now developing a global infrastructure for human resource management, a worldwide system in order to ensure efficiency in resource management as well."[45]

Internationalization meant deepening polarization between Nokia's U.S.-based and Finland-based employees, however. The design of Nokia's options and bonuses was identical worldwide, but local circumstances determined their level. "In our salary policies, we must work according to the markets. We can't pay more than the markets, nor can we pay less." The trend was toward performance-based hires.

"Apparently, firms are shifting fixed expenditures into variable expenditures in order to ensure that employees truly bring in added value. In this regard, the United States is ahead of the Nordic countries."[46] Furthermore, Nokia's HRM may have been very attractive in the Nordic countries, but it was quite ordinary in the United States. The faster and more extensively Nokia sought to build new capabilities in the mobile Internet, the more it engaged in M&A activities and strategic coalitions in California, Texas, and New York. With the strategic transition, HRM issues became more complex and harder to execute.[47]

In the long run, Nokia was vulnerable in compensation issues. As long as the company was growing, such problems remained suppressed. When the tide would turn, things might look quite different.

Part III

Toward the Mobile Information Society

Nokia's R&D: Focusing and Globalizing

IN late 1999, Nokia's leadership seemed almost invincible. It commanded nearly 30 percent of the world's mobile phone market, compared to Motorola's 25 percent and Ericsson's 14 percent, and the market was expected to double in volume within the next three to four years. The extra scale ensured volume efficiencies that smaller players would find hard to match. Nokia's market capitalization had soared to $106 billion, 5.4 times its revenues (by spring 2000, it would climb to $250 billion).[1] However, sustaining these results would require a new kind of strategic maneuvering in the mobile Internet. In this quest, Nokia was critically dependent on R&D efforts, which were dramatically accelerating.

From Finnish Innovation to Nokia's R&D

When Ollila replaced Vuorilehto as CEO in 1992, he quickly ramped up R&D activities in Helsinki, Tampere, and Oulu. At the same time, he tightened relationships with key suppliers, building Nokia's U.S. headquarters in Fort Worth, Texas, near chip supplier Texas Instruments. Focusing the company on mobile communications, Ollila's strategy required speed and timing. As the digital GSM standard took off in Europe, Nokia introduced easy-to-use cell phones to the world market. Influenced by the Japanese mass-customization approach, Nokia engineered its phones so that the same models could be adapted to the varying frequencies and standards around the world. Through the 1990s, Nokia strengthened and solidified its market positions in Europe, the United States, Asia-Pacific, and Latin America. Concentrating on the fragmented U.S. market, Motorola continued to pump research into analog technology. That left Europe and the growing digital markets in Asia largely to Nordic mobile vendors, Nokia and Ericsson. This R&D posture boosted Nokia's fortunes throughout the 1990s, but by the end of the decade, this strategy was no longer enough to sustain Nokia's market leadership.

In most companies, technology development encompasses a range of activities that reflect efforts to improve products and processes. At Nokia, R&D has been understood more broadly than in many other companies, applying to the *entire* value chain rather than just the traditional engineering department. Innovation has also influenced both the upstream (operations, new product development, logistics) and downstream processes (marketing, sales, service). This approach to R&D is unique, and the company's strategic R&D decisions demonstrate how technology-intensive companies can optimize the use of capital allocations in complex, fast-cycle industries.

Finland's National Innovation System

Nokia's R&D initiatives in Finland, especially during the 1980s and the first half of the 1990s, must be considered against the background of the national innovation system. While science and research have long been priorities of the economy, investments in R&D began to rise steadily only in the 1990s.

In the mid-1980s, electrical engineering manufacturers were experiencing stagnant markets and fierce competition. Still, electronics grew rapidly, and product range expanded from consumer electronics to include computers; communications equipment; and monitoring, control, and measuring equipment. Although electronics was still small compared to other industries, many Finns believed that it had good long-term prospects. At this time, both industry and government entities began paying greater attention to the development of high technology, especially in the electronics industry (see Exhibit 8-1).

The major players in electronics were intent on specializing in high value-added products and banded together to optimize R&D efforts and share expenses. The government, in turn, facilitated this cooperative effort by establishing the National Technology Agency (TEKES) in 1983. Despite this, Finland's R&D remained less than 1.5 percent of the GDP (well behind the OECD average of 2.2 percent in 1985). This figure rose to more than 2 percent in 1991. However, it was only after the collapse of the Soviet Union that the Finns could truly participate in European R&D projects and initiatives. Unlike many other European countries, Finland had missed out on the Marshall Plan and the ensuing technology transfer programs due to the Cold War. Now the Finns were rushing to catch up. "Technology provides keys for growth," argued Martti Mäenpää, former director general of

Exhibit 8-1. Milestones of Finnish technology policy.

1979	National technology committee
1982	Council of State resolution on technology policy
1983	Founding of TEKES
1984	Technology programs started
1985	EUREKA started
1986	OECD assessment of Finland's science and technology policy
	EU framework agreement on research cooperation
1990	Report of the technology program committee
1991	Finland becomes a member of CERN
1992	Finland chairs EUREKA
	Founding of Finland's EU R&D secretariat
1993	Ministry of Trade and Industry national industrial strategy
1994	EEA agreement intensifies research cooperation with the EU
1995	Finland becomes a member of the EU
	Finland becomes a member of the European Space Agency (ESA)
	Funding of energy technology transferred to TEKES from the Ministry of Trade and Industry
1996	Government decision to increase R&D funding
1997	Founding of Employment and Economic Development Centers
1998	Finland's R&D funding reaches 3% of GDP
1999	Finland becomes president of the EU

SOURCE: Finland's National Technology Agency (TEKES).

TEKES.[2] With the new national cluster strategy, the domestic innovation system became a key priority in the government agenda between 1992 and 1994. This effort boosted the national competitive advantage, placing the small country among the most competitive nations in the world.[3] The proportion of R&D investments of Finland's GDP increased from 1.4 percent to 3.01 percent between 1984 and 1998, which was more than that of Germany, Japan, or even the United States. The country also assumed a more active role in international technology cooperation. In the 1990s, Finnish companies in particular increased their R&D investment by 15 to 20 percent annually.[4] By 2000, the volume of European cooperative R&D in Finland was nearly FIM 1 billion (EUR 170 million) per year.

In 1995, the value of high-technology exports in Finland exceeded that of its imports, a historical milestone for the country.[5] Three years later, high-technology products accounted for nearly 19 percent of total Finnish exports, compared to only 4 percent in 1988. Today, Finnish high-technology exports consist primarily of telecommunications equipment, computers, instrumentation, space equipment, and chemicals. With the rise of R&D, the electronics and electrical industries have together become the third supporting pillar of Finland's economy.

In 1998, Finland's investments in R&D amounted to FIM 19.7 billion, while Nokia's R&D expenditures had reached FIM 6.8 billion, accounting for approximately 35 percent of the entire country's R&D investments. The figures, however, were not entirely comparable. Nokia's R&D expenditures included investments in domestic and foreign research institutions, universities, and companies. In interviews, Ollila has suggested that these expenditures account for about a third of the company's FIM 6.8 billion in R&D. On the other hand, a number of Finnish technology funds, in particular TEKES, invested in R&D programs that also benefited Nokia as it has sought to strengthen bilateral cooperation, particularly with the United States and Japan.[6]

When Finnish authorities initiated a critical review of future technology expenditures in 2000, Ollila called for an even "deeper dialogue between the private sector and the research and educational institutions": "Knowledge and expertise have become key determinants in economic and social development. Those countries that are able to specialize in information-intensive industries will succeed in the future. The winners and losers will be selected by the decisions that are made today. . . ."[7] Until the early 1990s, Finland's innovation system was a strong supporter of Nokia's R&D initiatives, but since that time R&D expansion has been driven by global R&D networks.

Nokia Research Center

Nokia's R&D unit has played a central role in the company's new-product development efforts, with R&D activities increasing rapidly through the 1990s. By the end of 1999, approximately one-third of the 55,000 Nokians worked in R&D. Of these 17,000 employees, only about 1,000 worked at the NRC, which had sites in six countries and R&D centers in fourteen.

Nokia did its utmost to integrate R&D into the whole corporate process, with activities taking place both within the individual business units and at the NRC. To monitor technological developments, the center maintained strong global contacts. It actively participated in the work of standardization bodies and various international R&D projects in cooperation with universities, research institutes, and other telecommunications and mobile companies. At Nokia, sustainable innovation now meant investing in R&D activities. The NRC sought to embody the entrepreneurial spirit of a small organization expanding to meet the needs of a global environment.[8]

At the end of the 1990s, the NRC was led by Senior Vice President Juhani Kuusi, who had been chief of TEKES until April 1995, when he answered Ollila's personal call. As far as Kuusi was concerned, Finnish technology policy emerged in 1982 when Finland's Council of the State decided to double technology funding to 2.2 percent of the GNP in only a decade. "At the time, that seemed impossible, but we did achieve it," Kuusi recalled.[9] Nokia's technology development has been directed by three veteran senior managers with long careers in telecommunications. Each had a different function in the corporate organization. Kuusi was in charge of the NRC, which gave him a two-year look into the future. Kaj Linden served as Nokia's research director and reported directly to Ollila. Finally, Yrjö Neuvo—who also served on the group executive board and played an important role in the 3G standardization talks—was in charge of product development in Nokia Mobile Phones and reported to Martti Alahuhta. As Ollila steered Nokia toward the "mobile information society," the company also appointed Erkki Ormala in April 1999 to lead Nokia's technology policy. Bringing extensive experience with the EU and OECD working groups in national innovation systems, he would focus on issues involving information technology and knowledge management.[10]

Globalization of R&D

Throughout the 1990s, the growth of Finnish R&D was, for all practical purposes, driven by the expansion of Nokia.[11] In the long run, the company's rapid globalization was bound to strain this virtuous circle. With the mobile Internet, Nokia has been forced to rely increasingly on external rather than internal R&D. As a result, Nokia's very success was bound to heighten tension at its Finnish home base.

The Expansion of Nokia's R&D

From 1983 to the early 1990s, Nokia's R&D expenditures grew steadily from FIM 267 million to FIM 1.2 billion (see Exhibit 8-2a). The decline that occurred in 1991 originated from the sale of Nokia Data to ICL. After a year or two of diminished investments, R&D expenditures began to increase again, but at a faster pace than in the previous decade. During the refocusing of 1993, R&D activities began to accelerate, and expenditures almost tripled to FIM 4.6 billion in just five years. As the company initiated its strategic transformation, R&D expenditures continued to rise, growing to FIM 10.4 billion in 1999.

R&D investments increased fivefold in the course of the 1990s, mirroring the explosive growth of the company itself. Nokia's R&D as a percentage of net sales remained below 5 percent throughout the 1980s (see Exhibit 8-2b). As the telecommunications/mobile segment

Exhibit 8-2. Nokia's R&D, 1983–1999.

(a) Expenditures

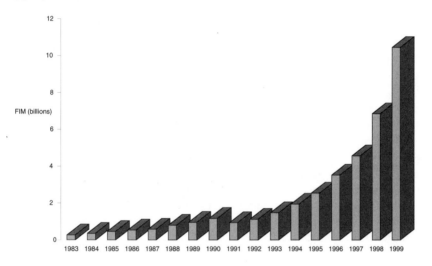

(b) Nokia's R&D as Percent of Sales

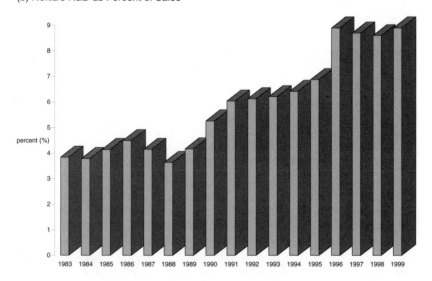

Exhibit 8-2 (continued).

(c) Nokia's R&D Per Segment

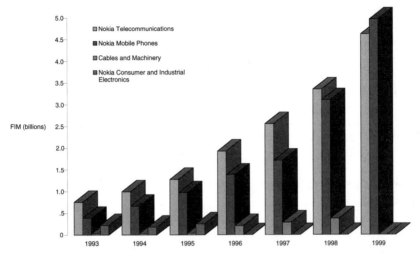

SOURCE: Company reports.

entered its growth course, R&D climbed quickly from 6 percent to 6.9 percent in 1995 and to 8.7–8.9 percent through the latter half of the 1990s (see Exhibit 8-2c). In terms of segments, R&D expenditures in NTC exceeded those of NMP from the early 1990s to 1998; the former grew sixfold, from FIM 752 million to FIM 4.6 billion, whereas the latter soared twelvefold from FIM 386 million to FIM 5 billion.

Between 1995 and 1997, at the height of its focus on cellular but before the transition to the mobile Internet strategy, Nokia spent some 4 to 7 percent of its revenue in R&D. While these investments had been steadily accelerating, they were behind those of Nokia's rivals, Motorola and Ericsson. By the end of the 1990s, Ericsson's R&D expenditures accounted for 16 percent of its revenues, whereas at Nokia the proportion was only half that. Ericsson invested in R&D three times more than Nokia (Ericsson's definition of R&D, however, was considered relatively broad). In Finland, more than half of Ericsson's employees were involved in R&D (615 to 715 of 1,100 employees).[12] "They joke that any problem can be resolved if only you lock 25 Finns in the same room long enough," said Rolf Svanbäck, Ericsson's chief of product development in Finland.[13]

Still, Nokia had a sophisticated and well-capitalized new product development division. In addition, many of its R&D facilities were strategically located within walking distance of those universities with which Nokia had strong ties. In this phase, Nokia's R&D strategy was to develop *generic* platforms that could be quickly adapted to different standards and to avoid development of proprietary component technology. Nokia chose to focus on software development, because software is the principal value-added component in a handset. This approach fit well with the company's overall strategy of speed to market with innovative products that covered multiple standards. In the past, Nokia had concentrated on channeling almost all R&D efforts into the development of high-margin, high-end handsets. The strategy worked well, as the company sold older models to the low-end market. What's more, as this market grew in size and sophistication, Nokia took the opportunity to familiarize these low-end customers with its quality products. This allowed the company to build its brand and induce customers to trade up to higher value phones.[14]

Since the 1980s, Nokia's R&D has played a critical role in executing the company's strategic intent, especially in scenarios for the future. However, the company's success was not achieved without some missteps.

Take, for instance, the "Nokia Future Watch," a state-of-the-art strategy and knowledge creating project, vital to the Nokia Telecommunications (NTC). The failure of the project does illustrate the fact that, in emergent markets, companies such as Nokia must often bet the future, and sometimes even the best jockeys choose the wrong horses.[15]

Standardization and Downstream Innovation

Throughout the 1990s, Nokia has closely aligned R&D and new-product development activities, but the nature and direction of this alignment has been unique in the industry. Unlike some of its key cellular rivals, Nokia has opted *not* to possess its own semiconductor production, choosing to buy its components. While this strategic decision has enabled Nokia to avoid the heavy expenditures and significant risks involved with semiconductors, it has rendered the company more vulnerable than its cellular competitors to distribution and market fluctuations. In terms of its value chain, this decision was typical of Nokia's emphasis on downstream innovation at the expense of upstream innovation. While its rivals have developed new technologies, Nokia has been more intent on listening to the customers.[16]

This focus on downstream innovation has not been the sole distinctive characteristic of Nokia's R&D. The absence of semiconductors and component production in its business segments has accounted for its concentration on and founding role in standardization and technology coalitions. Nokia has very often been the initiator in these activities; Ericsson, Motorola, and an array of other major industry giants have been involved as well. In the press, this aspect of Nokia's strategy has often been mistaken for an ethical dictum. By the close of the 1990s, for instance, Linus Torvalds, the founder of Linux, and Nokia joined forces against Microsoft. When Torvalds's company, Transmeta, unveiled its technology plans and launched the Crusoe family of processors in January 2000, it aimed to compete against the chip giant Intel with two processors used for distinct classes of devices. With its two chips, Transmeta was attacking the crumbling Wintel empire that had united Intel and Microsoft. Certainly, there has been and remains a certain moral dimension to open standards. In practice, they have been Nokia's only viable strategic option, after the company decided to reject in-house component production and reduced its role on the upstream innovation side of the value chain.

The Global R&D Network

By 1994, the mission of the NRC was to "enhance Nokia's technological competitiveness, core competencies and knowledge of new systems."[17] In order to support company-wide strategic objectives, the center has had to be a step or two ahead of strategic execution, particularly in the GSM and development of the 3G mobile communications standard, the UMTS.[18]

By 1998, approximately 70 percent of the center's funding came from other Nokia businesses vis-à-vis contracted R&D projects. Some 10 percent of the R&D funding originated from public sources, in particular TEKES and the EU, and another 10 percent from the Nokia Group. By the end of 1999, Nokia's R&D exceeded the budget of all Finnish universities and academic institutions. That year, the NRC invested over EUR 1.750 billion into R&D, up by 53 percent over the previous year. By then, about one-third of Nokia's more than 55,000 employees worldwide were involved in R&D activities. Yet, it is difficult to estimate the true expenditures of the NRC or the geographic distribution of its R&D globally. Of the more than 17,000 employees in Finland, only 1,000 worked at the NRC, which had sites in six countries.[19]

In the past, many industry leaders have located their R&D activities in their home base, thinking that it is important to keep R&D close to the place where strategic decisions are made. By the end of the twentieth century, however, many established R&D networks were housed in foreign countries in order to tap the knowledge there or to commercialize products for those markets quickly. Adapting a global approach meant aligning R&D strategy to the company's overall business strategy. Given its efforts to build effective R&D capabilities abroad, Nokia had become the great exception in Finland. Viewed from a global perspective, however, it conformed to the norm. By the late 1990s, senior managers of the most successful R&D networks understood the dynamics of global R&D and linked corporate strategy to R&D strategy. Having picked the appropriate sites, they staffed them with the right people, supervised the sites during start-up, and integrated the activities of the different foreign sites to ensure that the entire network functioned as a coordinated whole.[20]

Understandably, Nokia has not released information on the location or on its key R&D programs. "Our competitors would love to read information on such things," Kaj Linden, Nokia's research director, has said.[21] From publicly available information, however, it is possible to draw the broad outlines of Nokia's worldwide R&D network, which emulated its basic manufacturing configuration and began to be in place in the mid-1990s (Exhibit 8-3). The network consists of three circles of networked activities. The primary R&D concentrations remain in Europe, i.e., Finland, Sweden, and some Western European nations. In the Americas, the primary centers of activity are in the United States. In Asia, similar concentrations are located in Japan, but in the long term, R&D may also operate in China and India.

The Functions of the R&D Sites

By 2000, the NRC had fifty-two R&D centers in fourteen countries in Finland and Scandinavia (Sweden, Denmark), continental Europe (Germany, the United Kingdom), Asia (China, Japan), the Americas (the United States, Canada), and Australia. In selecting new sites, contemporary global companies tend to find it helpful to carefully articulate each site's primary objective.[22] In this regard, Nokia was hardly an exception (see Exhibit 8-4).

Many of Nokia's key R&D resources can be found in close proximity to the company's largest, and critical, production sites in Salo (Finland), Bochum (Germany), Dallas (United States), and Beijing (China). The majority of these sites are typically home-base–augmenting sites, which had been established to tap knowledge from rivals, markets, and universities around the globe. In these sites, information flows from the laboratory to the NRC at home or to key centers worldwide. Since production facilities are also located in Pecs (Hungary), Mexico, Brazil, Dongguan (China), and South Korea, it is reasonable to assume that some R&D functions are located in these regions as well. Only in India did Nokia invest in R&D without production; in this case, the company may have had a long-term view of India's regional market potential.

Most of these sites are home-base–exploiting sites, which had been established to support manufacturing facilities in foreign countries or to adapt standard products to the needs of regional markets.

Exhibit 8-3. Nokia worldwide: Sales offices, production and joint ventures, and R&D (1995).

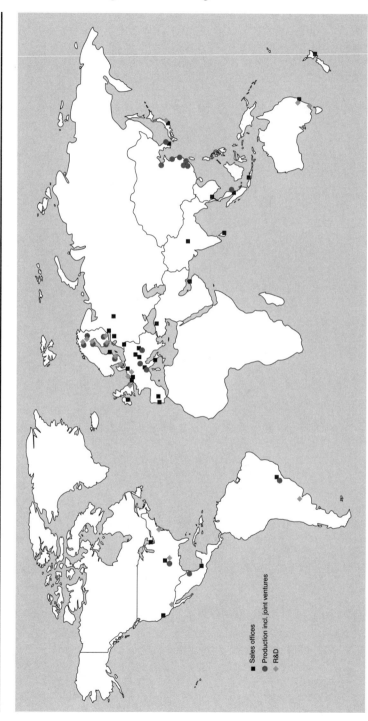

Sales offices
Production incl. joint ventures
R&D

SOURCE: Nokia Annual Report, 1996, p. 74.

Exhibit 8-4. Nokia's worldwide R&D concentrations (1998).

■ Primary R&D concentrations

● Production-related R&D concentrations

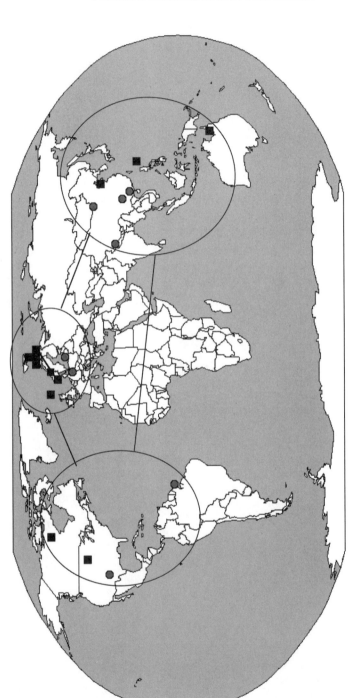

Source: Nokia annual reports.

In these sites, information flows from the NRC to the foreign R&D labs and key centers worldwide.

Typically, home-base–augmenting sites are located in regional clusters of scientific excellence through participation in formal or informal meeting circles, hiring employees from rivals, or sourcing equipment and research services from the competition's suppliers. In contrast, home-base–exploiting sites are located close to large markets and manufacturing facilities in order to commercialize new products rapidly in foreign markets. As a result of the different strategic function of these two kinds of sites, the type of information that is shared differs. Between home-base–augmenting R&D sites and the NRC, technology-related information reigns, whereas between home-base–exploiting sites, information on markets and manufacturing counts the most (see Exhibit 8-5).[23]

R&D and Business Units: Technology Integration

True to its emphasis on leadership and individual respect, the "Nokian Way" has paid less attention to formal manuals and weekly reports than to agreements between R&D functions and their contractors. Also, the NRC has encouraged the rotation of personnel between R&D and other functions, and in fact, the center's activities have been

Exhibit 8-5. Nokia's R&D spheres: information flows between home-base and foreign R&D sites.

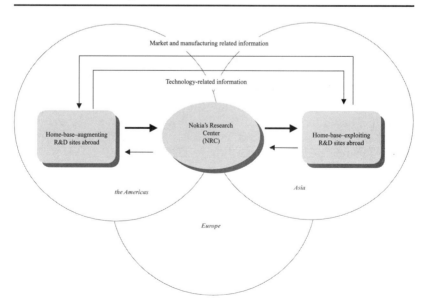

closely aligned with those of all of Nokia's business units. All R&D sites interact on a daily basis, not only with each other but also with all other parts of the company, including those units responsible for strategic planning, production, sales, and marketing functions.

Analysts often use the amount a company spends on R&D as an indicator of its competitive strength. However, despite R&D investments that are lower than some of its competitors, Nokia has proven to be more competitive than Ericsson in cellular handsets. More important than R&D allocations in determining a company's strength is the ability to rapidly and efficiently translate R&D efforts into products that satisfy market needs. It is superior technology integration that best reflects a company's competitive strengths. Nokia's success in the late 1990s paralleled that of U.S. companies that prevailed in the computer industry by abandoning traditional R&D and creating a radically new approach that relied on three central tenets:[24]

Focus on applied science. While industry leaders did not stop conducting basic research, they did shift the focus of these efforts to applied science. Similarly, at Nokia throughout the 1990s, the R&D function became increasingly focused, practical, and applied and continued to be extended globally through networked research communities and intensified collaboration.

Diverse base of suppliers and partners. In addition, new industry leaders have turned to an increasingly diverse base of suppliers and partners in order to generate and multiply technological possibilities. At Nokia, the importance of the platforms triggered a wide array of technology and standards coalitions.

Tightly knit teams. Finally, industry leaders often formed tightly knit teams of experts to develop new generations of major products and processes. Retained over multiple product generations, these team members become the company's repository of integrated system knowledge and provide continuity over several generations of products. At Nokia, in particular, the significance of the group executive board as well as the key product process and customer commitment process teams has been extraordinary.

At Nokia, it is the ability to listen to customer needs and be responsive to them that has defined technology integration in both upstream and downstream processes.

Small, Flexible R&D Teams: Concurrent Engineering

In the technology sector, Nokia's R&D system has often been considered more reasonable and flexible than systems in some large U.S.

companies, where time schedules have not been realistic. Kaj Linden, Nokia's research director, considered fifty employees an ideal size for research units. While Nokia did have smaller subunits, these were typically parts of larger units. Unlike Philips and Siemens, which have massive research centers in Eindhoven and Munich, respectively, Nokia favors smaller, more flexible R&D units. "Bigness just results in a lot of apparent optimization," Linden has argued. "When thousands of people are aggregated into one location, bureaucracies grow and may even regulate when each employee can come to work or take a lunch break. It is better to have 50 rather than 1,000 people in a single location. A large unit is an office, not a voluntary job. Such [an] environment will not be exciting to individuals."[25]

According to Kaj Linden and others, the common denominator of Nokia's R&D stems from concurrent engineering efforts in which product development, sales, and production units cooperate significantly. When product development begins, so does marketing planning. Meanwhile, sales might intervene to explain how features could be embedded in a product so that they are easy for customers to use. While the various business units might approach R&D differently, the R&D process chain itself consists of three phases:

1. Research and technologies, the initial generic development level
2. Technology and platforms, a more focused level involving defined goals and looking beyond immediate product development
3. Concurrent engineering, in which advanced product development is focused on creating products that fulfill customer needs

The timing of the evolution of concurrent engineering (CE) in the United States during the second half of the 1980s is significant. For two decades, American industrial productivity had failed to respond to the Japanese companies that captured world dominance in industry after industry. CE emerged as a new method of product development capable of being continuously upgraded and modified and was expected to reduce cost and development time significantly without sacrificing quality. CE also promised to be simple to comprehend, easy to implement, and easy to adapt to a diverse array of product development activities.[26] Hence, the oft-cited definition of CE:

> Concurrent engineering is a systematic approach to the integrated, concurrent design of products and their related processes, including manufacture and support. This approach is intended to cause the developers, from the outset, to consider all elements of the product life cycle from con-

ception through disposal, including quality, cost, schedule, and user requirements.[27]

From its inception, focus on customer needs and satisfaction penetrated CE. Top quality was considered to be built into the product, the result of continuous improvement of a process. CE envisioned translating the "tiger team" concept to big organizations; such teams would work with a unified product concept. If the team members were at geographically different locations, far-reaching changes in the work culture and ethical values of the organization were required.[28]

The lessons inherent in CE prepared Nokia for a leadership position in the mobile cellular industry,[29] but to dominate the market in the mobile Internet industry the company would have to strengthen its core capabilities and build new ones.

The Genesis of the Single Flexible Standard

Nokia perceived itself among the developers of the information society and continued to build and invest upon extensive know-how through cooperation with leading centers of excellence. The more R&D reached out to the future, the more Nokia and its NRC centers collaborated with business partners. By the close of the 1990s, networking with other companies, research institutes, and universities had become a central part of Nokia's global R&D. In addition to these efforts, its R&D underwent rapid globalization. In January 1997, for instance, Nokia joined the Microelectronics and Computer Technology Corporation (MCTC), becoming the first member headquartered outside North America. To extend its collaborative activities in Asia, the company accelerated research cooperation in China, India, and Japan.[30]

Such activities rapidly transformed Nokia's R&D into a truly global operation, which precipitated changes in other units as well. Yet, at the close of 1999, 70 percent of Nokia's research employees were still Finnish.[31] Although globalization was affecting the NRC, the number of foreign employees in other business units was still higher. At this time, Nokia was rushing to the convergence segments, combining the efforts of its global R&D network with those of its global R&D partners. In public, Nokia's rhetoric for open standards, industry partnerships, and R&D collaboration coincided with stabilizing the R&D function through cooperation. To paraphrase Carl von Clausewitz, the function of these alliances has been competition through other means.

By 2000, Nokia's International Mobile Telecommunications 2000 initiative (IMT-2000)[32]—or 3G in the U.S.—was expected to provide a platform for distributing converging services (e.g., mobile or fixed, voice and/or data, telecommunications, content and/or computing).[33] How could Nokia position itself in a competitive industry that did not yet exist?

Nokia's Initial 3G Efforts

The 1G and 2G cellular systems had been designed for national and regional networks with limited roaming capabilities. While the ITU had issued technical recommendations for how these systems should work together, it had not issued standards for the early systems. Starting in the late 1980s, the ITU began to develop 3G systems that stressed the need for harmonized frequency spectrum and radio interface standards worldwide. The goal was to achieve a global standard for 3G through IMT-2000.

Europe had developed mandatory standards during the 2G period, but the United States followed voluntary standards. The Europeans put their faith in standards they felt would generate markets, while American companies expected the markets to generate the standards.[34] Eventually, the Europeans adopted digital cellular far earlier than the Americans. However, American companies and markets pioneered the Internet revolution while European and Asian companies were compelled to engage in imitation strategies.

Not surprisingly then, the EU saw the 3G competition as the most important opportunity for European companies to reverse strategic positions with Silicon Valley and consumer electronics giants in Japan. In Europe, the objective became to ensure the compatibility of GSM with the 3G standards. The stakes were immense; ITU expected the platform to give rise to 2 billion users worldwide by the year 2010. The first 3G services were expected to launch commercially in 2001, with widespread global deployment by 2005. Even while the 3G licensing was already under way in several countries, early experimental systems were being field tested by the world's leading vendors. In the case of Nokia, work toward a 3G future had started thirteen years earlier.

The idea of strategic intent provides the basis for strategic insights as well. First, a future winner must compete for intellectual leadership. Second, it must compete to shape and shorten the migration paths from the current markets to those of the future. Third, it must compete for market power and position once the new opportunities take off and an industry structure begins to form.

The European Telecommunications Standards Institute (ETSI) played an integral role in the future of the mobile business.

Because of the strong role of politics in European standardization activities, the ETSI has been viewed with suspicion outside Europe, yet the organization has played a key role in the 3G standardization process,[35] with Nokia participating in all its phases. The initial steps of the 3G rivalry were taken in summer 1987, after Heikki Ahava, department chief at the NRC, heard an inspiring presentation by a Philips researcher on broadband digital networks. In Finland, the Defense Forces had become interested in broadband CDMA a year before and funded a research project that began in 1987. At Nokia's request, the project was kept secret. After a stint at Omnitele, which built the world's first GSM network for the Finnish Radiolinja, Ahava returned to Nokia and became its representative at the ETSI in the early 1990s.[36]

As GSM growth took off, Nokia and other mobile vendors used their increasing bargaining power against the powerful telecommunications monopolies, which might have preferred a different standard altogether. Still, as far as Nokia was concerned, the ETSI moved too slowly in GSM-related matters; it would have to be more proactive, and it would have to support competitive mobile vendors rather than monopolistic PTTs. At the ETSI, Ahava began lobbying for Juha Rapeli, who had a reputation of "getting things done." By the mid-1990s, Rapeli became chairman of a technical committee in charge of 3G standards in Europe.[37]

In the 3G rivalry, however, the stakes were far higher than those of the 2G digital cellular competition in the 1980s. Even a regional trading bloc would not suffice to resolve the standards issue, but *two* blocs out of three might be adequate. Nokia had been triumphant in Europe, but now it would have to find an appropriate partner.

Mobile vendors and operators in the United States were not pioneers of the 3G market. Although they knew how to compete, the markets were fragmented and innovation lagging due to diverse 2G standards. Vendors, operators, and consumer electronics giants in Japan had relied on proprietary standards in the 2G rivalry and failed. In the competition for the 3G standards, however, they were among the first movers. The Japanese were pioneering a 3G digital wireless system based on wideband code division multiple access (W-CDMA). Nokia opted for Japanese partners.

The Nordic-Japanese Alignment

Even Kairamo might have been stunned by the extent of Nokia's expansion in the 1990s. He was convinced that the company could thrive among the global giants, but he did not foresee Nokia becoming the dominant world player. Like other Nokians, he thought that the Japanese would capture global leadership in 2G communications, just as they had in consumer electronics:

> We can hardly expect to make it to the top of the world in any industry; it hardly makes sense to even invest in such

things. But in the adaptation of the technology we can be among the first and thrive. In order to accomplish that objective, we can benefit from those very factors that have always been against us, that is, the small size of Finland and Finnish companies. We are flexible. We can develop and change products frequently. We can achieve several production cycles annually.[38]

One of the Nokians' greatest surprises in the late 1980s and 1990s was the weak performance of Japanese competitors in the 2G rivalry. Initially, Japanese players had hoped to use the proprietary PDC standard to cover the Asian markets in response to Europe's GSM challenge. These hopes and visions crashed with the burst of the Japanese bubble economy. Through the 2G rivalry, Japanese consumer electronics giants, such as Panasonic, Sony, and NEC, failed to gain more than a few niche shares in the mobile markets, just as the R&D of the PDC exhausted the resources of Japanese mobile vendors.[39]

Nokia's Efforts to Access the Japanese Markets

At Nokia, the preparation for competition by the Japanese had been in play years before the inception of 3G. After Ollila took charge of Nokia, the company established a presence in Japan, first creating a sales organization with Mitsui, a $134 billion trading company. In just two years, Nokia founded its own research center in Tokyo. As the cellular business was about to explode, the Finns had overcome a severe recession and Nokia was again expanding, while Japan was swept by a painful downturn.

Despite their GSM success, however, Nokia had not been able to fully penetrate the Japanese markets; it competed with mobile phones but not with networks. At first, its PDC sales rose rapidly, and market share in Japan increased to 12 percent by the mid-1990s. By the end of the decade, however, it had declined to 5 percent. In Europe, even the most lightweight phones were more than 100 grams. Although Nokia's new models weighed about 92 grams, market leaders in Japan such as Panasonic sold phones of less than 70 grams. "We underestimated the significance of the smallness and lightness," admitted Olav Stang, chief of Nokia's Japanese activities in early 1999.[40] In the 3G rivalry, neither Nordic nor Japanese players could win on their own; each needed the other to succeed (see Exhibit 8-6).

NTT-DoCoMo and W-CDMA

Formed in 1952 by the Japanese Ministry of Communications to rebuild Japan's war-ravaged phone system, Nippon Telegraph and

Exhibit 8-6. From fragmented 2G markets to the Nordic-Japanese 3G alignment (ca. 1998).

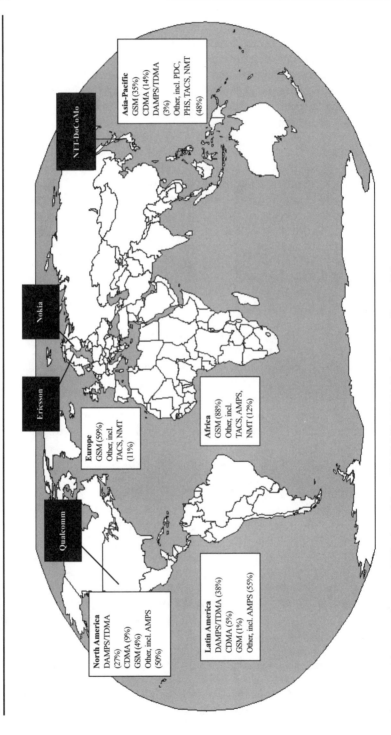

North America
DAMPS/TDMA (27%)
CDMA (9%)
GSM (4%)
Other, incl. AMPS (50%)

Latin America
DAMPS/TDMA (38%)
CDMA (5%)
GSM (1%)
Other, incl. AMPS (55%)

Europe
GSM (59%)
Other, incl. TACS, NMT (11%)

Africa
GSM (88%)
Other, incl. TACS, AMPS, NMT (12%)

Asia-Pacific
GSM (35%)
CDMA (14%)
DAMPS/TDMA (3%)
Other, incl. PDC, PHS, TACS, NMT (48%)

Qualcomm

Ericsson

Nokia

NTT-DoCoMo

SOURCE: Nokia annual reports; ITU, adapted from GSM MoU, CDMA Development Group, Ericsson.

Telephone (NTT) enjoyed a monopoly on fixed-line local and long-distance phone services until the 1990s. Spun off from NTT, DoCoMo ("anywhere") was Japan's leading wireless phone provider. NTT had first gone into mobile communications with a maritime telephone service in 1959, and a decade later the company began offering paging services. Mobile telephone service followed in 1987. DoCoMo took over NTT's personal handphone services (PHS) unit at that time.

In the early 1990s, Nokia had supplied cell phones to NTT-DoCoMo. Just as Nokia hoped to access Asian markets, NTT-DoCoMo was eager to enter European markets. By 1995, the Finns and the Japanese were in talks regarding an alignment. Two years later, Nokia and other European companies declared their support for frames multiple access. EU had funded these projects, which ultimately led Ahava and Yrjö Neuvo to choose a 3G digital wireless system based on W-CDMA. The choice meant an alignment with the Japanese.

Nokia's Scenarios

By 1997, Neuvo and Ahava opted for an alignment with the Japanese and the choice of W-CDMA. First, Neuvo and Ahava had to obtain Nokia's commitment, which proved difficult. Employed by NMP, the two represented the "cell Nokians." Since NMP manufactured cell phones for all major standards, they were the first to embrace the W-CDMA option. The "network Nokians" were a different story. Employed by NTC, they were familiar only with GSM. "Why don't we stick to the basics?" was the argument of the network Nokians, who wanted to focus on what the organization knew best and what the customers wanted. It was a tempting argument but applicable only to sustaining innovation, not disruptive innovation. The 3G rivalry represented a new inflection point. It was all about disruption. Nokia debated the options and then moved ahead.[41]

The final decision was made in February 1997, when Ollila and other board members saw a presentation by Lauri Melamies, the head of Nokia's vision group. He presented three future scenarios. In the first, the markets fragmented, and diverse standards emerged in Europe, Japan, and the United States; competition would be regional, not global. In the second, the standardization project failed and there would be no third generation—everybody would lose; it was a doomsday prediction. In the third scenario, CDMA would be the radio technique between the cell and the base station, *if* NTT-DoCoMo would accept GSM in its 3G infrastructure for traffic between base stations and the switching office. Only this scenario, a "historical compromise," was to the Nokians' liking. As a CDMA convert, Melamies thought that Europe could thrive in competition with the United States, but only as Japan's partner. Conversely, the Nokians thought that Europe would *not* succeed in competition with the Japanese, even if they had U.S. partners.[42]

Nokia's strategic choice was not unique. Previously, Ericsson had opted for a similar strategy. To their great surprise, the two 2G rivals found themselves in the same 3G camp. For decades they had competed with each other; now they would have to cooperate with each other in order to bring about the future of 3G. Together they would persuade the Japanese into a compromise. The Japanese front was not homogeneous, however. NTT-DoCoMo was internally split. NTT, the monopolistic parent, did not want GSM in its infrastructure. DoCoMo, NTT's competitive mobile subsidiary, was eager to cooperate with Nokia and Ericsson.

In May 1997, the representatives of Nokia, Ericsson, and NTT-DoCoMo met in Stockholm. In the aftermath, the Japanese continued to debate the Nordic proposals. Although the talks had been intense, the Nordic partners were optimistic—until they found out they were no longer alone in the competition for the future.

The Crumbling of the European Front?

In 1997, U.S. manufacturers led by Qualcomm announced that they would develop a technology for the 3G cell phones. In 1985, Mark Jacobs, Andrew Viterbi, and several other executives left M/A-COM Linkabit, a digital-signal-processing equipment company they had founded, to launch Qualcomm (*qua*lity *com*munications), a maverick challenger. For years, Jacobs, CEO and chairman of Qualcomm, had dreamed of modifying CDMA for commercial use. By 1989, when the company unveiled its version of CDMA, it had defense contracts worth $15 million. A year later, it interrupted the Cellular Telecommunications Industry Association's (CTIA) plans to adopt a rival technology (TDMA). Instead, NYNEX (now part of Verizon) and Ameritech made plans to use CDMA. Following Qualcomm's PR blitzes, Motorola, AT&T, Clarion, and Nokia signed product development and testing agreements with the company in 1991. Two years later, the CTIA adopted CDMA as the North American standard for wireless communications. By 1996, most major U.S. cellular carriers had upgraded to CDMA, and Jacobs had turned the new corporate entity into a $3 billion, Fortune 500 company.

Qualcomm's surprise announcement shook old coalition boundaries. Of the Nordic partners, Ericsson was familiar with the company, having been engaged in patent conflicts with the R&D company for years. In order to neutralize the U.S. initiative, Nokia and Ericsson rushed to publicize their agreement. At first, the objective prompted an unfortunate reverse reaction, splitting the European front. The Nokia-Ericsson alliance gave rise to opposition by Siemens. Instead of joining the Nordic alliance, the German electric giant decided to oppose it. Siemens had slipped to ninth among worldwide mobile vendors by 1998, and company shares fell 23 percent as net income slumped two-thirds from its 1996 peak of $1.36 billion.[43]

In August 1997, NTT-DoCoMo's CEO, Kouji Ohboshi, and R&D chief, Minoru Kuramoto, visited Finland and promised to join the Nokia-Ericsson camp. A month after Siemens heard of the partnership, it announced—with the French Alcatel and the Canada-based Nortel—that *they* had prepared a proposal of their own for Europe's new standard. Over the summer, Siemens had been in talks with U.S. manufacturers with the objective of forming an alliance between Europe and the United States that would force the Japanese to compromise. By the end of 1997, Motorola and other major equipment vendors had joined the new alliance.

Having struggled for liberalization of European telecommunications since the 1980s, the EC became concerned about the conflict among Europe's leading equipment manufacturers. In the late 1980s, the concept of GSM had matched the EC's objectives of providing comprehensive pan-European services and standards, as well as its willingness to transform European telecommunications from domestic monopolies into a fully competitive environment. At first, GSM had been promoted to achieve pan-European ideals rather than as an instrument for competition, but eventually it was presented as a mechanism for launching competition in European mobile and telecommunications operations, products, and services.[44]

For years, the EC had worked to unite European companies against their competitors in both the United States and Japan. The Internet revolution had enabled the United States to seize leadership in the *wired* digital economy, but GSM had turned Europe into the most *mobile* digital continent. Still, an internal trade struggle threatened to weaken regional competitive advantage, and the European front appeared to be crumbling. At the end of August 1997, Jacques Santer, chairman of the EC, invited the parties to Brussels. Despite the EU's effort, the conflict grew worse. In November, Martin Bangemann, EC commissioner for telecommunications affairs, organized another conference, yet the polarization persisted and became public. Siemens organized a conference in Munich, while Nokia and Ericsson invited most European telephone operators to Amsterdam.

The standardization of CDMA progressed well all over the world, with Nokia as one of its leading contributors.[45] In 1998, Nokia developed and integrated a W-CDMA experimental system consisting of a mobile phone, a base station, and switching equipment. A year later, it was building and expanding these experimental networks for field testing in China, Finland, and Japan to demonstrate further the system's capabilities to existing and new customers. It sought to develop and provide full-system offerings for 3G communications infrastructure in the future, thus providing an evolutionary path to existing *and* new customers. Concurrently, the NRC continued to develop new mobile data services for GSM in addition to its R&D and standardization work on 3G systems (see Exhibit 8-7).[46]

By the end of January 1998, the ETSI voted for the standard. While

Exhibit 8-7. Nokia's future 3G scenarios: first in GSM and first in 3G.

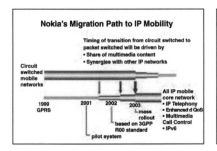

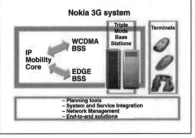

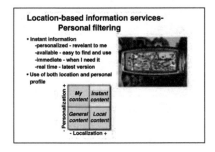

SOURCE: © Nokia 2000. Nokia and Nokia Connecting People are registered trademarks of Nokia Corporation.

Nokia and Ericsson received 61 percent of the votes, a win required 71 percent. Following intense, private talks, Nokia, Ericsson, and Siemens prepared to reach a compromise, and the ETSI agreed on a 3G mobile standard based on both W-CDMA and TDMA-CDMA proposals. Suddenly, the European standards struggle was over. Led by a slate of new products, Siemens was on track to triple its sales of mobile phones in 2000 to 30 million. It surpassed Alcatel and Ericsson, taking the third position behind Nokia and Motorola in Europe.[47] Meanwhile, the agreement with the Japanese served to open doors in Asia for Nokia and Ericsson.

The U.S. had been played out from the 3G competition. European players had united their front, just as they had managed to discourage opposition by U.S. industry leaders. Or so it seemed.

Trade Threats

In 1998, Qualcomm spun off its interests in wireless phone service operators, creating Leap Wireless International. It also formed Wireless Knowledge, a joint venture with Microsoft that provided products and services for Internet access from portable PCs. This joint venture kept the leading mobile vendors uneasy. Microsoft's emergence as a committed player in the mobile Internet would drastically reconfigure the playing field once again. Now Qualcomm argued that 3G needed a single standard. The European CDMA and its own technology (cdma 2000) would have to be combined, or the ITU would choose among them.

Because of American market fragmentation, the United States sent four different standards proposals to the ITU. As Qualcomm argued that the EU was about to lock American technology out of the European market, the Clinton administration began to examine the standards conflict.

To avoid trade conflicts, Nokia needed greater visibility in the United States. Since the mid-1990s, advertising, including Super Bowl commercials, had made the brand known on Main Street. The company's hyper growth of the late 1990s had also turned it into a Wall Street darling. Now the company needed friends in Washington. In August 1998, *Business Week* published a cover story on Nokia, portraying the company as the way of the future: "While Nokia, Ericsson, and Motorola are all preparing to battle one another with Internet phones and intelligent base stations, they've been forced to join forces on the Third Generation. . . . Ollila claims not to be worried. 'The market will be big enough for all of us,' he says.'"[48]

After success on Main Street and Wall Street, Nokia was about to arrive on Capitol Hill. The story provided great publicity, and a host of other triumphant cover stories soon followed. Nokia began to invest more in its government relations with Washington. For some time, Veli Sundbäck, a member of Ollila's group executive board and a veteran diplomat, had pushed for such efforts. A year before, the Nokians had also recruited Bill Plummer to lead their lobbying efforts. Though only thirty-three years old, Plummer had served eight years in the U.S. Department of Foreign Affairs and often did business with telecommunications companies. He had been influential in mobilizing Nokia's efforts to neutralize the early signs of trade conflict.[49]

As *Business Week* released its Nokia cover story, the EU announced a preliminary decision requiring all EU members to use the ETSI 3G technology. Qualcomm's PR campaign portrayed the EU decision as old-style protectionism, and by the fall of 1998, the conflict grew worse. While Ericsson and Qualcomm continued their court fight over patents, Qualcomm threatened to use its patent portfolio to prevent the implementation of the ETSI decision. Meanwhile, Plummer began an active lobbying campaign presenting Nokia as an American company. After all, it employed thousands of people in the United States. In the aftermath of the *Business Week* publicity, Plummer's lobbying expenditures multiplied accordingly.

In mid-December 1998, the EC lent its support to the ETSI decision, triggering yet another negative response in the United States, which now accused the EU of restricting competition in 3G mobile phones. EU Commissioner Bangemann received a letter from the U.S. government, signed by Secretary of State Madeleine Albright; U.S. Trade Representative Charlene Barshefsky; Secretary of Commerce William Daley; and FCC Chairman William Kennard. The U.S. was threatening the EU with a trade war. Meanwhile, the ITU published a press release expressing its concern over a "holy war" that could destroy the promise of 3G mobile communications and indicating a weariness regarding the Qualcomm-Ericsson patent wars.

In January 1999, Bangeman responded to the U.S. government with a letter refuting the accusations. The EU decision had not said that all EU member states would have to use only the European technology. According to Bangemann, there would have to be at least one operator in each member state that would use the European technology. The objective was to ensure that all European mobile phones would work across Europe, just as the GSM phones did, not to lock out the U.S. players. Bangemann's interpretation appeared to appease the U.S. government, but it did not neutralize Qualcomm's initiatives.

In December 1998, Finland's Ministry of Transport and Communications (MTC) initiated the 3G licensing process in Finland. In February 1999, Molly Foerster, Qualcomm's development director in Europe, met Harri Pursiainen, deputy director general of the MTC. She requested the Finns not to link licenses to European technology. In mid-March, Finland became the first country in the world to grant licenses for 3G mobile networks, opting for a technology-agnostic position:

> The decision did not include a final position on the technology to be used, since it will be determined by future international standardization decisions (IMT-2000). . . . Finland is the first country in the world to have granted licenses for third-generation mobile networks. The Ministry of Transport and Communications trusts the early start will speed up the start of operations elsewhere in the world. . . .[50]

Even as Finland became the first country to license 3G operators, Japan was expected to offer the first operational 3G network. Struggling with congestion in their current networks, the Japanese sought to launch their 3G network as early as 2001. Because the United States introduced digital wireless systems only in the late 1990s, 3G systems were not expected to emerge until 2003 to 2005.

Following the 3G press release, the MTC received a "verbal note" announcing that the United States was observing with great interest Finland's licensing process for the 3G mobile telecommunications services:

> We appreciate Finland's commitment to an open and non-discriminatory selection process. The U.S. government is concerned that 3G licensing activities in Europe and elsewhere should not prejudice the multilateral process of approving third-generation wireless standards to be completed at the International Telecommunications Union (ITU) before the end of 1999. . . . Additionally, we have some concerns with the speed of the licensing process. The rights holders of CDMA are embroiled in a dispute over intellectual property rights that could affect Finnish license holders and make them vulnerable to legal action, i.e., the current Qualcomm/Ericsson case. Finally, there could be an appearance of discrimination if sufficient time is not given to applicants new to the market. This does not appear to be in the interests of either consumers or potential service providers.[51]

Though unsigned, verbal notes typically reflect conflictual disagreements and play a role in international trade and politics. During the Cold War, however, the Soviets had used similar instruments to intervene in Finland's internal affairs. The Finns were puzzled; they did not expect such notes from the United States. Furthermore, the MTC had been admired worldwide for its early-mover initiatives in liberalization and competition. Many of these had been inspired by early precedents in the United Kingdom and the United States.[52] Now the ministry felt it was being lectured by the U.S. government, and for all of the wrong reasons.

After the Cold War, Finland had finally been able to participate in European integration. In telecommunications, however, the small country had been liberalizing faster than most of Europe; in the mobile industry, it was the pioneer in Europe and served as a role model of sorts for European competitiveness.[53] As most European countries lagged behind Finland in liberalization and deregulation, the Finns had had to re-regulate in order to harmonize their regulatory system with EU directives and policies. The 3G licensing process, thus, was vital to Finnish interests; first-mover advantage was also critical to Nokia's strategy (see Exhibit 8-8).[54]

In mid-February 1999, the Trans-Atlantic Business Dialogue (TABD) held a conference in Washington, D.C. With the support of Ron Brown, then U.S. secretary of commerce, the TABD had been formed to serve as an organizational safety valve; its function was to assist companies and governments to resolve trade conflicts without trade wars.[55] This was the right arena for the standards dispute, including participants from the top worldwide equipment manufacturers and operators as well as IBM and Hewlett-Packard. In the conference, T-Mobil, a major German operator, made a compromise proposal that suggested an "umbrella" solution. The 3G technology umbrella would be based on CDMA and cover major technologies; operators could make their own informed choices. The idea of a uniform single standard was buried, and the concept of a single flexible standard was born.

The TABD solution was formalized at the ITU conference in Fortaleza, Brazil, in March 1999, where the key players decided to develop IMT-2000 into a single flexible standard with a choice of multiple access methods including CDMA, TDMA, and combined TDMA/CDMA. It was agreed that IMT-2000 radio interfaces should be able to interact with both of the major 3G core networks under development. Meanwhile, Qualcomm and Ericsson settled their bitter dispute over the use of CDMA as an industry standard by signing a cross-licensing deal. Concurrently, Qualcomm unveiled a chipset for use in 3G wireless networks that would enable advanced functions such as video communications; that year, Qualcomm's stock soared beyond recognition, gaining 2,600 percent in twelve months. Although it had been the leading seller of mobile phones in the United States, the company, unable to compete with the triumvirate of Nokia, Ericsson, and Motorola,

Exhibit 8-8. From 3G to the first Nokia World Phone.

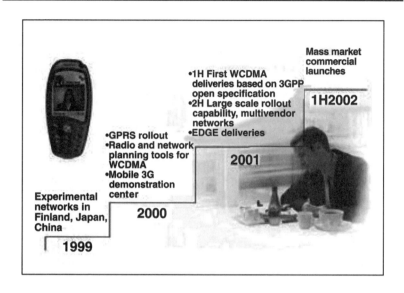

sold its phone-manufacturing operations to Japan's Kyocera.[56] In April 1999, the U.S. government sent one more verbal note to the EU, but the standards struggle was over and trade wars had been avoided.

■ ■ ■ ■ ■

Although the story of Nokia's success through the second half of the 1990s followed that of the GSM, the 3G decision played well at the company. Through Ollila's leadership, it had favored "technology agnosticism." The point had not been how a given *technology* works, but what it could do for the *customer*.

In Japan, Nokia and Ericsson were cooperating with the DoCoMo Research Center at the Yokosuka science park. In R&D activities, both Nokia and Ericsson worked together with Japan Telecom, Japan's third-largest phone company behind NTT and DDI. Both IDO and DDI had opted for Qualcomm's 3G standard in an effort to break DoCoMo's de facto mobile monopoly in Japan.

With rapid price erosion, the adoption of multimedia, and the return of consumer electronics companies to the mobile competition, Nokia was facing a new kind of Asian challenge—one no longer confined to Japanese companies.[57] Asian manufacturers were tightening their grip on home markets and increasing sales of their products abroad. For the three major mobile vendors (Nokia, Ericsson, and Motorola), new competition loomed as Asia's handset makers expected the coming shift to 3G would support them worldwide.

Pekka Tarjanne, a Finnish politician and veteran telecommunications executive, had led the ITU through the 2G rivalry. In the 3G era, his successor was Yoshio Usumi, Japan's former minister of Post and Telecommunications. Some industry observers viewed this transition as symbolic.

Upstream Innovation

OVER the course of the PC revolution between 1980 and 1994, more than 580 technology companies went public, creating more than $240 billion in net market capitalization. By January 1999—in just half a decade—the Internet had grown from a $34-billion industry to one worth $257 billion.[1] But, Ollila prophesized, the best was yet to come: "I firmly believe that Nokia is ideally placed to bring the benefits of the convergence of Internet and mobility to the markets."[2]

The year 1999 was the third consecutive year in which Nokia exceeded its overall growth and profitability targets. As Nokia's CEO Ollila and President Ala-Pietilä noted in 2000, the company was about to play *the* leading role in the emerging mobile era:

> We are at the beginning of something very significant. Not just for our company. Not just for our industry. But for everyone. And for all aspects of our lives. We are using the twin drivers of the Internet and mobility to break through the limits of time and place. These are very powerful forces. . . . This is what we mean by the Mobile Information Society.[3]

The two believed that Nokia had the necessary will to succeed, had the global presence and the key capabilities in mobility and other enabling technologies to make the transformation happen. They also thought it had the culture to cope with the required scale of change and the vision to point the company in the right direction. Ollila and Ala-Pietilä knew that the impending transformation would be even grander than the one the company experienced during the restructuring of the early 1990s. Most important, for Nokia, no longer local but global, the stakes were far greater. Still, the two executives were confident that Nokia would be the driving force in this change.

> Our culture and our vision have taken us this far. But this is only the beginning. We recognize that there is still a long

225

way to go. We believe that we are well positioned to meet the challenges. To meet what others may see as confusion and uncertainty with confidence and leadership. To adapt and evolve as required. And to bring the benefits of change to all of our lives. Life is about to change forever. And we want to be a driving force in that change. We know that there are no limits to what can be achieved with will, vision and determination. And we have all three in abundance.[4]

Building New Capabilities

Nokia's vision of the mobile information society originated from its first efforts to manage digital convergence. Around 1992, the company hatched a telecom project with the code name Responder and formed a secret unit to execute it. Approximately twenty-five researchers, managers, and scientists gathered discreetly in Tampere and were given a broad mission: "Look at the next challenge" in tapping the exploding world of wireless communications. The challenge was to combine Internet, computer, and telephone technologies to produce a *portable* machine that could use each technology equally. When presented with the idea, Nokia's top management pressed their engineers to move quickly to outpace the company's key competitors, Motorola and Ericsson. The first result of these efforts, the Nokia Communicator, hit stores in the United States in 1996 (see Exhibit 9-1). As the Communicator project progressed, the focus became to create the world's first pocket-size mobile office. The device would allow users to conduct conference calls, receive and send faxes, handle e-mail, and surf the Internet—whether from a moving car, a train, or a sidewalk cafe. It would, said Yrjö Neuvo, senior vice president for product creation, "turn one-plus-one into more than two," which he dubbed Nokia's corporate culture credo.[5]

Managing Development Capabilities

In the turbulent cellular environment, superior management of development capabilities was the key to competitive advantage. Viewed strategically, Nokia had been triumphant in the 2G rivalry because it had successfully integrated technology and commercial applications. For most companies, development projects (product and process) tend to fall into one of five categories (see Exhibit 9-2):[6]

1. *Applied research or advanced development projects* that aim at inventing new science or capturing new know-how for application in specific development projects.

Exhibit 9-1. The Nokia 9110 Communicator.

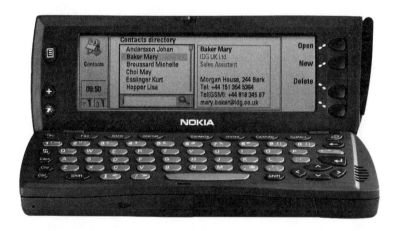

Source: © Nokia 2000. Nokia and Nokia Connecting People are registered trademarks of Nokia Corporation.

2. *Alliance or partnered projects* (e.g., Symbian, Bluetooth, WAP), in which the firm "buys" a newly designed product and/or process from another firm. Such subcontracting of development projects to partners can leverage in-house efforts but requires the resources for coordination and integration.
3. *Breakthrough development projects* (e.g., Nokia's WAP phone, the Communicator) that involve creating the first generation of an entirely new product and process. Their core concepts and technologies break new ground for the organization.
4. *Platform or generational development projects* (e.g., Nokia's digital GSM platform phones) that typically have a design life of several years and establish the basic architecture for a set of follow-on derivative projects.
5. *Derivative development projects* (e.g., Nokia's digital GSM phone accessories, niche product lines) that tend to be substantially narrower in scope and resource requirements than platform projects. Reflecting "incremental" advancements, they tend to refine and improve selected performance dimensions to better meet the needs of specific market segments.

In the turmoil of the early 1990s, Ollila had bet the future of Nokia on the emerging cellular market; by the end of the decade, he was betting on the mobile Internet. In the first instance, a new strategy led

Exhibit 9-2. Types of development projects: the evolution of Nokia's portfolio from R&D to incremental products (ca. 2000).

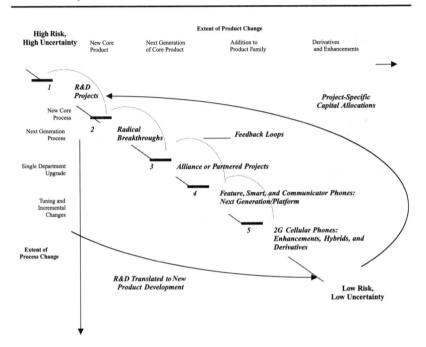

to restructuring the organization. For the new challenge, the company's cellular capabilities would have to be supplemented by new Internet capabilities. The company faced yet another reorganization to install a new repertoire of strengths to the company.

From Capabilities to Product Development

At Nokia, highly skilled people who embodied critical technological capabilities were seen as the key to the company's long-term success. In many industries, acquirers seek ownership of physical assets and brands; in the technology sector, however, successful acquisitions tend to focus on people. Of course, long-term success depends on the sustained ability to build on excellent products, but due to rapid product life cycles, first movers could easily lose their leadership position in future product generations if they are unable to develop new, critical capabilities.[7]

In the late 1990s, this "dual development of capabilities" proceeded in five phases (see Exhibit 9-3). In the first phase, the focus was on assessing acquisition needs (market developments, available technologies, product and technology road maps). These predevelop-

Exhibit 9-3. Development of capabilities: acquisitions and new product development—Nokia's early purchases in Silicon Valley (1997–1999).

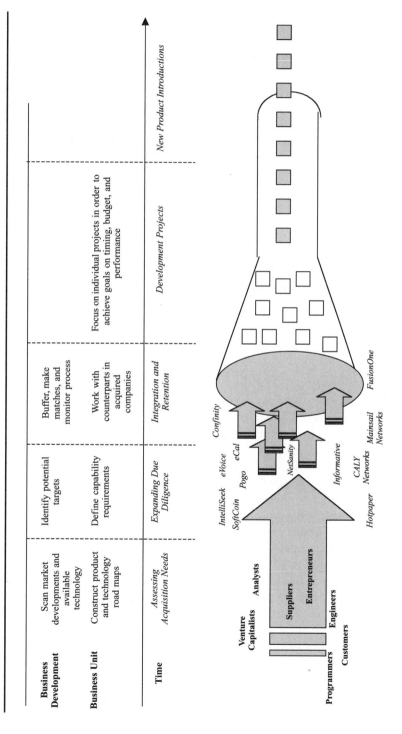

				New Product Introductions
Business Development	Scan market developments and available technology	Identify potential targets	Buffer, make matches, and monitor process	
Business Unit	Construct product and technology road maps	Define capability requirements	Work with counterparts in acquired companies	Focus on individual projects in order to achieve goals on timing, budget, and performance
Time	*Assessing Acquisition Needs*	*Expanding Due Diligence*	*Integration and Retention*	*Development Projects*

ment investigations made use of information available among venture capitalists, analysts, suppliers, entrepreneurs, channel intermediaries, engineers, programmers, and customers. In the second phase, the focus was still outside the acquirer's organization (identification of potential targets, definition of capability requirements). In the third phase, the focus moved from the external environment to internal organization (matching, monitoring, cooperative work efforts). The objective was to integrate the target company into the acquirer's organization as well as retain key employees who embodied critical capabilities. In the fourth phase, the focus shifted to individual projects seeking to meet goals on timing, budget, and performance. In the last phase, the role of the business unit diminished as the focus shifted toward introducing new products into the marketplace. Conversely, other units (e.g., logistics and distribution, marketing, sales, and service) began to play a more prominent part.

In many technology acquisitions, the initiative is driven by the need to add new capabilities quickly to existing ones. Typically, older high-tech companies that serve established customers tend to develop rigidities that prevent them from responding quickly to new markets. In contrast, smaller, younger companies acquired for a specific capability are expected to transform the acquirer into a more flexible competitor.[8]

It was precisely this view of a transformational acquisition that would motivate Nokia's interest in Silicon Valley toward the late 1990s.

By 2000, the competitive environment of mobile cellular was increasingly global and had become highly volatile. New product and process development had become the focal point of competition.[9] Nokia, Ericsson, Motorola, and Samsung as well as a host of minor players competed through development capabilities. Competitive advantage went to companies that reached the market fastest and more efficiently with products that best fit the customer. Between 1998 and 1999, Nokia widened its global market share from 22.5 percent to 26.9 percent[10] and nearly doubled its total sales from the prior year's figure of 38.6 million. These increases were spurred by the company's ability to introduce models quickly, distribute them better than their competitors, and offer premium pricing. Conversely, companies that were slow to get to the market or introduced products that did not match customer expectations saw their market positions erode and financial performance falter.[11]

Although Nokia had been investigating and investing in new businesses and technologies within diverse business groups since 1995, the company elevated these activities to the corporate level in 1998 by establishing the Nokia Ventures Organization.

Corporate Venturing

A separate organization running parallel to the three business groups (Nokia Telecommunications, Nokia Mobile Phones, and Nokia Communications Products), the Nokia Ventures Organization (NVO) aimed to foster growth opportunities beyond the current scope of the existing business groups. In 1999, the NVO's net sales rose to EUR 415 million; in the first three months of 2000, the division earned EUR 211 million in net sales, only 3 percent of the Nokia Group's consolidated net sales. Despite the NVO's losses, Ollila expected profitability for the unit. "Perhaps in 2001 or at least in 2003, fast GPRS networks will spread. That will stimulate markets."[12]

Unlike the NRC, where the time-frame was only two to three years, the NVO sought to develop areas with growth potential over the next five years. It explored new business areas facilitating future growth and boosting Nokia's product and long-term business development. The unit was comprised of several organizational building blocks (see Exhibit 9-4): Nokia Internet Communications, Nokia Home Communications, Nokia Mobile Display Appliances, Nokia Multimedia Terminals, Nokia Venturing Unit (NVU), and the Nokia Ventures Fund (NVF).

The strategic target of Nokia Internet Communications consists of what Nokia calls the "enterprise and managed Internet service provider" markets. Created in October 1999, it combines a number of de-

Exhibit 9-4. Nokia Ventures Organization.

Nokia Internet Communications (NIC)	Nokia Home Communications
Wireless application protocol (WAP)	Nokia Mobile Display Appliances
IP application and connectivity platforms	
IP network appliances	Nokia Multimedia Terminals
Security	
Wireless LAN and mobility management	Nokia Ventures Fund
IP telephony and intelligent applications and solutions	
	Nokia Venturing Unit

velopments already taking place within Nokia and seeks to build a powerful channel to the enterprise market through Internet virtual private networks and e-business products and solutions. Nokia Home Communications, created in November 1999, aspires to develop digital platforms and communications solutions for the home environment. It builds upon Nokia's expertise in technologies, such as wireless local-area networks, IP, and digital broadcasting. The third unit focuses on the development of mobile display devices that would enable visually rich, Internet-based communications.

Representing largely internal venturing, these three units concentrate on existing value activities. The other two (NVU and NVF) focus on potential activities, reflecting mainly external venturing.

The mission of the Venturing Unit is to explore new business areas. It serves as a greenhouse for new business ideas that would not otherwise arise within the company, and it runs pilots and other early-stage venturing, often with one or more partners. Based in Silicon Valley, the Nokia Ventures Fund invests in attractive start-ups and new market opportunities. With an initial capital allocation of $100 million, it is constantly on the lookout for disruptive technologies and emerging business models. By early 2000, examples of Nokia Ventures Fund investments included start-ups such as eVoice, Pogo.com, Confinity, FusionOne, and Informative.[13]

Early Acquisitions

With its cellular strategy in place, Nokia began to shop around for acquisitions that would help the company develop its online capabilities. It was certainly not among the first seeking to make a purchase in Silicon Valley. In the late 1990s, the acquisition activity in much of the United States had focused on the technology sector. Since the first Internet IPO waves of 1995 and 1996, market corrections have triggered several bursts of consolidation in the technology sector, stimulating M&A activities. By the end of the decade, the pace and scale of purchases accelerated. In June 1999, Alcatel Alsthom snapped up DSC Communications Corporation for $4.4 billion. Soon thereafter Nortel nabbed Bay Networks in a $9.1 billion deal.

In December 1997, Nokia acquired several newer high-speed IP companies, including Ipsilon Networking, a router enhancement maker ($120 million); DiamondLane, a Digital Subscriber Line (DSL) equipment maker ($125 million); Vienna Systems, an IP-to-voice gateway company ($90 million); and InTalk, a wireless Local Area Network (LAN) vendor. Despite these purchases and grand strategic objectives, many industry observers considered Nokia a lightweight when it came to Internet technology.

A powerhouse in handsets, Nokia risked becoming an also-ran in the telecommunications systems business, which represented a third of its sales. This rapidly growing segment was dominated by bold equipment manufacturers, such as Cisco Systems, Lucent Technologies, and Nortel, rushing to build the nerve centers for mobile networks in the coming century. To respond to the M&A challenge, Ollila had the board prepare a plan to issue $9 billion of new stock, yet Nokia intended to resist the "me-too" M&A activities that, to Ollila's mind, characterized those industry leaders who were getting into the wired Internet. Instead, Nokia would focus on the *wireless* niche. "Going head to head in Cisco's market is not the way to do it," Ollila said.[14] Such statements precipitated cooperation with Cisco.

Nokia did not engage in focused large-scale acquisitions. Like so many other acquirers, Nokia also stumbled with some of its smaller scale acquisitions—at least initially. The acquisition of Ipsilon Networking is one such example. By winter 1997, Ipsilon's senior managers had concluded that the company could not make it on its own. The company had been working on IP switching technology, but without market momentum.[15] "So we began to look for an acquirer because the industry was not moving toward a direction we'd thought," acknowledged Ipsilon's Tom Lyon. Nokia expected the acquisition to strengthen its data communications capabilities,[16] but critics and rivals believed Nokia had wasted money on a useless technology and a bankrupt company.[17]

Nokia's first acquisition proved to be something of a learning experience. When Nokia acquired Vienna Systems in December 1998, T. Kent Elliott came along with the deal. A year later, Elliott was heading up Nokia Internet Communications (NIC), which was expected to play a critical role in Nokia's convergence activities. "I've been asked to couple together certain know-how as well as launch activities in business markets," Elliott stated in late 1999. "We don't have to possess everything. We are experts in the network margins. But we must own the technology that pertains to our own special field."[18]

In Silicon Valley, Nokia remained something of an enigma. It was widely admired, but it had proven itself to be vulnerable. Why, then, did the company resist the kind of M&A activities so many had expected? Partly, Nokia was simply late. Pulled by soaring prices, risk premiums had climbed too high, but even more important, Ollila did not want Nokia to become too big. "We will not become a company with more than 100,000 people," he had said in one interview after another. Nokia had to remain flexible, and enormous companies were conspicuously slow. Instead of hiring more people, Nokia outsourced more of its processes.

Similarly, potentially costly M&A activities were not necessary if

Exhibit 9-5. Nokia's strategic positioning: linkages and coalition scope
(2000).

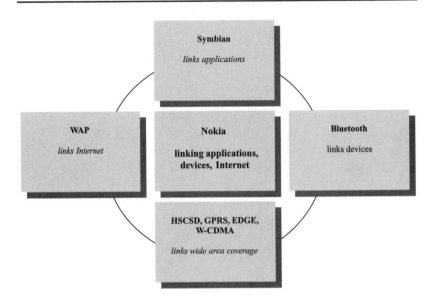

externalization accomplished identical objectives, which meant establishing more strategic coalitions and partnerships.

Standards Coalitions

To realize its vision of the mobile information society, Nokia stepped up its efforts in all relevant industry forums and arenas. Ollila had learned early to co-opt rivals into strategic alliances; identifying key technologies led to the creation of key coalitions (see Exhibit 9-5). In the 3G era of mobile communications, Ollila thought that such coalitions were inevitable. Complexity required cooperation. If the internalization of appropriate capabilities had become too costly in terms of strategic flexibility and financial resources, Nokia would have to obtain these capabilities externally. As vertical value chains crumbled, new horizontal ones would emerge. Ollila explained:

> The convergence of Internet to mobile phones will not lead into one single player becoming master of the universe. You're likely to see the horizontal value chain, like in computers. You've got to find your place in the value chain. Our special edge will be in voice and data terminals, where the

radio link is a crucial element. Voice terminals, to a major degree, will be wireless. That will mean that our weight in the industry will grow. Still, the future is all full of question marks and surprises. That's part of the fun in this industry.[19]

These activities, as well as Nokia's coalition formation in general, must be understood in the context of its highly focused overall strategy. Not surprisingly, Nokia's coalition activities were focused as well. Nokia's process chain consisted of three basic categories: *R&D* (critical support activities), *upstream processes* (platforms/standards, NPD, and logistics), and *downstream processes* (branding, segmentation, design). If the industry environment were to change, strategy and structure would shift accordingly. By 2000, Nokia was busy redesigning itself into a nimble administrator of partnership networks, apparently emulating the model of Cisco Systems. At the same time, it was slicing up the organization into "process modules" that could be set up to run operations on very short notice. In the past, Nokia, like some other cutting-edge technology companies, had been eager to modularize its product development; now it was after much more—it sought to modularize the entire organization in order to optimize strategic flexibility.

Nokia had engaged in downstream innovation since the mid-1990s and began the globalization of its R&D units soon thereafter, but the company approached the problem of upstream innovation differently. While it exercised tight control over new-product development and logistics, Nokia engaged in extensive coalition formation primarily focusing on standards.

Throughout the 1990s, R&D alone did not dictate Nokia's technology coalitions; the latter were motivated by product development. The company was not interested in basic capabilities, which could be acquired or imitated with relative ease; it sought *specialized* capabilities that were less vulnerable to trade and harder to duplicate.

In the old diversified Nokia, strategic coalitions had been each different in terms of their duration and intensity of cooperation. The joint venture with Tandy, for instance, ended after five years and another with Matra after eight years. In these cases, continuation was no longer needed because, as far as Nokia was concerned, the cooperation function had been fulfilled.[20] By the close of the 1990s, however, Nokia was building strategic coalitions that had very different functions.

The Functions of Nokia's Strategic Coalitions

In principle, strategic coalitions can be launched to perform any process or set of processes in the value chain. They tend to arise when performing a process with a partner is superior to performing the activity internally (organizational mechanism), externally in arm's-length transactions (market mechanism), or through a merger with another company.[21] Nokia expected the coalitions to unlock benefits that it did not expect to obtain by internal development, mergers, or arm's-length transactions. In particular, it sought five kinds of benefits. Four are fairly typical, but the fifth is unique to Nokia:

1. *Access to expertise.* Strategic coalitions enable the participants to acquire, pool, or sell access to the knowledge or ability to perform activities. Typically, such coalitions tend to grow out of first-mover effects (one competitor is significantly ahead of the others on the learning curve), comparative advantage effects (a specific country is a preferred location for performing an activity), desire for local ownership, or a combination of the three. To Nokia, for instance, access to knowledge may have contributed to its involvement with Symbian, which allowed the company to catch up quickly with segment leaders, such as Palm or Handspring.[22]

2. *Scale economies and learning.* Nokia hoped to gain economies of scale or learning. Pooling volume serves to raise the scale of the activity or the rate of learning about how to perform over that of each company operating separately. When, for instance, Internet-linked mobile phones arrived in Finland in the fall of 1999, Finnish companies rolled out a host of services designed to capture a new market for information on demand. Among others, insurers, airlines, yellow-pages publishers, and traffic police expected the wireless application protocol (WAP)—the communication standard allowing mobile phones to access the Internet—to change the way people did business throughout Europe and, later, around the world. Together, these companies came up with a preliminary WAP business model.[23] The introduction of WAP in Finland, thus, promoted scale economies and learning among the first movers.

3. *Shaping rivalry.* Strategic coalitions could also be used to influence the basis of competition as well as the competitors. Viewed in narrow terms, such motivation can be framed in terms of facilitating collusion. Viewed in broader terms, companies employ coalitions to facilitate others entering an industry to develop a technology that would affect its competitors' cost structure or to shape competition in their favor. When, for instance, Nokia co-founded Symbian to accelerate developments in wireless information devices in 1998, it and other founding members were seeking to reposition themselves by marginalizing the bargaining power of Palm Inc. and Microsoft in the rapidly evolving industry segment.

4. *Risk reduction.* Strategic coalitions also offer risk reduction. Because no single partner bears the full risk and cost of the coalition activity, these partnerships provide an attractive mechanism to hedge risk. For instance, when Ericsson, IBM, Intel, Nokia, and Toshiba founded the Bluetooth alliance in 1997, they did not just create a forum to enhance the Bluetooth specification and provide a vehicle for interoperability testing. They were also diversifying risk while ensuring extensive development activities.

5. *Upstream standardization.* In addition to these typical coalition-formation motives, Nokia may have had a fifth benefit in mind. Unlike its major 2G rivals, Motorola and Ericsson, it excelled in downstream innovation. Nokia's direct rivals—as well as those of its new and indirect 3G competitors—were strong in upstream innovation. Not surprising, Nokia has initiated upstream coalitions while its rivals have often been followers. By promoting open standards built upon externalization, Nokia has weakened its competitors' strengths (upstream innovation) while increasing its own (downstream innovation).

While no single technology can enable a mobile vendor to dominate the future, several key emerging technologies could play a critical role.[24] At Nokia, internal R&D activities and participation in standards creation are deemed necessary, but in the long term, the company must also build new capabilities through externalized R&D, i.e., geographic and coalition scope, and appropriate acquisitions. The function of these capabilities is to establish a foothold in critical emerging technologies as well as to build "Nokia Mobile Internet Technical Architecture"; hence Nokia's strategic coalitions with partners and rivals.

As far as Nokia was concerned, these coalitions were win-win opportunities. Where they generated positive results, it would benefit. Where they generated negative results, the failures would be more costly to its rivals. In terms of strategy—and particularly Nokia's view of strategic architecture—these building blocks were critical and relied on open standards that the company has actively been developing. As a founder of coalitions, it would be able to shape these initiatives; as a participant, it could continue to steer its development paths. Each of these technologies had its own place and mission in the 3G terminal; all were vital building blocks for mobile multimedia terminals:

- WAP made Internet content accessible with mobile devices.
- The EPOC operating system, developed by Symbian, provided an optimal platform for wireless information devices and future media phones.

- Bluetooth enabled short-range connectivity between devices in a totally digital environment.
- SyncML served as the synchronization solution for the mobile information society.

Wireless Application Protocol

In 1997, Nokia was one of the founding members of the wireless application protocol, an open standard that brought Internet-based advanced services to mobile phones and other wireless terminals. WAP was Nokia's link to the Internet. The technology originated from several years of cooperation among Nokia, Ericsson, and Motorola. In 1998, Nokia contributed actively to the first WAP standard. The technology had the potential to bring the Web to mobile handsets and other Internet-enabled devices with a microbrowser.[25] In Western Europe, WAP services are expected to take off in 2001.[26]

Nokia's WAP Vision and the WAP Value Chain

At Nokia, WAP was considered the leading global open standard for applications over wireless networks. By summer 2000, the company offered operators, manufacturers, developers, and corporations an ever-growing, innovative range of products, software, and solutions designed to help them capitalize on the WAP evolution. These encompassed WAP-compliant handsets such as the Nokia 6210, Nokia 6250, Nokia 7110, Nokia 9110, and iCommunicator.

The WAP platform facilitated the strategic transition from the 2G to 3G environment. These products were also vital to the extent that they anticipated the rise of the mobile Internet services. As a result, Nokia pushed the *entire* WAP value chain. The more players in the emerging WAP space, the more demand for Nokia's products and services. Prior to WAP, this chain consisted of providers who offered content and service, network operators who provided connectivity solutions and access networks, and end users who bought mobile terminals (see Exhibit 9-6a). With WAP, the value chain grew more complex as emerging channel intermediaries found new business opportunities. While content providers continued to offer content and services, they were also moving into service packaging, portals, and connectivity solutions. Conversely, network operators began struggling for the very same business. As boundaries blurred between the businesses of traditional content providers and network operators, value-added service players began to provide focused offerings (see Exhibit 9-6b).

Value-Added Transitionary Services

Nokia did not expect to cross the chasm from the niche and early adopter markets to mass markets until the mobile terminals could offer higher speeds. Even before true 3G competition, Nokia was pushing value-added services (e.g., general packet radio service [GPRS], high-speed circuit-switched data [HSCSD], enhanced data rates for global evolution [EDGE]) that would stimulate the transition from cellular to mobile Internet.

IP Delivery: GPRS. In the past, GSM operators had offered value-

Exhibit 9-6. Changing value chains.

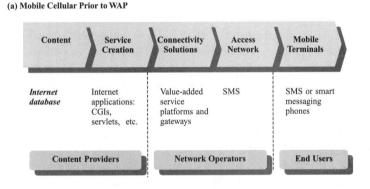

(a) Mobile Cellular Prior to WAP

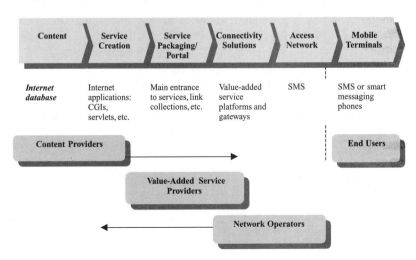

(b) WAP-Compliant Mobile Cellular

added services by providing mobile access to existing telecommunications services. With GPRS, argued Nokia, mobile operators possessed
a superb IP delivery vehicle that enabled them to re-evaluate and transform their position in the value chain, not only to preserve existing
business but also to grow revenue. Nokia urged operators to focus on
the changing markets, concentrate on high-performance radio access,
become a full-fledged service provider, or try to achieve all three. Comprehensive end-to-end solutions required new partnerships with solutions and content providers.

Mobile Data Service: HSCSD. With HSCSD, Nokia urged operators to begin the transformation to true mobile data service providers.
With it, providers could prepare their organizations and subscribers
for the coming 3G services. With these services, Nokia argued, subscribers would start to learn about the possibilities of high-speed data
over the mobile Internet. As users' mobile data behavior evolved and
usage patterns became clear, operators would be better positioned to
learn from early trends and thereby influence how subscribers would
use the many new applications. Such first-mover advantages would be
difficult to replicate because user behavior and usage patterns were
cumulative by nature. With its HSCSD, Nokia also expected fast access
to the Internet to become the norm, and GPRS would complement and
enhance the value of HSCSD. Nokia foresaw applications for both circuit-switched and packet-switched.

Mobile Multimedia: EDGE. As end-user services were about to
move into mobile multimedia, Nokia introduced a new technology,
EDGE, to boost network capacity and increase air interface data rates.
EDGE offered packet-data user rates up to 473 kbit/s and circuit-
switched data user rates of 64 kbit/s. For GSM providers, Nokia expected this new technology to increase data rates of both circuit switching and packet switching up to threefold.[27]

Unlike these transitional options, however, WAP was not a temporary stage but an open standard for the Internet era. By 2000, after
months of industry hype and inflated expectations, some frustrated
Nordic operators considered WAP to be a bug-infested pilot experi-
ment. The protocol remained critical, but its successful commercialization would require more time.

Symbian

In 1998, Nokia cofounded Symbian, a company designed to speed
up the evolution of wireless information devices. Featuring palmtop
computer maker Psion's software unit, Symbian shareholders included

Psion (28 percent); mobile phone leaders Nokia, Motorola, and Ericsson (21 percent each); and consumer electronics giant Matsushita (9 percent). Together, the alliance's electronics heavyweights made 85 percent of the world's mobile phones and sought to ensure the interoperability of application platforms, content, and services. The alliance was Nokia's link to applications.

Symbian provided core software, including the operating system, application frameworks, and applications and development tools for all EPOC licensees. EPOC was an advanced real-time, multithreading, scalable operating system designed especially for small handheld communications devices. Along with 3Com's Palm Computing and Microsoft's Windows CE (and products of some fifteen other competing companies), EPOC was an operating system for handheld mobile devices. Over time, Symbian was expected to provide solutions that deployed key industrial mobile standards and technologies such as an Internet technology suite, WAP, Java, and Bluetooth. Psion's palmtop computers were the bestselling devices in Europe (60 percent of the market), where cellular markets were ahead of the United States.

Symbian envisioned three types of terminals in the future—featurephones, smartphones, and communicators—and Nokia moved rapidly into each in order to dominate developments in the category and to fill any gaps in product portfolios that new challengers might use to gain a foothold.

Featurephones. The featurephone provided high voice quality together with text messaging and Internet browsing capabilities. By 2000, these phones represented the high end of the market. In the coming years, they will form the basic product offerings and the core of Nokia's existing products and will lead to future product introductions.

Smartphones. Smartphones have capabilities similar to featurephones but contain larger displays. If the mobile Internet represents the convergence of mobility, imagining, and the Internet, smartphones would have to provide staple offerings coupled with imagining capabilities. It is a category that Nokia, along with other current market leaders, would have to monitor carefully. If the Asian consumer electronics players (e.g., Panasonic, Sony, NEC) were to mount a significant challenge, many of them would likely begin with smartphones, most likely from a low-end corner of the emerging market.

Media Screen. In this category, the prototype of Nokia's Media Screen stole the spotlight in a German trade show in September 1999. Strategically, its function was to initiate dominance in the category and deter attacks. Nokia's Media Screen was a prototype featuring a totally new concept design combining digital television (DVB-T), Internet, and mobile phone technology (see Exhibit 9-7). Interestingly, the Media Screen ran the Linux operating system and featured its own software (the Nokia Navibards). Clearly, Nokia wanted to establish an open platform that did not belong to one service provider but could integrate many different kinds of services. Hence Linux was the platform of choice. This truly open operating system could be downloaded from the Internet. Nokia thought it might take another two years before the Media Screen would become a marketable product.[28]

Communicators. The communicators were designed for use by mobile professionals. This phone category coupled the basic cellular

Exhibit 9-7. Nokia's Media Screen.

SOURCE: © Nokia 2000. Nokia and Nokia Connecting People are registered trademarks of Nokia Corporation.

staple with advanced functionality, including a large display and touch-screen capability. It also offered access to the Internet and the corporate Intranet. Whereas smartphones would appeal to passive media use among consumers, communicators, with their robust features and rich functionality, would serve business-to-business markets. In this category, Nokia had to move fast as well. It was the key to lock in business markets, which in turn would ensure leadership in the future consumer markets as product innovations gradually trickle from the high end of the former to the low end of the latter.

Nokia Communicator. In March 1996, the company introduced the revolutionary Nokia 9000 Communicator, which combined digital voice and data services and personal organizer functions into a single, small, easy-to-use unit. Initially, the product was targeted to people on the move who needed access to various digital communications applications in multiple ways.[29] Nokia sought nothing less than category dominance with its Communicator 9000 series. "Digital cellular technology and the quality of networks have matured to a stage where Nokia sees a global opportunity for taking a giant leap towards the wireless pocketable office," stated Pekka Ala-Pietilä, president of Nokia Mobile Phones. "In Europe alone, GSM networks cover more than 300 million people, millions of which have a need for a versatile, simple, convenient and extremely compact communications tool. PCs revolutionized data processing, while fax machines, copiers and email systems transformed office automation. In a similar way, the Nokia 9000 Communicator will start a new era of wireless digital communications."[30]

Nokia and Palm Computing. In mid-October 1999, Nokia and the Palm Computing unit of 3Com announced that they would join forces to combine their products, including their operating systems. The broad joint development and licensing agreement were expected to create a new pen-based product category in the American market and subsequently on a worldwide basis, most likely in 2001. Indirectly, the cooperation between Nokia and Palm marginalized the bargaining power of Microsoft's Windows CE. Through this coalition, then, Nokia was skillfully shaping the competition in its favor.

Bluetooth

In 1998, Nokia also colaunched Bluetooth, a new consortium for wireless connectivity. The moniker referred to King Harold of Denmark, a.k.a. Harold Bluetooth, who unified his empire under Christianity in A.D. 986. This historical reference was a thinly veiled reference to the Nordic countries' leadership in the mobile Internet. At the end of the year, Bluetooth consisted of more than 250 active members; by early 2000, there were more than 1,200. The consortium aimed to create an open standard for short-range communications between different electronic devices (see Exhibit 9-8).[31] As a radio-based link, Bluetooth did not require a line-of-sight connection in order to establish communication. This capability enabled the creation of completely new applications such as personal devices that synchronize information without user intervention. The Bluetooth special interest group was led by a nine-company promoter group that included 3Com, Ericsson, IBM, Intel, Lucent Technologies, Microsoft, Motorola, Nokia, and Toshiba.[32]

Synchronization

By the end of the 1990s, mobile computing and communications devices promised to deliver information to users almost anytime and anywhere. This information could then be modified and updated in various locations and later synchronized by compatible applications when the user was back in the office or at home. Consequently, Nokia developed SyncML, its synchronization solution for the mobile information society.

SyncML aimed to deliver an open, industry-wide specification for the universal synchronization of remote data and personal information across multiple networks, platforms, and devices. The objective was to develop and promote a single data synchronization protocol that could be used in every compatible device and application. With SyncML-compatible applications, critical information such as e-mail, calendars, to-do lists, and contact information would be accessible and up-to-date regardless of the platform, manufacturer, or application.

The Discontents of Strategic Coalitions

These strategic coalitions played a critical role in Nokia's strategy to create a mobile information society. From Symbian and Bluetooth to WAP and other critical building blocks of the mobile future, Nokia built extraordinary sources of value that benefited a wide variety of existing and new industry players. Yet this cooperation may have benefited Nokia the most. Ultimately, the coalition partners served as Nokia's de facto technology suppliers. Although not vertically integrated, they filled empty slots in the process chain, which they also supported. The competitive advantage of Nokia's direct and indirect rivals was critically dependent on success in technology development, whereas the Finnish mobile vendor's advantage originated from downstream processes—where it initiated *no* strategic coalitions—

Exhibit 9-8. Wireless, Internet, and future applications: the enabling function of Bluetooth.

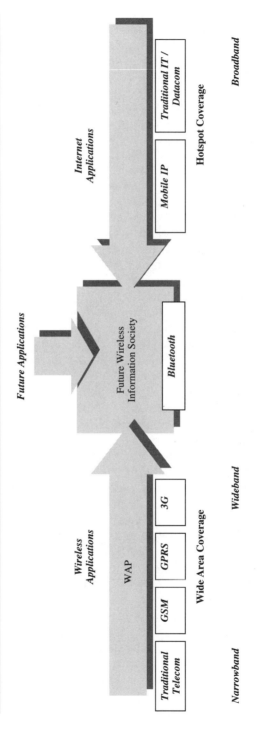

building and nurturing its brand as intently as Sony or Disney did with theirs.

With each strategic coalition, Nokia sought industry leadership through standardization and first-mover advantage. Such a coalition strategy is highly complex, based on the operational effectiveness of Nokia's in-house activities, including mobile phones, networks, communications products, and, more recently, venture capital. But it also relies on competitive scope through strategic coalitions. These facilitate such processes as competitive intelligence in scanning technology and environmental changes and technology and standardization initiatives through industry arenas and strategic partnerships. However, as the stakes grow, problems also emerge.

In January 2000, wireless technology provider Geoworks announced it would begin seeking fees for wireless data server systems and software utilizing the increasingly popular WAP, which the company believed was based partly on its patented technology. Geoworks's strategic move was a first among members of the WAP Forum. While the news sent its stock more than 100% higher, analysts considered the royalty debate a disastrous sign that could slow the industry's rapid growth. If other companies that owned pieces of the technology were to emulate Geoworks, the ensuing licensing struggles could stifle innovation from the estimated 30,000 WAP developers.

"The whole point of the WAP Forum is for everybody to work together and provide their intellectual property to each other at reasonable rates," said Cherie Gary, a Nokia spokeswoman.[33] Privately, the leading WAP Forum members, particularly Nokia and Phone.com, began consulting their lawyers. A strategic counterresponse followed in April 2000 when Phone.com filed a lawsuit against Geoworks in response to what it referred to as its rival's "aggressive" licensing plan. The suit sought a court order declaring that the patents were "invalid and unenforceable."[34]

In early March 2000, Geoworks stock reached a record-high $55. By August, it had decreased and stabilized at about $12. While the markets thought the leading WAP Forum players could somehow keep the members from breaking the ranks, the détente might not be a long-term solution. After all, the WAP standard was built on technology from several different companies, and many of them have rights to claim some intellectual property ownership (at least in theory). If these companies were to pursue their legitimate rights, that would interfere with industry growth and, ultimately, with their long-term interests. If they ignored their potential licensing rights, however, the scale economies of the industry growth would benefit lead coalition players, such as Nokia and Ericsson, more than smaller players, such as Geoworks. The royalty battles, then, were *not* just about esoteric intellectual property issues nor even about the difficulties inherent in coalition formation. These struggles reflected the constant tension among the entrenched industry giants and the innovative start-ups—the shifting balance of bargaining power that could make *and* break strategic coalitions.

Yet, these strategic coalitions continued to be a win-win situation for Nokia, which viewed the success or failure of upstream coalitions to be less critical to its own needs than to those of competitors. If Nokia's coalition strategy were viewed as a system of interdependent processes, the mastery of such a complex whole required subtle strategic maneuvering where the boundaries of competition and cooperation were blurred by design. Nokia's supplier and partner management was a case in point.

Supplier and Partner Management

Because Nokia has not integrated into semiconductors, it has nurtured solid and efficient long-term supplier relationships over two decades. In turn, the suppliers have significantly benefited from the company's rapid growth.

By 1997, Nokia functioned as a growth engine for the entire Finnish information, communication, and technology (ICT) cluster, whose value chains consisted of ICT equipment, networks, and related services (FIM 57 billion and 44,400 employees); telecommunications services (FIM 15.5 billion and 17,000 employees); and components and contract manufacturing (FIM 8 billion and 10,000 employees). In the equipment, networks, and related services segment, Nokia served as the growth core, with turnover of FIM 35 billion and 19,300 employees. In the Finnish cluster revenues, Nokia's contribution was an estimated 40 percent; of cluster exports, this share amounted to 80 percent.[35] By the end of the 1990s, the impact of globalization had permeated the entire value chain.

Nokia's strategy ensured that its suppliers extracted *more* value than did suppliers in other industries. Consider, for instance, the similarities and differences between Microsoft and Nokia. Through its dominance in operating systems and applications software, Microsoft was able to influence the evolution and expansion of personal computers from the late 1980s to the late 1990s. In mobile wireless, Nokia played a parallel function throughout the 1990s, defining technical agendas, setting standards, driving down costs, and dispersing affordable handsets to a broad base of users. But more than Microsoft, Nokia has invested in cooperation, strategic coalitions, and open standards.

It nurtured suppliers through procurement, which contributed to its growth.[36]

Since the beginning of the Ollila era, Nokia has patiently built a sophisticated supply chain, which also contributed to its global leadership and ensured the rapid growth of its suppliers. In 1999, the company had an estimated 15,000 subcontractors in Finland alone, where the number of Nokia's own employees was 21,000.[37] The subcontractors possessed little strategic flexibility. Business models were customized according to Nokia's requirements. Consequently, most suppliers relied on cost-focus strategies in which margins were highly dependent on high volumes.[38] Just as Nokia accelerated standardization in upstream innovation, its bargaining power compelled suppliers to seize cost-focus strategies. In the former case, it could clone new technology innovations; in the latter case, it could choose among elite suppliers. Concurrently, upstream innovators have been left with operational effectiveness that at best resulted in fleeting and short-term strategic advantages, whereas only Nokia has managed to thrive in strategic differentiation.

In 2000, Nokia's subcontractors consisted of electronics contract manufacturers, component suppliers, software and product development companies, production equipment suppliers, and service companies that were indirectly dependent on Nokia. To some extent, the sources of competitive advantage among suppliers emulated those of their lead customers, i.e., price (annual price erosion amounted to 20–30 percent in base station products), quality, flexibility and responsiveness, customer service, and globalization. In practice, partnership meant that the suppliers were willing to take risks in servicing their lead customers.

Toward the end of the 1990s, consolidation accelerated among contract manufacturers, in particular. U.S.-based SCI purchased Nokia factories in Oulu and Motala, Finland, while Flextronics bought Kyrel, and Sweden-based Essex acquired Finland-based Enviset. As big players concentrated on mass production, small ones were specializing, and mid-size competitors were squeezed out of the markets. "The pace is frenetic and the competition is tough," said Antti Jokitalo, the marketing chief of Essex. "During the past two years, international big manufacturers have arrived in the Nordic countries, where they have bought factories and subcontractors of their lead customers."[39]

Components and Contract Manufacturing

Nokia's success has not automatically translated into supplier success. The more dependent a supplier is on its lead customer, the more diminished its bargaining power and the greater the risk. In the late 1990s, for instance, Allgon, a Swedish maker of cell phone antennas, was swept by tight margins as production costs soared. In contrast, STMicroelectronics was thriving; its largest customer, Nokia, accounted for only 10 percent of its sales of flash memory and other components. Furthermore, the French chipmaker was also supplying Alcatel, Nortel, Motorola, and Ericsson.[40]

In the course of the 1990s, several successful subcontractors grew and internationalized along with Nokia. They followed their lead customer while expanding their customer base and new market potential. Such was the case for Elcoteq Networks, JOT Automation, Eimo, and Perlos, for which mobile phones were the common denominator. Eimo and Perlos manufactured molded plastic covers, Elcoteq produced mobile phones and phone parts, and JOT Automation built the equipment that Elcoteq and NMP used to manufacture their phones. Most earned 80 to 90 percent of their revenues from mobile phone-related products. All served as subcontractors for Nokia and Ericsson.

Elcoteq Networks

Through its rapid globalization, Nokia exerted powerful influence abroad with a number of contract manufacturers and subcontractors.[41] Elcoteq, for example, was the leading European provider of electronics manufacturing services, with headquarters in Helsinki and Lohja, located in southern Finland.[42] Following Nokia's example, its mission was to continuously improve the performance of the value chains it participated in through its customers and suppliers. Tuomo Lähdesmäki, Elcoteq's managing director, had worked at Nokia through the 1980s. Elcoteq Networks produced electronics subassemblies and end products for a variety of different customer applications.

Built upon the latest components and mounting technologies, Elcoteq's operation was supported by technology, purchasing and logistics, procurement, and postmarketing services. "Opportunities are immense in the North American marketplace," asserted Ilkka Pouttu, Elcoteq's chief of operations in the Americas (and a veteran employee of Motorola and Nokia's Mobira). "We're surfing on three growth waves—electronics, contract manufacturing, and telecommunications."[43] By the end of the 1990s, Elcoteq also followed Nokia's footsteps in internationalization (see Exhibits 9-9 and 9-10), which cost the company some EUR 14 million and hurt its share price until the end of 1999.

Elcoteq's customers were global high-technology companies engaged in telecommunications, IT, and selected fields of industrial and consumer electronics. In addition to Nokia, its key customers included ABB, Allgon, Axis, Benefon, Ericsson, Kone, Micronas, Optrex, Philips,

Exhibit 9-9. Elcoteq's strategy and structure: international expansion and global matrix.

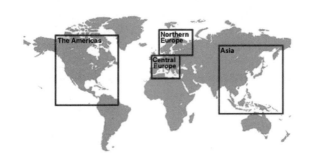

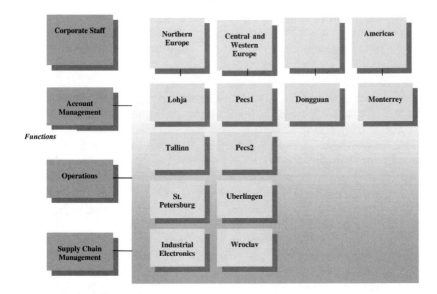

SOURCE: www.elcoteq.fi

Planar, Vaisala, and Viking. Like Nokia, Elcoteq considered customer satisfaction its ultimate value. By 1999, it had more than 9,000 employees, operations in twelve countries, and net sales in excess of EUR 750 million. "We're today the world's 16th largest contract manufacturer, but, at this pace, our ranking will soon improve," argued Pouttu. "We've become a global player, and there are no alternatives to these developments."[44] The world leaders in contract manufacturing—companies such as SCI, Solectron, and Flextronics—were far bigger

Exhibit 9-10. Elcoteq's milestones.

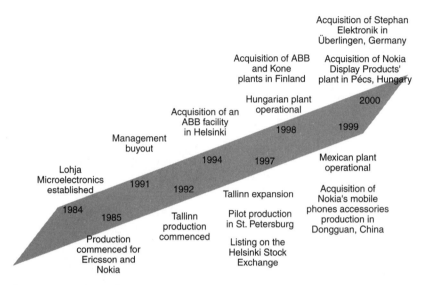

SOURCE: www.elcoteq.fi

than Elcoteq. Unlike these big players, however, the company favored strategic focus, concentrating only on digital communications.

Like so many other suppliers, Elcoteq took the idea of coevolution seriously and understood it as a way of working together with customers and other partners such as R&D institutes and materials suppliers.[45] Through coevolution, it aspired to define with all parties the objectives necessary to optimize the value chain and to set out the tasks and responsibilities to achieve these objectives. Unlike the weaker Finnish players, Elcoteq had managed to leverage its capabilities and served both Nokia Mobile Phones and Ericsson. It was critically dependent on these two incumbents, which accounted for an estimated 87 percent of its revenues in 2000. In the future, Elcoteq also hoped to do business with Motorola.

Eimo

Founded in 1959, Eimo at first turned out buttons (six at a time) with a small manual press and sold them to local dressmakers. Early expansion did not proceed in a planned manner. "At the time, I had no grand idea about the fact that a company must focus, concentrate on what it can do the best," said Jalo Paananen, the founder of Eimo.[46] With five injection-molding plants, one mold factory, and more than

700 employees in 2000, the start-up had evolved into a rapid-growth technology supplier with a turnover of EUR 78 million (50 percent exports).

Eimo perceived itself as a primary supplier to the mobile communications industry. Its objective was "to become a globally significant manufacturer of precision plastic components."[47] Like Nokia, Eimo paid great attention to reliability, flexibility, and rapid response. Mobile communications accounted for 91 percent of its turnover in 1999. Eimo's markets were global; the company supplied components for mobile telephones and their accessories in Europe, America, and Asia. In mid-July 2000, Eimo used stock valued at $161 million to purchase the bigger U.S.-based Triple S, thus creating a significant global supplier to the telecom industry (see Exhibit 9-11).

Net sales for the combined group totaled approximately $167 million. Based in Lahti, Finland, it employed a staff of 1,500 in Europe and North America. While the mobile sector generated over 90 percent of Eimo's sales, Nokia accounted for more than 50 percent of these sales and made up 60 percent of Triple S's. Expected cost synergies were not the prime factor in the merger, which sought to create benefits by pooling the company's expertise and customer base, but globalization was. "Eimo has a lot of technologies that Triple S does not have and which are sold to customers in the U.S. and neighboring regions," said Eimo's executive vice chairman, Elmar Paananen.[48]

Exhibit 9-11. The internationalization of Eimo/Triple S.

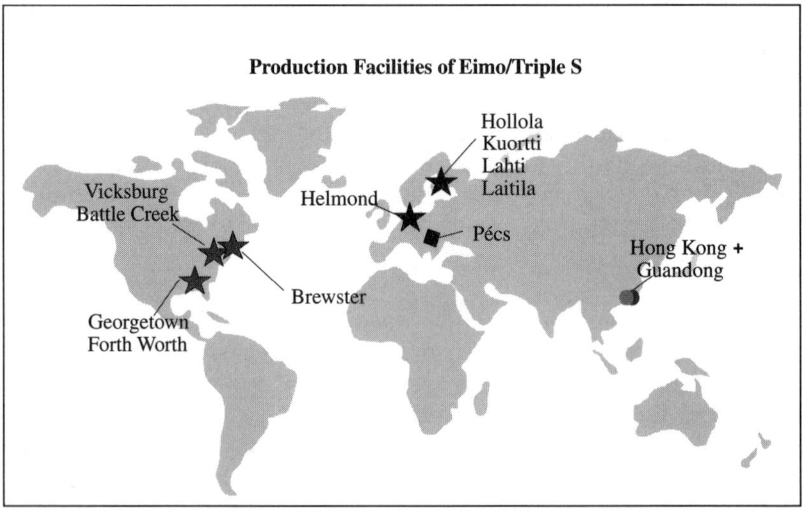

Production Facilities of Eimo/Triple S

Hollola
Kuortti
Lahti
Laitila
Pécs

Vicksburg
Battle Creek

Helmond

Hong Kong +
Guandong

Brewster

Georgetown
Forth Worth

SOURCE: www.eimo.fi

The new entity still trailed Perlos, another Nokia supplier, but Eimo remained interested in more acquisitions in Asia, Brazil, and Mexico. Worldwide, Eimo and Perlos competed with Nolaton, Ericsson's lead supplier, and the U.S.-based Nypro, Motorola's lead supplier in China. In the Nordic region, the two Finnish companies had smaller rivals that included Iplast in Norway, Wilden and Balda in Germany, and Rosti in Denmark. Yet, *all* suppliers remained critically dependent on their lead clients—Nokia, Ericsson, and Motorola, in particular, but also Philips, Alcatel, Lucent, NEC, Siemens, and the new Asian players.

Wecan

"Your Global Partner in Electronics Manufacturing" was the slogan of Wecan Electronics. It applied equally to most of Nokia's lead subcontractors. Founded in 1970, Wecan operated in electronics contract manufacturing. By 1999, its turnover amounted to FIM 185 million, and the estimate for 2000 was FIM 285 million.

With 450 employees, the company manufactured products for telecommunications and control systems and maintained production facilities in Finland, Estonia, and China (see Exhibit 9-12) as well as service units in the United Kingdom and Helsinki, Finland. The company offered customized partnership and full production services in

Exhibit 9-12. The internationalization of Wecan Electronics.

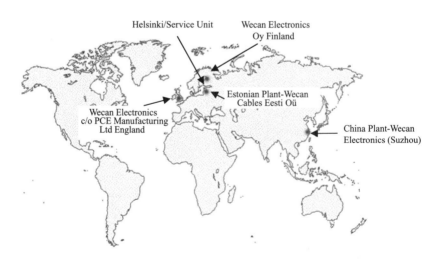

SOURCE: www.wecan.fi

addition to effective quality, planning, and control initiatives, which included quick response time to requested improvements.

Like Nokia, it continuously measured customer satisfaction. To increase flexibility, efficiency, and speed and to widen its technology base, it had built up a network with suppliers and strategic partners (see Exhibit 9-13).[49] When Nokia experienced business problems, however, that left little strategic flexibility for Wecan and other similar small to medium-size suppliers. While each sought to diversify risk, most remained dependent on Nokia's fortunes and had to endure great volatility amid strategic inflection points.

Elektrobit

Founded in 1985, Elektrobit initially worked in the software engineering field but grew to become involved in RF communications, cellular communications technology, and more recently, spread-spectrum technology. Special applications became a separate business area, drawing on the strengths of the company's experience in various technologies to fulfill contracts in the military and industrial automation fields. By 2000, Elektrobit had seven business segments, ranging from research and telecommunications projects to embedded communications and various regional services. It also had subsidiaries in the United States, Japan, and Switzerland (see Exhibit 9-14). Headquartered in Oulu, Elektrobit's engineers and designers were experts in telecommunications and industrial control.[50]

Others

Certainly, Nokia's expansion would not have been as smooth without efficient manufacturing partnerships, i.e., JOT Automation and PMJ Automec. These two Finnish companies automated final assembly and packaging to eliminate labor-intensive bottlenecks in the production process. By the fall of 1999, Nokia accounted for less than half of the earnings at JOT, which was now supplying other industry leaders, including Compaq, Intel, and contract manufacturers in Asia. Nokia's growth of new product lines translated into new production lines and ultimately into earnings for JOT.[51]

At Logica, the U.K. provider of IT support and software, the Aldiscon division put together the software that allowed wireless operators to sign up prepaid customers, a rapid-growth segment. In Finland, with more than ten years of experience in mobile data communication design and production, Aerial—yet another Nokia supplier—produced computer hardware for the vehicle environment. As vehicle fleet operators were becoming increasingly aware of the benefits of in-

Exhibit 9-13. Nokia and Wecan Electronics Oyj (formerly Pohjanmaan Tele Ky): milestones of an ecosystem.

1970s

The Start-Up Years

- 1970 Elsa and Pekka Aakula founded Pohjanmaan Tele Ky ["the company"] in Ylivieska, Finland. Initially, the company employed 15 people. The first customer was Televa.
- 1972 The company was able to expand its customer base with ITT and Siemens. A 450 m² plant was built.
- 1975 A plant extension was finished; now the surface area amounted to 600 m².
- 1978 Finland was swept up in the worldwide recession (oil crisis). At worst, the company was forced to reduce the staff to only 5 people. The company tried to sell out the plant and to move to smaller leased premises; fortunately, the plan failed. The city of Ylivieska assisted Pohjamaan Tele Ky by giving a longer loan period for the premises.

1980s

The First Nokia Subcontracting Activities

- During the 1980s, the company employed 25 to 50 people.
- 1980 The company experienced new growth thanks to cable coils, which it manufactured for Nokia. At first, the operation employed 5 people; in the mid-80s 20–30 people were manufacturing these products. The company also had small-scale R&D activities.

- 1982 The company received orders from Rosenlew (switchboards).
- 1984 The company received an order from Vestösuojaliitto (Civil Defense Center Authority), which ordered internal phone center planning and manufacturing for Helsinki subway shelters.
- 1985 The company received a FIM 5 million order from HPY, the largest Finnish local telephone operator. The company supplied HPY with voice-frequency receivers. With more R&D, the company sold these products to other operators as well for the next 3–5 years.
- 1987 The company received contract manufacturing for NMT from Nokia.

1990s

The GSM Era

- 1991 Finland was swept by a severe recession and the company was forced to reduce its staff to fewer than 30 employees.
- 1992 The company landed a GSM-standard contract manufacturing for Nokia that initiated a new growth period.
- 1996 The company changed its name to Wecan Electronics Ky and then to Wecan Electronics Oy. Its main products were backplanes, cables, and modules.

- 1997 Wecan Electronics Oy opened a cable plant in Prnu, Estonia.
- 1998 Wecan Electronics Oy launched Wecan Electronics Corp. Service Unit in Dallas, Texas, to support Nokia's and its own subcontractors.
- 1999 Wecan Electronics established a factory in Suzhou, China, to meet Nokia's needs in Asia. The company also established the service unit to Milton Kaynes, England, together with its English partner, PCE. It was a breakthrough event for Nokia Network's supply chain in England. Turnover in 1999 increased by 42% and amounted to EUR 31.4 million.

2000

- Wecan Electronics employed approximately 450 people: 200 in Finland, 200 in Estonia, and 50 in China.
- Extension of the Finnish plant completed; the surface area now amounted to 4,500 m².
- Nokia Network announced that it would close the base station factory in Dallas. Consequently, Wecan also closed its Service Unit there.
- The company launched its Service Unit in Helsinki to coordinate cable logistics with its Estonia plant.
- Wecan Electronics Oy became Wecan Electronics Oyj and had its IPO. Wecan Electronics Oyj shares were listed on the Helsinki Stock Exchange.

formation systems, it provided the means to connect the vehicles of its customers to their operative information systems. In effect, Aerial originated from Nokia in 1990 as a spin-off of the Mobile Data Unit of Nokia Mobile Phones. Today the company has "grown around and expanded from this core." By 2000, it operated internationally, its domestic market area covered all of Europe, and its target was to expand operations globally.[52]

Exhibit 9-14. The internationalization of Elektrobit.

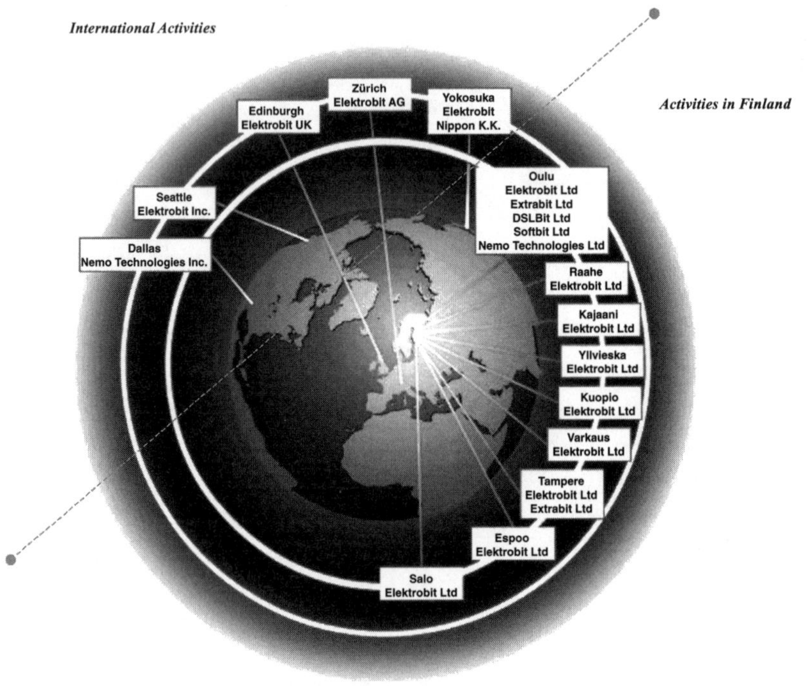

International Activities

Activities in Finland

Zürich
Elektrobit AG

Yokosuka
Elektrobit
Nippon K.K.

Edinburgh
Elektrobit UK

Seattle
Elektrobit Inc.

Dallas
Nemo Technologies Inc.

Oulu
Elektrobit Ltd
Extrabit Ltd
DSLBit Ltd
Softbit Ltd
Nemo Technologies Ltd

Raahe
Elektrobit Ltd

Kajaani
Elektrobit Ltd

Ylivieska
Elektrobit Ltd

Kuopio
Elektrobit Ltd

Varkaus
Elektrobit Ltd

Tampere
Elektrobit Ltd
Extrabit Ltd

Espoo
Elektrobit Ltd

Salo
Elektrobit Ltd

SOURCE: www.elektrobit.fi

The Swedish Allgon was not Nokia's sole antenna producer. Aerial had some 30 years experience in the design, production, and testing of antennas.[53] Its service concept includes antennas and antenna products, consultation, design, and measurement. From the very beginning of the industry, Nordic cellular networks had relied on Aerial's antennas.

Operators and Services

In addition to components and contract manufacturing, Nokia's value chain consisted of telecommunications/mobile services.

Sonera

Starting in the 1970s, Sonera—then still Finland's PTT—was Nokia's first major client in the telecommunications segment.[54] By the fall of 1999, Sonera had evolved into a growth company that played a critical role in Finland's "Wireless Valley." It had diversified geographically, buying 8 percent of Voicestream, an American cellular operator; it also had several minority stakes in emerging mobile markets.[55] It was considered the most technologically progressive operator in Europe, and it introduced a slate of mobile Internet applications, giving rise to mobile commerce and new value-added services. Sonera had become a major player in mobile portals (Sonera 2ed) and in the security segment (Sonera/SmartTrust) encryption technology for wireless networks, a system that could potentially compete with credit cards by letting users charge purchases on their phones. By the end of the 1990s, Sonera was no longer "just" a Nokia customer. Seeking to become a leading mobile commerce facilitator, it cooperated with the leading mobile vendor but had also become its competitor in mobile wireless services.

Merita-Nordbanken: Mobile Banking

In the late 1990s, KOP, along with other Finnish banks, had struggled for corporate control of the old, diversified Nokia. By 1998, it had been reconfigured and renamed Merita. The Internet rapidly became a central component of the bank's strategy and identity. The 136-year-old Finnish bank, newly merged with a Swedish lender, recognized several benefits in the Internet: lower costs through a smaller workforce, better customer retention through added convenience, and greater ability to lure new customers away from competitors that did not offer Internet service. By a general consensus, no banks in either the United States or Europe had been as proactive in this process as Merita, which first offered home banking over the phone as early as 1982.[56] By the summer of 1998, 420,000 of Merita's customers (roughly 27 percent of its active client base) were banking online. Deutsche Bank AG was more than ten times the size of Merita in terms of assets but had only around 300,000 customers banking online (less than 10 percent of its customer base). In the United States, Citicorp had 400,000 clients banking online, but the giant slated to merge with Travelers Group Incorporated was many times larger than Merita.[57]

Merita-Nordbanken teamed up with Sonera to explore new financial business opportunities spawned by the mobile Internet. Following a merger with Unidanmark, the number of online customers increased to 1.4 million, and the bank claimed to have the largest number of online banking customers and transactions in the world. Merita-Nordbanken had considerable experience in mobile commerce because its customers had been using their mobile phones for bill payment since 1992. The arrival of WAP, however, meant the acceleration of new opportunities through mobile commerce.

ICT Equipment, Networks, and Related Services

Although Nokia played the key role in the core ICT segment, it relied on others as well.

Satama Interactive

By 2000, Satama Interactive, the dot-com subsidiary of Talentum (the leading Finnish business and IT magazine publisher), was the country's pioneering digital consulting and design company; its parent had pumped nearly EUR 25 million into Internet and new media investments. Satama helped its clients to build better customer relationships through wireless and wired technologies. Ambitious to internationalize rapidly, Satama Interactive employed almost 400 e-business professionals in six countries. In 1999, for example, Nokia.com and Nokia Club service solutions were created for Nokia. Satama Interactive grew along with Nokia, its key customer.[58] In addition to Satama Interactive, Nokia relied on ICL Finland for its e-commerce solutions. Unlike Satama, ICL had adequate critical mass, technical expertise, and client bases.

F-Secure

In 2000, F-Secure had become a leading provider of data security solutions,[59] developing, marketing, and supporting a broad range of centrally managed and widely distributed best-of-breed antivirus and encryption software applications as well as the F-Secure Framework, a data security architecture for corporate computer networks. The company had entered into a number of strategic original equipment manufacturer (OEM) agreements pursuant to which Data Fellows's best-of-breed data security applications were integrated into the services and products of leading communications and IT companies. These companies included Cisco Systems, Digital Island, Fujitsu, IBM, Ericsson, and Sonera in addition to Nokia.[60] Indeed, Olli-Pekka Kallasvuo, Nokia's CFO, sat on the F-Secure board.

■ ■ ■ ■ ■

By 2000, Nokia was making every third cell phone in the world. Coupled with market leadership, the global focus strategy strengthened its supplier relationships. Suppliers prioritized and concentrated the bulk of their production for Nokia, which was able to introduce new models faster than its rivals. Further, while close to 70 percent of Finns already had cell phones, only 7 percent of the world population owned them.

If Nokia were to survive the transition from the 2G communications to the 3G era, then, as Ollila often put it, the "best was yet to come."

Nokia had evolved in a rapid-growth industry by driving innovation in product and process development and supplier/partner management. In particular, its supplier relationships had been characterized by typical growing pains. Through the mobile Internet, Nokia sought to create a new growth cycle. "What's important to us is that the supplier chain as a whole is cost-efficient, agile and can rapidly respond to demand fluctuations," said Jorma Nyberg, materials chief of NTC, who estimated the number of subcontractors at "several hundreds" in 1999. Over time, the company had tightened its supplier criteria. It no longer needed smaller contractors, which often failed to expand their production fast enough. Like many other Nokians, Nyberg avoided the term subcontractor. "It's old-fashioned. We speak of cooperators and partnerships."[61]

Given its cooperative approach, Nokia's supplier ties were deep and strong. Yet in the long run, maturation was bound to affect supplier relationships as well. The suppliers sought to protect themselves by rapid growth and expansion of their customer portfolios, which promised to reduce dependency on a single customer. As long as Nokia continued to grow, few cracks were visible in the armor, but when the growth slowed down, friction accelerated rapidly.

Even if Ollila and Nokia's group executive board had greatly contributed to the overall design of these strategic coalitions, the company relied significantly on decentralization within the corporate organization and cooperation with suppliers and partners, just as it was dependent on first-mover advantages. Since the mid-1990s, Nokia had been able to control "the whole," but this would be more difficult in the long term, as evidenced by the stock market slides of 2000. In late July 2000, Nokia's shares of the mobile vendor fell twenty-five percent as investors dumped shares after a warning about third-quarter results. On July 27, Nokia started the day with a market capitalization of about $257.2 billion and finished at about $192.9 billion in New York Stock Exchange composite trading. In the course of the day, some $64.3 billion was erased from the previously soaring market value.

Only a month before, some of Nokia's key suppliers in Finland had released warnings about their own third-quarter results. "At the same time, Nokia is growing explosively," reported the leading Finnish morning daily, *Helsingin Sanomat.* "Is Nokia's success based on the losses of its suppliers?"[62] As analysts explored the relationships between Nokia and its publicly owned suppliers (JOT, PMJ, Elcoteq, Eimo, Perlos), they found that the ratio between working capital and revenues had decreased at Nokia but increased at its suppliers. This, they argued, indicated that Nokia might be squeezing its suppliers, which had to wait for payments longer than before. On the basis of indirect evidence, however, it was difficult to assess the true nature of these supplier relationships.[63]

Certainly, these suppliers might characterize their role vis-à-vis Nokia as "coevolution," and it would not be a misrepresentation; the internationalization and expansion of Nokia's suppliers were stimulated by Nokia's hypergrowth. Still, the coevolution members did not share equal bargaining power. The highly cost-efficient value chain was designed under the terms of the mobile vendor rather than its suppliers.

Downstream Innovation

BY 2000, Nokia was known for its expertise in global segmentation, branding, and design. The emphasis on process configuration had shifted from technological innovation to customer fit. However, only a decade before, the company knew relatively little about the significance of market segmentation and possessed a brand that was known primarily only in the Nordic countries; in addition, design was still secondary to technology considerations.

Nokia was known for most of the 1980s as an OEM, acting as a supplier for several industry giants, such as IBM, Control Data, Tandy, Northern Telecom, Hitachi, Olivetti, Ericsson, and British Telecom. The OEM strategy was useful as long as Nokia did not have adequate marketing experience of its own. In the late 1980s, however, the company had exhausted this strategic route. As a Finnish industry observer noted, "Price competition is tough, and quality maintenance is difficult. Marketing is Nokia's number one problem. Surely, it is using acquisitions to accumulate marketing experience and distribution channels."[1]

By the end of the 1980s, Nokia initiated efforts to revise its marketing approach. Until then, most of its American sales had consisted of low-price car phones sold through the 5,000 RadioShack stores of Tandy Corporation, which owned a 50 percent stake in Nokia's plant in South Korea. Nokia's most expensive product, a Finnish-made phone that could be used outside the car, had been peddled through its Mobira subsidiary. Meanwhile, Mobira set out to sell the Korean phones as well, not in competition with Tandy but perhaps through phone companies. These more direct sales were expected to boost margins. Other suppliers were able to match Nokia's trend-setting products until the 1990s.[2]

Discontinuous developments in the mobile cellular rivalry forced Nokia to move from traditional volume business toward market segmentation years before the concept of the mobile Internet emerged. These innovations occurred in a small telecommunications unit that was considered strategic in the future Nokia but had little impact on the company's corporate-level strategy through the 1980s. At head-quarters, things began to change dramatically when Ollila took charge in 1992.

Market Segmentation

By the end of the 1990s, the mobile market was rapidly expanding while the composition of sales was changing as well. In addition to an increasing number of people buying their first phones, there was a growing upgrade market. A third evolving market was that for multiple handset ownership. In 1999, upgrades accounted for some 40 percent of unit sales, and the share was likely to rise to about 50 percent in 2000 and to around 70–80 percent in the next few years. Equipment manufacturers were struggling to design handsets for all actual consumer segments, from hiking enthusiasts' water-repellent, shock-resistant Gore-Tex phones with rubber gaskets to colorful, interchangeable plastic covers for fashion-conscious teens and easy-to-use models for the twelve-year-old set. Precipitating the trend, Nokia had introduced its colorful snap-on covers for mobile phones in the mid-1990s. By the end of the decade, its phone covers were available in a rainbow assortment of bright colors with names like meteor yellow and zircon green. Following the colors came graphic design. Again, Nokia anticipated the future by hiring a group of emerging young artists to design its latest batch of snap-on jackets.[3] Yet, generic needs were quite different in different segments. While snap-on covers could contribute to the purchase decision of some consumers, business users required functionality.

Nokia excelled in segmentation, which was relatively new to the company; it had been adopted along with the focus strategy only in the 1990s. Throughout the Kairamo era, Nokia had been driven by the imperative to internationalize. Near the end of the 1980s, the mobile phone division was crafting a global strategy. As Ollila focused the company, the strategic issues of the mobile unit became those of the corporation itself. Concurrently, the momentum in mobile communications was moving from business markets to consumer markets, i.e., from niche strategies to segmentation. As a result, the segmentation issues of the mobile unit became corporate-level issues at Nokia head-quarters, which was now rapidly moving toward global markets. The imperatives of globalization and segmentation became one through *global segmentation.*[4]

The distinctive issues of Nokia's new global strategy can be illustrated in the two fundamental ways a company chooses to compete internationally. *Configuration* refers to the location where each process in the value chain is performed, including the number of such places. *Coordination* refers to how like or linked processes performed in different countries are coordinated with each other. In both cases, a company has a wide array of options for each process in the value chain, i.e., both support processes (management, control, HRM, and R&D) and primary processes (product and customer commitment processes). While configuration options range from highly concentrated (e.g., performing a process in a single location that serves worldwide markets) to dispersed (e.g., performing a process in many countries), coordination options range from none (low coordination) to many (high coordination).

Through the Kairamo era, Nokia had for all practical purposes relied on an export-based strategy with decentralized marketing. The company was driven by a deep-seated motivation to internationalize, but the direction of this internationalization remained unclear. It was still largely a domestic company competing via a country-centered strategy. Foreign investment was relatively low, and there was minimal coordination among the subsidiaries. Kairamo's Nokia was a Finnish technology conglomerate with great international ambitions. But starting with the Ollila era, the new, focused Nokia seized on a global strategy that relied on extensive coordination among subsidiaries and increasing foreign investment (see Exhibit 10-1a).

There were two intriguing alternatives to this approach. A simple global strategy would have required high coordination among subsidiaries but low foreign investment. But it conflicted with Nokia's need to establish market presence to ensure responsiveness. Conversely, a multidomestic strategy would have built upon high foreign investment but minimal coordination among subsidiaries. That did not conflict with Nokia's market imperative, but it would have conflicted with its strong corporate culture and values, which required high coordination to enable market responsiveness. In mobile communications, all international strategies that were based on low process coordination would be doomed to extinction in the long run. Consider, for instance, the takeoff of mobile activities in Europe in the early 1980s. In contrast to the tiny Nordic countries that lacked appropriate resources and critical mass, Germany, Italy, and France—three of the largest European countries—chose to develop their own proprietary systems in cooperation with their preferred domestic telecommunications suppliers. With minimal resources and no critical mass initially, Nokia's *strategic* decisions and the favorable Nordic environment enabled the company to globalize more quickly and efficiently than its rivals in Western Europe.

An alternative approach to internationalization is to explore geographic and market reach in a global industry (see Exhibit 10-1b). Ab-

Exhibit 10-1. Dimensions of international strategy.

(a) Types of International Strategy

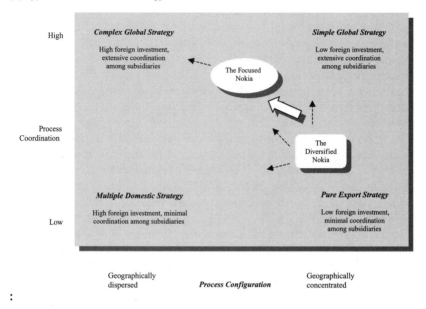

(b) Geographical and Segment Scope in Global Industry

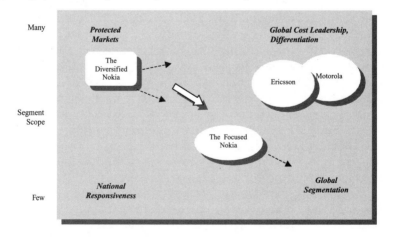

stracting from a specific configuration/coordination framework, there are four broad kinds of strategies in a global industry. Any competitive strategy involves a choice of the type of competitive advantage sought (low cost or differentiation), just as it requires the choice of the competitive scope within which the advantage is to be achieved. In global industries, competitive scope includes two factors: first, the industry segments in which the company competes and, second, whether it seeks the benefits of configuration/coordination across countries or a country-centered approach to competing. These dimensions generate four generic global strategies.

In *protected markets,* companies seek out countries where market positions are protected by host governments. In the past, regulation, lax or absent competition policies, and national industrial policies provided havens for protected-markets strategies in select industries, particularly telecommunications. In mobile communications, however, deregulation and accelerating international rivalry have boosted competitive markets. In *global cost leadership,* and *differentiation,* companies seek cost, differentiation, or both advantages of global configuration/coordination through a wide line of products to buyers in all of the lead markets. Historically, the global strategies of Motorola and Ericsson, Nokia's primary direct rivals, can be situated in this dimension.

Since the early 1990s, Nokia's focus strategy has required concentration on only a few industry segments. Thus, it has not opted for protected markets, global cost leadership, or differentiation. In *national responsiveness,* companies focus on those industry segments that are most affected by local country differences, even when the industry as a whole is global. While the protected-markets strategy rests on government impediments, the national-responsiveness strategy is based on economic impediments. It is driven by the company's efforts to meet unique local needs in products, channels, and marketing practices in individual countries and, thus, must neglect the competitive advantages of a global strategy. While national-responsiveness strategies, to a different extent, have been characteristic of some of Nokia's lead markets (such as Japan and China), they have not been used by Nokia. Because the Finnish company has opted for a truly global strategy, national responsiveness would have denied it the very advantage it sought. Hence, Nokia has been interested primarily in global segmentation.

In *global segmentation,* companies serve a particular industry segment worldwide or compete in a subset of countries where the advantages of concentration/coordination are particularly favorable. As a strategy, global segmentation fit Nokia's goals and aspirations perfectly. It captured the advantages of a truly global strategy but did not prescribe the kind of resources the company initially lacked. Instead, it enabled Nokia to optimally allocate its resources by focusing on a narrow segment. Global segmentation had been typical of the early phase of the "Japanese challenge" in the 1960s and 1970s; at the time, it served as the first step in a sequenced strategy to move from a domestic or multidomestic strategy toward a global strategy.[5]

Establishing an initial foothold at the low end of the product line, many Japanese challengers later expanded into full-line positions (just as in the Internet revolution many U.S.-based pure online players initiated their activities in the low-end market segments that served as footholds for later full-line attacks).[6] Instead, Nokia, throughout the 1990s, consistently stuck to its preferred industry segments (mobile phones, telecommunication networks) but extended them rapidly and aggressively across multiple locations, especially in the lead markets.

Since the early 1990s, then, Nokia's focus strategy has been global and has taken advantage of global segmentation. With the transition to the process organization in the first half of the 1990s, these strategic characteristics have fit Nokia's value chain particularly well. After all, the upstream parts of the business (e.g., production, procurement, relevant technologies) tend to be relatively similar, and standardization has made them even more so. As a result, the real differences have emerged in the *downstream* parts, where the leading rivals interact with customers. Indeed, Nokia has purposefully homogenized the upstream part of the value process while it has captured market and mind share in the downstream side of the value chain by creating new bases of competitive differentiation (i.e., branding, design). As standards coalitions have contributed to the increasingly homogeneous technology base of the leading mobile cellular players, the downstream function has become critical in industry rivalry. In order to respond to market evolution, and given its market-making strategies, Nokia has shifted competitive differentiation from upstream to downstream (see Exhibit 10-2).

In relative terms, Nokia's key rivals have exhausted resources in manufacturing, operations, and logistics, where industry similarities reign. They have concentrated on upstream processes that are increasingly characterized by cost-leadership rivalry. They have also invested relatively more in upstream innovation globally, i.e., homogeneous and standardized technologies. In contrast, Nokia has sought optimal allocation of resources by concentrating on industry differences in branding, design, and marketing. It has seized downstream processes as bases for competitive differentiation, and more than its rivals, it has invested in regional, in some cases even domestic, downstream activities. Nokia's product development process has been built upon operational effectiveness, whereas its strategic maneuvering has focused on the customer commitment process.

Exhibit 10-2. Global segmentation and competitive differentiation: Nokia and industry rivals.

Product Development Process   *Customer Commitment Process*

Inbound Logistics	Operations	Outbound Logistics	Branding and Design	Marketing	
					Segment 1
					Segment 2
					Segment 3
					Segment 4
					Segment n

- Industry similarities in manufacturing, operations, and logistics
- Upstream cost-leadership rivalry
- Homogeneous, standardized technologies
- Stress on global innovation

- Industry differences in branding, design, and marketing
- Downstream bases for competitive differentiation
- Heterogeneous, unique product differentiation
- Stress on regional/domestic tailoring

Nokia's focus strategy has been global, taking advantage of global segmentation while stressing the downstream parts of the value chain. In this process, marketing strategy has played a critical role—particularly in terms of the type (lifestyle segmentation) and timing (technology-adoption life cycles) of segmentation.

Lifestyle Segmentation

The central segmentation variables are well known in marketing literature. Usually, they are said to encompass demographic (age, gender, occupation, income, education, family size), geographic (region, city/metro size, density, climate), psychographics (lifestyle, personality), and behavioral segmentation (benefits, user status, usage rate, occasions).[7] These segmentation variables are not mutually exclusive and are, in fact, most often used in combination. In the 1998 U.S. market, for instance, more women than men were wireless users (55 percent vs. 45 percent, respectively). Similarly, young adults (eighteen to thirty-four years old) were the most active age group (31 percent of users). In terms of income, occupation, and education, the core categories made $30,000 to $50,000 per year, were professionals and managers, and had college or advanced degrees. Consumers typically used their cell phones for personal needs (61 percent) more than business (21 percent), spending some $26 to $50 per month.[8]

Indeed, the use of demographics, geographics, and behavioral segmentation has been fairly typical in most mobile industry studies, whereas lifestyle segmentation has required far more specific information on user populations. The more the vendors have aspired to differentiate on the basis of their customers' real-life usage patterns, the more they have required market research to listen to, understand, and satisfy the market needs.

That has been the objective of Nokia's market strategy. Like other major mobile vendors, Nokia has used the segmentation variables in combination. However, as the mobile cellular industry has begun maturing in the traditional key markets, Nokia has increasingly stressed lifestyle variables.

By 2000, Nokia's mobile phone had become Janus-faced. On the one hand, it was a critical personal communications device (function); on the other, it had aesthetic appeal (design). Initially, as long as business markets were more important than consumer markets, *function reigned over design.* Launched in 1984, the Mobira Talkman, for instance, was the first transportable phone. Heavy by today's standards, it was nonetheless 5 kilos lighter than its predecessor, the Mobira Senator of 1982, which had weighed 9.8 kilos. By 1987, Nokia had cut the size of its phones dramatically, introducing its first handheld model, the Mobira Cityman, which weighed only 800 grams with its battery (refer back to Exhibit 4-10). By the end of the 1990s, the handsets had become very light indeed, and single product categories had been replaced with extensive product families (see Exhibit 10-3).

New breakthrough or platform products often emerged first in high-end business markets but then ultimately trickled down to the low-end consumer markets. In addition to the nature of the markets (business vs. consumer), demographics and increasingly lifestyle determinants segmented demand in the mobile cellular business. Further, segmentation remained subject to competitive time (product life cycles were shortening) and geographic scope (lifestyle factors often mattered more than distances). To the Japanese, for instance, Nokia marketed small retro lifestyle phones that enabled communication over Japan's PDC network and dialed by voice. For European frequent flyers, Nokia furnished everything from dual-mode GSM 900/1800 phones to the Communicator, the first handheld device that let users make calls, surf the Web, and transmit data and faxes (refer back to Exhibit 9-1).

As momentum in mobile cellular shifted closer to consumer markets, segmentation accelerated accordingly, and *design began to reign over function.* Because functions and features no longer distinguished mobile vendors, consumers purchased phones that suited their different lifestyles. Well before its rivals, Nokia understood that the phone would be as much a fashion accessory as a tool. Consequently, Ollila hired designers from Europe and California to give Nokia phones their distinctive look and feel. Of course, both function and design contributed to the rapid growth of the mobile subscriber base, but the transi-

Exhibit 10-3. Nokia's mobile phone categories from the early 1980s to 2000.

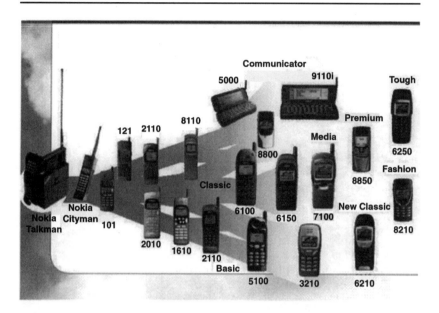

tion of the mobile phone from a business niche device to a global consumer product required a new approach to producing and marketing mobile phones. At Nokia, segmentation came to be considered a prerequisite for success:

> Today, everyone is a potential mobile phone customer. As the market has become increasingly segmented, the ability to master various product categories has become crucially important. In a segmented consumer market with high volumes, critical success factors include comprehensive product portfolio, a strong and appealing brand as well as efficient global logistics. We will continue to focus in these areas with the aim of sustained brand leadership.[9]

By late 1998, Nokia was already pumping out new models every thirty-five days. The approach was tested in Japan, where Nokia launched many of its niche systems. Just as Procter & Gamble engaged in segmentation and micromarketing to fill up supermarket shelves, Nokia proliferated segments to dominate categories. In consumer markets, both Nokia and Ericsson (due to the pioneering role of Nordic markets) anticipated trends better than their rivals did. However, because of its foresight and effectiveness in execution, Nokia excelled in taking advantage of these trends. Unlike its rivals, Nokia truly listened to its key corporate customers, such as AT&T, who wanted their customers to be able to communicate across frequency bands used by different formats.[10] Such service capabilities represented highly complex challenges in innovation; yet successful solutions paid off in the downstream processes as products moved from business-to-business to consumer markets.

In any product differentiation, such variables as quality, features, and services are critical dimensions, but not the only ones. Others include product variety, brand name, packaging, size, warranty, and returns. Near the end of the 1990s, mobile vendors seized ever-new dimensions to gain a competitive edge. At Nokia, design, in particular, has played an increasing role since the mid-1990s.

Design

Until the end of the 1980s, design was largely a neglected strategic tool, yet as competition intensified, it often provided a potent way to differentiate and position a company's products and services. While some marketers define design in narrow aesthetic terms, it should be considered more broadly as an integrative force, encompassing the totality of features that affect how a product looks and functions in terms of customer requirements.[11]

In 1990, Nokia's product marketing defined the nascent design strategy on the basis of three basic characteristics: identifiable, global, and soft design language. In the process, the company moved from geographic segmentation to customer segmentation classifications. Additionally, Nokia began to emphasize value-based segmentation after its marketing managers recognized that several attractive segments (e.g., small and medium-sized enterprises, self-employed persons) resisted cellular phones that they associated with a yuppie image. "The customer grabs the most attractive product, whatever that means to him or her," explained Nokia's marketing director, Wilska. "We talk about sexy appearance. The next step is when you have the phone in your hand. It must feel good and it is only then that other issues become relevant. . . . Products are no longer bought on the basis of functional values."[12] At the same time, Nokia began to move toward continuous product launches. The transition did not evolve from esthetic interests; the latter were subject to the needs of the sales organization. "Nokia had 50 competitors in the early 1990s, and each was launching new products every 2 to 3 years. As a result, about 20 new products were launched each year. As Nokia's sales organization did not get any new products for 2 years in the late 1980s, motivation and enthusiasm decreased. That was enough to justify the increased role of design in Nokia: to highlight the role of design, to indicate that something new has been launched, and to help our sales organization to sell."[13]

Design appears to be particularly important in making and marketing durable equipment, apparel, retail services, and packaged goods. It is not surprising, then, that its significance in the mobile cellular business has coincided with the transition from the institutional and business markets to consumer markets. Further, Nokia has had two inspiring models to encourage its concentration on design— Japanese product development and branding, in particular Sony's Design Center, and Finnish design, especially Marimekko.

For years, Nokia's senior managers have been ardent admirers of Sony, the Japanese consumer electronics giant. More than most Japanese challengers, Sony has had an international outlook. By the end of the 1990s, Sony Design Center, a consortium of some 300 top industrial designers from Tokyo to San Francisco to Cologne, had made a great contribution to Sony's widely recognized brand names and product lines, thus exerting a strong influence on popular culture and current trends in industrial and graphic design. Like Sony's founders, Morita and Ibuka, the Nokians concentrated on innovation, doing what has not been done before. Second, they wanted to lead, not follow. Like

Sony's Design Center, they were willing to make bold moves, pursue markets with products that no one else had, invent rules rather than follow them, and develop management structures and processes that nurtured talent and initiative. Similarly, Sony's "Sunrise/Sunset" strategy, which guided the design and development of virtually all of its products, had something of a parallel in Nokia's combination of branding, design, and technology-adoption life cycles.[14]

In addition to Sony's example, there was an older, more indigenous influence at work in Nokia. At the height of the Nixon-Kennedy race for the U.S. presidency in the summer of 1960, newspapers across the United States reported that Jacqueline Kennedy had bought some bright, hand-printed cotton dresses imported from an obscure Finnish company called Marimekko. The Finnish dresses were simple yet bold. Thus began the American fascination with Finnish minimalism. A similar awareness of design has helped to catapult Nokia to prominence in global markets. Just as Marimekko had rethought the idea of the dress, Nokia rethought the idea of the telephone.[15]

Like Italy's prominence in apparel and furniture design, Nordic countries have long been design leaders for their functionality, esthetics, and environmental consciousness.[16] Take, for instance, the case of IKEA, one of the world's leading furniture retailers and another Nordic company. With its strategic vision of dedication to quality, a distinctive design style, and convenience, it has grown to be a global network of 150 stores in thirty countries and four continents.[17]

At Nokia, the breakthrough design was the classic 2100 cell phone of 1994. The phone's size was actually increased to give it an elliptically shaped top and a rounded keypad, in hopes "it would be friendly, like a companion, not a little, square, hard box," said Franck Nuovo, vice president and chief designer at Nokia Mobile Phones, who led Nokia's seventy-member design team (Exhibit 10-4). "Putting a brick up to your face was not something I thought would be good."[18] Nuovo saw Finnish design as unique. It was based on a very utilitarian approach but with an appreciation of beauty. His background was in the automobile industry, where styling is considered very emotional. That approach, he believed, would work well with Finnish function and form. In April 2000, Nuovo's sleekly designed Nokia phones arrived in Hollywood.

Cell Phones as Fashion Statements

After the introduction of Nokia's 8860, Nuovo became a fashionable subject of *Vogue*, which praised him as "the designer who made wireless technology a fashion statement." Now cell phones were chic:

Exhibit 10-4. Frank Nuovo: vice president of design, Nokia Mobile Phones.

Source: © Nokia 2000. Nokia and Nokia Connecting People are registered trademarks of Nokia Corporation.

Nuovo's newest phone is the big hit in the world of wireless communication, the hottest cell phone on the charts. It is the sleek, streamlined, and aerodynamic phone that's a little Le Corbusier, a little Matrix—the first fashion phone. In the eighties, when cell phones began to infect the population, they were big and cumbersome, like something a platoon leader would use to call in an artillery strike. But in the nineties, cell phones shrank right under our ears. Before, just having any cell phone at all was cool. Now you have to have the right cell phone to get the call. There are more and more cool ones to choose from as digital time passes. . . . Nokia's 8860 . . . is the phone of the roaming designer who made moment, the phone that looks as if it were made to be retrieved chirping from a clutch purse. And at $799, it's the perfect neo-eighties status thing, the logo-as-object that is— almost as a bonus crackling with the sound of your best friend. . . .[19]

The "first fashion phone" appealed to the exclusive yet rapidly expanding membership of the 8860 club in which *Vogue* listed Lauryn Hill, Christy Turlington, Donny and Marie Osmond, Tom Cruise, Nicole Kidman, Janet Jackson, Barbara Walters, Minnie Driver, Paul Newman, Tom Hanks, Steven Spielberg, Steven Tyler, Niki Taylor, Ted Danson, and Sarah Michelle Gellar. Many of these celebrities provided the stage for a carefully orchestrated marketing campaign in which opinion leaders encouraged the use of Nokia phones among their fans. Hence, cameos of the 8860 appeared in everything from *Sex and the City*, a suggestive television show, to *Hanging Up*, a recent Diane Keaton movie. In addition, Nokia gave its 8860 phones as gifts to all the presenters at the Emmy Awards. The 8860 was preceded by the 8210, which was introduced in Members of Paris during Fashion Week. "That's our haute couture phone," said Nuovo, who described the objective of his design team as "humanized technology." For him, the goal was to meld style and reliability.[20]

Like its popular predecessor the 6110, the 8810 came with a calendar and an alarm to remind one of important engagements, three video games, and an infrared port for shuttling data effortlessly between the phone, PC, printer, or other phones.[21] Weighing as little as 98 grams and billed by its maker as the most elegant mobile phone ever, the 8810 made its official Asian sales debut in Hong Kong in September 1999 amid a frenzy of pent-up consumer demand that seemed to defy the city's somber economic outlook.[22] Unlike previous products, the 8810 was more about style than substance, just as it represented a new era of cellular competition in which style *was* substance. This "Porsche of mobile phones," as the *Wall Street Journal* called it, came with a metal "door" that protected the keypad, then slid down to bring the phone's microphone closer to the user's mouth. The 8810 was about 16 percent smaller than the 6110, and the antenna was enclosed inside the phone.[23]

With its flashy designs, Nokia, again, had its finger on the pulse of the times. In March 2000, the cover story of *Time* heralded the "design economy":

> So where design used to be considered vaguely precious, the province of the Sub-Zero-refrigerator-owning elite, it's now available to all. . . . If we learned anything from the barbaric old '80s, we learned that more is not enough. We want better—or at least better looking. . . . [The design economy] is the crossroads where prosperity and technology meet culture and marketing. These days efficient manufacturing and intense competition have made "commodity chic" not just affordable but also mandatory. Americans are likely to appreciate style when they see it and demand it when they don't, whether in boutique hotels or kitchen scrub brushes.[24]

As industries were increasingly competing at equal price and functionality, design was seized as yet another dimension of differentiation. In the 1930s, Raymond Loewy, founder of industrial design to many, said that the most beautiful curve was a rising sales graph. Some six decades later, Nokia saw the significance of design and the rising sales curve in handsets well before its rivals. The designs of Nuovo and other Nokians were patented, becoming intellectual property and contributing to switching costs (see Exhibit 10-5).

In addition to seamless solutions and virtual presence, Nokia considered human technology one of the three strategic cornerstones of global IP mobility. Technologies in themselves have no value; they attain value in the context of fulfilling human needs. Buyers must gain real benefits from them. Because such benefits remain, by definition, *perceived* benefits, design had a strategic function.

Designing in Teams

In 2000, Frank Nuovo, who had been doing contract work with Nokia since 1989, still considered the mobile phone in its relatively early formation stages, which ensured an exciting environment for a designer. The design team provided form and discipline for Nokia's bold vision. "Teamwork gives birth to new ideas," said Nuovo. "You cannot fall in love with your first idea. You have to be able to explore openly and accept input from lots of people. It is very important to be flexible. There are many influences to our work, but we do not follow trends at Nokia. We try to set them. So where does the inspiration for inspired designs come from? It can be anything from a beautiful tree to a motor car or a building. But the most inspiration comes from working in a good creative team with plenty of interaction."[25]

Under Nuovo's leadership, the design team did a lot of sketching and sharing of ideas with others, "like a jazz band." Though autonomous, the team reflected the overall strategic objectives at functional levels, emulating the relationship between the CEO and the executive board. Take, for instance, the parallel concepts of fashion trends in design and industry foresight in corporate strategy. Argued Nuovo, "Being at the forefront means that you really have to be in tune with what's happening in fashion, architecture, etc." Even more important, the emphasis was on teamwork instead of individualism at the top. Similarly, Nuovo sought to "keep pushing [Nokia's] talented staff in the right direction to support them and to contribute to the collective creative pool."[26]

The focus on design had the solid support of Nokia's strategic leadership. In effect, Jorma Ollila already saw Nokia's industry as an "experience industry": "We are in business, which offers people experiences. In this regard, we compete with entertainment, candy, fashion, and retail clothing. People expect communication to be an experience.

Exhibit 10-5. Nuovo's U.S. patents on Nokia phones.

US00D407398S

United States Patent [19]

Nuovo et al.

[11] Patent Number: Des. 407,398

[45] Date of Patent: **Mar. 30, 1999

[54] FRONT COVER FOR A TELEPHONE HANDSET

[75] Inventors: Frank Nuovo, Los Angeles; Tom Arbisi, Newbury Park; Dale Frye, Port Hueneme, all of Calif.

[73] Assignee: Nokia Mobile Phones Limited, Espoo, Finland

[**] Term: 14 Years

[21] Appl. No.: 83,317

[22] Filed: Jan. 30, 1998

[51] LOC (6) Cl. 14-03
[52] U.S. Cl. D14/138; D14/250
[58] Field of Search D14/137, 138, D14/147–148, 247–248, 250, 140–142; 379/433.434, 419, 420, 428, 441; 455/550, 575, 90, 556, 558

[56] References Cited

U.S. PATENT DOCUMENTS

D. 357,250	4/1995	Ifuji et al.	D14/138
D. 365,818	1/1996	Iuie et al.	D14/138
D. 365,819	1/1996	Sawaguchi et al.	D14/147 X
D. 385,554	10/1997	Nuovo	D14/138
D. 385,887	11/1997	Park	D14/250
D. 386,188	11/1997	Park	D14/250
D. 387,083	12/1997	Richards et al.	D14/138
D. 398,081	12/1997	Lohring et al.	D14/138
D. 398,784	1/1998	Phillips et al.	D14/138
D. 394,439	5/1998	Mischenko	D14/250 X
D. 395,316	6/1998	Mason	D14/250
D. 396,230	7/1998	Phillips et al.	D14/138
D. 396,713	8/1998	Nuovo et al.	D14/138
5,745,566	4/1998	Petrellu et al.	379/433
5,752,204	5/1998	Epperson et al.	455/575
5,768,370	6/1998	Maeda et al.	379/433

Primary Examiner—Jeffrey Asch
Attorney, Agent, or Firm Perman & Green, LLP

[57] CLAIM

The ornamental design for a "front cover for a telephone handset," as shown and described.

DESCRIPTION

FIG. 1 is a front elevational view of a front cover for a telephone handset with the cover closed showing our new design;

FIG. 2 is a right side elevational view thereof;

FIG. 3 is a bottom plan view thereof;

FIG. 4 is a rear elevational view thereof;

FIG. 5 is a top plan view thereof;

FIG. 6 is a left side elevational view thereof;

FIG. 7 is a top, rear and left side perspective view thereof;

FIG. 8 is a bottom, front and right side perspective thereof;

FIG. 9 is a front elevational view thereof with the cover open;

FIG. 10 is a top plan view thereof;

FIG. 11 is a bottom plan view thereof;

FIG. 12 is a left side elevational view thereof;

FIG. 13 is a rear elevational view thereof;

FIG. 14 is a right side elevational view thereof;

FIG. 15 is a bottom, front and right side perspective view thereof; and,

FIG. 16 is a top, rear and left side perspective view thereof.

1 Claim, 9 Drawing Sheets

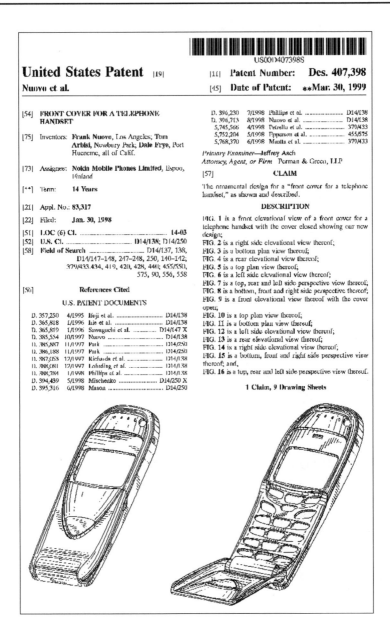

Exhibit 10-5. (continued).

US00D385554S

United States Patent [19]

Nuovo et al.

[11] Patent Number: **Des. 385,554**

[45] Date of Patent: **∗∗Oct. 28, 1997**

[54] MOBILE PHONE HOUSING

[75] Inventors: **Frank S. Nuovo**, Los Angeles; **Andy Siew Vong**, Venice, both of Calif.

[73] Assignee: **Nokia Mobile Phones Limited**, Espoo, Finland

[∗∗] Term: **14 Years**

[21] Appl. No.: **53,316**

[22] Filed: **Feb. 22, 1996**

[51] LOC (6) Cl. **14-03**

[52] U.S. Cl. **D14/138**

[58] Field of Search D14/137, 148, D14/140, 142, 147, 138, 149–151, 240, 248; 379/428, 440, 419, 420, 433–436, 58–61, 454–455; 455/89, 90

[56] **References Cited**

U.S. PATENT DOCUMENTS

D. 327,059	6/1992	Chu et al.	D14/148 X
D. 339,338	9/1993	Tattari et al.	D14/148 X
D. 353,809	12/1994	Nuovo et al.	D14/138

D. 354,284	1/1995	White	D14/138
D. 363,483	10/1995	Tanaka	D14/138
D. 369,796	5/1996	Crewe	D14/147 X
D. 370,673	6/1996	Happo et al.	D14/138
D. 374,007	9/1996	Tattari	D14/138

Primary Examiner—Jeffrey Asch
Attorney, Agent, or Firm—Perman & Green, LLP

[57] **CLAIM**

The ornamental design for "a mobile phone housing", as shown and described.

DESCRIPTION

FIG. 1 is a front perspective view showing the top and one side of our new design with the sliding cover closed, the opposite side being a mirror image thereof;

FIG. 2 is a front perspective view showing the top and one side of the new design with the sliding cover open, the opposite side being a mirror image thereof;

FIG. 3 is a rear perspective view showing the top and one side of the new design with the sliding cover open, the opposite side being a mirror image thereof; and,

FIG. 4 is a plan bottom view.

1 Claim, 4 Drawing Sheets

It is this idea that has given rise to many design concepts in the mobile cellular."[27]

Nokia's highly visible design had become a key segmentation variable. In more traditional industries, lifestyle segmentation has served strategies well. In the technology sector, however, even intricate information on target segments is not enough if the marketer lacks understanding of competitive time—i.e., technology-adoption life cycles.

Technology-Adoption Life Cycles

The ideas of Geoffrey A. Moore are hardly new; they originate from the classic technology-adoption life cycle frameworks.[28] Still, Moore has used them in a distinctive way by applying them in the technology sector and consumer marketing.[29] Nokia's marketers studied these ideas diligently. In *Crossing the Chasm* (1991), Moore introduced the idea of a "chasm" that innovative companies and their products must cross to reach the lucrative mainstream market. In *Inside the Tornado* (1995), he illustrated how technology companies could capitalize on the potential for hyper-growth beyond the chasm.[30] In both cases, the focus was on how the market forces behind the technology-adoption life cycle caused the need for radical shifts in market strategy and necessitated appropriate tactics for succeeding in each stage of the cycle.[31]

Moore's frameworks for marketing strategies fit Nokia's efforts at market-making strategies, which were founded on taking advantage of discontinuities in emerging technology markets. Similarly, Ollila's "new management paradigm" required foresight: reading the market and correct timing. His execution required speed in anticipating and fulfilling emerging customer needs, high quality in products and processes, and openness with people and to new ideas and solutions. In Nokia's marketing strategies, then, the chasm framework has enabled the company to tailor appropriate approaches for the early-adopter and the late-adopter markets.[32] The distinction is crucial. When technology companies have stressed upstream activities (technology innovation) at the expense of downstream activities (marketing innovation), they have often mistaken success among early adopters for mass-market adoption. Conversely, when these companies have focused on downstream at the expense of upstream innovation, they have had a tendency to expect mass-market adoption without success among early adopters.

Transitioning between these two phases was anything but smooth. Instead of an externally imposed, linear model of innovation, the chasm framework focused on the gaps between different life-cycle markets. Both aspects appealed to Nokia, for obvious reasons. On the one hand, it was moving from business-to-business to consumer markets. On the other hand, as the industry leader its future depended on the successful introduction of new product generations—cellular families representing continuous *and* discontinuous technologies.[33]

Through the second half of the 1990s, Nokia became a first mover and more successful than any of its rivals in segmentation. What, however, made it unique was its combination of a segmentation model with the technology-adoption life cycles. Today, this mix is widely known, almost a cliché, not least because of Moore's revival of the classic theory. But that was not the case in the early 1990s when Nokia began its segmentation efforts. Assisted by its British ad agency, it developed a model of its target customers. It paid special attention to the four most important segments: "poseurs," "trendsetters," "social contact seekers," and "high-fliers." If Nokia managed to capture these lead segments, the phones would rapidly trickle down to other segments as well.[34]

Loyal to its strategic view of inflection points, Nokia focused on the transition from the small early adopter segments to the critical mass markets. As far as Moore was concerned, Nokia and its rivals would have to overcome the kind of switching costs that make crossing the chasm difficult.[35] That is where branding came into the picture.

Branding

In 1905, Nokia's name still evoked a river in Finland. Over time, however, the brand name proved so strong that by the 1920s the Finnish Rubber Works started to use it. Galoshes branded the early Nokia, and rubber boots and winter tires represented the company until the end of the 1970s. In Finland, Nokia has been a strong brand since the early twentieth century, yet the global brand name has become powerful only in the 1990s as a result of the focus strategy.

Preceded by a two-year planning phase, Nokia's most intensive brand-building efforts were conducted between 1993 and 1995. Nokia Mobile Phones used the full range of marketing elements.[36] In addition to print advertising, Nokia was the first cellular company to invest in pan-European television advertising, from MTV Europe to sponsoring the Science and Technology program on CNN. The objective was to make Nokia mobile phones a global brand product, with the key messages being inspired technology, ease of use, and durability.

In September 1996, Nokia received a significant pan-European advertising award for long-standing brand building.[37] That year, market research indicated that Nokia had become the strongest cellular brand in Europe with regard to brand awareness and image. In effect, it was one of the very few global brands that had made its breakthrough during the 1990s. "We are especially satisfied that as a result of long-standing and holistic brand development we have achieved and even surpassed the global consumer electronics brands in awareness and recognition," said Anssi Vanjoki, then senior vice president of Nokia Mobile Phones, Europe and Africa.[38] In effect, Vanjoki had played a key role in the brand-building effort that originated in a far-reaching strategic decision in 1991—like Nokia's many other triumphs in the course of the 2G rivalry.

Mastering the Art of Branding

By the spring of 1999, American cellular users were far more familiar with Nokia's mobile phones than they had been only two years before. Some 43 percent of mobile users knew Nokia (compared to 58 percent of those familiar with Motorola, a veteran American company), and 14 percent had high regard for its products. The Finnish brand was particularly well known among heavy users and those who had owned mobile phones longer than seven years. Nokia's design appealed to sixteen–to–twenty-four-year-old users; one out of two considered the brand "cool."[39] It was a remarkable marketing accomplishment, but even more important, it was a *strategic* feat.

Prior to his role as Nokia's CEO, Jorma Ollila had run the mobile phone division. At the turn of the 1990s, he and several colleagues concluded that mobile phones were about to move from business markets to consumer markets. To some extent, the observation reflected the Nokians' acute industry foresight, but it was also rooted in the local telecommunications mobile cluster conditions. Along with other Nordic countries, Finland had become the lead market in the cellular rivalry, and the realization that market momentum was shifting was the result of everyday observations. Due to the powerful role of strategic intent in Nokia's corporate strategy and the chasm framework in its marketing strategy, Ollila understood the significance of prescient insight as strategic leverage.

If consumer marketing held the key to success in the 2G rivalry, Nokia would have to master the art of branding. Not only was this insight ahead of the times, but it required the kind of capabilities that were less known in pre-EU Finland, where consumer markets were just beginning to enter an era of truly market-driven competition. Through the 1980s, branding had at best been an afterthought, as Nokia's phones had been sold under a wide variety of names, including Mobira, RadioShack, and cellular operators' private labels. During the restructuring years, the company concentrated on cost cutting. The brand issue first emerged in the mobile phone unit, although Ollila's prescient observations would pertain to the entire company in time.

In 1991, Ollila's team decided that Nokia would have to be marketed as a *single* brand and hired a young 3M marketing executive, Anssi Vanjoki, to figure out how to make Nokia a household name. Prior to joining the cellular company, Vanjoki had served in marketing and sales functions at Sampo, a major Finnish insurance firm, and at 3M from the late 1970s to the late 1980s. He joined Nokia Mobile Phones as vice president of sales. As Vanjoki researched the history of companies that had developed successful brands, he discovered a common denominator among brand leaders such as Nike, Daimler-Benz, and Philip Morris. The crucial element, he believed, was a "holistic" approach. In these companies, brand was not a side effect or a function of the marketing department. Instead, these companies thought about the brand in every aspect of the value chain, including design, production, and distribution. In contrast to the classic functional perspective, these companies treated advertising as a kind of afterthought—they got around to it only when all the other elements were in place.[40] The insight was not new, but it allowed Vanjoki to shape new markets.

As Nokia was undergoing a transformation into a process organization, a holistic brand approach would have to encompass product development process, customer commitment process, and management, control, and HRM processes. In brief, it would have to penetrate the entire organization.

Branding in Mobile Cellular

Branding has been researched for decades. After all, it has characterized consumer marketing since the late nineteenth century. Furthermore, by the late 1980s, branding had become one of the hottest topics in strategic management. As Nokia's CFO in the late 1980s, Ollila had seen how, in the course of the M&As, companies paid substantial premiums for brand names because alternative development of new brand names was either not feasible or simply too costly. Second, in many industries the excessive use of price promotions had led to increasing price pressures diverting resources from brand building to developing points of differentiation. Finally, many senior managers had not fully exploited their assets, in particular brand equity, to maximize the performance of their businesses.[41]

There was little new in Nokia's branding. Instead, the uniqueness in its branding involved the industry itself. Previously, branding had not been applied to mobile phones. It was relatively new even in Finland, which was pioneering the digital cellular environment. Nokia was also branding far more than products or product portfolios; it was branding an entire company.

While Nokia's success in the 1990s was almost identical with the triumph of the GSM standard (which the company was about to launch), Ollila and his colleagues saw even further into the future. In 1991, Nokia decided to create a phone for all three digital standards: GSM in Europe, TDMA in the United States, and PDC in Japan. In the 2G rivalry, Nokia certainly sought to exploit optimally the GSM, but it would not bet the 3G competition on a sole standard.[42] Yet, what on the surface seems like an extraordinary bet or a lucky guess followed naturally from Nokia's premise to always "listen to the customer." In anticipation of the new products and markets, Nokia did not proceed from upstream to downstream processes (technology over customers), but from downstream to upstream processes (customers over technology). The point was not "how" this or that technology worked, but whether or not it contributed to *customer satisfaction*. Cellular standards would change and shift, brand awareness would not.[43]

In keeping with the holistic approach, Nokia's branding would make sure that the look and feel of mobile phones were the same everywhere worldwide. "We developed a new strategic direction for advertising across all our markets in Asia Pacific only after careful market study to help us better understand what the Asian mobile phone user wants and needs," stated Colin Giles, Nokia's regional director of marketing, in 1996. "The study told us that although each market has its own unique requirements, there are sufficient similarities for a single, unified approach to work across the region." In many markets, mobile phones had evolved over the years to become personal accessories. Consumers wanted to feel satisfied with their choice, and the Nokia campaign was designed to tell them that Nokia offered them that personal choice. "The key challenge," noted Giles, "is in creating modular components within the TV campaign that can be put together to create cost effective and consistent brand advertising for application in different markets, each of which has varying levels of sophistication and needs."[44]

In the past, mobile phone advertisements had been engineering-driven and focused largely on the technical features of the product. Instead, Nokia's approach sought to communicate the emotional benefit of buying a Nokia product. "Our position is that our phones are the 'most human.' They are designed for you and I. They are easy to use. They are there for you, in good times and in bad. For instance, our campaign features simple messages that cajole the consumer to 'talk to me,' 'hold me,' 'I'm with you.' "[45] In 1996, that unique approach was used in all Nokia advertisements that ran in twenty-one markets in Asia—from India, China, and Australia to Southeast Asia.[46]

Through the first half of the 1990s, the average wholesale price of low-end phones fell from $518 to as low as $136. Meanwhile, Dataquest projected that the number of mobile phones shipped globally each year would more than double to 100 million in 1999. That growth was likely to draw in powerful new competitors in addition to current ones such as Motorola, Ericsson, and NEC; it also contributed to price erosion. "If you get a company like Sony with the right product, the power of that brand is enormous," argued Dataquest's Dean Eyers. "Its phone sales went from nowhere to 16% of the U.K. market in 15 months. It could do that anywhere in the world."[47] Similarly, Ollila and his colleagues at Nokia thought they could make up what the company was losing on margin by boosting volume, but that required making Nokia a powerhouse global brand—just like Sony.

In the course of the 1990s, Nokia invested almost $1 billion in building its brand, whereas a new factory might have taken only a few hundred million dollars. By 2000, the company was better known worldwide than in the country in which it was based. In keeping with Nokia's globalization strategy, which evolved in the late 1980s and early 1990s, this quest for awareness and recognition was motivated by global branding.

Global Branding

Pursuing a global branding strategy, Nokia has systematically used its brand name across many countries. Like brand leaders such as Sony, Nike, Coca-Cola, Microsoft, and Heineken, Nokia invested significantly in building and maintaining its brand name worldwide, usually coupled with a common slogan—"Connecting People"—for immediate global recognition. Unlike most other brand leaders, however, Nokia's global brand is quite recent. It was created in the 1990s when U.S.-based Internet pioneers such as America Online and Yahoo! also achieved global brand awareness; it was also one of the few Europe-based global brands. Finally, unlike some of the current brand leaders, Nokia did not consider branding a product-related activity only. In effect, there was a curious linkage between recruiting new talent and branding. Both product and corporate branding had a dual objective: one focused on product markets and the other on labor markets. The more attractive the company, the more it could choose from those who selected the company.[48]

As Ollila expected competition to become even more intense and commodity-like in the near future, Nokia rushed to differentiate itself from its rivals. "Essentially, people's behavior doesn't differ that much in different markets," noted Anssi Vanjoki in 1999. "The secret is in the ability to discover the global uniformities. As such, it is easy to observe local differences and understand the basic culture. But it is difficult to observe in time the truly global megatrends." As competitors' product technology and quality had become almost homogeneous, brand emerged as an appropriate base of differentiation. As a result, marketing would have to understand human behavior in product functions and design. "Who buys a watch just because it shows the time?" Vanjoki asked. "The basic function of the watch has become secondary. Today, a cellular phone still remains a phone, but, in the future, the phone will be a side effect."[49]

According to the special report on world brands by *Advertising Age* in 2000, Nokia's branding relied on three major ad agencies: Grey Advertising (twenty countries), Ogilvy & Mather Worldwide (ten countries), and Bates Worldwide (twelve countries). In the report's ranking, these agencies held the third, fourth, and twelfth positions, respectively. In 1998, Nokia ranked ninety-one among the top one hundred global marketers; by 1999, it had climbed to sixty-seven.[50] In 1998, Nokia's media spending outside the United States amounted to $144 million (45 percent annual growth); its spending in the United States had climbed to some $32 million (15 percent annual growth). Nokia spent $176 million worldwide in media. Budget allocations reflected its priorities in terms of geographic segments: Europe received 45 percent, Asia 29 percent, and the United States 18 percent.

Like so many other global brands, Nokia occasionally stumbled. In 1995, Nokia sponsored the Tyrell team in Formula 1 racing. Unfortunately, it bet on the wrong horse despite FIM 20 million in expenditures. In 1996, Nokia's worldwide television advertising did not focus on a single product but on a slate of products; the ad was unsuccessful and was withdrawn. Also that year, Nokia launched its RinGo youth phone, but when the "Bimbo" phone was marketed to women, Swedish consumers responded negatively. In 1998, the company marketed its multicolor mobile phones in Germany with the very same phrase as on the gate leading to Buchenwald's concentration camp. The mistake triggered a protest from a Jewish organization in the United States. That same year, Nokia also had to apologize in China, where local vendors responded negatively when they realized that in the instructions booklet, Hong Kong, Taiwan, and Macao had been portrayed as distinct countries. Finally, Nokia's marketing in the Austrian magazine *Zur Zeit* triggered yet another wave of protest, for the publication was known for its neo-Nazi sympathies.[51] In most cases, Nokia reacted appropriately by apologizing and withdrawing the controversial ads. Still, such stumbling sparked some debate on complacency in its global brand coordination.

By 2000, Nokia had the world's fifth most valuable brand, as ranked by the consulting firm Interbrand. A strong brand equity reinforced soaring stock equity. By April, Nokia's market value had climbed to $250 billion, the highest of any European company. In 1988, there had been some 310 million mobile phone users worldwide. By the end of 1999, there were over 50 percent more, approximately 480 million. By the end of 2002, Nokia expected there to be over a billion.[52]

Processes and Performance

Going into 2000, Nokia had developed into a corporate giant that continued to grow rapidly. Organizationally, its processes had become highly specialized, but while it had created appropriate performance and control measures, the company had also evolved into a highly interdependent system that posed increasing challenges to strategic management.

The more quickly the markets grew, the more quickly they matured. In the long run, Nokia's success with dominant designs and ability to take advantage of strategic inflection points would not suffice. In the past, Nokia had benchmarked its rivals; now they were benchmarking Nokia. (At the same time, all were glancing nervously behind their backs, scanning for new challengers.) To thrive in increasingly competitive markets, the company had to subject its activities to rigorous performance measurement and control processes.

Control Systems

With the maturation of the markets, the significance of management accounting systems was bound to accelerate at Nokia. The group executive board has continued to stress the role of its values—customer satisfaction, respect for the individual, achievement, continuous learning—in all activities and every business segment. But it has also sought the implementation of these values through meticulous performance management and control, which have thus been aligned to corporate strategies and Nokia's values—from the headquarters to individual business units and to business processes, including new-product development.[53]

Performance Measurement: From the Headquarters to Business Units

Nokia's overall performance measurement system has been designed to be consistent with the strategic and operational planning process of the company, which can be divided into several phases:

- Each January and February, the strategic and operational planning process begins with company-wide vision planning.
- Next, strategic planning continues at the business unit and functional levels.
- In March, senior management meets again to decide which businesses the company wants to be part of in the future.
- Around April and May, the visions and key strategic goals are operationalized into long-term plans for the next three years.
- Starting in August, the business planning process continues through annual planning; the first year of the three-year plan is brought into focus; an operational plan is drawn to the cost-center level; and the need for additional employees is determined.[54]

In the rapid-growth mobile industry, the heavy control systems have surprised many industry observers. At Nokia, however, these systems have not only structured the everyday operations but also created a compact for the key participants. "The more turbulent the market," Nokia's corporate planning director has explained, "the more important it is to have a shared understanding of the future so that there is a clear reference point to which everyone can reflect his or her observations."[55] In accordance with the implications of its 1992 IT study, NTC moved toward harmonizing the different performance measurement systems in the mid-1990s.[56]

Nokia Telecommunications. Since the early 1990s and the adoption of process-based management, NTC has worked hard to align its corporate strategy, values, and performance management.[57] On the one hand, each business unit has defined and prioritized its own targets and performance indicators for customer satisfaction (correct time to market, price vs. performance and features, field reliability, delivery accuracy, and lead time), operational efficiency (cycle time, first time pass yield, cost efficiency, working capital in days), and people involvement (target setting and understanding, communication, empowerment, teamwork). On the other hand, these objectives and indicators have been measured and linked to Nokia's two core processes—product development and customer commitment—as well as its management and support processes.[58] Each performance area has been measured for each core process. The product process includes activities from identification of needs to development and launching of new systems, products, and features. The customer commitment process comprises activities from tendering to order delivery, implementation, and after-sales (see Exhibit 10-6a).

Nokia Mobile Phones. At NMP, the performance measurement matrix paralleled that in NTC. Again, customer information has been in a central position while controllership has followed current reporting structure (regions and functions) and business environment and dimensions (customers, business lines, and processes). The core processes within NMP have encompassed product creation, product delivery, and management processes. Most important, the starting point for each process has been the customer. At NMP, controllers have played a management function, but not a policing one. Instead, they have proactively sought future opportunities (see Exhibit 10-6b).[59] Apparently, performance measurement was becoming increasingly significant as a control mechanism in the NPD and NMP. There has been a keen need for financial and *non*financial indicators because the relationship between the input and output of the process was complex.[60] NMP discouraged traditional cost management and stressed profitability. The notion of product life cycle was predicated on the idea of satisfying customers' needs and increasing investors' profits during the life cycle of profitable new products. In the future, controllers were expected to play an increasingly strategic role in the 3G competition, successive generations of mobile communications, and new wireless data applications.

Exhibit 10-6. Performance measurement matrices at Nokia.

(a) NTC

	Performance measures:			
Core processes:	Customer satisfaction	Operative efficiency	People involvement	Market position and profitability
Product process				
Customer commitment process				
Management and support processes				
Overall				

(b) NMP

	Performance measures:					
	Regional measures			Functional measures		
Business lines:	Region 1	Region 2	Region 3	Product creation process	Product delivery process	Management process
Business line 1						
Business line 2						
Business line 3						
Business line 4						
Business line 5						
Business line 6						
Business line 7						

Customer information

SOURCE: As presented in Erkki K. Laitinen and Rolf Leppänen, *Global Success and the Role of Strategic Steering and Management Accounting Systems: Case Nokia Group* (University of Vaasa, Department of Accounting and Business Finance, 2000).

Customer Life Cycle and Profitability Analysis

Loyal to its overall strategic approach, Nokia in general, and its business units in particular, have been highly selective in their use of management accounting systems. Take, for instance, NTC.[61] Apparently, the unit has not utilized strategic cost management or strategic investment appraisal. While there have been some uses and applications of target cost management and activity-based costing, these were either minor or not regarded as useful or beneficial. Value-based pricing was implemented, but considered technically difficult to execute. Life-cycle accounting has been applied on an ad hoc basis and with difficulties in cost allocation.

In effect, if these various approaches were to be visualized according to NTC's process chain, it is quite obvious that the company focused on strategic management accounting systems that stressed the customer and profitability. As a result, customer profitability analysis and nonfinancial performance measurement have been widely adopted and considered strategic. Similarly, customer business analysis has been actively conducted by account teams and considered increasingly significant in the future. The emphasis on customer profitability has also been present indirectly. Life-cycle accounting has been deemed interesting to the extent it has enabled profitability calculations for the customer life cycle (see Exhibit 10-7).

■ ■ ■ ■ ■

By 2000, Nokia, the cellular leader rushing into the mobile Internet, hardly resembled the old, diversified Nokia. Starting in 1992, it had moved toward a process organization, which grew rapidly and became increasingly complex as the company captured industry leadership six years later. Throughout this era, Nokia's capabilities were based on a global focus strategy. Soon Nokia initiated the transition from the cellular industry to the mobile Internet and began building new capabilities through accelerating upstream innovation (technology development, internal investments, acquisitions, and strategic coalitions) and downstream innovation (segmentation, branding, and design), and its processes grew even more complex. In this new strategic era, Nokia's objective has been to build new capabilities to bring about the mobile information society.

In the first era, the company had not engaged in unique positioning. It was better and faster (though not necessarily cheaper) than its rivals, but it was not very different from them. In the second era, it began to move toward unique positioning. In effect, through its eagerness to use competitive time as a strategic leverage, it was intent on

Exhibit 10-7. Strategic management accounting systems at Nokia Telecommunications: "The Customer Is Always Right"

Life-Cycle Accounting (LCA)
Applied on ad hoc basis; difficulties in
cost allocation; interest in profitability
calculations for the customer life cycle

Value-Based Pricing (VBP)
Implemented but technically difficult to
carry out

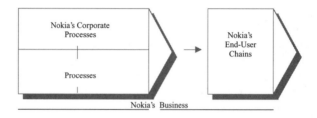

Nokia's Corporate
Processes

Nokia's
End-User
Chains

Processes

Nokia's Business

Target Cost Management (TCM)
Some elements applied, but implicitly

Activity-Based Costing (ABC)
Applied in some units; not regarded as
useful; low benefits

Customer Profitability Analysis (CPA)
Widely adopted; strategically critical

Customer Business Analysis (CBA)
Actively made by account teams; increasing significance
in the future

Nonfinancial Performance Measurement (NPM)
Widely applied; strategically important

Strategic Cost Management (SCM)
No observations.

Strategic Investment Appraisal (SIA)
No observations.

SOURCE: Based on data in Marko Järvenpää, *Strateginen johdon laskentatoimi ja talousjohdon muuttuva rooli* (Turku: Turku School of Economics and Business Administration, 1998), pp. 233–236.

arriving in the future well before its key rivals in the cellular, IT, and consumer electronics industries.[62]

To understand where Nokia was by 2000 and where it intended to go, it is necessary to go beyond the study of its history or strategy. It is vital to analyze what Nokia was actually *doing* (see Appendix B). In such an analysis, the premise is that the capabilities the company has built or is building are determined by its long-term vision or strategic intent, whether explicit or not. This task can be achieved by mapping Nokia's capabilities, which form a specific configuration encompassing a wide array of systems. As a strategic whole, the configuration is made by a number of high-order strategic themes implemented through clusters of tightly linked processes.

"In three to four years, after all processes have become Internet-driven, nobody will any longer speak of electronic commerce, "Ollila predicted in 2000. "There will be an internal Intranet, but external customer and contract partner relationships will be 'Webified' as well."[63] In particular, the developers of Nokia's electronic business model reported directly to Jorma Ollila. Reportedly, they approached the task from the perspective of the customer. On the one hand, the Internet forced Nokia to homogenize its activities. Products and services had to be homogeneous across the world. On the other hand, Nokia was chopping up its business processes into modules that enabled the company to quickly assemble, set up, transform, and run down operations. According to Mikko Kosonen, Nokia's senior vice president for strategy and information management who worked on Nokia's corporate strategy, this remodeling emulated the pattern set by Cisco Systems. In business meetings, the Nokians were often supplemented by the employees of their contract partners. "We shall outsource more of the mobile phone production, but we shall keep the core production capabilities in-house," said Ollila. (More than 70 percent of Nokia Networks' production had already been outsourced.) In product development, however, the company controlled "all central elements, and the brand, which is a part of the company's soul, it belongs to us."[64]

Logistics played a critical role in the organizational whole. Preemption required first-mover advantages, which required rapid responsiveness. During the 1G rivalry of the 1980s, Nokia's organization had been input-focused, budget-driven, and functional. During the 2G rivalry of the 1990s, it became output-focused and market-driven. These developments became possible with process organization. Toward the end of the 1990s, Nokia initiated still another organizational transformation, brought about by the Internet revolution. Now the objective was to become network-focused and customer-driven while the entire structure would be, as Ollila put it, "Webified." Concurrently, the processes were chopped up into modules to ensure strategy flexibility. The organization would be seamless and transparent. Despite extraordinary complexity, it would be able to meet the challenges of customer service, time compression, industry globalization, and organizational integration (see Exhibit 10-8).

In the late 1990s, as Internet stocks endured several corrections and Asian markets suffered a currency crisis, Nokia's stock price kept going higher and higher. Unlike the pure Internet players, Nokia had a strong and growth-driven cash flow, but unlike "old-economy" stocks, it also had a future as an Internet player. It was enjoying the best of both worlds, at least until the summer of 2000.

How long can Nokia's market leadership continue?

Exhibit 10-8. Technology generations and Nokia's organizational changes: structure and rivalry.

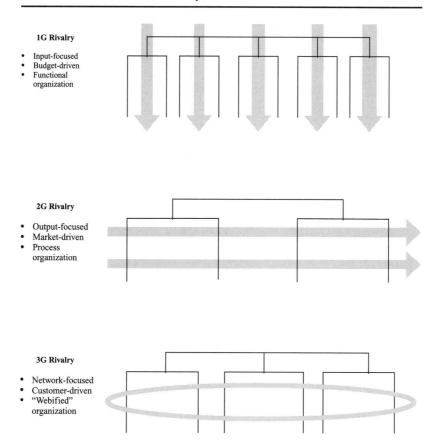

1G Rivalry

- Input-focused
- Budget-driven
- Functional organization

2G Rivalry

- Output-focused
- Market-driven
- Process organization

3G Rivalry

- Network-focused
- Customer-driven
- "Webified" organization

Nokia's Secret Code

WHEN MIT economist Bengt Holmström joined Nokia's board in 1999, he asked Ollila, "Mikä on sinun salaisuutesi?" (*"What's your secret code?"*). Holmström added, . . . *"because you've got to have something."* *"We went on for an hour or two on what it could be,"* Ollila recalls he responded. *"There is no secret code. But it is a good way of asking the question."*[1]

Is there indeed a Nokia secret code?

Incumbent Challenger

Throughout the 1990s, Nokia came out with better products again and again, and more often than its competitors. As a result, it could command a premium price. Like its Japanese precedents, it built upon a global focus strategy, moved rapidly from low-end niches to high-end segments, and skillfully exploited strategic inflection points amid industry shifts. It was bold, risky, aggressive, and it became a corporate giant with the mindset of an industry challenger.

By May 2000, Nokia's stock traded at about one hundred times earnings, but that was the tip of the iceberg. Over the past decade, Nokia's performance was magnificent; now the company was rushing toward a future that it was able and willing to shape. It would make handsets that were connected and personalized and it would put the Internet in consumer pockets. That was Nokia's vision, but what were the drivers of its strategic success? And were these success drivers renewable in the new environment?

Historical Success

Nokia's strategy has evolved through half a dozen competitive stages in the past 140 years. Starting in the 1860s (innovation, early-mover strategies), initial capabilities (forestry), and market opportunities (focused niches), the company has moved from the initial focus strategy to diversification, growth, global focus, and now a mobile Internet strategy. In each case, the transition from one strategy to another has taken place through strategic inflection points and/or shifts in the macroeconomic stage of competitive development. Similarly, in each case, the company has built its strategic advantages upon the capabilities of the previous competitive stage (see Exhibit 11-1).

Despite Nokia's strategic success and extraordinary performance, which have translated into a high shareholder value and market capitalization, the era of its very high profitability has been relatively brief in relation to its history. Though the company has thrived for years, it has been the darling of Wall Street for less than a decade. Its recent success originates from the early 1990s, when, after the institution of the process organization, Nokia's management, HRM, R&D, performance measurement, and control processes were aligned with its rapid-growth strategy. As the company successfully entered world markets and developed a global mind-set, these central corporate processes have been globalized accordingly. The story of Nokia's R&D, in particular, foreshadows the future developments of the company as a whole. Similarly, the core business processes—product development and customer commitment—have penetrated Nokia's key business segments (Nokia Mobile Phones, Nokia Networks), as well as its new expanding

Exhibit 11-1. Nokia's strategic maneuvering.

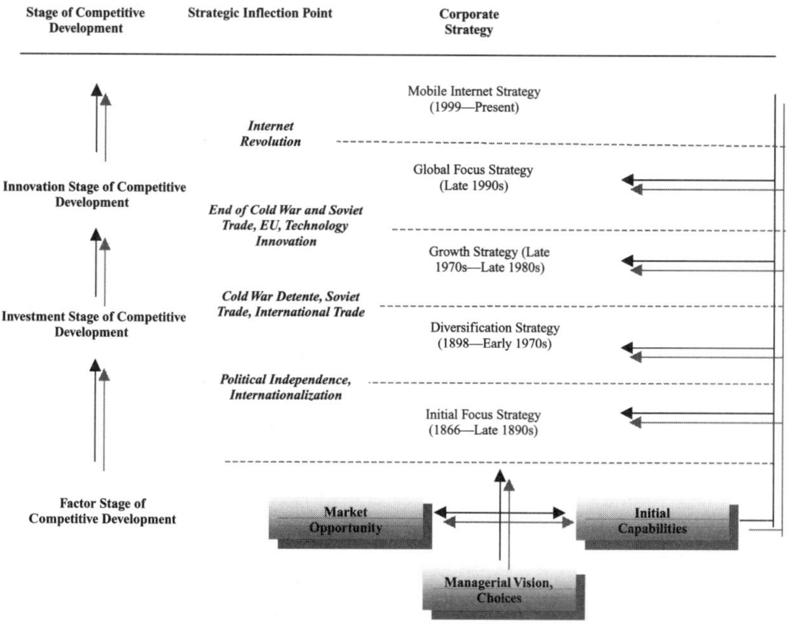

units (Nokia Communications Products, Nokia Ventures Organization).

Within a process chain that was designed to satisfy existing and potential customer needs, Nokia has been active in both upstream and downstream innovation, but in very different ways. On the upstream side, its focus has *not* been technology innovation, which has been far more prominent for Ericsson and Motorola, but standards coalitions. As far as Nokia is concerned, these strategic coalitions (WAP, Symbian, Bluetooth, SynchML, and many others) have unlocked benefits that it has not expected to obtain by internal development, mergers, or arm's-length transactions. At the same time, the coalitions have played a critical role in Nokia's stated strategy to create a mobile information society. Ultimately, these strategic coalition partners have served as Nokia's de facto technology suppliers. While not vertically integrated, they have filled the empty slots in the process chain that they also enabled. For instance, as Nokia decided not to invest directly in semiconductors or component production, it had to ensure solid and efficient long-term supplier relations in order to avoid strategic vulnerabilities.

Since the early 1990s, Nokia's focus strategy has taken advantage of global segmentation. The upstream business processes (e.g., logistics, operations, new product development, relevant technologies) tend to be similar, and standardization has made them even more so. The real differences have emerged in downstream business processes. Nokia has purposefully homogenized the upstream part of the value process while it has captured market and mind share in the downstream side of the value chain by creating a new basis of competitive differentiation (i.e., segmentation, branding, design). As standards coalitions have contributed to the increasingly homogeneous technology base of the leading mobile cellular players, the downstream function has become critical in industry rivalry.

While its competitors have debated and agonized over first-mover strategies, Nokia has decisively rushed for new markets and opportunities, products and services, seemingly without hesitation. The boldness of its initiatives should not be trivialized as merely personal extensions of its CEO or other chief executives. Instead, it should be analyzed against Nokia's dynamically changing competitive landscape. As a small Finnish company with few resources, Nokia had few alternatives at first. Doubt and indecision were privileges of industry incumbents. To claim its share of worldwide markets, it had to move more quickly and decisively than its entrenched competitors. That was its *only* chance.

Nokia began as a focused forestry business, moved quickly toward diversification, engaged in a growth strategy and an M&A binge thereafter (investment stage), until Ollila implemented the global focus strategy in the early 1990s (transition into the innovation stage).[2] These historical developments illustrate the success of Nokia's strategy from the late nineteenth century to the early twenty-first century, but they do not explain the strategy drivers of this success—i.e., the specific set of determinants or the interplay of those determinants that have made contemporary Nokia so successful. While they may point to some individual elements of a "secret code," they do not reveal its workings.

Three Possible Explanations

When *Fortune* published a dialogue between Bengt Holmström and Jorma Ollila, it could not help but speculate on the potential response. It posited three possible explanations for Nokia's extraordinary success: "(1) Nokia was very lucky; (2) Jorma Ollila is really smart; or (3) something about the way Nokia works makes it more pragmatic, more focused, and more flexible than other companies. There's truth in all three explanations, but when you talk to Ollila about the company's secret, it's clear he's partial to the third."[3]

Certainly Nokia has been lucky, especially with timing, but chance is a fickle success factor. It may explain some success some of the time, but not all success all of the time. In effect, *no single determinant can account for Nokia's success*. Take, for instance, Nokia's entry into mobile communications, which took place in the late 1960s through trial and error. Near the end of the decade, Nordic public authorities joined forces to work for joint standards, decisions that Nokia had little control over, yet the company went for the first mobile technologies just as it had gone after the telecommunications technologies. Without the persistence of its early "digital gurus," these early efforts would have ended rapidly. In effect, had the corporate parent evaluated them using common indicators of profitability (discounted cash flow, revenue generation), it *should* have divested the electronics unit very early. Nokia's senior managers, however, had been trained in U.S. management approaches (learning curve, portfolio management) that encouraged the parent to nurture and subsidize promising segments with cash flow from mature units. Kairamo's sheer determination, the digital gurus' technology extrapolations, and Ollila's impressive management abilities—all these factors and many others empowered Nokia's extraordinary performance in the 1990s.

From Fredrik Idestam's focus strategy in the forestry business of the late nineteenth century, to the diversification strategy through the first half of the twentieth century, to the M&A strategy of Kairamo in the 1980s, and to Ollila's global focus strategy in the 1990s, Nokia has always been in the vanguard of new markets, products, and services, but not by chance. It is an inherent part of Nokia's strategic innovation—and its mystique.

When Idestam was touring the local sights and factories of Germany in April 1863, he happened to travel to Mägdesprung. This was not something he had planned, but his eye was trained for new opportunities. He knew of Lüders, who had created a new process to manufacture pulp based on the work of Keller and Völter. When Idestam visited Lüders's factory and asked the workers to demonstrate the operations of the mill, he did not necessarily expect that they would actually do so, yet they did. Lüders threw Idestam out for what he deemed industrial espionage, but not before the Finn had seen enough. Whether the story is true or just another corporate myth is irrelevant. Through the persistent determination and practical ingenuity of Idestam, Mechelin, and several generations of Nokia chief executives, the company has insisted against all odds on being the *innovator*. Time and time again, this posture has meant taking a dive into the unknown and the willingness to cannibalize the company's current sources of success in the name of a future opportunity.

If, then, "chance" is a poor explanation, the reduction of Nokia's success to Jorma Ollila's management style is hardly better. On the surface, it may be tempting to believe because it is relatively easy to periodize the evolution of a given company on the basis of its successive chief executives. The problem is that such an explanation tells everything and nothing. Everything, because now the management style of the corporate leader appears to penetrate even the most intricate processes of everyday operations. And nothing, because in practice no chief executive has such power and influence. Furthermore, Nokia has ridiculed all such efforts with disdain, pointing to the significance of teamwork, the nature of the process organization, and the proliferation of cross-functional activities. Even more important, the group executive board—half a dozen highly capable senior executives—rather than Ollila alone has developed, formulated, and implemented Nokia's strategy since the early 1990s. Certainly, Ollila has taken responsibility and should be given credit for the crucial strategic decisions, not all of which have been exactly painless, especially in the first years of his leadership. It is almost impossible to understand Nokia's magnificent success at the end of the twentieth century without reference to Ollila's role in its strategy. When Ollila became Nokia's CEO and chairman in 1999, his power, at least formally, only increased, yet even this formal designation should be balanced against the scale and scope of the changing company. In 1992, when Ollila was appointed Nokia's CEO, Nokia's revenues were about $3.5 billion, net losses amounted to almost $80 million, and it had fewer than 27,000 employees. By 2000, its revenues had soared to almost $20 billion, net income was at $2.6 billion, and it had more than 51,000 employees. At that time, Ollila was already delegating responsibilities to his second-in-command, Pekka Ala-Pietilä.

If neither chance nor management style can explain Nokia's success, perhaps there is something about the way Nokia works that has made it more pragmatic, focused, and flexible than other companies. Even this explanation, however, does not lead very far, as *Fortune* explained:

> "It's the way the organization creates a meeting of minds among people," [Ollila] says. "How do you send a very strong signal that this is a meritocracy, and this is a place where you are allowed to have a bit of fun, to think unlike the norm, where you are allowed to make a mistake?" Yes, this sounds kind of squishy and vague. And it may seem a slender reed upon which to balance $250 billion in market cap. But spend time around Nokia asking what has made the company so successful, and it's as definite an answer as you'll get. Not that people who work at Nokia dislike talking about the place; they, too, just seem to have trouble putting a finger on what's different about it.[4]

It is the dynamic evolution of Nokia's highly complex process configuration (refer to Appendix B), the elusive interdependent whole that so many industry observers and investment analysts have had so much trouble putting their fingers on.

The Drivers of Nokia's Strategic Success

Instead of searching for a single all-powerful success factor or even a set of such success factors, it is far more productive to examine the interplay of several systemic determinants.[5] From this standpoint, Nokia's strategy—or any strategy examined against a longitudinal or dynamic perspective—is a function of overdetermination, i.e., multiple, highly interdependent variables. This, precisely, is the logic of the process configuration.[6] Yet, even this configuration is a still picture of a moving target; it cannot portray the impact of change. In order to capture the strategic postures that have made Nokia so successful, it is necessary to delineate the current drivers of this configuration, whose dynamic truly encapsulates Nokia's elusive "secret code" (see Exhibit 11-2).

As important as Nokia's historical strategies may be to illustrate its dogged persistence in innovation and bold first-mover strategies, they explain little of Nokia's success. When trying to understand No-

Exhibit 11-2. The drivers of Nokia's strategic success.

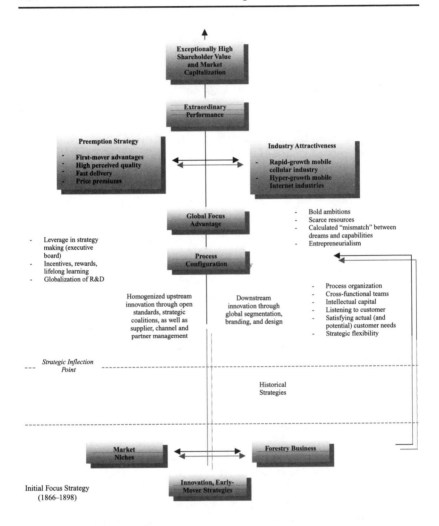

kia's shareholder value and market capitalization, for instance, Idestam's innovation in the forestry business of the 1860s is merely a
historical curiosity. Nokia's "secret code" cannot be found in its historical strategies, but in its strategic history. However, because strategic
advantages are built upon capabilities, it is vital to pay attention to the
competitive stages (the growth strategy of the 1980s, the M&A spree,
technology focus, restructuring) that have made possible the current
success (global focus, mobile Internet strategy). Among these capabilities are Nokia's process organization, cross-functional teams, emphasis
on intellectual capital, ability to listen to the customer, boldness to en-

vision and satisfy both actual and potential customer needs, and strategic flexibility in the corporate organization. During its global focus and after its transition to the mobile Internet strategy, Nokia has exploited these very drivers. However, while old capabilities may provide the base for new strategic advantages, far more is needed.

Nokia's process configuration has not evolved haphazardly. Despite seemingly chaotic growth, Nokia's expansion has a logic that has penetrated its process chain as well as the entire vertical system in which it operates. Product and corporate branding reinforced efforts to create a global network of specialists. Along with mobile vendors like Nokia, this vertical system included component suppliers, independent dealers, service operators, mobile Internet content providers, and value-added service providers. By 2000, the challenge was to make the global company transparent in order to provide seamless high-quality service to the customer. While the company is widely considered innovative, the term is so inflated that few observers have successfully specified its precise meaning.

Nokia has purposefully sought to homogenize upstream innovation through open standards and strategic coalitions as well as skillful supplier, channel, and partner management. This strategic posture has enabled the company not only to solidify its own strengths (downstream innovation) but also to weaken those of its most powerful competitors (upstream innovation). Similarly, Nokia's R&D has not only been globalized, but leveraged through extensive collaboration with vital research institutions worldwide. At the same time, Nokia has focused on downstream innovation through segmentation, branding, and design. Like Procter & Gamble, it has shrewdly filled the shelves with new and innovative products to dominate categories. Like Coca-Cola, it has become ubiquitous, but far more rapidly. Like Sony, it has used its umbrella brand to sell new products and services and to create footholds in new markets. In each case, it has additionally engaged in preemptive strategies to keep competitors at bay and skim the cream before its rivals.

As long as the preemptor enjoys first-mover advantages, it will be successful. What may be termed the *preemptor's dilemma* is the other, darker side of this equation. If the preemptor *fails* to deter its rivals, it will have to deal with first-mover *dis*advangages. In addition to early and risky resource commitments and capacity issues, preemption requires that the company successfully deter competitors, avoid disastrous price competition, and sustain its early leadership. These are extremely difficult tasks to accomplish simultaneously in competitive circumstances, where cost advantage and differentiation rivals launch counterattacks while focus players nibble away profits in the niche markets seeking to out-focus the focusers.[7]

Preemption requires risk taking, bold dreams and ambitions, and ceaseless innovation and strategizing. But none of these is new to Nokia. Despite its size, it has favored small and agile teamwork and entrepreneurialism. Unlike most large corporations, it has internalized the logic of Silicon Valley by rewarding success and using failures as cases from which to learn rather than as sources of punishment. Incentives, rewards, and lifelong learning now permeate the entire company. When the company's capabilities have not sufficed, it has bought new capabilities and created new organizational arrangements to do so (corporate innovation). Yet unlike most of its direct and indirect rivals, Nokia has not engaged in substantial M&A activities. While some observers have considered this fact a fatal flaw, others—those who are more skeptical about the alleged benefits of inflated M&As in the technology sector—see it as still another virtue or as Nokia's unwillingness to engage in conventional capability building. If size and rigidity discourage strategic flexibility, the company should avoid both.

Even more importantly, throughout the Ollila era the company has purposefully nurtured a mismatch rather than a fit between its scarce resources and bold ambitions. The former works better for a small-country challenger in emergent industries, whereas the latter has been more advantageous in established American, European, or Asian corporations. Similarly, Ollila's Nokia has skillfully exploited leverage in strategy making. Instead of depending on a single CEO/chairman or a small cadre of top-down administrators, the company has managed to rely on its group executive board in which each member brings something unique to the table. With Ollila's guidance and steering, this "collective mind" crafts and refines Nokia's corporate strategy in which vision remains steady but details are subject to constant revision. Ollila and his chief executives have been able to communicate their vision to each Nokian as well as galvanize the company around it. Yet, Nokia—like its Japanese precedents—has also had to deal with the other side of this calculated mismatch, leverage and strategic intent. In extreme cases of exhaustion and agony, it has lost executives whose bold dreams of the future have been mugged by the realities of current markets and organization. Through the personal example of discipline, initiative, family life, and personal time, Ollila and the other members of the group executive board have sought to suppress the potential of anomic crises, but not all Nokians are Ollilas.

Through its process configuration and drivers, then, Nokia has built its global focus advantage. Success in strategy formulation and implementation, as well as a certain degree of attractiveness in the industry structure, have also been required. Since the early 1990s, Nokia has engaged in a bold and risky preemption strategy, seeking first-mover advantages through perceived high quality, fast delivery, and price premiums. Over the decade, Nokia benefited from high attractiveness in the rapid-growth mobile cellular industry. As the key markets in the developed countries have become saturated, the company has rushed to future volume markets, including China, to ensure continued growth. Even more important, Nokia has fully embraced the World Wide Web through its mobile Internet strategy. This strategic decision is hardly unique. After initial resistance, Microsoft, another industry giant, embraced the online markets, extending its current capabilities in a new marketspace in the mid-1990s. But unlike Microsoft, Nokia has managed its corporate and government relations far more considerately, just as it has been able to avoid high-profile and costly antitrust or competition policy struggles in the courts. Unlike Microsoft, Nokia has also been bold enough to engage in preemption strategies that are predicated on early-mover postures in highly uncertain and risky markets. Instead of trying to buy or crush potential rivals and creating animosity on all sides, Nokia has skillfully co-opted most of its actual or potential rivals and thereby created goodwill on most sides.

At the close of the 1990s, the results of these drivers, process configuration, strategy, and industry attractiveness were manifested in Nokia's extraordinary performance, which translated into magnificent shareholder value and market capitalization. It is this highly interdependent system that accounts for the company's extraordinary success—and *is* its "secret code."

Disruption and Success

Nokia became the world's largest supplier of mobile phones in 1998. A year later, it strengthened its global market position even as the mobile phone market grew by more than 60 percent. The company estimated about 275 million mobile phones were sold worldwide in 1999, compared to about 168 million in the previous year. Nokia's sales volume growth exceeded that of the market with sales of 78.5 million units, up 92 percent from the previous year's 40.8 million. By 2000, Nokia was triumphant, and its strategy seemed almost invulnerable.

But is Nokia's code invulnerable? Certainly not. In May 1996, for instance, Nokia posted a 70 percent plunge in first-quarter pretax profit to FIM 399 million (about $84 million), as sales of mobile phones and related gear slowed. Ollila issued an earnings warning and blamed the tumbling earnings on problems at the group's flagship mobile phone business, whereas some Finnish analysts went further, calling the results a catastrophe. Another reminder of Nokia's mortality—perhaps far more telling in terms of potential negative scenarios—followed on

July 28, 2000, when the company lost some $64.3 billion of its market capitalization.[8]

The moral of the story? As long as Nokia can keep up its extraordinary performance, which will translate to exceptionally high shareholder value, the mobile powerhouse will continue to exceed market expectations and thereby delight investors. But should this growth falter, markets will punish swiftly and severely.

The Drivers of Nokia's Strategic Failure

What *could* go wrong with Nokia's secret code? Anything and everything, or more precisely, the individual elements and drivers of the complex profit-generation system, the interdependent system as a whole, or both. To understand the drivers of Nokia's potential strategic failure, the strategist must simply reverse the drivers of its current strategic success. The company, thus, would suffer in the following overall circumstances:

- If one or more drivers were exhausted in upstream processes (e.g., failures in coalition formation, proprietary instead of open standards)
- If one or more drivers were exhausted in downstream processes (e.g., weaknesses in segmentation, complacency in brand execution, or lack of appropriate investments in branding, design mistakes, or more attractive competitor designs)
- If individual elements of the process configuration fail to work together or conflict with one another (e.g., R&D bets on "wrong" technologies, coalitions, products, and services)
- If the preconditions of global focus advantage stumble (e.g., new logistics crises, exclusion or weak performance in critical existing or future lead markets)
- If the company were to have problems with its preemption strategy (e.g., first-mover disadvantages, product/service quality issues, problems in delivery, loss of the ability to command price premiums)
- If Nokia's powerful "twin drivers" (mobility and the Internet) were to experience significant difficulties (e.g., significant perceived health risks of cellular use, rapid saturation of the lead markets coupled with slow replacement demand, infrastructure or traffic problems in the use of the cellular and/or the Internet)

At the end of the 1990s, for instance, the arrival of the 3G competition was widely perceived as the great accelerator of Nokia's profit machine. By 2000, however, many observers and analysts learned to factor in the huge fees that telephone and network operators around the world were paying for 3G cellular licenses that would allow them to offer mobile data communications services. They came to suspect that these fees might cut into the funds available for developing and marketing such services. While European countries had started auctioning off those licenses, thus drawing tens of billions of dollars in bids by mid-2000, the United States joined the process in the fall.

Ever since Ollila took charge of Nokia in 1992, the company has rushed from one success to another. Even when it has stumbled, it has quickly learned from its mistakes and moved on. The more quickly and the larger the company has grown, the more complex and harder it has become to manage the entire organization. Of all the drivers and elements of the interdependent process configuration, it is perhaps the overall strategy that can either make or break the company. What if Nokia's preemption strategy falls apart? What if it can no longer deliver the kind of first-mover advantages that have significantly contributed to its extraordinary performance and thereby to its exceptionally high shareholder value?

According to conventional strategy wisdom, a company can outperform competitors if it can establish a difference that it can sustain. It must deliver greater value to buyers, create comparable value at a lower cost, or both.[9] Nokia does not comfortably fit into this schematic view, and it may not be an exception in this regard.

First, *sustainable* competitive advantage may have been typical of many industry leaders in industries characterized by domestic rivalry, low use of information systems, hierarchical organizations, low service, and regulation. By the same token, it may be far more difficult to realize in contemporary industries driven by globalization, information, flexibility, speed, and deregulation. To Nokia, as well as to its key rivals such as Ericsson and Motorola, stable sustainability has become nearly impossible in an industry where even the dominant players have to renew their competitive advantage with each new technology platform. The competitive requirements have been quite different in the 1G, 2G, and 3G environments.

In addition to the problem of sustainability, many contemporary technology industries and companies, Nokia in particular, pose another difficulty for classic notions of differentiation and cost leadership. The classic framework of competitive strategy is a classification that suppresses historical and evolutionary factors. *Competitive time* plays a critical role in the industry rivalry. It does not exclude differentiation, cost leadership, or focus strategies, but it must be incorporated with each.[10] Certainly, a company can outperform competitors if it can establish a difference that it can sustain over the short or long term. For superior performance, it must deliver greater value to buyers, create comparable value at a lower cost, or do both before its competitors. In other words, differentiation, cost leadership, or focus strategies no longer operate in a static environment, but dynamically. In such circumstances, competitive time is vital for superior performance.

Nokia's industry dominance has not been structural, but behavioral; it lies not in the uniqueness of its strategic maneuvering but in its faster, better, and cheaper execution.

No strategy is invulnerable; all represent compromises among business processes, drivers, capabilities, process configurations, competitive advantage, industry attractiveness, performance, and valuations. In theory, then, many things *could* go wrong at Nokia, but as of late July 2000, none have. This, more than anything else, serves to illustrate how carefully, ingeniously, subtly, and presciently the company has orchestrated its business processes since the early 1990s. It is the extraordinary performance of this interdependent organizational whole, along with bold dreams and entrepreneurial willingness, that is a tribute to Nokia's strategic leadership and has rightly earned the admiration of industry observers and investment analysts worldwide.

In the course of three decades, Nokia has divested declining segments, focused on growing ones, relied on cash cows, and bet futures on question marks. Yet, what makes its success so elusive to comprehend is the role of strategic inflection points in its evolution, transitional shifts that have both affirmed and refuted history. Not everything, however, is under Nokia' s strategic control. Although the company may seem invincible, there is no assurance that its future will be as magnificent as its recent past and present.

Which Customers to Listen To?

For decades, Nokia has excelled in its ability and willingness to "listen to the customer." Under Ollila's leadership, this capability has been perfected into an art through strategy, structure, and resource allocation. But, really, the dictum begs the question: *Which* customers should the company listen to?

By 2000, Nokia was an indisputable industry leader in the mobile cellular industry, but performance trajectories were affected by two kinds of innovation.[11] Sustaining innovations maintain a trajectory of performance improvement that has been established in a market. These innovations give customers more and better examples of attributes they already value. Through the 2G rivalry, Nokia had been engaged in sustaining innovations. In the GSM competition, it had been the leading company and ahead of its rivals in developing and adopting sustaining innovations, from incremental to radical. That is how it ensured success among its most lucrative customers.

In contrast, disruptive innovations introduce an entirely different value proposition; they bring about a different package of attributes to a marketplace from the ones that mainstream customers historically have valued. Initially, the new products tend to perform far worse along one or two dimensions of performance that are vital to the *existing* customers. Consequently, mainstream customers are seldom willing to use disruptive innovations. Initially, then, these are used and valued only in new markets and applications, and they often trigger the emergence of new markets. While they typically underperform along traditional metrics of functionality, disruptive products and services are often cheaper, simpler, and more user friendly than their predecessors. In the 3G rivalry, Nokia was after disruptive innovations even while it sought to retain industry leadership in sustaining products and services (i.e., the GSM world). With most companies that, precisely, has been the recipe to failure, but unlike Nokia, they have failed to exploit the strategic inflection points.

Usually, once disruptive innovators have secured a foothold in a low-end or emerging market where the product is valued, they have attacked and penetrated mainstream applications from the underside after rapid improvements. In the course of these competitive revolutions, many industry leaders that had been "built to last" stumbled and ultimately lost their positions of prominence. Why should Nokia be any different? Unlike most incumbents (and despite its advanced corporate age), Nokia has been an attacker itself and has operated in a relatively young industry.

Certainly, Nokia has not been just another industry leader, but has it been *different enough?* Take the 1G and 2G rivalry. "The giants do not invest enough in the small markets of this [mobile] industry that they could achieve a leading position," said Jorma Nieminen, Nokia-Mobira's chief in the 1980s. "This is a side business for them and that is why it will not achieve a leading position. . . . There is more reason to be afraid of small unknown competitors than well-known giants."[12] This powerful insight came ahead of its time and has enabled Nokia to pay careful attention not just to entrenched telecommunications monopolies but also to the competitive fringe of small start-ups, those mobile vendors and operators that became the industry pioneers of the 1990s.

Similarly, more than a decade before the adoption of the single flexible standard for the 3G rivalry, Nokia initiated the vital technological and political efforts that were deemed necessary for strategic positioning in what is today known as the mobile Internet. The stakes were immense. Potential trade wars came with the territory. But if one could not take the heat, one was not in the right business. The proactive stance was a matter of pride and an obsession to Ollila. Humility, humility, humility, he would preach to his troops; only the paranoid survive. He would repeatedly warn against pride brought by success. Tomorrow was today. There was no time for sequential strategic planning and implementation; both had to move ahead, hand in hand. There was no need for self-satisfaction; that was the privilege of those who were about to be overthrown.

In the 1980s, Nokia had exploited the strategic inflection into analog cellular. At first, it had thrived, then it had stumbled. In the 1990s, it had overcome a different inflection point into digital cellular. At first, it had stumbled, then it had thrived. In 2000, Nokia was an industry leader as well as an agile competitor. Prophetically, it had begun preparations for the 3G future some eleven to thirteen years before that future became a reality. Market leadership was secured in premarket maneuvering, including government and trade relations. After all, regional trading blocs were no longer passive bystanders; election victories were about jobs, and trade surpluses meant employment, which translated into votes. The industry was global, the number of competitors had proliferated, and the technology had grown increasingly complex and specialized. Strategic coalitions were held together by a mix of trust and suspicion. Today's cooperators were tomorrow's competitors. New potential attackers entered the industry frequently and did so across the globe.

In 1975, the young Bill Gates formulated a vision statement for a tiny unknown software company: "A computer on every desk and in every home." Less than a decade later, Apple's Steven Jobs declared another radical vision: "A personal computer to every household." Following the PC revolution, the Internet pioneers, such as Cisco Systems, America Online, and Yahoo!, set out to network every household PC, unleashing the Internet revolution. After its acquisition of McCaw Cellular, AT&T, for its part, announced a new era of communications in which demand drove innovation, not vice versa. In this environment, people would be able to communicate anytime, anywhere. At the end of the 1990s, Ollila decided to push the markets far beyond the early visions of digital convergence. In Nokia's vision, the mobile phone was a natural vehicle for "putting the Internet into everybody's pocket."

Despite years of preparation for the mobile Internet—or as Ollila would say, "sweat and agony"—Nokia was in for a new ball game. Unlike most industry leaders, however, it thought big and was willing to take bold risks. That was its only viable option; a big company in a small country could not conduct itself otherwise among big companies in big countries. A preemptor has to pay to play. No risks, no rewards. Such thinking has always been Nokia's greatest strength, just as it will remain its greatest potential source of its vulnerability.

Chronology of the European Integration of the Nordic Countries and Finland

1945 Finland's Communists win a great victory in the parliamentary election and enter the government.

1947 Announcement of the Truman Doctrine by the U.S. government. The Marshall Plan is launched for the economic reconstruction of Europe.

1948 Creation of the Organization for European Economic Cooperation (OEEC) with sixteen member states. Finland is pressured to ratify the Treaty of Friendship, Cooperation, and Mutual Assistance with the Soviet Union.

1949 Signing of the Washington treaty founding the North Atlantic Treaty Organization (NATO). The Council of Europe is established as an intergovernmental consultative forum on all nondefense matters. The start of the Cold War reduces membership to the states of Western Europe.

1950 The Schuman Plan calls for the French and West German coal and steel industries to be placed under one common authority.

1951 The Treaty of Paris establishes the European Coal and Steel Community (ECSC).

1954 The 1948 Brussels Treaty is modified and the Western European Union (WEU) is established.

1955 Finland joins the United Nations and the Nordic Council.

1956 Urho Kaleva Kekkonen is elected president of Finland.

1957 The United Kingdom proposes a European free-trade association. The Treaty of Rome establishes the European Economic

Community (EEC). To avoid an economic rift between the founding states of the EEC and non-EEC states, the Maudling Committee is established by the OEEC to secure agreement on a free-trade zone in Western Europe.

1960 The signature of the Stockholm Convention establishes the European Free Trade Association (EFTA) with seven founding member states: Denmark, Sweden, Norway, Austria, Portugal, Switzerland, and the United Kingdom. The OEEC is reorganized into the Organization for Economic Cooperation and Development (OECD), following the failure of the Maudling Committee.

1961 The United Kingdom and Denmark apply for membership in the EEC.

1962 Norway requests negotiations on membership in the EEC.

1964 The Kennedy Round of the GATT trade negotiations opens, and EEC member states attend the negotiations as a single delegation.

1966 Major gains in the parliamentary election by the Finnish Left. Communists and Social Democrats form a coalition government, to which conservatives stand opposed until the late 1980s.

1967 Norway applies for EEC membership.

1968 A treaty creating the Nordek Customs Union (NCU) among member states of the Nordic Council is ratified.

1970 The Nordic states abandon the NCU.

1971 Nordic countries implement all the measures planned for NCU without a formal alliance.

1972 The United Kingdom, Denmark, and Ireland conclude membership negotiations with the EC. Norwegian electorate rejects EC membership in a referendum, but the Danish electorate accepts. The Paris Summit agrees to the Economic and Monetary Union (EMU) in 1980.

1973 Accession of United Kingdom, Denmark, and Ireland to the EC. Norway and the EC sign a "special relations" agreement.

1975 Conclusion of the Conference on Security and Cooperation in Europe and the signing of the Helsinki Final Act.

1979 Establishment of the European Monetary System (EMS).

1982 Mauno Koivisto succeeds Kekkonen as president of Finland.

1983 EC and EFTA member states establish a common free-trade zone, and the European Parliament approves a draft of the Treaty on European Union.

1985 The European Council agrees to the creation of a single European market by the end of 1992.

1986 Finland becomes a full member of EFTA.

1987 The conservative National Coalition Party in Finland, which had been in opposition for two decades, and the Social Democrats form a majority government that remains in power until 1991.

1989 The fall of the Berlin Wall, and Communist governments begin to collapse in Eastern Europe. The EC signs a ten-year trade and cooperation agreement with the Soviet Union.

1990 Germany is unified, and the first phase of the EMU begins. The first signs of Finland's worst recession in the post–World War II era and a dramatic decline in trade with the Soviet Union begin.

1991 Sweden applies for EC membership. The Soviet Union is dissolved. The European Council meets at Maastricht and agrees to the Treaty on European Union. Nordic prime ministers propose a thorough re-evaluation of Nordic cooperation. Finnish trade relations with the EC accelerate. At first, the Finnish government favors pursuing relations with the EC through the European Economic Agreement (EEA), but after Finland's elections, the Social Democrats are left in opposition; a new government is formed by the conservatives and the Center Party.

1992 Finland recognizes Russia as the successor to the Soviet Union, and the two countries conclude a treaty containing no military articles; the Treaty on Friendship, Cooperation, and Mutual Assistance is declared null and void. Finland applies to the EC. The Treaty on European Union is signed in Maastricht, but the Danish electorate rejects it. The ERM crisis begins. Norway applies to join the EC. The European Council opens accession negotiations with Austria, Finland, Sweden, and Norway.

1993 Finland opts for a change in its foreign ownership legislation, and foreign direct investment in Finnish companies accelerates quickly.

1995 Austria, Finland, and Sweden become members of the EU.

1999 Finland becomes president of the EU.

SOURCES: Adapted from "Chronology," in *The European Union Handbook*, ed. Philippe Barbour (Chicago: Fitzroy Dearborn Publishers, 1996); Virtual Finland, available at http://virtual.finland.fi

Nokia's Process Configuration

IT is the process systems that tell Nokia's strategic story in the cellular era (through the 1990s) and in the mobile Internet era (starting in the late 1990s). Indeed, these process-system maps indicate the kinds of activities Nokia was engaged in, how they were conducted, and where they were located. In particular, these maps illustrate how the company's strategic position—or more precisely, maneuvering toward a strategic position—was contained in a set of tailored processes.

The Peak of the Cellular Era (1997)

By 1997, Nokia had found its strategic course in the mobile business (see Exhibit B-1). That year proved to be the peak of the company's cellular era. Under Ollila's leadership, the group executive board served as a model of teamwork and job rotation for the entire company. With its willingness and increasing ability to shape its own future, Nokia had not only become a tough competitor but also a heavily involved collaborator, lobbyist, and coalition builder in technology, government relations, and international trade relations.

As logistics problems disappeared and Nokia began to assume industry leadership, its stock price began to soar. The process organization was now in place, enabling the cross-functional teams to be appropriately networked. While branding had been initiated nearly six years before, the global campaigns finally began to pay off. As Nokia moved from business markets to consumer markets, it seized segmentation. Previously, the company had been quick to establish client relationships with new operators; now it was implementing customer commitment processes in consumer markets.

With process organization in place, Nokia could also optimally

Exhibit B-1. Nokia's process configuration: the peak of the cellular era (1997).

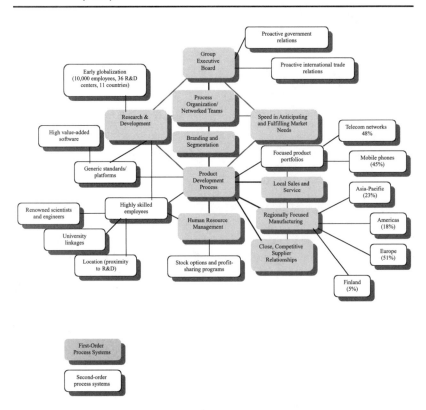

benefit from its product development process. Nokia was faster and more agile than its rivals in anticipating and fulfilling market needs. Its regionally focused manufacturing was coupled with close but competitive relationships with a web of suppliers that were internationalized in its footsteps. In the business segments, product portfolios had grown focused while revenues of telecommunications networks (48 percent) still rivaled those of mobile phones (45 percent). In its geographic segments, Europe reigned (51 percent), but the growth markets were in Asia-Pacific (23 percent) and the Americas (18 percent). In the long term, Japan's significance had grown as the first major test field of 3G competition, whereas China's 1.2 billion inhabitants promised extraordinary volume potential. As a test laboratory for new mobile products and services, Finland remained significant (more than 50 percent of the production efforts were still concentrated in Finland), but its revenue fraction declined rapidly (to 5 percent).

On the upstream side, the product development process increasingly concentrated on generic standards/platforms and high value-added software. In the long term, Nokia's new-product development process depended on HRM and R&D. In the 1990s, Nokia had gained clout as a challenging and inspiring employer that stressed meritocratic values. It sought the best and brightest by keeping close to universities, renowned scientific and engineering communities, and other academic institutions. Once it attracted an appropriate, highly skilled workforce, it sought to retain the talent by offering generous stock options and profit-sharing programs. In Finland, the company created an expanding pool of "Nokia millionaires."

Although the center of Nokia's R&D activities remained in Finland, its technology development had entered a period of rapid globalization, with more than 11,000 employees and thirty-six R&D centers in eleven countries. Such developments precipitated changes in other units as well. Starting in the HRM division, the number of foreign-born senior vice presidents increased. Nokia's headquarters may have been in Finland and the company may have cherished the old egalitarian Nordic values, but it was hardly a Finnish company any longer. In fact, it had not been controlled by Finnish banks for several years; it was owned now by international, primarily American and European, institutional investors.

Beginning of the Mobile Internet Era (2000)

By 2000, Nokia was intent on building new capabilities for the mobile Internet as well as moving toward the mobile information society well before its rivals (see Exhibit B-2). Having consolidated his role as Nokia's CEO and chairman, Ollila delegated some authority to Pekka Ala-Pietilä, Nokia's president, who was widely considered Ollila's successor. Except for job rotation, the composition of the group executive board remained the same. With Nokia's first stumbling steps in Silicon Valley, some industry observers had begun to question the depth of the company's globalization initiatives. Although the R&D employees and general workforce of Nokia were rapidly diversifying, the chief executives remained all Finnish. However, as long as the company's performance was superior vis-à-vis its rivals, the negative tones stayed in the background.

If anything, Nokia had become an even tougher competitor. Near the end of the 1990s, it was also widely considered *the* model for the coming European technology challengers, which would (the EC hoped) challenge U.S. dominance in computers and the Internet and Asian dominance in consumer electronics. Under Ollila's cautious diplomacy, Nokia enjoyed the benefits of its dominant position in Eu-

Exhibit B-2. Nokia's process configuration: the beginning of the mobile Internet era (2000).

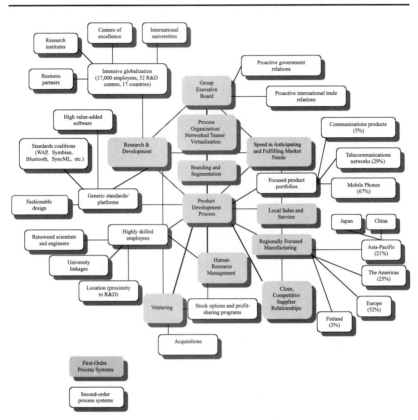

rope but kept its doors open in the Americas and Asia-Pacific. Now the company had a significant role not just in the Nordic countries or even Europe, but as a global company that was increasingly involved in precompetitive activities, through the EU and the OECD, for instance. Similarly, Nokia's high-profile maneuvering had accelerated drastically vis-à-vis the standards coalitions; it had either founded or cofounded every new industry partnership that would have relevance in the 3G and mobile Internet rivalry. In the process, it shifted the basis of competition in the cellular business from product development processes to customer commitment processes, where its differentiation was more favorable and its bargaining power greater.

At the peak of the cellular era, Nokia's stock price rose; on the eve of the mobile Internet era, it seemed to go through the roof. It was the industry leader in the cellular business, and its strategic intent was to lead mobile Internet as well. Many analysts saw Nokia as a "double gorilla" of sorts. As valuations caught up with the perception, it suddenly became Europe's most valuable company.

The process organization and the cross-functional teams worked as before, but now there were more of them and most had been networked online. Indeed, Nokia's corporate Web site was one of the first in the industry and had proved highly useful in various processes, from internal publishing to recruiting new talent. As a global brand, Nokia was now among the industry leaders of the era, in the company of Nike, Intel, Coca-Cola, and Procter & Gamble. Although it did not enjoy a sustained competitive advantage, it had become *the* mobile vendor. Through its customer commitment process, Nokia had learned to excel in lifestyle segmentation and was pushing design as well. Toward the end of the 1990s, Nokia's new models became subjects of importance from fashion magazines to the Emmy Awards and Hollywood cocktail parties.

By 2000, Nokia's new-product development was considered both innovative and revolutionary. The company was faster and more flexible than its rivals, and now it was also learning how to use the World Wide Web as an instrument of customer commitment (Nokia Club). It was rapidly expanding its regionally focused manufacturing, just as it needed more new suppliers to build capabilities in the mobile Internet. In its business segments, the composition of revenues had shifted drastically. By 2000, the emphasis was clearly on handsets (67 percent), even if telecommunications networks still had an important role to play (29 percent). The emergence of communication products (5 percent) precipitated the mobile Internet and entirely new products. However, this segment was also burning cash and was expected to continue to do so for a few years to come.

Through strategic partnerships, Nokia quickly co-opted potential rivals, such as Palm and Microsoft. Stressing open standards, it was actively shaping not just cellular or the mobile Internet, but computing systems as well. In the long term, Nokia now saw itself primarily as a software company rather than a cellular supplier. As Nokia established its venture organization and venture fund, it made no secret of its determination to build new capabilities in a new environment for a new kind of industry. At first, its acquisition program faltered, but it was designed as a long-term commitment of new-product development. Still, the absence of significant Internet properties triggered speculation over Nokia's real strengths in the "new economy." Indeed, the larger Nokia grew, the harder it was to attract and retain exceptional talent. At the same time, the importance of new employees, especially in the strategic Internet segments, was growing rapidly. Globalization was rapidly transforming the company.

In just two years, the number of its R&D employees had increased from 10,000 to 17,000. Instead of thirty-six R&D centers in eleven countries, it had now had fifty-two in seventeen. Perhaps not surprisingly, the chief of HRM became Nokia's first non-Finnish senior vice president. The faces of its employees were rapidly becoming as diverse as the lead markets in which it had a significant role. The more heterogeneous the workforce, the more Ollila and other chief executives would emphasize Nokia's egalitarian values and vision.

Nokia's process configuration was a pragmatic solution to environmental changes. If there were to be more external shifts, the internal environment would have to adapt. In the spring of 2000, Mikko Kosonen, Nokia's senior vice president for strategy and information management, spoke to Finnish managers about the power of change. He advised the Finns to rethink everything, starting with the basic concepts and benchmarks of business. The talk was not mere rhetoric, nor did it reflect only those efforts to accommodate the Internet transition. For years, indeed for decades, Nokia had lived as it preached. In the past, life had been slow-paced; now it had become rapid paced. Significant changes in the environment required significant changes in strategy and structure and the conceptual maps to comprehend both.

A Note on the Finnish Sources

TO understand Nokia's success, it is necessary to understand Nokia's role and function in both the global rivalry *and* the Finnish telecommunications/mobile cluster. In the absence of an adequate understanding of each of these, industry observers, investment analysts, and journalists have typically either encouraged inflated expectations due to a lack of knowledge of Nokia's real competitive circumstances (e.g., international portrayals of Nokia's success), or they have examined Nokia solely as a Finnish company within the Finnish environment, which has often resulted in the trivialization of the company's competitive circumstances (e.g., Finnish debates on stock options and the "Nokia millionaires"). Also, some international journalists inadvertently have relied on very selective information sources, which have served to further mythologize the company.

I have relied primarily on typical international sources of business information as well as direct, indirect, and related sources, when they illustrate key aspects of Nokia's corporate and/or business processes. Here I shall only focus on the most central sources and their basic characteristics. Full documentation can be found in the chapter references.

In Finland, the organizational precursors of Nokia have been studied in several corporate histories. In fact, most early Nokia scholarship is historical. In 1929, Karl Ekman published *Nokia bruk 1868–1928* (in Swedish), the classic story of the early Nokia. It was followed by Victor Hoving's *Suomen gummitehdas osakeyhtiö 1898–1948*, which tells the story of the Finnish Rubber Works. The origins and growth of the Finnish Ropery Works and the Finnish Cable Works have been studied by Eige Cronström et al. in *Puoli vuosisataa kaapeliteollisuutta 1912–1962*. A more recent and beautifully illustrated work was produced in 1998 by Ritva Palo-Oja and Leena Willberg, *Rubber: The History of Rubber and the Finnish Rubber Industry*. It provides important information on the

Finnish Rubber Works, a precursor of the current Nokia. In addition, Lauri Saari's *Valcoinen kirja* (1981) offers a tabloid-style account of the Valco debacle, including some interesting facts on the efforts to socialize Finland's nascent electronics industry in the 1970s.

From the late 1970s to the end of the 1980s, the most important Finnish studies on Nokia or by Nokians on related themes consist of those by Nokia's chief executives. In the early 1980s, Jorma Ollila, later Nokia's CEO and chairman, wrote two theses: "International Trade Under Uncertainty" (Helsinki University) and "Optimization of Economic Growth" (Helsinki University of Technology). Both works illustrate his central concerns for the future and, perhaps even more important, his strategic way of thinking. In 1983, Sari Baldauf published a study of disinvestment, *International Divestments as the Reallocation Process of Productive Assets*. She joined Nokia soon thereafter and later became a member of Nokia's group executive board.

Near the end of the 1980s, amid Nokia's struggle for growth, internationalization, and corporate control, two key Nokian executives— Timo H. A. Koski, Kari Kairamo's right-hand man, and Matti Alahuhta, one of Nokia's executive insiders today—published dissertations. Koski's "Ownership Strategy and Competitive Advantage" (HUT, 1988) illustrates the growing pressures of financial control and corporate governance. As Kairamo's heir apparent, Koski anticipated many of the key problems that Ollila would have to resolve in the late 1990s. Two years after Koski, Matti Alahuhta completed his own dissertation at the HUT, "Global Growth Strategies for High Technology Challengers." While Alahuhta has not been the only globalization expert of Nokia's senior leadership, the dissertation provides a concise introduction to the prime motives of Nokia's globalization in the early 1990s.

In the aftermath of the Finnish banking crisis of the early 1990s, several books were published in Finnish on the key players, some of whom were plotting the takeover of Nokia before its restructuring. The most important and controversial of these figures remains Pentti Kouri. In 1991, Harri Saukkomaa, a business journalist, published one of the most influential in a long series of "revelations," *Kuka tarvitsi Pentti Kouria?* In 1996, Pentti Kouri wrote his biography, *Suomen omistaja ja elämäni muut roolit*, in which he sought to clean his tarnished reputation and "put things right." Two years later, Antti Mikkonen's *Rahavallan rakkikoirat* provided a vivid picture of these financial plots and corporate raider wannabes.

The first substantive accounts of the present-day Nokia were released only in the mid-1990s, right after the company had found its new strategic course around 1993. One of the most important of these remains Mikko Koivusalo's *Kipinästä tuli syttyy: Suomalaisen radiopuhel-*

inteollisuuden kehitys ja tulevaisuuden haasteet, which tells the story of Finland's wireless industry, focusing on Nokia's triumphant growth. While Koivusalo's account is based on fragments of old annual reports and internal company documents and is therefore less narrative than many in-depth studies, it provides organizational details on Nokia's expansion and core processes.

Although the Nokian CEOs are very well known in Finland and have often been interviewed in the Finnish business press and media, none has yet published a book-length study on the topic. According to some observers, however, Jorma Ollila may write one. In the fall of 2000, Matti Saari published the first book-length biography on Kairamo, *Kari Kairamo: Kohtalona Suomi,* a study of the pioneer Nokian who in so many ways made possible the preconditions of Nokia's future success. (I am grateful to Saari and Risto Väisänen, manager of Gummerus Publishing, for allowing me to explore the manuscript prior to its release in Finland.)

After I had to decline an offer to write Nokia's corporate biography in the early 1990s, the company invited Marco Mäkinen, an advertising professional and author of *Nokia saga: Kertomus yrityksestä ja ihmisistä jotka muuttivat sen,* to write the book. In Finland, some have criticized the approach of that biography for a certain "softness" in its treatment. The book is an oral history based on interviews with key players of the company in various phases of its history, and it provides much interesting anecdotal material. At the end of the 1990s, it was the only comprehensive Finnish book on the company, due in part to Mäkinen's direct access to Nokia's senior managers. In 1996, Lasse Kivikko, a technology consultant, and Juhani Hokkanen, then director of Nokia's human resources, published a brief essay, "In the Eye of Rapid Growth," an account of strategic flexibility at Nokia Mobile Phones. In 2000, Anja Kivimäki-Kuitunen published *Work, Rest & Play: Matkaevästä Nokian nuorilta esimiehiltä,* a short collection of interviews with the product development managers of Nokia Mobile Phones.

Academic research on Nokia did not really begin in Finland until the late 1990s. This delay is somewhat odd and may have less to do with Nokia than with the general gap between industry and the academic community that has been characteristic of Finnish business schools until recently. Unlike their American counterparts but like many European universities, Finnish schools have kept a certain academic distance from the practical world of everyday business. In my book *The Competitive Advantage of Finland* (1998), I explored these delays in scholarship in the context of distortions caused by Finland's political economy through the Cold War.

Another factor that may explain the delay of Nokia scholarship in the Finnish academic communities is groupthink. Until the end of the

Cold War, Nokia's struggle for internationalization was perceived as "American," which many Finns—even well-known academics—did not necessarily consider a good thing. Such caution and conformity were relics of the old neo-Stalinist intellectual fashion. With the eclipse of the Cold War, many of these "progressive" academics have struggled to "redefine" themselves in the new Finnish political economy. Consequently, moderate caution and uncritical positivity have replaced constructive criticism. Both postures reflect the kind of groupthink that is unfortunately prevalent in a small country where "everybody knows everybody else."

In the academic community, Raimo Lovio's dissertation, "Evolution of Firm Communities in New Industries" (1993), was among the first to study Nokia, although indirectly. It tells the story of Finnish electronics and thus illustrates the rise of electronics within the company. Concurrently, dozens of Finnish business scholars participated in an extensive national research project that sought to craft a new national strategy amid Finland's most severe recession since the 1930s. Many of these scholars came from or had been involved with the Research Institute of Finnish Economy (ETLA), the Helsinki School of Economics and Business Administration (HSEBA), the Finnish National Fund for Research and Development (SITRA), and Finland's National Technology Agency (TEKES). Finland's Ministry of Trade and Industry, as well as several other ministries, government agencies, and public organizations, also played vital roles in these developments. In their work, *Advantage Finland: The Future of Finnish Industries* (1996), Hannu Hernesniemi, Markku Lammi, and Pekka Ylä-Anttila portrayed a cluster gallery of the Finnish economy, from the old forestry sector to the emerging information communication technology (ICT) cluster. Their analysis of the Finnish ICT cluster provided a framework for many more recent Nokia studies. (Notably, even Mäkinen's *Nokia saga* built upon such ideas as clusters, locational advantage, enlightened buyers, and public policies.) In this stream of research, the role of Pekka Ylä-Anttila, research director of ETLA, has been crucial.

In 1996, Tarmo Lemola and Raimo Lovio edited a collection of essays, *Miksi Nokia, Finland,* analyzing Nokia's success through academic research from several perspectives. "The Breakthrough of Nokia Mobile Phones" (1997), Matti Pulkkinen's dissertation, illustrates the "success factors" of Nokia as the company's senior managers have understood them. A year later, I published *The Competitive Advantage of Finland,* a continuation of the *Advantage Finland* project that explores more recent developments of Nokia and Finnish telecommunications. In 2000, Jyrki Ali-Yrkkö, Laura Paija, Catherine Reilly, and Pekka Ylä-Anttila of ETLA, in cooperation with TEKES, published *Nokia: A Big*

Company in a Small Country, which focuses on Nokia's impact on Finnish exports, R&D, and GDP.

Since the mid-1990s, interviews with Nokia's leadership in leading American and international business newspapers and magazines have typically been conducted by specific members of the press. The good news is that these arrangements have allowed some journalists to gain a longitudinal perspective and learn more about Nokia's key executives. The bad news is that the very same arrangements have given rise to vested interests. In order to retain their access, journalists often fail to dig deeply enough. So long as Nokia thrives, these arrangement will probably work for all parties, but should Nokia face difficulties, markets will discipline inflated expectations, and new arrangements will be instituted.

At the same time, Nokia hired a Finnish historian, Martti Häikiö, to research and write its "official" corporate history. Prior to the end of the Cold War, political historians played a critical role in the national discourse on foreign policy; after the eclipse of the Cold War, the role of political historians in Finland has become far more marginal. Among astute Finnish historians, Häikiö repositioned himself as a corporate historian. In Finland, he is known for the histories of major telephone operators, as well as his personal connections with the political center and conservatives, reflecting also Nokia's political affiliations— and those of its key executives. Since Häikiö is a historian, not a business analyst, Finnish industry and policy observers expect him to write a solid historical account that will incorporate the richness of Nokia's history while reflecting the views of the current leadership.

In 1999, two Swedish journalists, Staffan Bruun and Mosse Wallen, published a different kind of account, *Nokian valtatie: Taistelu tiedosta, tulevaisuudesta ja optioista.* Tammi, one of the leading Finnish publishers, was supposed to release the Finnish version of the book, but the book was ultimately published by Gummerus, a smaller Finnish publishing house. The authors argued that Ollila, a member of Tammi's board, was behind the decision. Unlike most Finnish or international journalists, the authors went beyond the official corporate biographies and examined the early years of Ollila as an influential student leader during the years of Finnish radicalism. They also dedicated several sections to Nokia's options program, a familiar incentive in the United States but a new and controversial method of compensation in Scandinavia, where egalitarian values and contemporary business ethics do not always go hand in hand.

In 2000, Erkki K. Laitinen and Rolf Leppänen, two academics with consulting experience in industry, published a concise review based on recent dissertations and academic publications on Nokia's steering and management accounting systems. Unlike past academic studies, it was driven by practical issues. Also in 2000–2001, I published several studies that indirectly explore the key drivers of Nokia's success, including a three-part *Finland's Wireless Valley* (Ministry of Transport and Communications), *Sonera's Evolution* and *Sonera's Strategy* (both Sonera Corporation), as well as a lengthy analysis, "Assessing Finland's Wireless Valley: Can the Pioneering Continue?" in *Telecommunications Policy* (2001).

In addition to Nokia's Annual Reports, which can be found on the World Wide Web (www.nokia.com), as well as decades of Nokia's corporate releases, I have relied on many feature stories and interviews, mainly in the Finnish and international business press. Among others, the major Finnish trade and business sources include *Talouselämä, Tietoviikko, Kauppalehti, Taloussanomat,* and *Forum for Ekonomi och Teknik*. Other sources include *Helsingin Sanomat, Suomen Kuvalehti, Seura, Hufvudstadsbladet, Ilta-Sanomat, Iltalehti,* and *Yliopisto*.

Indeed, dozens of Finnish business journalists continue to report on Nokia's activities, while those that are better-positioned—for instance, Päivi Vihma (*Talouselämä*) and Anssi Miettinen (*Helsingin Sanomat*), and several others—have taken commentator roles. With Nokia's success, these reports have become something of a cottage history in the small country.

Notes

Introduction

1. On the Finnish telecommunications/mobile cluster and public-sector strategies, see Dan Steinbock, *Finland's Wireless Valley* (Helsinki: Finland's Ministry of Transport and Communications, 2000); Dan Steinbock, "Assessing Finland's Wireless Valley: Can the Pioneering Continue?" *Telecommunications Policy*, vol. 24, no. 11, January 2001.
2. For the context of the Finnish sources, see Appendix C.
3. Kenneth Klee and Jennifer Bensko, "The Future Is Finnish," *Newsweek*, June 21, 1999.
4. Steve Silberman, "Just Say Nokia," *Wired*, September 1999.
5. Klee and Bensko, "The Future is Finnish."
6. Justin Fox, "Nokia's Secret Code," *Fortune*, May 1, 2000.
7. Linturi lives according to his words. A while ago, he had a house built for his family on the shore of the Gulf of Finland. It has sensors in each room to control air circulation, and it lights up when someone walks in. He can lock or unlock his front door by calling a number on his mobile phone, and if someone rings his doorbell when he is away, his phone rings so he can ask who it is. Some 10 kilometers of wires run through the house. See Dan Steinbock, personal correspondence with Risto Linturi, September 22, 1999.
8. In spring 2000, SMS was still little known in the United States, where GSM phones accounted for only 4 percent of all cell phones, while they represented 89 percent of the European mobile phone market. Compare Bruno Giussani, "Text Messages, Though Short, Catch on with Cell Users," *New York Times*, March 14, 2000.
9. See Chapter 7.
10. Fox, "Nokia's Secret Code." The market share estimates are from Dataquest; the brand valuations from Interbrand.
11. Compare George Stalk, Philip Evans, and Lawrence E. Shulman, "Competing on Capabilities: The New Rules of Corporate Strategy," *Harvard Business Review* (March/April 1992).
12. It is this historical persistence that certainly makes it tempting to compare Nokia with the successful "visionary companies" or with the longstanding "living companies." On the surface, the affinities seem overwhelming, but scratch the surface and the dissimilarities come into view. Like the famous visionary companies, for example, Nokia has thrived for over a century; however, unlike these giants, its global success is very recent in terms of its corporate history. On visionary companies, see James C. Collins and Jerry I. Porras, *Built to Last: Successful Habits of Visionary Companies* (New

York: HarperBusiness, 1994). On living companies, see Arie De Geus, *The Living Company: Habits for Survival in a Turbulent Business Environment* (Boston, Mass.: Harvard Business School Press, 1997).

13. While the Finnish telecommunications/mobile cluster may be critically dependent on Nokia, the company is no longer as dependent on Finland. It has grown beyond its home base. In Finnish business and politics, this is a source of great national pride and concern.

14. As the value of the output produced by a unit of labor or capital, productivity depends on both the quality and features of products, which dictate the price premium they can command, as well as the efficiency with which they are produced. On the stages of competitive development, see Michael E. Porter, *The Competitive Advantage of Nations* (New York: The Free Press, 1990). On the Finnish cluster studies, see Hannu Hermesniemi, Markku Lammi, and Pekka Ylä-Anttila, *Advantage Finland—The Future of Finnish Industries*, ETLA Series B: 113 (Helsinki: ETLA/SITRA, 1996); Dan Steinbock, *The Competitive Advantage of Finland: From Cartels to Competition?* (Helsinki: ETLA/SITRA, 1998).

15. The literature on the competitive advantage of nations has identified four distinct stages of national competitive advantage: factor-driven, investment-driven, innovation-driven, and wealth-driven. The first three stages relate to the successive upgrading of a nation's competitive advantages and are usually associated with progressively rising economic prosperity. The fourth stage involves drift and ultimate decline. See Porter, *The Competitive Advantage of Nations*, pp. 543–573. While nations do not inevitably pass through these four stages, the Finnish experience in general and Nokia's history in particular do reflect the progression through the first three stages.

16. Jorma Ollila, "To Our Shareholders," Nokia Corporation Annual Report 1998, pp. 6–7.

17. Jorma Ollila and Pekka Ala-Pietilä, "To Our Shareholders," Nokia Corporation Annual Report 1999, p. 7.

18. On preemption as a generic strategy, see Dan Steinbock, *Dynamic Advantage* (forthcoming).

Chapter 1

1. On the basic characteristics of factor-driven economies, see Michael E. Porter, *The Competitive Advantage of Nations* (New York: The Free Press, 1990), pp. 546–548.

2. On the "old" Nokia, see Lars G. von Bonsdorff, *Nokia Oy 1865–1965* (Helsinki: Nokia Oy, 1965); Karl Ekman, *Nokian Tehdas 1868–1928* (Helsinki: Nokia Oy, 1928).

3. The government of Finland was directly controlled by the tsar, who appointed a governor general as his advisor. With one brief exception, all of the governors general were Russian. See Hugh Seton-Watson, *The Russian Empire, 1801–1917* (Oxford: Clarendon Press, 1967), p. 774.

4. The Diet derived from the dual kingdom of Sweden-Finland. For centuries, Finns had enjoyed the common Nordic right to manage local affairs by themselves. After 1435, they began sending representatives to the kingdom's governing body, the Diet of the Four Estates (*Riksdag*), which anticipated the emergence of the Finnish Parliament, *Eduskunta*.

5. For an account of Idestam's German experiences and the creation of the precursor of Nokia, see Bonsdorff, *Nokia Oy 1865–1965*; Ekman, *Nokian Tehdas 1868–1928*.

6. On the role of vision as a precondition of strategy, see James C. Collins and William C. Lazier, "Organizational Vision for Small to Mid-Sized Companies," in *Managing the Small to Mid-Sized Company: Concept and Cases* (Chicago, Ill.: Irwin, 1995), pp. 23–42.

7. Bonsdorff, *Nokia Oy 1865–1965*, p. 34.

8. In 1872, Mechelin left the board. Given his own business activities, the membership raised conflict of interest issues.

9. Bonsdorff, *Nokia Oy 1865–1965*, p. 69.

10. Such circumstances continued until the end of the factor-driven stage in the 1930s and 1940s. Compare Risto Tainio, "Finland Between Two Systems: Emergence, Reproduction, and Change of Governance Structures," unpublished paper, 1996.

11. Compare Seton-Watson, *The Russian Empire, 1801–1917*.

12. The struggle against Russification culminated in the Great Strike that spread from Russia to Finland near the end of 1905. A year later, Finland obtained a unicameral parliament, partially due to Mechelin's crusade for political independence.

13. See Joan Magretta, "Governing the Family-Owned Enterprise: An Interview with Finland's Krister Ahlström," *Harvard Business Review* (January/February 1998). In Finland, Ahlström's great-grandfather, who created the company, was a farmer's son who started out in shipping some two decades before Idestam.

14. In only a few months, about 30,000 Finns perished, less than a quarter of them on the battlefield, the rest in summary executions and in detention camps. These deaths amounted to about 1 percent of the total population of Finland. By comparison, the bloodiest war in the history of the United States, the Civil War, cost the lives of about 2 percent of the population, but that loss was spread out over four years. See Eino Jutikkala and Kauko Pirinen, *A History of Finland* (New York: Praeger, 1962), p. 152.

15. Compare Markku Kuisma, "Government Action, Cartels, and National Corporations: The Development Strategy of a Small Peripheral Nation During the Period of Crisis and Economic Disintegration in Europe (Finland 1918–1938)," *Scandinavian Economic History Review* 91, no. 3 (1993): 242–268. See also Markku Kuisma, *Metsäteollisuuden maa* (Jyvaskylä: Gummerus, 1993).

16. On the origins and growth of the FRW, see Victor Hoving, *Suomen Gummitehdas Osakeyhtiö 1898–1948* (Helsinki: 1948); Ritva Palo-Oja and Leena Willberg, *Rubber: The History of Rubber and the Finnish Rubber Industry* (Tampere: Tampere Museums, Association of Rubber Industries Registered Associations, 1998).

17. Quoted in Ritva Palo-Oja and Leena Willberg, *Rubber: The History of Rubber*, pp. 41–74.

18. On these early decades of Finnish rubber, see in particular Palo-Oja and Willberg, "The Rubber Industry in Finland," in *Rubber*, pp. 41–74.

19. A year of physical absence, however, did not mean the end of his influence. Through correspondence, he continued to propose innovations. Furthermore, it was during this time that he devised the company's future direction. Seeing the number of automobiles soar in the 1910s, Polon believed that, over time, the company would have to shift its production from galoshes to tire manufacturing.

20. On the origins and growth of the Finnish Ropery Works and the Finnish Cable Works, see Eige Cronström, Holger Ström, et al., *Puoli vuosisataa kaapeliteollisuutta 1912–1962* (Helsinki: Suomen kaapelitehdas osakeyhtiö, 1965).

21. Compare Markku Kuisma, "Metsässä syntynyt, puusta pudottautunut," in *Miksi Nokia, Finland?* eds. Tarmo Lemola and Raimo Lovio (Helsinki: WSOY, 1996), pp. 16–35.

22. See Juhani Laurila, *Finnish-Soviet Clearing Trade and Payment System: History and Lessons*, Bank of Finland Studies A:94 (Helsinki: 1995).

23. With a population of only 3.5 million, Finland itself was not a threat to the Soviet Union, but its territory, located strategically near Leningrad, could be used as a base by the Germans. See Anthony F. Upton, *Finland in Crisis, 1940–41: A Study in Small-Power Politics* (London: 1964), p. 22; D. G. Kirby, *Finland in the Twentieth Century* (Minneapolis: 1979).

24. Approximately 86,000 Finns died in the war, about three times the losses suffered during the civil war. In addition, about 57,000 Finns were permanently disabled. The vast majority of the dead and disabled were young men in their most productive years. The war also left 24,000 war widows, 50,000 orphans, and 15,000 elderly. In addition, about one-eighth of the prewar area of Finland was lost, including the Petsamo area with its valuable nickel mines. One-half million Finns were refugees, including more than 400,000 from the ceded or leased territories and about 100,000 from Lapland, where their homes had been destroyed. During the war years, approximately 70,000 children were evacuated from Finland, primarily removed to Sweden. Although most returned to Finland, some remained in Sweden and Denmark.

25. In Finland, the years between World War II and the peace treaty (1944–1948) have often been called "years of danger." As some Finnish Communists proclaimed that the "Czechoslovakian model" fit Finland as well, many Finns feared a Communist takeover. In order to contain the pro-Soviet zeal of Finnish Communists, the Central Party and the Social Democrats allowed the Communists to participate in the government coalitions in the coming decades.

26. As Finnish observers have noted, "The procedures and institutions used were created so as to match the approach followed in the Soviet administration." While the sell and buy decisions were made by Finnish companies and the Soviet trade corporations, the clearing currency was the Soviet ruble. See Laurila, *Finnish-Soviet Clearing Trade and Payment System*, p. 30.

27. The FCW had evolved in four stages. Through the 1920s, it endeavored to build an adequate production line for markets; by 1926, the company reportedly controlled some 48 percent of the domestic marketplace, whereas the proportion of largely German imports amounted to 52 percent. From the late 1920s through the 1930s, the company focused operations on cable production, while the expansion efforts sought to deter foreign competition and, in some segments, to invade the domestic markets. Prior to the war years, the size of the domestic cable markets had tripled, and the company's domestic sales quadrupled. As a result, the proportion of imports declined from more than 50 percent to less than 30 percent. From the mid-1930s to the end of the reparations in 1948, the FCW concentrated on open-wire lines and power cables. With the end of the war reparations, the growth of the open-wire cable segment remained solid, and growth of the power cable increased, but phone cable exhibited

explosive growth. See Cronström, Ström, et al., *Puoli vuosisataa kaapeliteolli-suutta 1912–1962*, pp. 145–155.

28. Compare Cronström, Ström, et al., *Puoli vuosisataa kaapeliteollisuutta 1912–1962*, pp. 145–155.
29. Historians have acknowledged the importance of these limiting factors: "It is perhaps not quite correct, vis-à-vis the company, to stress the favorable role that war, periphery and the unique post-war market conditions were compelled to play in the stages of the company." Ibid.
30. The changing composition of Nokia's leading foreign customers of pulp from 1934 to 1963 reflects the abrupt impact of changes. In the 1930s, Great Britain was Nokia's key customer; over the course of the decade, its demand shrank from a peak of more than 10,000 tons to nil. Throughout the war years, Germany, Finland's military ally, replaced Great Britain as the key customer. As the war ended, so did exports to Germany, until the mid-1950s, when the former ally took a new place among Nokia's customers. Toward the end of the 1950s, Great Britain, as well as France and the United States, rapidly grew in importance for Nokia's pulp segment.
31. While this solution prepared the way for the modern Nokia, it also created a limiting ownership arrangement that frustrated both Kari H. Kairamo and his senior executives from the late 1960s to the late 1980s. When the national financial crisis paralyzed banks in the early 1990s, Jorma Ollila restructured the ownership arrangements of the company. Not only did Nokia gain international institutional investors, it also eliminated the Finnish banks' control.
32. See Bonsdorff, *Nokia Oy 1865–1965*, p. 531.
33. See Marco Mäkinen, *Nokia saga: Kertomus yrityksestä ja ihmisistä jotka muuttivat sen* (Helsinki: Gummerus, 1995), especially Chapter 6.

Chapter 2

1. Throughout the Cold War, one was either for the Paasikivi-Kekkonen foreign policy line or against it. If one dared to question its rationale in public, one was against it. Few Finns did. In the 1980s, Nokia was among the first Finnish companies to test the dark waters—not in questioning the policy line, but opening doors to Europe and through Europe to the worldwide markets.
2. The first and second articles of this treaty required Finland and the Soviet Union to undertake military cooperation in the event of an attack or threat by Germany or its allies. This quasi-military treaty was often used as a political deterrent to aggression but was never really consulted.
3. Finland refrained from memberships in international organizations, including the United Nations, through 1955, because such commitments would have obliged the country to take sides in conflicts between the superpowers. On the other hand, Finland became a member of the International Monetary Fund (IMF) in 1948 and the General Agreement on Trade and Tariffs (GATT) in 1950 to boost export policies but not to facilitate market and trade liberalization.
4. On the basic characteristics of the investment-driven stage, see Michael E. Porter, *The Competitive Advantage of Nations* (New York: The Free Press, 1990), pp. 548–552.
5. As prime minister, Urho Kekkonen had attempted to persuade the Nordic

countries to declare their neutrality. Now his goals included the Nordic nuclear–weapon-free zone and the organization of the Conference on Security and Cooperation in Europe. These initiatives were prepared in cooperation with representatives of the Soviet Union.

6. Finnish business scholars and historians initiated a more critical analysis of such arrangements only *after* Finland had left Moscow's sphere of political influence and joined the European integration process. See Risto Tainio, "Finland Between Two Systems: Emergence, Reproduction and Change of Governance Structures," unpublished paper, 1996.

7. The report relied heavily on the contemporary European discourse, the presumed success of some socialist countries in heavy industries, and the highly *dirigiste* French national plans in particular. See the *Report of the Committee on Industrialization* [in Finnish] (Helsinki: VAPK, 1951).

8. Urho Kekkonen, *Onko meillä malttia vaurastua?* (Helsinki: Otava, 1952).

9. Ibid., pp. 58–59.

10. Concurrently, competitive advantages widened to include low-cost as well as more advanced factors, such as university-trained engineers, and well-functioning mechanisms for factor creation, such as educational institutions and research institutes. On the role of the technocracy in the Finnish political economy, see Pertti Ahonen, *Valtion liiketoiminta, hallinnon teoriat ja finanssihallinto* (Turku: Åbo Academy Press, 1987).

11. "Right after World War II the Finnish decision-makers prepared a development plan which placed a heavy emphasis on the role of investment in promoting the standard of living. . . . This national model of economic development was based on the tight regulation of the labor and capital markets." See Matti Pohjola, *Tehoton Pääoma: Uusi näkökulma taloutemme ongelmiin* (WSOY: Porvoo, 1996).

12. Due to the simultaneous rise of income policies, the Finnish policy never achieved the high efficiencies of the "Asian tigers." A parallel national consensus was explicit in both Japan and Korea in which spectacular growth was based on rapid growth in inputs. See Paul Krugman, "The Myth of Asia's Miracle," *Foreign Affairs* (November/December 1994): 62–78.

13. See Kari Kairamo, "Puhe Suomen Ulkomaankauppaliiton vuosikokouksessa," May 1987; Kari Kairamo, "Education for Life: A European Strategy," London 1989. For a historical interpretation on the Kairamo era, see Karl-Erik Michelsen, "Kari Kairamon unelma: Eurooppalainen Suomi," in *Miksi Nokia, Finland?* eds. Tarmo Lemola and Raimo Lovio (Helsinki: WSOY, 1996).

14. After two weeks of treatment and medication, Kairamo returned to work. This episode of depression precipitated another in the late 1980s, when he no longer could hide the alternating symptoms of manic activity and depressive withdrawal. Concerned about negative publicity, he decided not to see a psychiatrist or rely on medication. That episode would prove fatal. See Matti Saari, *Kari Kairamo: Kohtalona Nokia* (Helsinki: Gummerus, 2000).

15. Saari, *Kari Kairamo*, p. 64.

16. On the mobilization of the invisible assets and the strategic reliance on human resources within corporate organizations, see Hiroyuki Itami, with Thomas W. Roehl, *Mobilizing Invisible Assets* (Cambridge, Mass.: Harvard University Press, 1987).

17. "Kari Kairamon ajatuksia Nokiasta ja isänmaasta: Vikkelä soveltaja pääsee melkein huipulle," *Talouselämä*, 33, 1981.

18. Ibid.
19. On the origins and role of the Schuman Plan and the ECSC, see William Diebold, *The Schuman Plan* (New York: Praeger, 1959).
20. It was not until the accession of Finland and Sweden to the European Union in 1995 that Nordic integration, which had expanded steadily since the beginning of the 1950s, was dissolved *and* affirmed through the EU, even though Norway had rejected membership once again in a referendum.
21. By the mid-1970s, the economic cooperation framework between the two countries was extended to fifteen years. See T. Keskinen, *Idänkauppa 1944–1987* (Porvoo: WSOY, 1987).
22. On Finnish economic policies and devaluation cycles, see Jukka Pekkarinen and Juhana Vartiainen, *Suomen talouspolitiikan pitkä linja* (Helsinki: WSOY, 1993).
23. The significance of Soviet trade, especially for the postwar development of Finland's engineering and light industry, is indisputable but should not be stretched thin. Finnish historians stress the beneficial nature of the trade from Finland's standpoint. This "success argument," however, ignores the fact of *resource dependency*—something that Nokia's electronics division sought to balance with exports to the West. In contrast to the United States and its Western allies, the Soviet Union was not a sophisticated customer; it ensured trade, but not necessarily innovation. In retrospect, then, the Finnish trade with Moscow may well reflect a foreign policy success, but over time it proved a hindrance to national competitive advantage. On the success argument, see Timo Vihavainen, "After the War: Finland's Relations with the Soviet Union 1944–91," available from Virtual Finland at virtual.finland.fi.
24. On the American aid program and its economic and political consequences, see Michael J. Hogan, *The Marshall Plan* (Cambridge: Cambridge University Press, 1987).
25. The reduction of trade barriers contributed to the process, but for small open economies, the indirect benefits or spillovers of foreign (U.S.) R&D by trade had an even larger effect on domestic productivity than did investments in domestic R&D—especially when the spillovers were coupled with U.S. foreign investment.
26. As Sylvia Ostry concludes in her important work, *The Post–Cold War Trading System*, ". . . after the Marshall Plan program ended in 1957 productivity programs became well established in Europe, technology issues a major element in OEEC and OECD activities, and technology policies a priority for most European governments. Furthermore, after studying the results in Europe, Japan asked for and received a similar program in 1955 . . . the enormous surge of American investment in Europe beginning in the late 1950s was important . . . in transferring American technology and management practices, . . . in furthering the technology gap debate in the OECD, and stimulating European industrial policy in promoting high-tech industries first at the national level in the 1960s and 1970s and then at the community level in the 1980s. . . . One of the most important indirect consequences was to shake up complacent, cartelized and inward-looking European business and to underline the importance of competition policy in the Treaty of Rome." See Sylvia Ostry, *The Post-Cold War Trading System* (Chicago: The University of Chicago Press, 1997), pp. 28–30.
27. Initially, the Soviet government had presented the idea of a European se-

curity conference in the mid-1950s. Despite reservations, the United States joined the Commission on Security and Cooperation in Europe (CSCE) process when the Soviet Union indicated its readiness to start negotiations on the reduction of conventional forces in Europe. In the short term, Finland's role in the organization of the CSCE process was regarded as pro-Moscow, hence the hawkish notion of Finlandization.

28. Finland had learned its lesson during the tenure of the "night-frost government" at the end of the 1950s, when the Soviet Union discontinued all trade and recalled its ambassador from Finland.

29. Unfortunately, many Finnish politicians had few inhibitions about discussing the positive and negative aspects of their own and other political parties with these "friends." "The KGB had become the channel of communication between Finnish political parties of the left and the right and the Soviet Union," argues Vihavainen. "The KGB's top official in Finland was always the Finnish President's confidant from the time of President Kekkonen to that of President Koivisto." The system worked routinely throughout the Cold War. See note 23.

30. Saari, *Kari Kairamo*, p. 69.

31. Ibid., pp. 108–109.

32. Quoted in Timo Anttila, "Kari Kairamo: Ei kukaan tarvitse takapajulaa," *Suomen Kuvalehti* 7 (1986).

33. Stephen D. Moore, "Nokia Has Vexing Problem With Image: Outside of Finland, It Doesn't Have One," *Wall Street Journal*, April 21, 1987.

34. Porter, *The Competitive Advantage of Nations*, Introduction.

35. Although Finland managed to delay austerity measures for five years, balance-of-payments considerations compelled the government to introduce in 1978 a far-reaching reform package designed to ensure the competitiveness of Finnish industry in world markets.

36. Dan Steinbock, interview with Gordon Moore, chairman emeritus, Intel Corp., March 24, 1999.

37. As early as 1957, the Finns felt confident enough to shift their policy toward Western Europe. The move was designed to protect access to traditional export markets, especially in Britain, as well as to shift economic activity to segments in which the country had a comparative advantage at a time when extensive economic growth was reaching its limits. Soviet opposition had blocked Finnish membership in the OEEC, leading the Finns to set up the "Helsinki Club," which the OEEC countries, agreeing to apply their liberalized import lists to Finnish goods, then joined. In 1958, Finnish authorities further liberalized trading conditions by making the Finnish markka convertible in European markets.

38. These broad-based coalitions—together with the package deals for regulating conflicts in the economy—made the period the most politically stable in the history of the Finnish republic. The core of the developing consensus politics was the participation of all market sectors in major economic decisions.

39. See *The Finnish Government's White Paper on Industrial Policy*, 2/1997, pp. 26–29.

40. See Dan Steinbock, *Finland's Wireless Valley* (Helsinki: Finland's Ministry of Transport and Communications, 2000).

41. Jacques Servan-Schreiber, *The American Challenge* (New York: Athenium, 1968), p. 3.

42. Compare Raimo Lovio, *Evolution of Firm Communities in New Industries:*

The Case of the Finnish Electronics Industry, Acta Academiae Oeconomicae Helsingiensis, Series A: 92 (Helsinki: The Helsinki School of Economics and Business Administration, 1993).

43. Typically, the cost estimates of Siemens and other companies were based on the Western exports, whereas Finnish politicians, Salora, and Hitachi expected Soviet trade to make Valco profitable.

44. Eero Rantala, then minister of Trade and Industry, noted, "The current electronics industry is one of the most rapidly growing industries. It is also an industry in which research and development, innovation and efficient marketing are crucial. Therefore, significant resources are needed. Thus strong public intervention creates security and confidence in the industry prospects in Finland." See the Annual Report of the State-Owned Companies, Finland's Ministry of Trade and Industry, 1976.

45. *Eletroniikka-Uutiset* 8 (1976).

46. According to Saari, the Finnish state, Salora, and Hitachi would form the component unit (i.e., Valco). The state-owned Televa, which was later acquired by Nokia, would become the concern's telecommunications unit. Valmet's instrument factory would provide its process and biotechnology units. Furthermore, the new state-owned electronics concern would rely on strong cooperation with Nokia in order to protect Finnish markets against foreign multinationals such as Siemens, ITT, and L. M. Ericsson. Compare Nils Eriksson, *Operaatio Valco-Salora* (Saarijarvi: Kustannuspiste Oy, 1979), Chapter 6.

47. In 1981, the Ministry of Finance established a working group to examine the status of the public enterprises organized as agencies. The Valco debacle led to the proposal to reform public enterprises. Toward the end of the 1980s, the Ministry of Trade and Industry began preparations for the large-scale privatization of the remaining state-owned giants.

48. Quoted in Saari, *Kari Kairamo,* p. 83. In Kairamo's inner circle, Sundqvist, despite his radical rhetoric, was considered the "all-time best" minister of Trade and Industry. In 1984, some Social Democrats insisted on the socialization of Nokia because of labor conflicts in the rubber factory, yet after the Valco debacle, the company would remain in the favor of the Social Democratic Party.

49. "Nouseva Nokia avoimista avoimin," *Talouselämä,* 11 (1981).

50. In 1982, Nokia also needed an attractive alternative to traditional pulp and paper making. In order to dominate the entire bleaching-chemical market in Finland, it acquired Finnish Chemicals. In 1989, industry observers still expected the electrochemical business to remain a solid part of the new high-technology Nokia. As one historian noted, "Sometimes it is fortunate that historians don't have to answer questions concerning the future. . . . Yet, something could be said about the future of Nokia Chemicals. . . . [It] will be a strong chemical producer for a long time to come." See Karl-Erik Michelsen, *Sähköstä ja suolasta syntynyt: Finnish Chemicals Oy Nokia Chemicals 1937–1987* (Jyväskylä: Gummerus, 1989), p. 307. By the late 1980s and early 1990s, all noncore segments were divested from Nokia, including Nokia Chemicals.

51. Quoted in "Vuorineuvos valvoo elektroniikkaa," *Talouselämä,* 33 (1984).

52. Most firms relied too much on intuitive strategies that were "based upon traditional patterns of behavior which have been successful in the past," argued Bruce Henderson, BCG's founder. "In growth industries or in a changing environment, this kind of strategy is rarely adequate." See Bruce

D. Henderson, *Henderson on Corporate Strategy* (Cambridge, Mass.: Abt Books, 1979), pp. 6–7.
53. See note 49.
54. On the limitations of the BCG concepts, see William J. Abernathy and Kenneth Wayne, "Limits of the Learning Curve," *Harvard Business Review* (September/October 1974). On the criticism of portfolio analysis and long-term resource commitments, see Robert H. Hayes and William J. Abernathy, "Managing Our Way to Economic Decline," *Harvard Business Review* (July/August 1980).
55. Quoted in "Vuorineuvos valvoo elektroniikkaa," *Talouselämä* 33 (1984).
56. Nokia's chief found himself struggling more than ever with issues pertaining to management and engineering talent. In order to execute its growth strategy, Nokia needed more and more high-skill human resources, but the small country provided a limited talent pool. "That is why, if it only could, Kari Kairamo's company would like to hire all Finnish electrical engineering graduates," noted one analyst. See "Kasvoi kolmanneksen, jäi budjetista," *Talouselämä* 13 (1985).
57. "Nokia kokosi palapelin," *Talouselämä*, 2 (1984).
58. "Nokian merkit esiin," *Talouselämä*, 41 (1987).
59. Quoted in "Vuorineuvos valvoo elektroniikkaa," *Talouselämä*, 33 (1984).
60. The distinction was important to Nokia's efforts to raise capital (corporate finance) and to keep to its growth strategy without the constraints imposed by the Finnish banks through the board (corporate governance). Compare Timo H. A. Koski, *Ownership Strategy and Competitive Advantage*, Acta Polytechnica Scandinavica, Mathematics and Computer Science Series, No. 49 (Helsinki: 1988).
61. Quoted in "Vuorineuvos valvoo elektroniikkaa," *Talouselämä*, 33 (1984).
62. "Aikamiespoika lähtee," *Talouselämä*, 13 (1988).
63. Kari Kairamo, "Puhe Suomen Ulkomaankauppaliiton vuosikokouksessa." In effect, the Finnish membership *was* under preparation in Finland's Ministry of Foreign Affairs. Apparently, Kairamo, through his extensive contact networks, had heard of the matter and gave his speech on the basis of the Ministry's memos. See Saari, *Kairamo*, p. 143.
64. Viktor Vladimirov, *Näin se oli . . . Muistelmia ja havaintoja kulissientakaisesta toiminnasta Suomessa 1954–84* (1993).
65. Jukka Ukkola, "Viiden tuuman Eurooppa, neljän tuuman Nokia," *Suomen Kuvalehti* 7 (1989); Jukka Ukkola, "Yhden miehen tungos," *Suomen Kuvalehti* 3 (1986).
66. Moore, "Nokia Has Vexing Problem With Image."
67. Ibid.

Chapter 3

1. "Kevätkuosia a la Kairamo," *Talouselämä*, 14 (1986).
2. "Uusi järjestys," *Talouselämä*, 13 (1986).
3. Initially, the nonsocialists aspired to form a government without Social Democrats or Communists. Conservatives would govern the country under the leadership of Paavo Väyrynen. Soon the plans changed. The new president, Mauno Koivisto, a popular veteran Social Democrat who insisted that Social Democrats join the government, considered Väyrynen a major political enemy.

4. See Matti Saari, *Kari Kairamo: Kohtalona Suomi* (Jyväskylä: Gummerus, 2000), p. 139.

5. On the deregulation in Finnish financial services and banking, see the publications of the Finnish Bankers' Association, *Bank of Finland Bulletin* (various issues); Risto Tainio, Kari Lilja, and Timo Santalainen, "Changing Managerial Competitive Practices in the Context of Growth and Decline in the Finnish Banking Sector," in *Regulation and Deregulation in European Financial Services*, eds. Glenn Morgan and David Knights (London: Macmillan Business, 1997), pp. 201–215.

6. See in particular Alfred Rappaport, *Creating Shareholder Value: A Guide for Managers and Investors* (New York: The Free Press, 1998), Chapter 4.

7. Jyrki Veranen first explored the issue in his dissertation in 1986. See Jyrki Veranen, *Active and Competent Ownership*, Working Paper W-56 (Helsinki: HSEBA,1993); Jyrki Veranen, *Tuottoa vaativat omistajat* (Porvoo: WSOY, 1996).

8. In particular, he drew from Michael E. Porter's works, globalization studies (Christopher A. Bartlett, Ghoshal Sumantra, Yves Doz), and resource theory (Gary Hamel, C. K. Prahalad). He read everything he found on Bruce D. Henderson, the strategist behind the BCG experience curve.

9. Timo H.A. Koski, *Ownership Strategy and Competitive Advantage*, Acta Polytechnica Scandinavica, Mathematics and Computer Science Series, No. 49, (Helsinki 1988). p. 141.

10. Ibid., pp. 144–145.

11. Finnish ownership of industrial companies has traditionally been dominated by banks, insurance companies, and other industrial entities, noted Koski, who considered the owner and investor groups cooperatives of sorts. The impact of these "limitations of ownership by banks and insurance companies," he argued, raised three critical questions for the future: "What have these cooperative groups *contributed* to the competitive advantage of Finnish industry, and what impact will the anticipated changes have? What will be the *sources of the domestic capital* needed to maintain the present balance of power and control as foreign ownership expands? Does this new legal situation *alter the behavioral patterns of banks and insurance companies* by changing them from cooperative to more speculative and interventionistic investors?" Ibid., p. 148.

12. On the microeconomic theory of the capital investment system, see the research of the Harvard Business School Council on Competitiveness, in particular Michael E. Porter, *Capital Choices*, June 1992. See also the reports of the Institutional Investor Project at the Columbia University Center for Law and Economic Studies, Institutional Investors and Capital Markets. On the transformation of the Finnish capital investment system, see Dan Steinbock, *The Competitive Advantage of Finland: From Cartels to Competition?* (Helsinki: ETLA/SITRA, 1998), Chapter 10.

13. Finnish researchers have come up with similar conclusions. See Risto Tainio, Matti Pohjola, and Kari Lilja, "Economic Performance of Finland after the Second World War: The Myth of Success?" (paper presented at the EMOT workshop on economic performance outcomes in Europe, The Role of National Institutions and Forms of Economic Organization, Berlin, January 1997).

14. Quoted in Saari, *Kairamo*, p. 129. Interestingly enough, the last sentence is a direct quotation from Michael E. Porter and Victor E. Millar, "How Information Gives You Competitive Advantage," *Harvard Business Review*

(July/August 1985). These ideas on IT's impact on the physical value chains were very much in the air in the mid-1980s, and Koski, as Kairamo's intellectual sparring partner, may well have been the source of the argument.

15. Quoted in Nan Stone, "The Globalization of Europe: An Interview with Wisse Dekker," *Harvard Business Review* (May/June 1989). Dekker considered the Roundtable's principal aim to help strengthen and develop Europe's competitive capabilities by encouraging the creation of a single European market, improving the European business climate, and promoting entrepreneurial drive through various market- and technology-driven initiatives.

16. In order to surpass the current deficiencies, Kairamo spoke for an extensive international exchange program and greater cooperation between schools and businesses.

17. Dekker considered Kairamo's work critical in preparing the European workforce to fight the competition battles that lay ahead. See Stone, "The Globalization of Europe."

18. In November 1989, the Helsinki-based *City Magazine* published a feature on Koski, "Story of the Chief Strategist of Nokia's European Conquest." At first, the story had been shelved, but as it was finally released at the peak of Nokia's problems, it had a strong impact on Kairamo's state of mind.

19. Stephen D. Moore, "Finnish Electronics Firm's Bold Strategy May Be Unraveling Since Two Acquisitions," *Wall Street Journal*, December 29, 1989.

20. See Staffan Bruun and Mosse Wallen, *Nokian valtatie: Taistelu tiedosta, tulevaisuudesta ja optioista* (Jyväskylä: Gummerus, 1999); Saari, *Kairamo*, pp. 209–210.

21. Ibid.

22. Kairamo, presumably, suspected that Kouri intended to break Nokia in pieces and sell the parts. He was also aware of the close affiliation between Kouri and KOP.

23. Kouri also published several pieces in the prestigious National Bureau of Economic Research, Inc. (NBER), including "The Effect of Risk on Interest Rates" and "Macroeconomics of Stagflation under Flexible Exchange Rates."

24. Kouri even talked about his role and intentions to the students at New York University.

25. In the process, Kouri became the biggest shareholder in KOP, Finland's second-largest bank, acting through a Virgin Islands–based partnership and his Helsinki-based holding company, Kouri Capital. He controlled about 6 percent of KOP's voting stock. See Stephen D. Moore, "Academic Turned Raider, Kouri, Plays Lead Role in Helsinki's Biggest Deal," *Wall Street Journal*, March 20, 1989.

26. Ibid.

27. Ibid.

28. Saari, *Kairamo*, p. 242.

29. Bruun and Wallen consider this deal between Nokia and *Helsingin Sanomat* "strange," and not entirely without reason. It does reflect the cozy arrangements between Finnish journalists and corporate executives at the end of the Cold War era. Compare Bruun and Wallen, *Nokian valtatie*, p. 46. In the aftermath, Virkkunen denied such a deal ever took place.

30. On the value of diversification in emerging markets, see Tarun Khanna and

Krishna Palepu, "Why Focused Strategies May Be Wrong for Emerging Markets," *Harvard Business Review* (July/August 1997).
31. "Kari Kairamon ajatuksia Nokiasta ja isänmaasta: Vikkelä soveltaja pääsee melkein huipulle," *Talouselämä* 33 (1981).
32. "Vanha elätti Nokiaa," *Talouselämä* 14 (1989).
33. "Nokia sähköistyy," *Talouselämä* 13 (1990).
34. Simo Vuorilehto, "Liiketoiminnan linjat säilyvät ennallaan," *Nokia Corporation Newsletter* 1 (1989).
35. Quoted in Bruun and Mosse Wallen, *Nokian valtatie*, p. 82.
36. On the structural causes of the Finnish recession, see Hannu Hermesniemi, Markku Lammi, and Pekka Ylä-Anttila, *Advantage Finland: The Future of Finnish Industries*, ETLA Series B 113: Helsinki (1996), pp. 17–35.
37. As economist Matti Pohjola put it, "As measured by relative standard of life, we lost in a few years the results of two decades worth of work and savings." See Matti Pohjola, *Tehoton pääoma* (Porvoo: WSOY, 1996), p. 9.
38. As Laurila notes, "Finland was, indeed, the last industrialized capitalist country to give up clearing trade with the Soviet Union and to dismantle its clearing arrangements with the (former) socialist countries, with Bulgaria in 1992 and with the Soviet Union at the end of 1990. Finland was preceded in this respect by Austria in 1971 and Sweden already in 1966." Still, in 1990, Ministers Ilkka Suominen and Konstantin Katushev signed a five-year agreement based on intergovernmental clearing. See Juhani Laurila, *Finnish-Soviet Clearing Trade and Payment System: History and Lessons*, Bank of Finland Studies A-94 (Helsinki: 1995), pp. 47–58.
39. After four decades, the status quo was so "natural" that when financial deregulation began in the 1980s and the Office of Free Competition was established to promote competition and efficiency, few understood the long-term implications.
40. From the standpoint of the OECD, the Finnish crisis was rooted in a combination of weak economic conditions, deregulation of financial markets, strong growth of bank lending with insufficient risk management, supervisory problems, and legislation governing the financial industry that was not commensurate with the conditions and demands of a liberalized financial market. See *OECD Economic Surveys: Finland 1996*, August 1996, pp. 47–49.
41. "Europe is going to be changing even faster, and European companies are going to emerge," Kairamo had said years before in an interview with the *Wall Street Journal*. "People like [Italian financier Carlo] De Benedetti have already begun, and Finnish companies have to try and play the same game." See Moore, "Nokia Has Vexing Problem With Image."
42. The most recent divestments took place in 1995 and 1996, when Nokia sold its cable-industry operations and television business.

Chapter 4

1. See "Mobile Telephone Density of Finland is the Highest in the World," Ministry of Transport and Communications Finland, February 20, 1997.
2. In 1886, the Finnish Senate issued a telephone statute, the Gracious Declaration, which effectively separated long distance (first managed by Russia's Imperial Telegraph Office, later by Finland's post, telephone, and telegraph [PTT]) from local telephone traffic (which would belong to the

private Finnish operators). At the time, this approach was a shrewd compromise. It stemmed from a political rather than economic rationality that focused on national security considerations—those of the tsarist empire, not Finland. The idea of a European-style national monopoly was out of the question. After all, Finland was not part of Europe, but a Grand Duchy of Russia. Paradoxically, it was the Telephone Statute of 1886—a Finnish arrangement under Russian authority—that gave rise to the extraordinary competition in the nascent Finnish telecommunications industry. See Dan Steinbock, *Finland's Wireless Valley* (Helsinki: Ministry of Transport and Communications, 2000).

3. On the early history of Finnish electronics, see Mikko Koivusalo, *Kipinästä tuli syttyy: Suomalaisen radiopuhelinteollisuuden kehitys ja tulevaisuuden haasteet* (Espoo: Cetonia Systems, 1995). See also Raimo Lovio, *Evolution of Firm Communities in New Industries: The Case of the Finnish Electronics Industry*, Acta Academiae Oeconomicae Helsingiensis, Series A: 92 (Helsinki: HSEBA, 1993).

4. Between 1962 and 1976, Televa's VHF radiophone revenues increased from FIM 0.6 million to FIM 6.8 million. Starting in the 1970s, the new car mobile telephone (CMT) network contributed to the revenues.

5. The failure of Valco contributed to Nokia's stepping up its electronics and radiocommunications activities. On the Valco debacle, see Chapter 2.

6. Near the end of the 1970s, there were some 37,000 VHF/UHF base and mobile stations in Finland. In the PMR networks, three leading domestic players (Salora, Televa, and Nokia) each held 25 percent market shares, while the remaining proportion consisted of Swedish and Danish imports. Although Swedish, Danish, German, English, and American rivals played a marginal role in the Finnish market, their role was significant in European exports. At Televa, exports were insignificant, but at Nokia, they accounted for 33 percent of revenues, mainly to the Soviet Union. Salora had a more significant role in the Scandinavian markets (more than 20 percent in Norway).

7. With the eclipse of the Cold War, Nordic prime ministers proposed a thorough re-evaluation of Nordic cooperation. Now cooperation also developed in foreign and security policy issues, which previously had less priority.

8. On the introduction of the first Nordic cellular services, see Garry A. Garrard, *Cellular Communications: Worldwide Market Development* (Boston: Artech House, 1999), Chapter 2.

9. Sonera (Finland's former PTT) originated with the construction of the first telegraph line in Finland in 1855. See Dan Steinbock, *Sonera's Evolution* (Helsinki: Sonera Corp., 2000); Dan Steinbock, *Sonera's Strategy* (Helsinki: Sonera Corp., 2000).

10. Compare Garrard, *Cellular Communications*, p. 8.

11. The term *cellular* refers to splitting the coverage area into many smaller areas (cells), each served by a low-power transmitter and receiver. In the precellular period, the conventional way to improve wireless capacity was to divide up frequencies, thus creating additional available channels. However, this reduced the bandwidth assigned to each user and resulted in poorer service. Instead of dividing frequencies, cellular divides up geography; it offers more efficient use of the radio spectrum.

12. For a concise introduction to mobile cellular, the three technology generations, and the current industry rivalry, see *World Telecommunication Development Report 1999: Mobile Cellular* (Geneva: ITU, 1999), Chapter 2.

13. See Koivusalo, *Kipinästä tuli syttyy*, pp. 54-55.
14. Quoted in Koivusalo, *Kipinästä tuli syttyy*, p. 55.
15. Quoted in Matti Pulkkinen, *The Breakthrough of Nokia Mobile Phones*, Acta Universitatis Oeconomicae Helsingiensis, A-122 (Helsinki: HSEBA, 1997), p. 108.
16. By 1983, Mobira's NMT products—Senator, Combi, and Quattro—made it the market leader in Nordic countries. It had 59 percent of the market in Finland, 21 to 23 percent in Sweden and Norway, and some 13 percent in Denmark. In England, Mobira was able to garner 60 percent in the System 4 network and some 20 percent in the TACS network. In early 1985, the specifications for a 900 MHz system had been released. Even prior to their release, Mobira and PTT had agreed on the construction of a Finnish test network, in which base stations were manufactured at Oulu. These public-private partnerships, coupled with bold technical solutions and aggressive pricing, enabled Mobira to establish market leadership in the Nordic countries.
17. Quote by Edward Mier, a telecommunications specialist in London for Dataquest Ltd., a consulting concern. Stephen D. Moore, "Nokia Has Vexing Problem with Image: Outside of Finland, It Doesn't Have One," *Wall Street Journal*, April 21, 1987.
18. Quoted in Pulkkinen, *The Breakthrough of Nokia Mobile Phones*, p. 76.
19. Mobira personnel magazine, 1980.
20. A joint venture between Nokia-Mobira and France's Matra Communication claimed 50 percent of the French cellular phone market. Meanwhile, Nokia and Alcatel were building a second cellular network in France that was expected to give Nokia access to 100,000 more phone customers. In West Germany, where the cellular market was approaching 100,000 phones a year, Mobira was waiting for a government license for its phone.
21. Quoted in Joyce Heard, with John J. Keller, "Nokia Skates into High Tech's Big Leagues," *Business Week*, April 4, 1988.
22. The market dominance of publicly owned telecommunications monopolies (the PTTs) meant duplication of R&D efforts and increased costs. Between 1979 and 1989, telecommunications equipment was 80 to 100 percent more expensive in Europe than in the United States. These pressures were expected to increase with the entry of Japanese competitors. As a company headquartered in Europe but still outside the EC, Nokia-Mobira had reason to be particularly concerned about both the emerging threat and opportunity. Compare Ilkka Lipasti and Martti M. Kaila, in association with John A. Quelch, "Nokia-Mobira Oy: Mobile Telecommunications in Europe," Harvard Business School Case 9-589-112, 1989.
23. Quoted in Pulkkinen, *The Breakthrough of Nokia Mobile Phones*, p. 133.
24. In Finland, the new emphasis on competition, productivity, and efficiency grew prior to and with the European integration in the early 1990s. While the EU industrial policies provided the rhetoric, the frameworks stemmed from *The Competitive Advantage of Nations* (New York: The Free Press, 1990) by Michael E. Porter. On the Finnish national cluster strategy and its extraordinary impact, see Michael E. Porter, foreword, "The Competitive Advantage of Nations: The Finnish Case," to *The Competitive Advantage of Finland: From Cartels to Competition?* by Dan Steinbock (Helsinki: ETLA/SITRA, 1998).
25. In Europe, cartels and managed trade reigned until the end of the 1980s. Throughout the 1990s, the industrial policy debate pitted advocates of

"old" industrial policies, who supported intervention with the market allocation of resources (the "verticalists"), against advocates of "new" industrial policies, who aspired to intervene only in the case of market or government failures (the "horizontalists"). During the latter half of the 1990s, the horizontalists dominated the debate in the EU. See Martin Bangemann, *Meeting the Global Challenge: Establishing a Successful European Industrial Policy* (London: Kogan Page, 1992), pp. 20–51; John Peterson, "European Union Industrial Policy," in *The European Union Handbook*, ed. Philippe Barbour (London: Fitzroy Dearborn Publishers, 1996), pp. 177–185.

26. In 1969, Finland had joined the OECD, the successor to the OEEC. When two important trading partners, Britain and Denmark, switched from EFTA to the EEC, Finland (like the other EFTA states) negotiated an industrial free-trade agreement with the EEC that went into effect in 1974.

27. European statesmen and chief executives found themselves squeezed between what they perceived as a former superpower (the United States) and a new economic power (Japan). The threat of American and Japanese companies heightened EC-level policies for competition, public procurement, external trade, and R&D. Compare Wayne Sandholtz, *High-Tech Europe: The Politics of International Cooperation* (Berkeley: University of California Press, 1992).

28. In the early 1990s, these efforts were initiated in the name of employment (White Paper on Growth, Competitiveness and Employment, 1993); in the second half of the decade, intervention and subsidies were justified in terms of the "information society" projects. On the rise of the EU technology policy, see Margaret Sharp and John Peterson, *Technology Policy in the European Union* (Basingstoke: Macmillan, 1996).

29. Around 1997, the only substantial difference between Nokia's strategy and the American electronic commerce policy involved the role of encryption. Jorma Ollila saw electronic commerce as a broad and powerful collaborative tool with the potential to bring broad benefits in improved productivity and cost efficiencies but requiring open access to encryption technology. As the Clinton administration began to relax its encryption requirements, the two positions were converging. Compare Dan Steinbock, "Dismantling the Barriers to Global Electronic Commerce," Turku, Finland, 19–21 November 1997; An International Conference and Business-Government Forum, OECD/ICCP, February 1998. See also Dan Steinbock, interview with Ira Magaziner, senior policy advisor of the Clinton administration, March 7, 1997.

30. See Porter, *The Competitive Advantage of Nations*, p. 552–556.

31. Among other things, the CEPT served as the principal forum for the development of telecommunications standards in Europe. On the GSM evolution, see Garrard, *Cellular Communications*, Chapter 5.

32. See Steven Silberman, "Just Say Nokia," *Wired*, September 1999.

33. See Steinbock, *The Competitive Advantage of Finland*, Chapter 10.

34. At the time of the NMT introduction, for instance, there was no real proof that sufficient demand would justify the very substantial initial investment.

Chapter 5

1. On Finland's Wireless Valley as a test laboratory, see Introduction.

2. Quentin Hardy, "A Wireless World," *Wall Street Journal* September 21, 1998.

3. "Telecommunications and information technology giants believe that, in the next few years, wireless Internet will transform people's lives and electronic commerce. . . . At the moment, Finland and Sweden are the most thriving locations in which these companies can seek this software gold. IT giants in particular are trying their best to find out, as early as possible, how Nokia and Ericsson envision the future." See "Langaton Internet syntyy Pohjolassa," *Talouselämä*, 5 (2000).

4. Stephen Baker, with Roger O. Crockett and Neil Gross, "Can CEO Ollila Keep the Cellular Superstar Flying High?" *Business Week*, August 10, 1998.

5. In reality, Nokia's logistics plan was not flawlessly executed. Another price for these inflated expectations followed a few years later, in July 2000, when Nokia's shares fell 25 percent as investors dumped Nokia's shares after a warning about third-quarter results. The decline was *not* due to earnings decline or fundamental weakness; rather, it followed as Nokia fell short of the "exceptional results" the market had come to expect.

6. In retrospect, this rebellion may have been far less political than generational by nature. Many of the student leaders were children of the war generation, which had fought for the independence of the country against the Soviets. What better way to shock their parents than with red flags and revolutionary rhetoric.

7. Staffan Bruun and Mosse Wallen, Nokian Valtatie (Helsinki: Tammi 1999), p. 110.

8. Jorma Ollila, speech delivered on November 14, 1974.

9. Rahul Jacob, "Nokia Fumbles, But Don't Count It Out," *Time*, February 19, 1996.

10. "Mies jolla on näyttöä," *Helsingin Sanomat/kuukausiliite*, June 1999.

11. Ibid.

12. Justin Fox, "Nokia's Secret Code," *Fortune*, May 1, 2000.

13. Ibid.

14. Jacob, "Nokia Fumbles, But Don't Count It Out."

15. Mark Landler, "Market Place: Nokia's Poor Quarter Shows How Tough Wireless Market Is," *New York Times*, May 13, 1996.

16. Tara Perker-Pope, "Nokia, Cell Phone Maker, Posts Plunge of 70 percent in First-Period Net," *Wall Street Journal*, May 9, 1996.

17. See Gail Edmondson, "Nokia's Signal Isn't Really Fading," *Business Week*, March 18, 1996.

18. Logistics, timing, pricing—it was a complex task to keep these and other critical determinants in place. At the close of 1995, Nokia had found itself with a large inventory of high-priced parts at a time when prices on mobile phone handsets were falling. That would translate to razor-thin profit margins until older phone models made with the high-priced components could be sold off. "The problems are largely of Nokia's own making," said Paribas Capital Markets analyst Peter Roe in London. "And these things aren't solvable overnight." Nokia was doing its best to buy time because it expected a boost in the second half of 1996 from several new products. Analysts were particularly interested in the performance of the company's new 8110 phone, which had been nicknamed the "banana" because it included a casing that covered the phone pad and slid down to provide a mouthpiece. Compare Perker-Pope, "Nokia, Cell Phone Maker."

19. See the section on "Performance Measurement," in Chapter 8.

20. Sirkka Järvenpää and Ilkka Tuomi, *Nokia Telecommunications: Redesign of International Logistics*, Harvard Business School Case 9-996-006, September 11, 1995.

21. Quoted in "Kaiken ytimessä on teleklusteri," *Talouselämä*, 20 (1999).

22. On value-chain analysis and process-chain analysis, see Dan Steinbock, *Dynamic Advantage* (forthcoming). Historically, both activity- and process-based frameworks originate from competitive cost analysis (McKinsey's Business System) and Michael E. Porter's value-chain analysis, which coupled customer analysis and cost analysis and thereby gave impetus to business system redesign.

23. See Gary Hamel and C. K. Prahalad, "Strategic Intent," *Harvard Business Review* (May/June 1989).

24. "Strategic Intent" triggered an extensive management debate between advocates of competitive strategy and the resource theory of the company. I focus here only on issues that pertain to Nokia's growth strategy; I have treated the subject more broadly elsewhere. See Dan Steinbock, *Dynamic Advantage*.

25. "On the one hand, strategic intent envisions a desired leadership position and establishes the criterion the organization will use to chart its progress. . . . The concept also encompasses an active management process that includes focusing the organization's attention on the essence of winning; motivating people by communicating the value of the target; leaving room for individual and team contributions; sustaining enthusiasm by providing new operational definitions as circumstances change; and using intent consistently to guide resource allocations." See Hamel and Prahalad, "Strategic Intent."

26. Building on the ideas of Hamel and Prahalad, some Finnish researchers have examined Nokia's triumph as a "breakthrough" process, focusing on product-market determinants. Certainly, the product development process has played a key role in the success of the company, yet it should not be isolated from the customer commitment process or the corporate processes (e.g., managerial activities, human resource management, R&D, government relations). It is the strategic whole and timing that counts. On Nokia's product development processes, see Matti Pulkkinen, *The Breakthrough of Nokia Mobile Phones*, Acta Universitatis Oeconomicae Helsingiensis, A-122 (Helsinki: HSEBA, 1997).

27. That is also precisely what Nokia decided at the close of the 1990s, when it again seized strategic intent to define its challenge, which would stretch the organization into its "leading, brand-recognized role in creating the Mobile Information Society." Whatever the obstacles, strategic intent would enable the company to transcend them. Hence, Nokia's slogan in the spring of 2000: "There are no limits."

28. Reported in Rolf Leppänen, "Nokia Group: Case Study in Strategic Steering System," TEKES Research Project A/555.

29. Gary Hamel and C. K. Prahalad, *Competing for the Future* (Boston, Mass.: Harvard Business School Press, 1994). See also C. K. Prahalad and Gary Hamel, "Strategic Intent"; C. K. Prahalad and Gary Hamel, "The Core Competence of the Corporation," *Harvard Business Review* (May/June 1990).

30. Hamel and Prahalad, *Competing for the Future*, p. 88.

31. Ibid., p. 89.

32. Quoted in Richard S. Dunham, "Q&A: Nokia's Ollila on CEO Profiles and the Company's Future," *Business Week*, August 10, 1998.

33. "For a challenge to be effective, individuals and teams throughout the organization must understand it and see its implications for their own jobs. Companies that set corporate challenges to create new competitive advantages quickly discover that engaging the entire organization requires top management to: *create a sense of urgency*, or quasi crisis, by amplifying weak

signals in the environment that point up the need to improve, instead of allowing inaction to precipitate a real crisis." See Gary Hamel and C. K. Prahalad, "Strategic Intent."

34. See Richard S. Dunham, "Q&A: Nokia's Ollila on CEO Profiles and the Company's Future," *Business Week*, August 10, 1998.

35. Compare Youssef M. Ibrahim, "Nokia: Made in Finland and Sold Just About Everywhere," *New York Times*, August 13, 1997.

36. Hamel and Prahalad argued that this stemmed from the strategic weakness of "Western companies," but the premise proved untenable. By the 1990s, U.S. companies had caught up with operational effectiveness and, unlike Japanese companies, were able to create new strong global franchises through the Internet revolution. Only two to three years after "Strategic Intent" was published, the Internet revolution generated the greatest entrepreneurial wave in U.S. history, leading to the creation of the first-mover online giants. In the 1980s, Japanese companies did manage to create new global brand franchises, but this had less to do with their strategic ingenuity than with their operational effectiveness. As American and European companies caught up in execution, Japanese companies ran into trouble.

Chapter 6

1. "To the Finland base station: The Finns are the world's most enthusiastic mobile-phone users. They have also created its most successful mobile-phone maker." *The Economist*, October 9, 1999.

2. Ibid.

3. Alahuhta was only one member of Nokia's group executive board. Ollila himself had been active in international business since the early 1980s, and his strategic ideas—from restructuring, global focus, and convergence efforts—have been prominent in Nokia's overall strategy. Furthermore, Nokia used consultants, such as Gary Hamel, who were known for their theories on global strategy. Similarly, the company applied the ideas of Geoffrey A. Moore, whose *Crossing the Chasm* (1991) introduced the idea of a "chasm" that innovative companies and their products must cross in order to reach the lucrative mainstream market (covered in Chapter 10). Finally, several other members of the executive board have left their impact on the company's globalization, in particular those senior managers (Sari Baldauf, Pekka Ala-Pietilä, and Olli-Pekka Kallasvuo) in charge of Nokia's expansion in the critical volume markets, i.e., the American and Asia-Pacific operations.

4. Born in 1952, Alahuhta earned his master of science degree in engineering in 1976. After gaining experience as an R&D engineer in Nokia Electronics (1975–1979) and as a team manager in the unit's information systems and market research, Alahuhta had served as sales director at Rank Xerox (1982–1984), only to return to NTC, where his career moved rapidly toward senior management. In 1990, Alahuhta earned his doctorate in engineering from HUT. As Ollila took charge of Nokia, Alahuhta was back in the company as executive vice president of NTC. From 1992 to 1998, he served as president of the unit, having joined the group executive board in January 1993. He also served as chairman of the Board for Federations of Finnish Electrical and Electronics Industry (1997 to present); vice chairman

for the Federation of Finnish Metal, Engineering, and Electrotechnical Industries (1998 to present); and vice chairman for the Technology Development Center of Finland's Ministry of Trade and Industry.

5. Alahuhta studied six high-technology challengers that had global growth between 1982 and 1989 significantly exceeding market growth. He divided the challengers into two strategic groups: (1) fast-growing global high-technology challengers in high-growth industries with rapid change driven by technological innovation (Logitech, Technophone, Olivetti/Office Systems); and (2) fast-growing global high-technology challengers in maturing industries with slow technological change (ABB Robotics, Nokia-Maillefer, Norsk Data). See Matti Alahuhta, *Global Growth Strategies for High Technology Challengers*, Acta Polytechnica Scandinavica, Electrical Engineering Series No. 66 (Espoo: The Finnish Academy of Technology, 1990).

6. See Dan Steinbock, *Dynamic Advantage* (forthcoming).

7. For instance, the wave of entry into the U.S. auto industry began in 1894, whereas the first wave of exits followed in 1923 and peaked only a few years later. Ford's Model T was introduced in the 1910s, and by 1926 some 80 percent of all American automobiles were all-steel, closed-body cars. In the "Internet time," advancements have occurred much more quickly, as evidenced by product innovation. See James M. Utterback, *Mastering the Dynamics of Innovation* (Boston, Mass.: Harvard Business School Press, 1994), Chapter 2. On product development in Internet time, see Marco Iansiti, *Technology Integration: Making Critical Choices in a Dynamic World* (Boston, Mass.: Harvard Business School Press, 1997).

8. Alahuhta, *Global Growth Strategies for High Technology Challengers*, p. 17.

9. See Michael E. Porter, "Competition in Global Industries: A Conceptual Framework," in *Competition in Global Industries* (Boston, Mass.: Harvard Business School Press, 1986), pp. 15–60.

10. Alahuhta, *Global Growth Strategies for High Technology Challengers*, p. 19.

11. In this case, the fast global growth of a company was triggered by exploiting a product-related industry shift. In order to manage such an opportunity, these challengers set early global objectives and entered lead markets early to be aware of technology trends and changes in customer requirements. The challengers in maturing/slow-change industries also set clear global objectives and entered lead markets early. In this case, fast growth was triggered by exploiting a nonproduct-related industry shift coupled with a well-planned acquisition program.

12. When Jean-Pierre Jeannet released his *Managing with a Global Mindset* in 2000, Matti Alahuhta was among the leading European CEOs whose recommendations were used on the back cover of the book: "Jean-Pierre Jeannet's book brings clarity to the development of global strategies." At the end of the 1980s, Alahuhta had written his dissertation on global growth strategies at IMD, cooperating closely with Jeannet and using his notions to conceptualize appropriate growth strategies for ambitious European small and medium-sized enterprises. See Jean-Pierre Jeannet, *Managing with a Global Mindset* (London: Financial Times–Prentice Hall, 2000).

13. The key sites that served as his "laboratories" over many years were mostly European companies with extensive global operations, including ABB, Electrolux, Lego, ICI, DSM, Novartis OTC, and, in particular, Nokia. See Jeannet, *Managing with a Global Mindset*, pp. xiv, xxi.

14. Ibid., pp. 14–15.

15. Ibid., pp. 164–166.
16. Rahul Jacob, "Nokia Fumbles, But Don't Count It Out," *Time*, February 19, 1996.
17. Jeffrey S. Young, "Wireless Wonderland," *Fortune*, March 25, 1999.
18. Peter Richardson, "Worldwide Mobile Terminal Market Shares, 1999: Nokia Knocks the Opposition," Dataquest February 3, 2000.
19. Ibid.
20. The ITU World Telecommunications Indicators Database.
21. In China, Nokia had supplied its GSM technology to the Beijing PTA, Henan PTA, Yunnan PTA, Changsha Unicom, Zhejiang PTA, Fujian PTA, and Shanghai Unicom. See "Nokia Supplies GSM Network Expansion to Jiangxi, China," *Wall Street Journal*, October 24, 1996.
22. According to press reports, prior to his retirement, Honkavaara returned to Finland, where Ollila promised him personally that he could stay in the company as a financial planner. After Honkavaara had been in the new job for a month, Ollila fired him. Soon thereafter Honkavaara shot himself. News of the suicide was suppressed at the company. See Jouni Flinkkilä, "Nokian tarkoin varjeltu julkisuus: Topin vaiettu lähtö," *Seura*, August 30, 1996.
23. "Nokia vetää ohjelmistoyritykset Kiinaan," *Talouselämä*, February 4, 2000.
24. Ibid.
25. Jorma Ollila, speech delivered September 1997.
26. "The Internet Revolutionizing Nokia," *Finns in Business 2000/Talouselämä*, July 2000.
27. Quoted in "Kaiken ytimessä on teleklusteri," *Talouselämä*, 20 (1999).

Chapter 7

1. See Jeffrey S. Young, "Wireless Wonderland," *Forbes*, March 25, 1999.
2. On the evolution of Nokia's geographic segments, see Chapter 6.
3. With total sales of $14.5 billion, Nokia earned $8.3 billion in cellular phones, a 51 percent jump in total sales over the previous year and a 74 percent increase in cellular phone sales alone. It was growing far more quickly than either Ericsson or Motorola.
4. Kent Elliott, "Moving Life into Digital Space," Nokia 1999 Annual Report, pp. 12–13.
5. Ibid., p. 13.
6. In office applications, a combination of wireless and wired networks was expected to link a variety of computer and computer-based devices, just as networked devices would gradually take hold at home. The Internet would unify all of these convergence opportunities.
7. "No Limits, No Borders," *Finns in Business 2000/Talouselämä*, July 2000.
8. "Ollila: Toimiva yhdistelmä," *Helsingin Sanomat*, March 18, 1999.
9. Sari Baldauf, *International Divestments as the Reallocation Process of Productive Assets*, FIBO Working Paper, 1/1983. By 2000, her interests extended from international business to international peace. At the initiative of Pär Stenbäck, a veteran Finnish politician, she was appointed to the board of the Balkan Youth Summit, which fought for the reconstruction of the Balkan region and aid to its children.
10. Justin Fox, "Nokia's Secret Code," *Fortune*, May 1, 2000.

11. Quoted in "The Internet Revolutionizing Nokia," *Finns in Business 2000/ Talouselämä*, July 2000.

12. "Kuka valvoo Jorma Ollilaa?" *Helsingin Sanomat*, March 21, 1999.

13. The first Finnish book on the subject of corporate governance—Ahti Hirvonen, Heikki Niskakangas, and Juha Wahlroos, *Hyvä hallitustyöskentely* (Sitra: WSOY: Juva)—was published only in 1997. Hirvonen had been Ollila's enthusiastic supporter at Nokia in the early 1990s.

14. "Nokiassa käyttöön 'valistunut diktatuuri,' " *Helsingin Sanomat*, March 19, 1999.

15. One incident that may have contributed to the criticism of Ollila's appointment as Nokia's CEO and chairman occurred in the spring of 1999, when Ollila spoke in the Future Managers seminar at Helsinki University and gave an interview to *Yliopisto*, a university publication. Afterwards, Nokia's corporate communications suggested some changes in the story prior to its release. (The title was purposefully ambiguous, "The Stretched Hand of the Godfather.") As a result, Pekka Matilainen, editor-in-chief of *Yliopisto*, criticized Nokia's public relations staff for excessive intervention. He mentioned the points the Nokians would not have preferred to see in the final story and called Nokia's group executive board its "central committee," a thinly veiled reference to the Communist Party elite in the former Soviet Union ("Radikaalisti improvisoiden," *Yliopisto* 7 [1999]). "Ollila got angry and called the rector of Helsinki University," wrote Matilainen to the author on February 15, 2000. "I was questioned by the rector and received a written warning." Soon thereafter, the story was picked up by Finnish press and media. In late June, *Kauppalehti*, Finland's leading business daily, released a story that indicated that Nokia had frozen its support of three research projects at Helsinki University. Some commentators felt that Kari Raivio, the rector of university, as well as Ollila, had overreacted.

16. Quoted in Fox, "Nokia's Secret Code."

17. The coordination alone was a challenge. Headquartered in Finland, Nokia had to follow the laws of its home country. Yet by 2000, American investors who were familiar with American investment rules owned an estimated 60 percent of Nokia. "The Finnish system is created for registered shareholders," acknowledged Ursula Ranin, Nokia's general counsel, "and it is inflexible about receiving foreign investors." A longtime Nokian, Ranin had grown with the company. Having joined Kairamo's Nokia in 1984, she was promoted in Ollila's Nokia from corporate lawyer to assistant director and, in 1992, to general counsel. Meanwhile, Nokia's legal unit grew from a handful of lawyers based in Finland to a global network of ninety lawyers. See "A Lawyer's Dream Job," *Finns in Business 2000/Talouselämä*, July 2000.

18. The following discussion is based, with some modifications, on Jorma Ollila, "Nokia's Strategic Intent," lecture delivered to the Finnish Strategic Society in Helsinki, Finland, January 20, 1999. See also Rolf Leppänen, "Nokia Group: Case Study in Strategic Steering System," TEKES Research Project A/555, 2000.

19. "Internet mullistaa koko Nokian," *Talouselämä*, 18 (2000).

20. In this strategy framework, the role of strategic intent coincides with that of vision in the V-I-E framework; see James C. Collins and William C. Lazier, *Managing the Small to Mid-Sized Company: Concepts and Cases* (Chicago, Ill.: Irwin, 1995), Chapter 2.

21. The following account on the mobile cellular industry and its dominant

design draws from Dan Steinbock, "Industry Rivalry in the Mobile Cellular," unpublished manuscript, Harvard Business School Case Project, 2000.

22. Quoted in Fox, "Nokia's Secret Code."

23. On innovation dynamics and dominant designs, see James M. Utterback, *Mastering the Dynamics of Innovation* (Boston, Mass.: Harvard Business School Press, 1994), Chapter 2.

24. These strategic inflection points, as Intel's chairman Andrew S. Grove has noted, refer to "a time in the life of a business when its fundamentals are about to change. That change can mean an opportunity to rise to new heights. But it may just as likely signal the beginning of the end." See Andrew S. Grove, *Only the Paranoid Survive: How To Exploit the Crisis Points That Challenge Every Company* (New York: Random House, 1996), pp. 3–4.

25. "Kari Kairamon ajatuksia Nokiasta ja isänmaasta: Vikkelä soveltaja pääsee melkein huipulle," *Talouselämä*, 33 (1981).

26. Riitta Weiste, "Human Resource and Development," Nokia, December 4, 1997.

27. On Nokia's human resource management policies, see its annual reports throughout the 1990s.

28. See Tim Burt, "Hello World, Helsinki Calling," *Financial Times*, March 24, 1999.

29. Quoted in Anu-Kaisa Ojanen, "Yrityksen arvot kansainvälisesti toimivassa yrityksessä" (master's thesis, University of Tampere, Finland, 2000).

30. The following account of the three critical challenges is indebted to an essay by Lasse Kivikko, a technology consultant, and Juhani Hokkanen, the former director of Nokia's human resources. See Kivikko and Hokkanen, "In the Eye of Rapid Growth" [in Finnish], in *Johtajana muutoksissa*, eds. Risto Tainio and Anneli Valpola (Helsinki: WSOY, 1996).

31. The emphasis on teamwork has been a fundamental characteristic of Nokia throughout Ollila's tenure. In 2000, a thin booklet was published (in Finnish) on the management rules of Nokia's product development unit in Oulu, Finland. This collection of interviews reinforces the prevailing impression of the central role of teamwork in Nokia. See Anja Kivimäki-Kuitunen, *Work, Rest & Play: Matkaevästä Nokian nuorilta esimiehiltä* (Maarianhamina: Mermerus, 2000).

32. On the evolution of intellectual capital management (ICM) in the United States, see Patrick H. Sullivan, *Value-Driven Intellectual Capital* (New York: John Wiley & Sons, 1999), pp. 225–265.

33. In 1986, Karl-Erik Sveiby published *The Knowledge Company* (in Swedish), a book that sought to explain how to manage intangible systems. For Sveiby's more recent statement, see Karl-Erik Sveiby, *The New Organizational Wealth: Managing and Measuring Knowledge-Based Assets* (San Francisco: Berrett-Koehler Publishers, 1997).

34. In 1999, the Center for Knowledge and Innovation Research (CKIR) was founded at the Helsinki School of Economics and Business Administration. In the process, Nonaka became visiting dean of the center. When CKIR held its first conference in May 1999, Nonaka served as one of the lead sponsors and as a senior manager (others were Erkki Ormala, director of technology policy, and Mikko Kosonen, chief of Nokia's corporate development).

35. On Nokia's current intellectual property resources strategy, see, e.g., "Motorola-kiista terävöitti Nokian patenttistrategiaa," *Tekniikka & Talous*, April 29, 1999.

36. Ibid. Through its Intranet, Nokia provided information on its own as well as industry-related patents. An in-house database allowed the company to focus content and retain control over indexing. "General databases are complicated," said Kristian Luoto, a patent engineer at the Nokia Research Center. "The interpretation of the results can be problematic." See "IBM tienaa patenttitiedolla," *Tekniikka & Talous*, April 29, 1999.
37. Under the Nokia Connecting People Bonus Plan, a total of EUR 70 million would be paid out based on 1999 performance.
38. These included the Individual Incentive Plan, the Program/Project Incentive Plan, and the Team/Production Incentive Plan. There were also incentive plans for production personnel as well as R&D and other work teams. In addition, there was a special achievement award given to individuals or teams in recognition of outstanding contributions, significant achievements, or exceptionally good performance. In 1999, some EUR 90 million was paid out under these schemes.
39. In *Nokian valtatie*, two Swedish journalists, Staffan Bruun and Mosse Wallen, suggest that Ollila had been involved in "insider deals." In Finland, critical business observers, including the editor-in-chief of *Talouselämä*, an influential business weekly, quickly repudiated such accusations. See Staffan Bruun and Mosse Vallen, *Nokian valtatie*. See also Pertti Monto, "Nokiaollila, Ollilanokia," *Talouselämä, 30* (1999). The debate also triggered a certain amount of hypocrisy. For instance, during his term as president (1994–2000), Martti Ahtisaari was firmly against stock option programs; after his term, he joined the board of Elcoteq Networks, a Nokia subcontractor, which granted him the right to subscribe to stock options.
40. In effect, Holmström noted that options were used often in the United States in the 1960s, whereas in the 1970s they disappeared. "The focus on shareholder value is a more constant phenomenon than the compensation of executives with options," he said. "Talouden muutos vaatii optioita," *Helsingin Sanomat*, February 21, 2000.
41. "Nokian johtaja yrittäjäksi: kommunikaattorin isä," *Talouselämä, 6* (2000).
42. "Internet mullistaa koko Nokian," *Talouselämä, 18* (2000).
43. Operating in China, Finland, Italy, and Singapore, the learning centers deliver training activities. These activities are considered necessary to maintain and improve the attractiveness of Nokia's working environment as the competition for talent grows more intense.
44. See "Nokia—Disconnecting Families? Mørk ei kanna huolta pitkistä päivistä," *Talouselämä*, February 4, 2000.
45. Ibid.
46. Ibid.
47. Take taxation, for instance. In 1997, according to Ollila, hiring an engineer in Finland cost the company about FIM 22,000 per month ($3,700 to $4,400), whereas hiring an engineer in Dallas cost perhaps FIM 2,000 more per month. Due to the taxation, however, a U.S.-based Nokia engineer might get FIM 16,500 in net income, whereas a Finland-based engineer would get only FIM 9,200. Just as Koski argued in the late 1980s and Ollila commented in the late 1990s, such taxation differences created insurmountable problems for Nokia and other Finnish technology companies. "The real problem is how to keep in-house a cumulative know-how of 15 years," Ollila argued. See "Nokia: Me tarvitsemme Suomea," *Helsingin Sanomat*, May 16, 1997.

Chapter 8

1. Deborah Orr, "How High Is High," *Forbes*, 4 October 1999.
2. Argued Mäenpää: "Technology policy seeks to strengthen the competitiveness of industry, and to create new products, new businesses and new jobs. "A balanced approach combining strengthening the competitiveness of basic industry and the development of new high-tech industries is Finland's strategic cornerstone." See Martti Mäenpää, "Technology Provides Keys for Growth" (2000). Available at http://virtual.finland.fi.
3. In 1999, the International Institute of Management Development (IMD) placed Finland third in overall competitiveness due to technology and research cooperation, technology development and application, utilization of new information technology, and good administration. The same were highlighted in the report of the World Economic Forum of the Western European Union (WEU), which states that the level of technology knowhow in Finland was highest of the fifty-three countries compared.
4. The private sector accounted for some 65 percent of overall R&D and the public sector for 35 percent. By 1998, investments in research and technological development amounted to FIM 19.7 billion (EUR 3.3 billion), which translated to 3 percent of Finland's GDP. Of this total amount, the private sector accounted for FIM 13.3 billion (EUR 2.2 billion) and the public sector for about FIM 6.3 billion (EUR 1.1 billion).
5. In 1998, Finnish high-technology exports were estimated at FIM 43 billion (EUR 7 billion), which was FIM 15 billion (EUR 2.5 billion) higher than imports.
6. In 2000, TEKES remained the leading organization in Finland for implementing technology policy, but it was subordinate to the Ministry of Trade and Industry. Founded in 1983, TEKES's primary objective has been to promote the competitiveness of Finnish industry and the service sector by technological means.
7. Jorma Ollila, "Tutkimuksessa ei ole varaa välivuosiin," *Helsingin Sanomat*, February 8, 2000.
8. One symbolic milestone was passed in June 1999, when the new main building of the NCR was opened in Helsinki. It had been designed to maximize contact and information exchange among the employees. Located in the center of the city, it was in close proximity to major universities, which were expected to provide a physical environment for the Nokians as they prepared to migrate from the company into a virtual environment.
9. Following the critical decision, TEKES was founded, and Kuusi became its first director general, once serving as the president of the EUREKA research program. "In 1982, forestry industry accounted for 75 percent of Finnish exports. Today, its role is about 25 percent and heavy metal industry another 25 percent. Of the new industries, the role of electronics is about 25 percent and biotechnology and chemistry about 10–12 percent. The electronics exports have doubled. No other country has achieved anything like this." See "50-Year Old Juhani Kuusi," *Helsingin Sanomat*, November 11, 1998.
10. After thirteen years as a research engineer in the Technical Research Center of Finland, Ormala had served twelve years as the chief planner in Finland's Science and Technology Council while consulting on industrial concerns. Ormala reported to Veli Sundback, executive vice president and a veteran diplomat in charge of Nokia's international trade issues. "It's nice

to have an opportunity to do things directly," Ormala commented. Typically, he did not describe his job description in greater detail. "These things go the way they go. In the next few months, I will learn new things. I won't say more." See "Nokia pureutuu teknologian ytimiin," *Talouselämä*, 12 (1999).

11. To ensure their role in the mobile Internet, Nokia and the NRC have been particularly interested in multimedia and 3G mobile communications systems. Research activities into multimedia cut across all technology areas at the Center. In connection with these efforts, Nokia organized a Finnish national program in 1994 on multimedia technology in conjunction with the Finnish National Information Highway Initiative.

12. Company reports.

13. Quoted in "Tuotekehittäjistä ei tapella," *Tekniikka & Talous*, March 4, 1999.

14. Due to price pressures, the margins exist only in the higher value phones. Because forecasting demand for a new phone is a very tricky business, the ability to unload inventory and make the customer trade up is essential for Nokia. See *Nokia*, Harvard Business School Case, May 12, 1998.

15. See Ilkka Tuomi, *Corporate Knowledge: Theory and Practice of Intelligent Organizations* (Helsinki: Metaxis, 1999), pp. 34–44.

16. On Nokia's upstream and downstream innovation, see Chapters 9 and 10.

17. Nokia Annual Report, 1994.

18. International standardization activities were under way, due in part to results from R&D projects carried out with the support of the EU. The NRC had participated in several key projects related to UMTS and intended to maintain an active role in its further development.

19. Finnish researchers have estimated that in 1999 some 60 percent of Nokia's R&D expenditure took place in Finland, although this percentage has fallen as the company expanded more rapidly abroad than in Finland. However, since this percentage takes into account only Nokia's direct R&D expenditures, it excludes the supplier impact and may significantly ignore the strategic impact of Nokia's global R&D networks. For Finnish estimates of Nokia's R&D expenditures, see Jyrki Ali-Yrkkö, Laura Paija, Catherine Reilly, and Pekka Ylä-Anttila, *Nokia: A Big Company in a Small Country* (Helsinki: ETLA, 2000), p. 12.

20. On these developments in global R&D, see Walter Kuemmerle, "Building Effective R&D Capabilities Abroad," *Harvard Business Review* (March/April 1997).

21. "Nokia peittoaa yliopistot," *Tekniikka & Talous*, March 4, 1999.

22. On the general characteristics of home-base–augmenting and home-base–exploiting sites, see Kuemmerle, "Building Effective R&D Capabilities Abroad."

23. The exhibit is a modified version of Kuemmerle's depiction of the way information flows between home-base and foreign R&D sites.

24. As product life cycles had shortened drastically, companies were forced to develop and commercialize new technologies more quickly than ever before. In such circumstances, competitive advantage did not necessarily go to the companies that created the vast array of technologies, but to those companies that were most adept at choosing among them. On the new and emerging R&D paradigm, see, e.g., Marco Iansiti and Jonathan West, "Technology Integration: Turning Great Research into Great Products," *Harvard Business Review* (May/June 1997).

25. "Nokia peittoaa yliopistot."

26. Initially, the CE approach was developed at the U.S. Department of Defense (DoD). As a consumer, the DoD thought that many American products took "too long to develop, cost too much to produce, and often [did] not perform as promised or expected." The problem, so the argument went, derived from the isolation of the design of the product from the design of the manufacturing processes employed later. In order to resolve the problem, the CE advocates argued that the design of the manufacturing and support processes should be undertaken in parallel to optimize efficiencies. Furthermore, fewer design mistakes would remain to be discovered at the stage of volume or prototype production. See R. I. Winner et al., *The Role of Concurrent Engineering in Weapon Systems Acquisition*, Institute of Defense Analyses Report R-338 (1998); K. J. Cleetus, *Definition of Concurrent Engineering*, Concurrent Engineering Research Center Technical Report Series, CERC-TR-RN-92-003 (1992).

27. Winner et al., *The Role of Concurrent Engineering*.

28. For an introduction to CE, see Suren N. Dwivedi, "Concurrent Engineering—An Introduction," Concurrent Engineering Research Center Technical Report Series, CERC-TR-TM-90-006 (1990).

29. At Nokia, the CE lessons have allowed the company to respond to the Japanese challenge by matching its overall accomplishments in operational effectiveness.

30. Nokia established research cooperation with the Beijing University of Post and Telecommunications (BUPT) in China and the Indian Institute of Science (IISC) in Bangalore, India. In addition to the relationship with BUPT, Nokia developed relationships with several other top-ranking universities in China, all with specific expertise in technology areas relevant to Nokia. Similarly, the company established R&D facilities in Beijing and Tokyo.

31. "Suurin osa Nokialle tutkimustyötä tekevistä on yhä suomalaisia," *Helsingin Sanomat*, June 12, 1999.

32. In Europe, IMT-2000 has been called UMTS, a concept developed by the European Telecommunications Standards Institute (ETSI) with the European Radiocommunications Committee (ERC) coordinating regulatory issues.

33. IMT-2000 had three particularly attractive characteristics. First, it would make possible seamless global roaming, enabling users to move across borders as well as make and receive calls while using the same number and handset. Second, it would translate to higher transmission rates offering a minimum speed of 2 Mbit/s for stationary or walking users and 348 kbit/s in a moving vehicle. (Second-generation cellular systems offer speeds ranging from 9.6 kbit/s to 28.8 kbit/s.) Third, it would offer seamless service delivery, for instance, via fixed, mobile, and satellite networks. See *World Telecommunication Development Report 1999: Mobile Cellular* (Geneva: ITU, 1999), pp. 21–22.

34. Supporters of the mandatory standards believed that without norms, market development would be hindered because customers would be confused and therefore unwilling to buy. Supporters of voluntary standards argued that customers were better positioned to select a standard through actual use than a group of industry specialists looking for consensus.

35. ETSI emerged in 1988 when the members of the Conférence Européen des Administrations des Postes et Telecommunications (CEPT) agreed to its formation and to the transfer of its role in developing standards. Instead of being an exclusive club with its membership restricted to the European

PTTs, ETSI opened its doors to most European telecommunications organizations. Ownership or country of origin was not the key factor; R&D activity in Europe was. Consequently, Motorola was granted full membership despite its American origins. Compare Rudi Bekkers and Jan Smits, *Mobile Telecommunications: Standards, Regulation, and Applications* (Boston: Artech House Publishers, 1999), pp. 70–72.

36. "Taistelu joka teki Nokiasta suurvallan," *Helsingin Sanomat/Kuukausiliite*, kesäkuu June 1999.

37. Prior to his chairmanship at the ETSI, Rapeli had served as a senior manager at Nokia Mobile Phones. Between 1991 and 1994, Rapeli served as chairman of several ETSI working groups involving the Digital European Cordless Telecommunication (DECT) system and equipment. Between 1994-1997, he was chairman of a subtechnical committee responsible for 3G standards in Europe. Later, he returned to NMP but moved to Philips Consumer Communications to serve as vice president and CTO of wireless technologies.

38. "Kari Kairamon ajatuksia Nokiasta ja isänmaasta: Vikkelä soveltaja pääsee melkein huipulle," *Talouselämä*, 33 (1981).

39. On PDC and Japanese mobile telecommunications, see Garry A. Garrard, *Cellular Communications: Worldwide Market Development* (Boston: Artech House, 1999), Chapter 10.

40. "The most important thing is to understand early what the markets want, especially the kind of applications the markets are after. That's what counts." See "Standardien sota ratkaisee miljardien tilaukset: Maailman-kännykän kisa alkaa," *Talouselämä* 3 (1999).

41. "Taistelu joka teki Nokiasta suurvallan."

42. Ibid.

43. Jack Ewing, "Siemens Climbs Back," *Business Week*, June 5, 2000.

44. Dan Steinbock, *Finland's Wireless Valley: Pioneering Regulation and Competition Policy* (Helsinki: Ministry of Transport and Communications, 2001).

45. Based on its continued communication systems research, Nokia had been actively involved in creating the three major 3G standards proposals that were submitted to the ITU: W-CDMA, CDMA 2000, and UWC 136 (universal wireless communications). All followed a path from the 2G cellular standards (i.e., GSM, CDMA One, and US TDMA). Indeed, at the end of the 1990s, Nokia was the *only* major equipment manufacturer that operated multiphone capabilities and made telephones in all three digital cellular standards: CDMA, TDMA, and GSM. The execution was not flawless, however. Nokia stumbled with the design of its TDMA chipset.

46. Nokia offered operators an opportunity to upgrade their networks step by step for personal mobile multimedia services, starting with 2G GSM enhancements, such as HSCSD, GPRS, and EDGE. W-CDMA will use the new 3G spectrum allocation and utilize the advanced and evolving GSM core networks.

47. Toward the end of the 1990s, Siemens no longer tried to fight the Nordic mobile vendors; it sought to overthrow them by emulating them. Like Nokia and Ericsson, it was paying increasing attention to marketing, design, and costs. See Ewing, "Siemens Climbs Back."

48. Stephen Baker, with Roger O. Crockett and Neil Gross, "Can CEO Ollila Keep the Cellular Superstar Flying High?" *Business Week*, August 10, 1998.

49. "Taistelu joka teki Nokiasta suurvallan."

50. "Finland Is the First Country in the World to Grant Licenses for 3G Mobile

Networks—Technology Will Be Determined by the Future ITU Standard," press release, Ministry of Transport and Communications, Helsinki, March 18, 1999. Four licenses out of an initial fifteen applications were awarded to existing operators Radiolinja, Sonera, Telia Mobile, and Suomen Kolmegee ("Finland's Three-G"), formed by regional telephone companies together with a Swedish telephone company, Tele2.

51. The verbal note was published in *Helsingin Sanomat/Kuukausiliite*, kesäkuu June 1999, p. 76.

52. On the role of the MTC in the emergence of Finland's telecommunications/mobile cluster, see Dan Steinbock, *Finland's Wireless Valley:* Pioneering Regulation and Competition Policy.

53. The shifts were codified in the Telecommunications Act of 1987 and the Telecommunications Market Act of 1997. The former reflected the Finnish players' search for first-mover advantages in telecommunications/mobile markets, whereas the latter represented efforts to "harmonize" these strategic moves with EU directives and reforms. Having just taken two steps forward, the Finns now had to take one step backward to participate in the EU developments. This worked against the pioneer strategies that, since the 1980s, generated great payoffs through first-mover advantages. Ibid.

54. The preemptive strategy of the emerging 3G markets was crucial to Nokia's group executive board, not only in competitive terms. If it were successful, it would also fulfill certain noneconomic objectives—most important, it would help the company retain its identity despite increasing internationalization. When Ericsson, Nokia's Swedish rival, announced its plan to move its headquarters out of Sweden because of high taxation, a debate followed in Finland as well. Like Ericsson, Nokia acknowledged that it had considered moving its headquarters to a foreign location in the previous two years. Such strategic decisions held substantial national significance in Finland. A year earlier, Nokia's exports accounted for 13 percent of the entire Finnish exports and were rapidly rising. Furthermore, although the proportion of Nokia's Finnish sales was only 6 percent at the time, some 55 percent of the entire production volume was in Finland (for Ericsson, the corresponding figure was only 3 percent). Throughout the 1990s, Nokia enjoyed a magnificent market ride. In the long term, however, the company also had to face difficult years. With increasing international institutional ownership, the ownership issues were almost certain to resurface.

55. In 1995, many political analysts and commentators were warning of a drift in trans-Atlantic relationships and the need to reassess common goals. That year, the Trans-Atlantic Agenda identified joint initiatives in four broad areas: promoting peace, development, and democracy around the world; responding to global challenges; contributing to the expansion of world trade and closer economic relations; and "building bridges" across the Atlantic, such as the TABD, through which companies could explore their conflict issues and thereby influence their governments.

56. In the process, Qualcomm also bought SnapTrack, a maker of software for locating cell phone callers, for $1 billion, and signed a major deal with China Unicom. This deal opened the door for Chinese carriers and equipment makers to use CDMA technology in China, where the GSM reigned. Later in 1999, Nokia and Motorola teamed up to push for the standardization of Motorola's 1Xtreme technology over Qualcomm's high-data-rate (HDR) format 3G networks. Qualcomm stood to gain either way—1Xtreme was based on its CDMA patents.

57. Still, new Japanese mobile operators, such as DoCoMo, were expected to play a critical role. The competition was intense in the Japanese telecommunications markets, where the old monopoly players—in particular NTT, which still owned a majority stake in DoCoMo—enjoyed superior bargaining power. Typically, Japanese mobile phones featured the name of the operator, not the mobile vendor. While Panasonic, the market leader, featured only the letter "P" in the lower corner of its mobile phone, Nokia managed to place its brand name in the same corner.

Chapter 9

1. Market value measures from Morgan Stanley Research, *The Technology IPO Yearbook*, annual editions.
2. Jorma Ollila, "To Our Shareholders," Nokia's Annual Report 1998, pp. 6–7.
3. Jorma Ollila and Pekka Ala-Pietilä, "Letter to Our Shareholders," Nokia's Annual Report 1999, pp. 6–7.
4. Ollila and Ala Pietilä, "Letter to Our Shareholders," p. 7.
5. Compare Youssef M. Ibrahim, "Nokia: Made in Finland and Sold Just About Everywhere," *New York Times*, August 13, 1997.
6. On the characteristics of these five basic development projects, see Steven C. Wheelwright and Kim B. Clark, *Revolutionary Product Development*, Boston, Mass.: Harvard Business School Press, 1992, Chapter 4.
7. On successful and unsuccessful acquisitions in the U.S. technology sector, see Saikat Chaudhuri and Behnam Tabrizi, "Capturing the Real Value in High-Tech Acquisitions," *Harvard Business Review*, September–October 1999. The following account seeks to integrate critical observations in two different research literatures: successful high-tech acquisitions and successful new product development. See Chaudhuri and Tabrizi, "Capturing the Real Value in High-Tech Acquisitions"; Wheelwright and Clark, *Revolutionizing Product Development: Quantum Leaps in Speed, Efficiency, and Quality*.
8. Compare Chaudhuri and Tabrizi, "Capturing the Real Value in High-Tech Acquisitions."
9. On the general characteristics of competing through development capabilities, see Wheelwright and Clark, *Revolutionary Product Development*.
10. On the industry figures, see Gautam Naik, "Nokia Widens Lead in Wireless Market While Motorola, Ericsson Fall Back," *Wall Street Journal*, February 8, 2000. Market share information from Dataquest, Inc.
11. While Nokia's sales soared, Motorola saw its market share fall from 19.5 percent to 16.9 percent. It had difficulties with the supply of certain components, and it needed to introduce more models to compete with jazzy offerings from Nokia. Similarly, Ericsson had a tough year, mainly because it too did not possess a product portfolio to match that of Nokia.
12. "The Internet Revolutionizing Nokia," *Finns in Business 2000/Talouselämä*, July 2000.
13. The IP telephone company eVoice was dedicated to providing convenient messaging solutions via the Internet. Pogo.com was the first service to target the emerging market of family Internet game players. Confinity concentrated on meeting the rapidly growing demand for strong cryptography on handheld computers and other small devices. FusionOne was developing Internet synchronization software and services that make in-

formation access seamless across multiple communications and computing devices. Informative was the leading provider of Web-based, real-time information solutions.

14. See Stephen Baker, "Nokia Is Shopping for a New Number: It Needs a Big Acquisition to Develop the Mobile Internet," *Business Week*, April 5, 1999.

15. Quoted in "Piilaakson kautta internetiin," *Talouselämä*, 34 (1999).

16. See "Nokia Acquires Ipsilon Networks, Inc., Strengthens Data Communications Capabilities," press release, Nokia Corporation December 9, 1997.

17. "All the key people who had something to do with the technology left Ipsilon in half a year," claimed Ken Fehrnström, senior vice president of Internetworking Systems at Lucent Technologies. From the strategic viewpoint, Nokia has done some good deals, but it's only 10 percent of the struggle. The remaining 90 percent is about execution. In that regard, I would give Nokia a poor grade, unless it has something in its sleeve that hasn't been seen yet." Quoted in "Piilaakson kautta internetiin," *Talouselämä*, 34 (1999).

18. "Nokia has done small acquisitions, in order to bring in certain know-how to couple our own technology," stressed T. Kent Elliott, "not to buy market shares." At Nokia, acquisitions were perceived as a way to accelerate new product development. Quoted in "Piilaakson kautta internetiin."

19. Richard S. Dunham, "Q&A: Nokia's Ollila on CEO Profiles and the Company's Future," *Business Week*, August 10, 1998.

20. Despite pragmatic motivations, not all ventures were successful. In the mid-1990s, Tarmo Lemola, a Finnish R&D expert (who was later appointed Nokia's chief of technology policy, argued that Nokia's most prominent failure may well have been Micronas, a semiconductor company that Nokia founded together with Aspo and Salora in 1979. After a decade of stumbling, Micronas was acquired by the Swiss Crosstec. See Tarmo Lemola, "Riittääkö kolme miljardia markkaa?" in *Miksi Nokia, Finland?* eds. Tarmo Lemola and Raimo Lovio (Helsinki: WSOY, 1996).

21. On value chains and the general characteristics of coalitions, see Michael E. Porter and Mark B. Fuller, "Coalitions and Global Strategy," in *Competition in Global Industries*, ed. Michael E. Porter (Boston, Mass.: Harvard Business School Press, 1986), pp. 315–343.

22. However, because Nokia's overall strategy depended on preemption and first-mover advantages, access to knowledge as a motivation for coalition formation was more typical of its competitors. To enjoy comparative advantage effects, many of these rivals toward the late 1990s launched subsidiaries or joint ventures in Finland's Wireless Valley, which for years had served as Nokia's test laboratory.

23. Sonera, the leading Finnish operator, served as a giant billing center for all WAP services, so mobile-phone users could purchase services or goods anywhere, anytime, and receive an itemized bill once a month along with the regular phone bill. See Almar Latour, "Finnish Firms Lead Wireless Revolution as Vanguard Companies Capture Market," *Wall Street Journal*, September 10, 1999.

24. Compare Jorma Ollila, "Evolving Toward a Mobile Information Society— Putting the Net in Your Pocket," Telecom 99, Geneva, Switzerland, October 14, 1999.

25. Almar Latour, "WAP Buzz Likely Will Fuel Service Providers' Shares," *Wall Street Journal*, September 3, 1999.

26. Until 2001, a number of factors combined to inhibit the upsurge of WAP in Western Europe, including growth in short messaging services (SMS),

handset replacement requirements, the move from time- to data-driven pricing for WAP services, lack of adequate content, the introduction of GPRS, and network providers' potential problems with technical issues. While some of these factors were also expected to drive WAP use, IDC thought that, in many respects, the market was not yet ready. "WAP Is on the Way, but Is Europe Ready?" IDC, London, August 27, 1999.

27. For TDMA/ANSI-136 providers, EDGE, coupled with the GPRS core network, would enable the introduction of new and high-bit-rate data services. In GSM systems, these higher speed data services were referred to as EGPRS (enhanced GPRS) and ECSD (enhanced circuit-switched data). In TDMA/ANSI-136, high-speed data services were referred to as EGPRS-136HS.

28. Nokia Corporate Communications; see http://www.nokia.com.

29. The Nokia Communicator was a fully featured GSM phone with enhanced communication and organizing capabilities. In addition to voice calls, the Communicator enabled users to send and receive faxes, e-mail, and short messages (online postcards) as well as to access Internet services and corporate and public databases. The new product also provided users with organization functions, such as an electronic calendar, address book, notepad, and calculator. It was available in a single stylish unit the size and weight of a hand-portable phone.

30. "Nokia pioneers new product category with the world's first all-in-one communicator," Nokia Corporate Communications, March 13, 1996.

31. It defined the air interface and communication protocols for a low-power radio link operating on the 2.4 GHz industry, scientific, and medical (ISM) band. By forming intuitive wireless networking to connect various devices, Bluetooth effectively replaced traditional cables and interfaces.

32. Bluetooth Special Interest Group to be Led by 3Com, Ericsson, Intel, IBM, Lucent, Microsoft, Motorola," press release, Bluetooth, December 1, 1999.

33. Quoted in John Borland, "Profit Squabble Mars Wireless Web Future," *CNET News*, January 21, 2000.

34. "Phone.com Sues Geoworks over Wireless Licensing Plan," CNET News. com, April 26, 2000.

35. Jyrki Ali-Yrkkö, Laura Paija, Catherine Reilly, and Pekka Ylä-Anttila, *Nokia: A Big Company in a Small Country* (Helsinki: ETLA, 2000), p. 27.

36. Take Oulu, a major city in northern Finland, where Nokia had initiated technology activities and built its very first telecommunications facilities. By the end of the 1990s, this city enjoyed economic growth of 9 percent a year, not least because of mobile start-ups and plants operated by Nokia.

37. "Nokia jakaa kasvun ja kivun," *Helsingin Sanomat*, August 1, 1999. The numbers are estimates based on Nokia's lead subcontractors in Finland. Not all subcontractor employees worked in Nokia-related projects. On the other hand, the aggregate number did not include all Nokia subcontractors. Finally, the number of overseas subcontractors was accelerating rapidly.

38. See Tomi Alkula, "Nokia Networks in tukiasemasopimusvalmistajan kilpailutekijät: Case Wecan Electronics Oyj" (master's thesis, Helsinki School of Economics and Business Administration, 2000). Based on a thorough understanding of Wecan's evolution and processes, Alkula's fascinating study illustrates the strategic strengths and vulnerabilities as well as the unique dependencies of Nokia's small and mid-size suppliers.

39. "Nokia jakaa kasvun ja kivun," *Helsingin Sanomat*, August 1, 1999.

40. As Nokia expanded, the supplier followed by adding capacity and resurrecting a plan to build $600 million chip plants in Singapore, France, and Italy (whose governments were major shareholders in STMicroelectronics). Compare Leslie P. Norton, "Ringing Up Gains: Nokia's Suppliers Have Prospered Along with Cell-Phone Maker," *Barron's*, November 8, 1999.
41. Nokia also attracted leading global contract manufacturers into Finland at the same, including SCI Systems.
42. On Elcoteq, see http://www.elcoteq.fi.
43. "Kolmen aallon Elcoteq," *Optio*, October 7, 1999.
44. Ibid.
45. The concept covered management of the entire life cycle of the products from research, technology development, and design through manufacturing, testing, purchasing, materials, and logistics and on to maintenance and aftermarketing services.
46. "Amerikka kutsuu, Paananen päättää," *Talouselämä*, 25 (2000).
47. See Eimo's Annual Report 1999, p. 1. On Eimo, see http://www.eimo.fi.
48. "Finnish Eimo to Buy U.S. Triple S," Reuters, July 14, 2000.
49. On Wecan, see http://www.wecan.fi.
50. On Elektrobit, see http://www.elektrobit.fi.
51. On Nokia's Finnish "inheritors," see "114 miljardin markan joukkue," *Talouselämä*, 20 (1999).
52. On Aerial, see http://www.aerial.fi.
53. Ibid.
54. On the history and strategy of Sonera, see Dan Steinbock, *Sonera's Evolution* (Helsinki: Sonera, 2000); Dan Steinbock, *Sonera's Strategy* (Helsinki: Sonera, 2000).
55. In addition to the United States, Sonera also owned 9 percent of Powertel, a Georgia wireless operator, as well as 41 percent of Turkish cellular operator Turkcell.
56. Although the bank was among the first to venture into cyberspace, its early use of new distribution channels allowed it to evolve gradually, making incremental investments rather than huge sums to implement the latest and greatest technological innovations.
57. On Merita's historical first-mover advantages in online banking, see Dan Steinbock, "Bo Harald (MeritaNordbanken): Banks as the Drivers of the Finnish Internet" [in Finnish], in Dan Steinbock, *Internet markkinointi Suomessa* (Helsinki: Edita, 1998), Chapter 8. Also see Christopher Rhoads, "Merita Vaults to the Lead in the On-Line Banking Race," *Wall Street Journal*, June 29, 1998. On Merita and mobile commerce, see Almar Latour, "Mobile Commerce Forces Banking, Telecom Industries to Transform," *Wall Street Journal*, February 28, 2000.
58. See Annual Review, Satama Interactive, 1999. For a case study on Satama Interactive, see Dan Steinbock, *Internet markkinointi Suomessa* (Helsinki: Edita, 1998), Chapter 5.
59. Founded in 1988, the company's early areas of expertise were the provision of data security consulting services and training. It had entered the antivirus software market in 1990. In 1996, it diversified into the emerging market of encryption software products, and it established sales and marketing subsidiaries in some of its most important markets.
60. DataFellows offering memorandum, November 1, 1999.
61. "Nokia jakaa kasvun ja kivun," *Helsingin Sanomat*, August 1, 1999.
62. "Huippukuntoinen Nokia kiristi 'renkiensä' toimitusehtoja," *Helsingin Sanomat*, June 3, 2000.

63. Analysis was complicated by the fact that suppliers avoided public comments on their contracts and did not release information on the proportion of orders among Nokia, Ericsson, and other mobile vendors. Furthermore, most suppliers were far more vulnerable to cyclical changes than Nokia itself. Finally, they were hardly a homogeneous group but comprised quite different companies that operated in quite different industries and with different roles in Nokia's vertical chain.

Chapter 10

1. "Nokia ottaa shokkihoitoa," *Talouselämä* 3 (1988).
2. Stephen D. Moore, "Finnish Electronics Firm's Bold Strategy May Be Unraveling Since Two Acquisitions," *Wall Street Journal*, December 29, 1989.
3. Compare Amanda Kaiser, "Express Yourself: Why Phone Makers Offer Something 'Special' for You," *Wall Street Journal*, October 11, 1999.
4. The following account of global segmentation builds on the literature on global strategies, which has greatly impacted Nokia's key executives, through the frameworks of configuration and coordination (Porter), global segment organizations (Jeannet), and transnational management (Bartlett and Ghoshal). For key contributions, see Michael E. Porter, "Competition in Global Industries: A Conceptual Framework," in *Competition in Global Industries* (Boston, Mass.: Harvard Business School Press, 1986); Jean-Pierre Jeannet, *Managing with a Global Mindset* (New York: Prentice-Hall, 2000); Christopher A. Bartlett and Sumantra Ghoshal, *Managing Across Borders: The Transnational Solution*, 2nd ed. (Boston, Mass.: Harvard Business School Press, 1998).
5. Ironically, Japanese challengers failed in the nascent mobile industry. The cellular remained strictly regulated in Japan until the mid-1980s. The first rival services were launched only near the end of the decade. In retail markets, the sales of CMT terminals for end users began only in 1994; previously subscribers could only rent phones from the operators. The spectacular failure of the Japanese mobile invasion stemmed from Japanese public policies—slow deregulation and absence of real competition.
6. In this case, global segmentation was reinforced with the transition from sustaining to disruptive technologies—or, more precisely, business models. Compare Clayton M. Christensen, *The Innovator's Dilemma: When New Technologies Cause Great Firms to Fail* (Boston, Mass.: Harvard Business School Press, 1997). See also Dan Steinbock, Interview with Clayton M. Christensen, December 4, 1998.
7. For an introduction to the segmentation variables, see, e.g., Philip Kotler, *Marketing Management: Analysis, Planning, Implementation, and Control*, 9th ed. (Upper Saddle River, N.J.: Prentice-Hall, 1997), Chapter 9.
8. *The Evolving Wireless Marketplace* (Peter D. Hart Associates, 1998).
9. Nokia's Annual Report 1998.
10. Serving AT&T, Nokia's multimode phones combined analog and digital services, which allowed subscribers to get cellular services in virtually all parts of the United States, switching between different systems depending on network coverage. See Stephen Baker, "The Best Wireless Phone on the Market," *Business Week*, August 10, 1998.
11. See Philip Kotler, "Design: A Powerful but Neglected Strategic Tool," *Jour-*

nal of Business Strategy (fall 1984): 16–21. See also Christopher Lorenz, *The Design Dimension* (New York: Basil Blackwell, 1986).

12. Quoted in Matti Pulkkinen, *The Breakthrough of Nokia Mobile Phones*, p. 146.
13. Ibid.
14. Since the mid-1950s, Sony's "Sunrise/Sunset" strategy had covered the design of hardware, software, packaging, media, and even the Sony logo itself. It perceived market development as a six-step process: creation (sunrise, early morning), penetration (late morning), market domination (noon), expansion (early afternoon, late afternoon, sunset), saturation (perpetual sunset), and exhaustion. At each step, target audiences were at different points in the technology-adoption life cycle. See Paul Kunkel, *Digital Dreams: The Work of the Sony Design Center* (New York: Universe, 1999), pp. 12–55.
15. On Marimekko's invasion in the United States, see Elizabeth Kendall, "Design: Fine Finnish," *Civilization*, June 1999.
16. Compare Kotler, *Marketing Management*, p. 288.
17. Compare Ingvar Kamprad, "A Furniture Dealer's Testament," in *Leading by Design: The IKEA Story* by Bertil Torekull (New York: HarperBusiness, 1998), Appendix B.
18. Quoted in Kendall, "Design: Fine Finnish."
19. Robert Sullivan, "Ring Leader," *Vogue*, April 2000.
20. On the genesis of 8810, see Nokia Corporate Communications, http://www.nokia.com.
21. In addition to its sleek, black-and-silver metal casing, the 8810 could store 250 names and telephone numbers; users could program it to ring differently in different situations, from vibrating silently in a meeting to blasting out one of thirty-six different rings; and the graphics menus could appear in thirty-two different languages.
22. See Connie Ling and Wayne Arnold, "Stylish Mobile Phone from Nokia Becomes the Rage in Hong Kong," *Wall Street Journal*, September 15, 1998.
23. The small body was a trade-off. Equipped with the lighter lithium battery that helped bring the 8810 down to 98 grams, the phone could last for only about forty-five minutes of conversation. To get the phone to last for just over two hours meant using a heavier battery and adding 20 grams to the package. The 6110, on the other hand, was 137 grams but boasted about four hours of talk time.
24. Frank Gibney, Jr., and Belinda Luscombe, "The Redesigning of America," *Time*, March 20, 2000.
25. Quoted in Nokia's Annual Report 1999, p. 18.
26. There was nothing wrong with individualism, but in industrial design the objective was most decidedly successful teamwork. "Many young designers go into industrial design thinking to get their own line of something. It is good to be ambitious, but you should always remember that most often a designer is more a part of the orchestra than a conductor. If you want personal expression only, then become an artist. As a designer, you will almost always be a part of a team, as in fact I am." See Nokia Corporate Communications, http://www.nokia.com.
27. Harri Saukkomaa, "Matkalla elamysmaailmaan," *Suomen Kuvalehti*, November 19, 1999.
28. For the classic statement on the diffusion of innovations, see Everett M. Rogers, *Diffusion of Innovations*, 4th ed. (New York: The Free Press, 1994).
29. See Dan Steinbock, *The Birth of Internet Marketing Communications* (Westport, Conn.: Quorum Books, 2000), Chapter 3.

30. Geoffrey A. Moore, *Crossing the Chasm: Marketing and Selling High-Tech Products to Mainstream Customers* (New York: HarperBusiness, 1991); *Inside the Tornado* (New York: HarperBusiness, 1995).
31. Starting in the early 1990s, Forrester Research, Inc., combined lifestyle, psychographic, and technology indicators to study in greater detail the adoption processes as entire industries began to migrate online. On technology, segmentation, and lifestyle, see Mary Modahl, *Now or Never: How Companies Must Change Today to Win the Battle for Internet Consumers* (New York: HarperCollins, 2000).
32. Despite the impact on Nokia of the life cycle model and chasm framework, Moore's works include no examples of the company, which he admired but thought different from the typical Silicon Valley companies. "Nokia is a great Nordic high-tech firm. Yet the telecommunications environment differs from Silicon Valley. To some extent, it is still a regulated market. Competition plays out differently in telecommunications. As data traffic begins to overwhelm the voice traffic, all networks must eventually build upon an IP network. That is going to be really difficult and challenging for the telecommunications industry." Dan Steinbock, interview with Geoffrey A. Moore, May 12, 1998.
33. One might add one more aspect: Nokia was comprised of engineers who were beginning to understand marketing rather than marketers who were beginning to understand engineering. "In a sense, the model looks at marketing through an engineer's eyes," argued Moore. "It tries to create markets as systems and thus gives the engineers a systemic model of markets so that they can understand how choosing different actions will have different impacts on the system. If the model had introduced technology marketing as advertising or branding, they would have less idea of how it works." Ibid.
34. Compare Adrian Wooldridge, "The World in Your Pocket: A Survey of Telecommunications," *The Economist*, October 9, 1999, pp. 23–27.
35. "At first, the cellular business crossed the chasm as an analog industry. Initially, then, the early adopters were wealthier and represented narrower business segments. After these early adopters, other segments have crossed the chasm as well. It has become a mass market. In such an environment, the problem with the introduction of a new standard may not be the digital infrastructure but marketing. The buyers should now pay a significant price premium and yet their digital phone experience is not *that* different from the analog one. In this situation, the technology is discontinuous, but the new experience does not significantly differ from the old one. The cellular companies must introduce an early market technology into what has become a relatively conservative customer base. That is why these firms are now struggling to overcome the problem. They must somehow get the consumers to pay for the transition." Ibid.
36. Nokia's partner during the five-year period of brand development had been the advertising agency SEK & Grey.
37. Successful brand building was judged on the basis of various numeric criteria relating to the development of market shares, sales and distribution channels, and marketing research results. Judging for advertising was based on the marketing strategy, the advertisements themselves, the media schedule, and evidence of achievement.
38. "Nokia Wins a Major International Advertising Award: Recognition for Long-Standing Brand Development," Nokia press release, September 27, 1996.

39. Press release. Strategy Analytics, April 12, 1999.
40. Compare Justin Fox, "Nokia's Secret Code," *Fortune*, May 1, 2000.
41. On the rise of branding in the late 1980s, see, e.g., David A. Aaker, *Managing Brand Equity: Capitalizing on the Value of a Brand Name* (New York: The Free Press, 1991).
42. When, in 1999, the ITU, leading mobile vendors, and global regulators decided on a single *flexible* standard, they essentially arrived at a compromise that the Nokian had anticipated in 1991. These eight years provided the company with vital strategic leverage.
43. By the end of the 1990s, some marketing researchers argued that, in contrast to half a century ago, supply outstripped demand. In such a environment, brands served as "assets that transcend product life cycles and technology obsolescence." See Jeffrey R. Rayport, introduction to *Branding: The Power of Market Identity*, by David E. Carter (New York: Hearst Books International, 1999).
44. "Nokia Named Advertiser of the Year by Media Magazine and Picks Up 'Most Creative Use of Media' Award for Excellence," Nokia press release, December 17, 1996.
45. Ibid.
46. The campaign was driven through consistently in various media including television, print, point-of-sale, Nokia's award-winning Asia-Pacific Web site, trade promotions, buses, and sponsorships of events like the Hong Kong Rugby Sevens. Nokia also introduced Chinese, Indian, Malay, and Caucasian talents in the various advertisements that were broadcast in different languages.
47. Rahul Jacob, "Nokia Fumbles, But Don't Count It Out," *Time*, February 19, 1996.
48. See Kivikko and Hokkanen, "In the Eye of Rapid Growth" (in Finnish), *Johtajana muutoksissa*, ed. Risto Tainio and Anneli Valpola (Helsinki: WSOY, 1996).
49. "Nokiaan kehittyy markkinamiehen sielu," *Talouselämä*, 35 (1999).
50. Top 100 marketers by media ad spending outside the U.S., *Advertising Age* Database. See http://www.adage.com.
51. "Nokian markkinoinnin harha-askelia," *Talouselämä*, 35 (1999); "Mainonnan tapaturmat tahraavat Nokiaa," *Helsingin Sanomat*, June 16, 1998.
52. Compare Nokia's Annual Report 1999, pp. 18–19.
53. Erkki K. Laitinen and Rolf Leppänen examined Nokia's use of management accounting systems on the basis of a concise literature review. Erkki K. Laitinen and Rolf Leppänen, *Global Success and the Role of Strategic Steering and Management Accounting Systems: Case Nokia Group* (Vaasa: University of Vaasa, Department of Accounting and Business Finance, 2000).
54. Marja Tahvanainen, *Expatriate Performance Management. The Case of Nokia Telecommunications*. Acta Universitatis Oeconomicae Helsiengiensis, A-134 (Helsinki: Helsinki School of Economics and Business Administration, 1999), pp. 100.
55. "Tärkeintä on nähdä tulevaisuuteen," *Talouselämä*, 21, (1999).
56. "Performance management is one of the most important human resource management processes," noted a NHR manager at Nokia headquarters, "and it has to be efficient and effective. We at NTC think that for our future success, having such a process is a basic requirement." See Tahvanainen, *Expatriate Performance Management*, p. 107.
57. The following draws from Mikko Kosonen, "Driving for Excellence in Per-

formance: The Role of the Controller," Business Controller Seminar, September 9, 1995, IIR Helsinki, Finland.

58. The management and support processes have included strategy setting (direction setting), finance and control (measuring), and HRM process (competence development). Customer satisfaction has been measured by customer surveys and internal measures (milestones), operative efficiency by internal measures that include traditional financial measures, and people involvement by employee involvement surveys. The goals for performance improvement have encompassed strong market position and good profitability that are consistent with the vision and the strategy.

59. Tapani Lehtinen, "Taloushallinnon ja controllereiden tehokas rooli liiketoiminnan ohjauksessa, suorituskyvyn mittauksessa ja tulevaisuuden oleellisen strategisen informaation tuottamisessa," Case Nokia Mobile Phones, seminar "Taloushallinnon uudistaminen kohti" "world class"—tasoa ja business partneruutta, IIR Finland Oy, May 27, 1997, Helsinki.

60. The performance matrix consisted of four kinds of measures: (1) financial: R&D costs/net sales, profitability, licensing, litigation, savings; (2) customer: new product revenue, warranty costs/sales, customer satisfaction, market strength, attractive product portfolio, standards, alliances; (3) process: time accuracy and speed, direct costs, process quality, market orientation and product-quality tools, innovations; (4) people, learning, and knowledge: process-quality tools, managing resources, technology tools and methods, technology strategies update, employee satisfaction, recruiting and retention, development learning. See Jani Taipaleenmäki, "Management Accounting in New Product Development: Case Study of Management Accounting and Knowledge Creation in Process-Oriented Product Development Environment," unpublished working paper, Turku School of Economics and Business Administration, 1999, p. 34.

61. The following account draws from Marko Järvenpää, *Strateginen johdon laskentatoimi ja talousjohdon muuttuva rooli*, Series D-1 (Turku: Turku School of Economics and Business Administration, pp. 233–236.

62. This logic matched that of strategic intent: "The strategist's goal is not to find a niche within the existing industry space but to create new space that is uniquely suited to the company's own strengths, space that is off the map." Compare C.K. Prahalad and Gary Hamel, "Strategic Intent," *Harvard Business Review* (May/June 1989).

63. "Internet mullistaa koko Nokian," *Talouselämä*, 18 (2000).

64. Ibid.

Chapter 11

1. Justin Fox, "Nokia's Secret Code," *Fortune*, May 1, 2000.

2. "Big players make biggest profits," *Finns in Business 2000/Talouselämä*, July 2000. By 2000, Nokia's share of Finland's exports had increased to 20 percent, while its share of the GNP amounted to about 3 percent. In Finnish big business, it had become the greatest investor and employer and generated the largest profits. Optimistic observers celebrated the increasing diversification of the production structure in the small Nordic country, whereas pessimists lamented the deepening dependency.

3. Fox, "Nokia's Secret Code."

4. Ibid.

5. As Pankaj Ghemawat has convincingly argued, strategic analysis has largely been about the search for success factors since the 1950s and 1960s, even if they provide only a "shaky foundation for strategy." See Pankaj Ghemawat, *Commitment: The Dynamic of Strategy* (New York: The Free Press, 1991), Chapter 1.

6. The methodological implications are critical. In most contemporary strategic analysis, students are trained *not* to understand the impact of strategic innovation. Business schools instruct students to conduct company case studies that are *not* longitudinal by nature. The discipline mirrors the "short-termism" in capital markets and corporate management. In the past decades, several pioneering studies in business history, strategic commitment, dynamic capabilities, and dynamic innovation have demonstrated the need to think dynamically. In the absence of such longitudinal understanding, the logic of the process configurations (i.e., the evolution and capabilities of a firm) will escape analysis. Compare David J. Teece, *The Selected Papers of David J. Teece*, Vols. 1–2 (Cheltenham: Edward Elgar, 1998); Alfred D. Chandler, Jr., *Scale and Scope* (Cambridge, Mass.: Belknap Press of Harvard University Press, 1994); Pankaj Ghemawat, *Commitment* James M. Utterback, *Mastering the Dynamics of Innovation* (Boston, Mass.: Harvard Business School Press, 1994).

7. Critical first-mover advantages include reputation, switching costs, benefits associated with the marketing mix (product, price, channel distribution, promotion, and advertising), proprietary learning curve and/or private information, institutional barriers, and rules of the game. Conversely, critical first-mover disadvantages include erosion of reputation, decreased switching costs, and so on. On preemption as a generic strategy, see Steinbock, *Dynamic Competition*.

8. Nokia reported second-quarter pretax profit of EUR 1.42 billion ($1.32 billion), up 62 percent from the year before and better than official market estimates of EUR 1.4 billion. Still, that was short of "unofficial expectations" of about EUR 1.5 billion. Revenue rose 55 percent to EUR 6.98 billion and earnings per share were 20 European cents, up 54 percent. Shares fell 25 percent as investors dumped Nokia's shares after a warning about third-quarter results. Nokia started the day with a market capitalization of about $257.2 billion and finished at about $192.9 billion at 4:00 p.m. in New York Stock Exchange composite trading. See Almar Latour, "Investors Punish Nokia After It Says that Profits Will Decline," *Wall Street Journal*, July 28, 2000.

9. On these premises of classic competitive strategy, see Michael E. Porter, *Competitive Strategy* (New York: The Free Press, 1998); Michael E. Porter, *Competitive Advantage* (New York: The Free Press, 1998); Michael E. Porter, "What Is Strategy?" *Harvard Business Review* (November/December 1996). Even as competitive strategy has been reframed and refined for strategic analysis in more dynamic environments, these premises continue to motivate the theory. See Michael E. Porter, "Towards a Dynamic Theory of Strategy," *Strategic Management Journal* (winter 1999): 95–117.

10. On competitive time and competitive strategy in dynamic markets, see Dan Steinbock, *Dynamic Advantage*.

11. On the distinction between sustaining and disruptive innovations, the following account draws from Clayton, M. Christensen, *The Innovator's Dilemma: When New Technologies Cause Great Firms to Fail* (Boston, Mass.: Harvard Business School Press, 1997).

12. Quoted in Matti Pulkkinen, *The Breakthrough of Nokia Mobile Phones* Acta Universitatis Oeconomicae Helsingiensis A-122 (Helsinki: HSEBA Helsinki School of Economics and Business Administration, 1997), p. 132.

Index